Anatomy of a Campaign

The British campaign in Norway in 1940 was an ignominious and abject failure. It is perhaps best known as the fiasco which directly led to the fall of Prime Minister Neville Chamberlain and his replacement by Winston Churchill. But what were the reasons for failure? Why did the decision makers, including Churchill, make such poor decisions and exercise such bad judgment? What other factors played a part? John Kiszely draws on his own experience of working at all levels in the military to assess the campaign as a whole, its context and evolution, from strategic failures, intelligence blunders and German air superiority, to the performance of the troops and the serious errors of judgment by those responsible for the higher direction of the war. The result helps us understand not only the outcome of the Norwegian campaign but also why more recent military campaigns have found success so elusive.

JOHN KISZELY served in the British Army for forty years, rising to the rank of lieutenant general. His operational service included Northern Ireland, the Falkland Islands, Bosnia and Iraq. He served three tours of duty in the Ministry of Defence, latterly as Assistant Chief of the Defence Staff. On leaving the Army he was for three years a visiting professor in war studies at King's College London, and from 2014 to 2017 a visiting research fellow on the Changing Character of War Programme at Pembroke College, Oxford.

Cambridge Military Histories

Edited by

> HEW STRACHAN, Chichele Professor of the History of War,
> University of Oxford and Fellow of All Souls College, Oxford
> GEOFFREY WAWRO, Professor of Military History, and Director of
> the Military History Center, University of North Texas

The aim of this series is to publish outstanding works of research on warfare throughout the ages and throughout the world. Books in the series take a broad approach to military history, examining war in all its military, strategic, political and economic aspects. The series complements Studies in the Social and Cultural History of Modern Warfare by focusing on the 'hard' military history of armies, tactics, strategy and warfare. Books in the series consist mainly of single author works – academically rigorous and groundbreaking – which are accessible to both academics and the interested general reader.

A full list of titles in the series can be found at: www.cambridge.org/militaryhistories

Anatomy of a Campaign

The British Fiasco in Norway, 1940

John Kiszely

John,

With best wishes.

John Kisz[ely]

25 November 2018

CAMBRIDGE
UNIVERSITY PRESS

CAMBRIDGE
UNIVERSITY PRESS

University Printing House, Cambridge CB2 8BS, United Kingdom

One Liberty Plaza, 20th Floor, New York, NY 10006, USA

477 Williamstown Road, Port Melbourne, VIC 3207, Australia

314–321, 3rd Floor, Plot 3, Splendor Forum, Jasola District Centre,
New Delhi – 1100025, India

79 Anson Road, #06–04/06, Singapore 079906

Cambridge University Press is part of the University of Cambridge.

It furthers the University's mission by disseminating knowledge in the pursuit of
education, learning, and research at the highest international levels of excellence.

www.cambridge.org
Information on this title: www.cambridge.org/9781107194595
DOI: 10.1017/9781108161046

First published 2017
3rd printing 2018

Printed in the United Kingdom by TJ International Ltd. Padstow Cornwall

A catalogue record for this publication is available from the British Library.

Library of Congress Cataloging-in-Publication Data
Names: Kiszely, John, author.
Title: Anatomy of a campaign : the British fiasco in Norway, 1940 / John Kiszely,
independent scholar.
Other titles: British fiasco in Norway, 1940
Description: 1st edition. | New York, NY : Cambridge University Press, [2016]
| Includes bibliographical references and index.
Identifiers: LCCN 2016049303 | ISBN 9781107194595 (Hardback)
Subjects: LCSH: World War, 1939–1945–Campaigns–Norway. |
Norway–Strategic aspects. | World War, 1939–1945–Naval operations, British. |
Norway–History–German occupation, 1940–1945.
Classification: LCC D763.N6 K48 2016 | DDC 940.54/2181–dc23
LC record available at https://lccn.loc.gov/2016049303

ISBN 978-1-107-19459-5 Hardback

Contents

Preface   *page* vii
Acknowledgements   x
List of Figures   xi
List of Maps   xii
British Operations   xiii
Abbreviations   xv

1 Introduction   1

2 'A Legitimate Side-Show'   20

3 Deciding to Decide   29

4 Warning Signs   39

5 'The Major Project'   47

6 'Hare-Brained'   55

7 Taking Stock   67

8 Weserübung   79

9 'Something Must Be Done'   87

10 The Jigsaw Puzzle   100

11 'Completely Outwitted'   110

12 'Boldness Is Required'   135

13 'An Even Greater Prize'   155

14 Maurice   168

15 Sickle   181

16 'We Must Get Out'   205

17 The Third Dimension   218

18 'In the Name of God, Go!'   230

19 'A Good Dividend'?   240

20 'No Time to Lose'   248

21 The Long Retreat   259

22 Finale   268

23 Conclusions   274

Appendix A: Operational Code Names   300
Appendix B: Who's Who (September 1939–June 1940)   301
Abbreviations Used in the Endnotes   305
Notes   306
Bibliography   360
Index   370

Preface

As we have discovered in the opening years of the twenty-first century, success in expeditionary military campaigns can be elusive. Circumstances conspire to frustrate the best of intentions; events take unexpected turns; decisions have unintended consequences; errors of judgment are made. Disentangling the reasons for failure can itself be far from easy, with closer examination often revealing an ever-greater complexity. Each campaign is, of course, unique, but all have some things in common, and some have many things in common.

The British campaign in Norway in the spring of 1940 – for British forces, the first land campaign of the Second World War – ended in ignominious failure. It is not a well-known campaign, being overshadowed, if not eclipsed, by events on the Western Front and the fall of France. It is perhaps best known, in the United Kingdom at least, as the fiasco which directly led to the fall of Prime Minister Neville Chamberlain and to his replacement by Winston Churchill.

Little known it may be, but a surprisingly large number of books have been written about the campaign or aspects of it. The books are broadly broken into four categories. First are those that cover the period prior to the German invasion, notably Salmon, *Deadlock and Diversion: Scandinavia in British Strategy during the Twilight War*. Second are those that focus on the conflict itself, doing so from a British perspective and confining themselves largely to the tactical level: Ash, *Norway 1940*; Adams, *The Doomed Expedition*; and Kynoch, *Norway 1940: The Forgotten Fiasco*. The third category contains wider accounts from a British perspective – some written not long after the Second World War – notably the official history by Derry, *The British Campaign in Norway*, published in 1952, and Moulton, *The Norwegian Campaign of 1940: A Study of Warfare in Three Dimensions*, published in 1966. More modern books in this category are Harvey, *Scandinavian Misadventure*; Rhys-Jones, *Churchill and the Norwegian Campaign*; and Dix, *The Norwegian Campaign and the Rise of Churchill*. The final category includes those that cover the campaign from a wider, non-British perspective: Kersaudy,

Norway 1940; Mordal, *La Campagne de Norvège*; and the comprehensive and detailed accounts by Lunde in *Hitler's Pre-Emptive War* and by Haarr in *The German Invasion of Norway* and *The Battle for Norway*.

All identify the main reasons for Allied failure: poor strategy, intelligence blunders, German air superiority, the weak performance of the troops involved and serious errors of judgment by those responsible for the higher direction of the war – namely, the War Cabinet and its military advisers, the Chiefs of Staff.

The underlying reasons have received less attention. For example, how and why did the perceived errors of judgment come about? Were they identifiable as errors at the time or only in retrospect? How was it that intelligent, hardworking individuals at the top of their chosen professions made such poor decisions? In addressing such questions, this book sets out to understand why the decision-makers made the decisions that they did based on the information available to them at the time, rather than that available with hindsight.

Military campaigns begin long before the first shot is fired. Indeed, by the time the first shot is fired, the outcome of the campaign may be largely preordained. It is, therefore, necessary to comprehend the campaign as a whole, to understand its context and to follow its evolution from inception. In particular, it is necessary to examine the anatomy of the campaign – the constituent parts and their relation to each other – to find out what worked or did not work, both individually and in combination, and the reasons one way or the other. To what extent were the policy and plans for the campaign founded on strategy – in the sense of the process and intellectual activity balancing the ends to be achieved with the ways and means available? How well did the policymakers assess and manage risk? Was the military advice, on which so much depended, sound and timely? If not, why not?

The answer to all these questions should help our understanding not only of this campaign as a whole but also of campaigns more generally, including (perhaps especially) recent ones. The British campaign in Norway had a number of similarities to more modern campaigns. It was an expeditionary, tri-service, multinational campaign with democracies pitted against a dictatorship, and it was the first land campaign after a long period of peace. There was, and is, no shortage of lessons to be learned from what Churchill dubbed 'this ramshackle campaign'.[1]

This book does not set out to give a comprehensive account of the Norwegian campaign. Its subject is very much the British role and British decision making. Its focus is at the strategic level, both the grand-strategic (national and Alliance) level and the level of theatre strategy (sometimes referred to as the 'operational' level). It looks at the tactical level, but mainly in terms of its relationship to strategy and policy, rather than seeking to give a blow-by-blow account of all the battles and engagements or to record the contribution of the units, ships and squadrons which took part. It is, therefore, important to acknowledge from the outset that in doing so, the book invariably overlooks the individual acts of courage and heroism that featured in every battle and engagement and, indeed, often in the periods in between. It is equally important to bear this in mind to see these events in perspective.

Acknowledgements

There are many people to whom I owe huge thanks for their help in the production of this book. I am particularly grateful to Professor Sir Hew Strachan for suggesting that I undertake a visiting research fellowship on his Changing Character of War Programme at the University of Oxford and to Dr. Rob Johnson, the programme director, who acted as my supervisor. Both of them devoted far more of their time to my work than I deserved and offered wise advice and encouragement throughout. My thanks, too, go to the fellows and staff of Pembroke College for their welcome and hospitality.

In the course of my three years of research, I received much support and a highly efficient service from the staff at all the libraries, archives and other research establishments that I consulted: the Joint Services Command and Staff College Library at the Defence Academy, Shrivenham; the National Archives at Kew; the Bodleian Library, Oxford; the Codrington Library at All Souls College, Oxford; the British Library; the Liddell Hart Centre for Military Archives at Kings College London; the Churchill Archives Centre at Churchill College, Cambridge; the Imperial War Museum; the National Army Museum; the Army Historical Branch of the Ministry of Defence; the National Museum of the Royal Navy; the Royal Marines Museum; the Royal Air Force Museum London; the Norwegian Armed Services Museum in Oslo; and the Combined Arms Research Library at Fort Leavenworth, Kansas.

I am grateful to the following who read all or part of my manuscript and provided helpful comments: Dr. Harald Høiback, Dr. Rob Johnson, Professor David French, Dr. Christina Goulter, Nigel de Lee, Air Vice Marshal Tony Mason, Professor Douglas Porch and Professor Sir Hew Strachan.

I would to thank my editor Michael Watson at Cambridge University Press. And my thanks to Angela Wilson at All Terrain Mapping for the maps. Others to whom I am grateful for their support and assistance are Geirr Haarr, Dr. Jan Lemnitzer, Ruth Murray, Lieutenant Colonel Russell P. Rafferty (U.S. Army) and Dr. Robin Woolven.

Finally, I am eternally grateful to my wife, Arabella, for her forbearance during the writing of this book, and for her love.

Figures

1.1 The War Cabinet, September 1939 (Standing: Hankey, Hore-Belisha, Churchill, Wood. Seated: Chatfield, Hoare, Chamberlain, Simon, Halifax) *page* 4
1.2 Air Chief Marshal Sir Cyril Newall 10
1.3 Admiral of the Fleet Sir Dudley Pound 11
1.4 General Sir Edmund Ironside 13
1.5 The Chiefs of Staff: Ironside, Newall, Pound 15
4.1 A key relationship: Churchill and Chamberlain 41
8.1 General Nikolaus von Falkenhorst 81
11.1 The heavy cruiser *Blücher* in Oslo Fiord, 9 April 132
11.2 German troops entering Oslo, 9 April 134
12.1 Major General Pierse Mackesy 140
12.2 Admiral of the Fleet the Earl of Cork and Orrery 140
12.3 Narvik from the north-west 144
12.4 Major General Eduard Dietl 149
12.5 A German machine gun post overlooking Narvik harbour 152
14.1 Major General Adrian Carton de Wiart at Namsos 171
14.2 British troops searching the ruins of Namsos 175
15.1 Major General Otto Ruge 184
15.2 Major General Bernard Paget 190
15.3 The remains of the attempt to establish an airfield at Lake Lesjaskog 193
15.4 The German attack held up at Otta 195
15.5 The fate of many: British prisoners being marched into captivity 202
17.1 A target-rich environment: Oslo's Fornebu airport 224
17.2 German reinforcements arriving by air 226
20.1 Under increasing pressure: German Gebirgsjäger in the mountains above Narvik 253
20.2 Naval bombardment of Bjerkvik prior to the assault, 13 May 255
20.3 Lieutenant General Claude Auchinleck with his air component commander, Group Captain Maurice Moore 257

Maps

1.1 Scandinavia   *page* 6
11.1 Norway   111
11.2 Fleet movements 7–9 April   130
12.1 Narvik Area   135
13.1 Central Norway   155
14.1 Namsos to Trondheim   168
15.1 Åndalsnes to Lillehammer   181
18.1 Trondheim to Narvik   232
20.1 Narvik   248
21.1 Mosjøen to Bodø   259

Map copyright: All Terrain Mapping

British Operations

1940	Narvik Area	South of Narvik	North of Trondheim	South of Trondheim
Apr				
8		British mines laid	Loss of *Glowworm*	
9	*Renown* v *Gneisenau* & *Scharnhorst*			*Karlsruhe* sunk off Kristiansand
10	Destroyer attack, Narvik			*Königsberg* sunk, Bergen
13	Warspite attack, Narvik			
14	First British troops land near Harstad		Naval party at Namsos	
15	24 Brigade at Harstad			
16			146 Brigade at Namsos	
17				Naval party at Åndalsnes
18				148 Brigade at Åndalsnes
19			Chasseurs Alpins land	
21			Action at Vist begun	Action at Lundehøgda Ridge
22				Action at Fåberg
23				Action at Tretten 15 Brigade at Åndalsnes
24	Bombardment of Narvik			
25				Gladiators at Lesjaskog

(*cont.*)

1940	Narvik Area	South of Narvik	North of Trondheim	South of Trondheim
				Action at Kvam begun
27				Action at Kjørem
28	Chasseurs Alpins land			Action at Otta
May				
2				Evacuation of Åndalsnes completed
3			Evacuation of Namsos completed	
4		No 1 Independent Company at Mo		
6	Foreign Legionnaires land			
8		Nos 4 & 5 Independent Companies at Mosjøen		
9	Polish brigade lands	No 3 Independent Company at Bodø		
13	Bjerkvik captured	No 2 Independent Company at Bodø		
15		Loss of *Chrobry*		
17		Loss of *Effingham* Action at Stien		
21	Gladiators at Bardufoss			
22		Action at Krokstranda		
25		Action at Pothus		
26	Hurricanes at Bardufoss	Gladiators at Bodø		
28	Narvik captured			
31		Evacuation of Bodø completed		
June				
4	Evacuation from Narvik & Harstad begun			
8	Evacuation completed Loss of *Glorious*			

Abbreviations

BEF	British Expeditionary Force
CIGS	Chief of the Imperial General Staff
CinC	Commander-in-Chief
JIC	Joint Intelligence Committee
KOYLI	King's Own Yorkshire Light Infantry
MI	Military Intelligence
OKW	Oberkommando der Wehrmacht
RAF	Royal Air Force
SIS	Secret Intelligence Service

1 Introduction

Genesis

Around the Cabinet table on the morning of 19 September 1939, just over a fortnight into the war, sat the nine men responsible for its strategic direction.

In the chair was Prime Minister Neville Chamberlain. Now aged seventy, he was politically in a strong position, and his Conservative Party had an overall parliamentary majority of more than 200. Although criticised for the failure of appeasement, his stock was riding high, both within his own party and in public opinion. Even Anthony Eden, who had resigned as Foreign Secretary over the Munich agreement, remarked earlier in the year that Chamberlain had the makings of a really great Prime Minister, provided his health held out.[1] For six years Chancellor of the Exchequer before he became Prime Minister in 1937, Chamberlain tended to sympathise with the Treasury point of view, a trait that hitherto had served him not entirely for the worse. He was known to be a master of his brief, and his private secretaries were 'amazed by his command of detail'.[2] Although outwardly self-confident, he was, even at this early stage of the war, deeply troubled by self-doubt. On 10 September he wrote to one of his sisters, 'Whilst war was still averted, I felt indispensable for no-one else could carry out my policy. Today the position has changed. Half a dozen people could take my place while war is in progress and I do not see that I have any particular part to play until it comes to peace terms.'[3] Within a few weeks, following the sinking of the battleship *Royal Oak* at Scapa Flow, he was confiding in his other sister, '[H]ow I do hate and loathe this war. I was never meant to be a war minister, and the thought of all those homes wrecked with the *Royal Oak* makes me want to hand over my responsibilities to someone else.'[4] And when it was mentioned in Cabinet that the Chiefs of Staff might be about to recommend 'gloves off' in the air war, 'he shook his head in a dull way as if it were too much to consider.'[5] By nature, Chamberlain was a conciliator – not just in foreign policy terms but also in his style of leadership and management. If confrontation or 'unpleasantness' with colleagues could be avoided, he would almost always favour that path, a policy which worked better for him in time of peace than it was to in time of war.

One of Chamberlain's first tasks on the outbreak of war had been to decide on the size and membership of his Cabinet. In 1916 Lloyd George had formed a War Cabinet comprising a very small group of ministers, almost all without departmental responsibilities.[6] Chamberlain may have been influenced to some degree by this, but his approach was essentially pragmatic – 'My sole purpose was to find a Cabinet that would work'[7] – deciding on a membership of six ministers, two of whom headed full departments of state. The first of the latter was the Earl of Halifax, the Foreign Secretary, aged fifty-eight. Born into an aristocratic Yorkshire family, Edward Halifax had embarked on an academic career as a Fellow of All Souls College, Oxford, before entering politics. Appointed Viceroy of India, where he served from 1926 to 1931, he had occupied a series of ministerial jobs on his return before becoming Foreign Secretary in 1938. From 1934, reflecting his continuing affinity with academia, he had, in addition, been Chancellor of the University of Oxford. He was also a keen Master of Foxhounds and a devout High Anglican (or, as Labour Party leader Clement Attlee put it many years later, 'all hunting and Holy Communion'.)[8] Halifax had been, and remained, a close colleague of Chamberlain, an architect of appeasement, who by nature preferred consensus and compromise.[9] As one historian has noted, 'Both men . . . had a striking, not to say naïve belief in the power of reason and reasonableness.'[10] Halifax, though, was not beyond scheming behind Chamberlain's back and was seen by some as a potential alternative Prime Minister.

The other departmental minister to whom Chamberlain turned was Sir John Simon, Chancellor of the Exchequer. Aged sixty-seven, Simon was another of the most experienced ministers in the peacetime Cabinet. Originally a member of the Liberal Party, he had founded and became leader of the breakaway Liberal Nationals and held two of the great offices of state – Home Secretary and Foreign Secretary – before succeeding his close political ally Chamberlain as Chancellor in 1938. Simon, too, was a leading advocate of appeasement. But his outstanding intellect and legal training were marred by what one biographer has described as 'his ability to see all sides of a complicated question [which] easily degenerated into an irritating inability to make up his mind'.[11] Nor was Simon's loyalty to be taken for granted; on the eve of war, he had suddenly and vociferously joined the group arguing for a more hawkish response to Hitler – a move prompted, it was said, because in it he 'saw his chance of becoming PM'.[12]

Also chosen by Chamberlain was the Home Secretary, Sir Samuel Hoare, aged fifty-nine, who had been in one ministerial office or another – including that of Foreign Secretary – since 1923.[13] A tireless worker, but lacking in charisma, it was said that his 'competence did not in public or private life make up for his lack of warmth'.[14] Although Chamberlain considered him to be an ally – Hoare was another supporter of appeasement – he would have known of Hoare's notorious ambition. According to one of Chamberlain's private secretaries, Hoare was known as 'Slippery Sam, . . . [and] his intelligence was matched, or even surpassed, by his natural bent for intrigue'.[15] The Prime Minister appointed him to the wide-ranging, but non-departmental, post of Lord Privy Seal.

A more surprising choice was a man virtually unknown to the British public: a sixty-two-year-old retired civil servant, albeit of immense distinction, Lord Hankey. Maurice Hankey's entire career, less five years as a Royal Marine, had been spent in the corridors of power, where he 'progressively became secretary of everything that mattered'.[16] For twenty-two years until 1938 he had been Cabinet Secretary and hugely influential as a military advisor and diplomatic confidant with an unsurpassed expertise in national defence matters. Indeed, in 1938 he had recommended the structure of a wartime government in his 'War Book'.[17] A professional bureaucrat to his fingertips, but with no experience as a politician, Hankey was appointed Minister without Portfolio.

Chamberlain also included the Earl Chatfield, aged sixty-six, because it would have been inconceivable for someone holding his appointment not to be. Chatfield was the Minister for Coordination of Defence, a retired Admiral of the Fleet[18] and former head of the Royal Navy. The job had been established in 1936 to oversee and coordinate the rearmament of British defences, and the Minister was expected to speak on behalf of all three services. The degree to which this appointment lived up its title will be discussed later.

Finally, Chamberlain invited someone whom he could not, politically, afford to leave out: Winston Churchill. Churchill, now two months short of his sixty-fifth birthday, had been the fiercest critic of appeasement, but his reputation and popularity meant that 'he would have been a most troublesome thorn in our flesh if he had been outside'.[19] Churchill rejected Chamberlain's offer of a non-departmental seat in the War Cabinet but agreed to become First Lord of the Admiralty (the minister for the Royal Navy) – the job he had held at the outset of the First World War.[20]

Figure 1.1 The War Cabinet, September 1939
(Standing: Hankey, Hore-Belisha, Churchill, Wood
Seated: Chatfield, Hoare, Chamberlain, Simon, Halifax)
(*Getty Images*)

This presented a problem. The other two service ministers – Leslie Hore-Belisha at the War Office and Sir Kingsley Wood at the Air Ministry – argued strongly, and successfully, for equal status. Both were admitted but knew that their membership was due entirely to Chamberlain's need to have Churchill on board, and this was reflected in their standing within the War Cabinet.

Chamberlain's War Cabinet was thus a hybrid – larger and with a greater proportion of departmental ministers than he would have wished. It also lacked the participation of the main opposition party, which had declined the invitation. (This was, in part, due to personal animosity. Attlee later recalled: '[H]e always treated us like dirt.')[21] The War Cabinet contained what had been described since 1938 as the 'inner Cabinet' – Chamberlain, Halifax, Simon and Hoare – with five additions. Its average age was, as Churchill observed to Chamberlain, '[o]nly one year short of the Old Age Pension!'[22] With one exception, Chamberlain had surrounded himself with like-minded ministers: calm, logical, sober, unemotional, reasonable and 'gentlemanly' – people he knew he could do business with. The exception, of course, was Churchill. Overall, Chamberlain's War Cabinet contained many seeds of rivalry and disharmony, but arguably no more so than most other Cabinets before or since. In A. J. P. Taylor's opinion, the government as a whole may have looked good on paper, but 'only on paper. The war machine resembled an expensive motor car, beautifully polished, complete in every detail, except there was no petrol in the tank.'[23] Anyway, Chamberlain seemed well pleased with his creation: '[W]e are working together very harmoniously and successfully', he recorded.[24]

This was the group that was sitting around the Cabinet table on 19 September, along with a few more junior ministers, the service Chiefs of Staff and sundry officials. They were considering for the first time a specific proposal for military action in Norway, and it was Churchill who had made it.

Norway

On 1 September Churchill had returned to the Admiralty 'to the room I had quitted in pain and sorrow almost exactly a quarter of a century before, when Lord Fisher's resignation had led to my removal from my post as First Lord and ruined irretrievably, as it proved, the important conception of forcing the Dardanelles'.[25] Indeed, the disastrous failure of the Dardanelles operation in 1915, and the major role that Churchill had played in it, was to cast a long shadow over the British campaign in Norway in 1940.

Clearly determined that the Royal Navy should take the fight to the enemy at the earliest opportunity (and be seen doing so), Churchill already had some ideas about how this might be achieved. The first of these was a scheme, uncannily reminiscent of the Dardanelles plan, to force a sea passage – this time into the Baltic with a small flotilla of large ships with specially reinforced armour plating and extra anti-aircraft guns. He had trailed this idea with a senior general two months earlier[26] and, on arrival at the Admiralty, had directed the naval staff to produce a report on Operation Catherine, as he christened it ('because Russia lay in the background of my thought'[27]).

The second scheme was already under consideration at the Admiralty when Churchill arrived there. This concerned the interdiction of the export of Swedish iron ore to Germany. The Foreign Office had been aware for some years of the dependence of German industry on the large

SCANDINAVIA

Tromsø
Kirkenes
Petsamo

Lofoten Islands

Narvik

Arctic Circle

Norwegian
Sea

Gällivare

Luleå

Trondheim

The Leads

SWEDEN

Gulf of Bothnia

FINLAND

NORWAY

Lillehammer

Bergen

Oslo

Stavanger

Kristiansand

Skagerrak

North
Sea

Ålborg

DENMARK

Helsinki

Stockholm

Oxelösund

Baltic
Sea

Copenhagen

Kiel

Hamburg

Danzig

0   100   200 Miles
0   100   200 Kms

Map 1.1 Scandinavia

quantity of high-grade iron ore imported from Sweden. In addition, in April 1939 the Foreign Office had drawn the Admiralty's attention to a book published in Germany ten years earlier by a highly respected strategist, Admiral Wolfgang Wegener. The book emphasised the strategic importance to Germany in any future war of seizing potential bases on the Norwegian western seaboard.[28] In 1939 a small, unofficial staff in the Admiralty[29] had been studying the implications of this, and of the trade in iron ore from the northern Swedish ore fields around Gällivare to Germany.[30] In summer, the ore was shipped direct from the Swedish port of Luleå, but in winter when the Gulf of Bothnia was frozen, the ore was transported by train to the Norwegian port of Narvik, thence in German freighters, avoiding British interference by using the Leads – the territorial inshore waters down the west coast of Norway. Attention had been drawn in several pre-war books to the potential for the fleet to interdict this trade.[31] Germany's dependence on imported iron ore had also been the subject of reports by the government's Industrial Intelligence Centre, and Churchill was already familiar with this subject as a result of the briefings he had been regularly receiving, with official sanction, from the Centre's head Desmond Morton, a close friend and neighbour.[32] Morton had written as early as 1937, '[W]ere Sweden alone to refuse to supply Germany with iron ore, German industry would come to a stop in a very short time, possibly measurable in weeks.'[33]

When Churchill and his senior staff discussed the Admiralty report on 18 September, they agreed that if diplomatic means to prevent the trade failed, 'we should be prepared to violate Norwegian territorial waters'.[34] There was a complicating factor. Negotiations were underway between the British and Norwegian governments for the charter by Britain of the large (and, for Britain, critically important) Norwegian merchant fleet, but these negotiations looked like they would be satisfactorily concluded in the near future. The way would then be clear for the action proposed. Churchill, enthused by the project, wasted no time. The very next day he put the idea to the War Cabinet. Having explained the overall problem, he set out his solution: If the desired result could not be attained by pressure on the Norwegian government, he would be compelled to propose a more drastic remedy, namely, the laying of mines inside Norwegian territorial waters to drive the ore-carrying vessels outside the three-mile limit, thereby opening them to attack.

What those around the table quite made of this is hard to judge. No discussion is recorded in the minutes; the Cabinet merely 'took note', and moved on.[35] Judging by subsequent recorded discussions, though, it is highly unlikely that their reaction was quite as Churchill reported back to the Admiralty: 'The Cabinet, including the Foreign Secretary, appeared strongly favourable to this action. It is therefore necessary to take all steps to prepare it. . . . Pray let me be continually informed of the progress of the plan, which is of the highest importance in crippling the enemy's war industry.'[36]

A fortnight later the War Cabinet returned to the subject, following a memorandum from Churchill calling for further plans to be made for prompt action. But the issue appeared to be overtaken by events. Halifax, no doubt to Churchill's embarrassment, reported that very little iron ore was, in fact, now being exported from Narvik, nor would there be through the winter.[37] The War Cabinet noted that no action would be necessary unless supplies from Narvik to Germany started moving again but agreed that, in that event, the Royal Navy would take 'drastic action'.[38]

And there the matter rested. But not for long.

The Strategy Makers

The War Cabinet was one of four levels in the higher direction of the war, and in the making of strategy. Above it, in terms of the Anglo-French Alliance, was the Supreme War Council. Modelled on the council which had proved successful in the final year of the First World War, it comprised the British and French prime ministers along with other ministers, and with military advisers in attendance, meeting on average monthly either in London or in France (usually in Paris). It was in turn served by a small standing committee, the Allied Military Committee, which lived and worked in London.

Immediately below the War Cabinet sat the Military Coordination Committee, established in October 1939.[39] The need for greater coordination of the three single services had been recognised for many years. Indeed, Churchill had been at the forefront of a campaign for a coordinating authority in the 1930s, resulting in the Prime Minister, Stanley Baldwin, creating a Minister for the Coordination of Defence in 1936. Whilst giving the appearance both of decisive political action and of a necessary improvement in the nation's defences, it was a façade and a compromise. On the one hand, the Minister was enjoined to exercise day-to-day supervision of the Committee for Imperial Defence, to consult with the Chiefs of Staff, to convene and chair meetings of the Chiefs of Staff Committee as necessary and to chair the Principal Supply Officers Committee. On the other hand, he was given no department, minimal staff, and had no executive authority[40] – or, in A. J. P. Taylor's words, 'one room, two secretaries and no powers';[41] and he was specifically forbidden from weakening the authority of the service ministers. Cynicism was further fuelled by Baldwin's selection as Minister of a man with no obvious qualification for the job - the Attorney General, Sir Thomas Inskip - prompting the unkind comment that it was '[t]he most remarkable appointment since the Emperor Caligula made his horse a consul'.[42] The purpose was to head off criticism that defence was uncoordinated, but without upsetting the vested interests of the services; its creation was a neat political trick, but little more than that. Inskip was succeeded in early 1939 by Lord Chatfield, who 'found it equally impossible to get things done, in spite of his vast experience in the politico-strategic field'.[43]

A further attempt to achieve greater coordination was the establishment in October 1939 of the Military Coordination Committee. Under Chatfield's chairmanship, it comprised the three service ministers and the Minister of Supply with the three service Chiefs of Staff acting as 'expert advisers'. The committee's remit was 'to keep under constant review on behalf of the War Cabinet the main factors of the strategic situation and the progress of operations, and to make recommendations from time to time to the War Cabinet as to the general conduct of the war'.[44] Again, its actual power to achieve coordination of defence was strictly limited.

Below the Military Coordination Committee sat the Chiefs of Staff Committee. The quality of advice of the three service Chiefs would play a critical role in determining the success of government strategy.

The chairman of Chiefs of Staff Committee, largely by virtue of longevity in post, was the Chief of the Air Staff, Air Chief Marshal Sir Cyril Newall.[45] Commissioned into an infantry regiment, Newall had transferred as a captain from the Army to the Royal Flying Corps in 1914 and was posted to France. There he had been awarded the Albert Medal (the then equivalent to the George Cross) for courageously leading a party of airmen in fighting a fire in an ammunition store. From early 1915 he filled a succession of command and management appointments, ending the war as Deputy Commander of the Independent Air Force deployed in France. Thereafter, he served almost exclusively in Britain, displaying his administrative skill in important Air Ministry jobs, such as head of the Royal Air Force (RAF) Supply and Organisation. Newall became Chief of the Air Staff in 1937 at the remarkably young age of fifty-one, selected personally by the Secretary of State for Air, Lord Swinton. This came as a surprise to many who believed that there were better men for the job, notably the stronger personalities of Air Chief Marshals Hugh Dowding of Fighter Command and Edgar Ludlow-Hewitt of Bomber Command, 'both of whom', in one historian's opinion, 'were his superiors in every respect'.[46]

Figure 1.2 Air Chief Marshal Sir Cyril Newall
(*National Portrait Gallery*)

An interesting pen-picture of Newall is given by Marshal of the Royal Air Force Lord Slessor, a long-serving member of Newall's wartime staff. Given that Slessor was writing when Newall was still alive, it is necessary to read between the lines:

In spite of an outwardly self-confident manner, he was at this time actually a rather reserved and self-effacing person, who took a bit of knowing, but in whom those who did know him well had great confidence. He had more force of character than appeared on the surface, and though he would be the last man to claim great intellectual qualities, was sound, level-headed and decisive. ... I have seldom met a man who was so good for one's morale.[47]

Other writers have been less kind, summing up Newall as 'a diligent office manager ... who proved to be an inadequate head of the RAF',[48] or commenting that '[t]here were too many much stronger characters amongst the senior air commanders to make his tenure as CAS an entirely happy one.'[49] Newall had never attended staff college, either as a student or instructor, and was somewhat narrow-minded in his understanding of warfare. In the Chiefs of Staff Committee, he confined himself mostly to matters pertaining to his own service, and in Cabinet, he was punctilious in representing the views of the Committee's

Figure 1.3 Admiral of the Fleet Sir Dudley Pound
(Getty Images)

members rather than attempting to offer wider or more personal advice or take the lead.

The head of the Royal Navy, or First Sea Lord, was Admiral of the Fleet Sir Dudley Pound. Pound's First World War service had included a spell as naval assistant to the First Sea Lord, Admiral of the Fleet Sir John 'Jackie' Fisher, command of a ship at the Battle of Jutland and further key staff appointments in the Admiralty. Between the wars, he had served at sea, notably as Commander-in-Chief (CinC) of the Mediterranean Fleet, and distinguished himself in several further Admiralty posts, latterly as Second Sea Lord, in charge of personnel and training. Pound was not expected to become First Sea Lord and in 1939 was due to retire.

According to one historian, Pound was an officer whose 'contemporaries judged a plodding second-rater, with a mind untroubled by large strategic visions' who came to the appointment 'only ... because sickness, premature death and early retirements had thinned the field of choice'.[50] According to his biographer, 'He was not prepared for the role he had to play. ... He took the job on because there was no-one else and he shouldered the burden as best he could.'[51] Pound, almost sixty-two years on appointment, was not in full health, suffering from increasingly serious osteoarthritis and growing deafness. He was, according to a contemporary who knew him well, already 'a tired man when he became First Sea Lord'.[52] Pound had a reputation for imperturbability but also as a workaholic, 'the supreme centraliser',[53] who had 'an obsession with detail'.[54] An officer who served on his staff observed, '[H]e would spend hours amending, re-writing and editing his minutes'.[55] Pound was dedicated to the navy but with few interests outside it and with 'narrow intellectual horizons'.[56] An officer who had served with him at sea remarked on 'the complete absence of books in Pound's cabin'.[57] Within the Chiefs of Staff Committee, his contribution to debate was sparing, and he, like Newall, tended to confine himself to matters of his own service. His major challenge would be his relationship with his political master, Churchill.

The Chief of the Imperial General Staff (CIGS) was fifty-nine-year-old General Sir Edmund Ironside. Superficially, Ironside might have appeared to be Central Casting's choice as professional head of the Army. Standing six foot four and squarely built, a former Rugby international, Army heavyweight boxer and a multilinguist to boot, 'Tiny' Ironside had had a colourful military career. As a junior officer, he had served in the Boer War, where he had been wounded three times and carried out clandestine work, dressed as a Boer; he was said to be the inspiration for John Buchan's character Richard Hannay. In the First World War, Ironside had held a number of front-line command and staff appointments, ending the war as a brigadier general with a Distinguished Service Order and six times Mentioned in Despatches. In 1919 he had commanded the Allied force in northern Russia, supporting the White Russians' fight against the Bolsheviks around Archangel, before a succession of short-term appointments heading military missions in Hungary, Turkey and Iran and surviving a plane crash in Iraq. He had then held the key appointment of Commandant of the Staff College, finding time there to write a book about the battle of Tannenberg.[58] In 1938 Ironside had been appointed Governor of Gibraltar, normally a pre-retirement sinecure, but had been brought back in May 1939 as Inspector of Overseas Forces. As a possible war approached, Ironside was convinced that he was supremely and uniquely qualified to be commander-in-chief of the British Expeditionary Force (BEF) in time of war and that his selection was a mere formality. Indeed, he 'did not hesitate to boast ... that he was the only officer left in the British Army who had experience of high command in war'.[59] The man actually chosen for this appointment, however, was the incumbent CIGS, Lord Gort. To the amazement of many, not least Ironside himself, he was chosen to be Gort's successor. Ironside was 'bitterly disappointed that

Figure 1.4 General Sir Edmund Ironside
(Getty Images)

I am not going to command the army in the field. My great ambition. I am not suited by temperament to such a job as CIGS, nor have I prepared myself to be such.'[60] The appointment had been contentious within government, the more so since there was another strong candidate, Lieutenant General Sir John Dill. Ironside's cause had received the significant support of Churchill (a friend, and something of a *confidant*),[61] as Hore-Belisha told Ironside.[62] One factor in the decision, at least for Hore-Belisha, who cared about these things, was Ironside's relatively high public profile. As one officer observed, 'Ironside's appointment was very well received. He was very much in the public eye at the time.'[63]

There were a number of drawbacks to Ironside as a potential CIGS. He had never served in the War Office, let alone at the interface between military-strategy and policy. He was a field commander by nature, temperament and experience, who was used to a simple environment where you either received orders or gave them, rather than having to make and justify your argument, work through committees and deal with the complexity, uncertainty and ambiguity that is inherent at the strategic level. He was not unintelligent, but he did not have a trained mind. One well-placed commentator described it as 'schoolboy intelligence', commenting that a discussion with him was very exhilarating if disorderly, 'like sitting under Niagara Falls – or watching a cricket hop from point to point'.[64] The War Office's Permanent Secretary, P. J. Grigg, waspishly observed: 'No doubt the new incumbent had many qualities and qualifications, but precision of thought and an orderly mind were not among them. Nor did he seem to me to have much idea about running a large machine',[65] describing him to a friend as 'a frothblower'.[66] Unfortunately, Ironside's self-confidence was often misplaced, sometimes to the point of arrogance, and he tended to rely on instinct rather than the advice of his staff. He also found it difficult to conceal his disdain for politicians. Although he believed that he had made a very favourable first impression on the Cabinet, word got back to the War Office that 'Far from impressing the Ministers he had annoyed them very much. . . . His manner with politicians was much too brusque.'[67] Chamberlain thought him 'a tactless man'[68] and, before the year was out, was asking Hore-Belisha whether he still had confidence in his CIGS.[69] Ironside was also highly disadvantaged by the timing of his appointment – the first day of the war – and the fact that some of the key members of the General Staff, in particular, the Director of Military Operations and Plans,[70] were removed at the same time. 'I protested', Ironside recalled. 'The DMO was the man who knew all the plans. I knew nothing.'[71] This upheaval and its timing were quite unnecessary. As Field Marshal Montgomery later observed, 'It is almost unbelievable that such a thing should have been allowed to happen. But it did.'[72] One result of this was that Ironside was in at the deep end.

A more favourable view of Ironside comes from Major General Sir John Kennedy, one of his staff officers in the early months of the war; but it is worth remembering that, like Slessor's assessment of Newall, Kennedy's was made while Ironside was still alive. 'I admired him immensely. The post of CIGS was uncongenial to him, and he made no secret of the fact. But in those bogus months between September 1939 and May 1940, he had injected into our preparations for war a virility and imagination and forcefulness which would have been lacking in Whitehall but for his presence.'[73]

Arguably as important (if not more so) as the individual competence of the Chiefs was the effectiveness of their combination in the provision of advice and the degree to which they worked as a team.

The photograph of the happy, smiling band of brothers walking down Whitehall belies a relationship between them that, beneath the surface, was inherently tense. Nor has this been an unusual state of affairs among the service Chiefs of Staff, either before or since. For example, before the First World War it was said that General Sir William Nicholson, CIGS 1908-1912, 'possessed a visceral loathing for the navy, a feeling which Admiral Sir John Fisher [First Sea Lord] heartily reciprocated'.[74] According to one historian, 'In the summer of 1939 personal relations among the COS [Chiefs of Staff] were as bad as during the Beatty-Trenchard era.'[75] Ironside had a low opinion of Pound – 'very deaf and hardly says anything except on naval subjects'[76] – and later referred to 'that creature Newall' as 'a sort of buffoon with no knowledge of modern war',[77] recording his performance at their first meeting with the French

Figure 1.5 The Chiefs of Staff: Ironside, Newall, Pound
(Getty Images)

Chiefs of Staff as 'weak and unconvincing'.[78] The reciprocal views of Pound and Newall about Ironside are not known. In the words of another historian, 'continual consultation among the COS had not produced a better understanding among the services; familiarity with each other's views had bred contempt rather than compromise'.[79]

The basis for the tension in the Chiefs' mutual relationship was their perspective on their individual responsibilities and loyalties. In common with many of their predecessors and successors, they saw their role and duty primarily as head of their own service and guardian of its interests, and despite having clear terms of reference about their remit to advise on defence policy as a whole, with 'all considerations concerning Single Service being subordinated to the main object of National and Imperial Defence',[80] believed that, quite to the contrary, they were doing their duty by putting the interests of their own tribe first. A running sore between the services was the competition for finite and scarce financial resources. The 'Ten Year Rule' – under which the armed forces were instructed to draft their estimates 'on the assumption that the British

Empire would not be engaged in any great war during the next ten years'[81] – may have been terminated in 1932, but strict financial stringency in defence funding remained. In the years leading up to the Second World War this competition had been particularly fierce, with successive governments keeping the services on very tight budgets – or, as the services believed, with justification, denying them the money they needed to operate effectively.

Each service manoeuvred shamelessly to secure a greater share of the funding. For example, in late 1938 the RAF had stated its case candidly:

[I]t is worth remembering that it is not enough to avoid losing a war. We have got to be able to win it. The Navy cannot win a war for us in less than a matter of years. We certainly cannot win it with an army of four or five divisions. We do not know that we can win it in the air. But a powerful air striking force seems our only means of providing a backing of immediate force behind our policy that might be effective within a reasonable time.[82]

At the same time, the Army's leaders were engaging in more covert subterfuge, lobbying for an increase in size of a BEF by planting questions with their French opposite numbers to be asked of British ministers visiting Paris, and surreptitiously denigrating the RAF's case with the Minister for Coordination of Defence.[83]

All three services were badly placed to face a war, for numerous reasons that are well explained elsewhere,[84] but each believed that it was particularly badly placed. The Royal Navy considered that it had been starved of money at the expense of the RAF which, by 1939, was consuming more than forty per cent of the entire annual defence budget. Following the ending in 1936 of the so-called building holiday – the moratorium on the construction of new warships – the Admiralty had sought approval for an ambitious programme to achieve a 'New Standard Navy', but this had been greatly curtailed by the government. By 1939 the Admiralty had many serious concerns: a high proportion of its ships were obsolescent; the first of its new King George V-class battleships was still in construction; the Fleet was seriously short of escorts, minesweepers and anti-submarine vessels; there were 'extremely serious deficiencies' in the Fleet Air Arm; and there was an overall shortage of skilled ratings.[85] For its part, the RAF, despite comparatively greater investment, was, with reason, far from confident of its readiness for war against a Luftwaffe that by 1939 was numerically superior to the air forces of Britain and France put together. Bomber Command was reported by its CinC to be lacking the strength and efficiency to go to war 'within any predictable period'.[86] Fighter Command was equipped 'in barely adequate numbers'. And Coastal Command was not only weak in numbers but also 'almost entirely equipped with obsolescent aircraft'.[87]

Finally, the Army, despite vigorous protest, had been bound by the policy of 'limited liability' – the planning assumption that, in the event of war, an expeditionary force would not be sent to France. It was an assumption that suited the other two services: financial provision for the self-styled 'Cinderella of the services'[88] had been restricted accordingly. When limited liability came to an abrupt end in February 1939, the Army was 'faced [with] the implications of . . . transforming itself from a small professional force concerned with imperial policing into a cadre to train and command a conscript force over a million strong to take part in large-scale continental warfare'.[89] It viewed its unreadiness with considerable alarm, aware that it was 'desperately short of all kinds of weapons, equipment and stores',[90] that its armoured forces were 'desperately weak'[91] and that there was a grave shortage of anti-aircraft guns.[92] The government's decision in March to double the size of the Territorial Army and the introduction in April of limited conscription – both without preparation, planning or financial provision – caught the headlines nicely, but caused considerable confusion, and for many months, did little to improve capacity or readiness. In August, Ironside calculated that the Army was still short of more than 1,300 officers and 41,000 men.[93]

A further and constant bone of contention[94] between the services throughout the 1930s had been the role and provision of air support. The Navy and Army both believed that, to be effective, air support should be an integral part of their own organisations. Responsibility for the Fleet Air Arm had been divided between the RAF and Royal Navy in 1918, but following a long campaign by the Admiralty, and much bitter wrangling in private and in public, all but a small part was returned to the navy in 1937. Although, at working level, liaison between the Fleet Air Arm and the RAF's Coastal Command may have, as some have claimed, been 'close and effective',[95] this did not prevent stealthy naval predatory moves on Coastal Command, including a proposal that a number of its airfields be transferred to naval ownership. This, in turn, focussed the RAF on 'defending ourselves against ever increasing encroachments'.[96] One result of this toxic relationship was that in the two years preceding the outbreak of the war, the Fleet Air Arm and Coastal Command held only two joint exercises.[97]

The RAF was also locked into 'acrimonious debate' on the subject of air support with the Army.[98] The latter had increasingly seen the need for direct air support for ground forces and resented both the low priority given to the resourcing of it by the RAF and the small air component dedicated to the role. In March 1939 the CIGS, Lord Gort, had demanded a much increased air component, including bombers, and insisted that the force should be an integral part of the deployed field force, under army control. Such a demand was anathema to the RAF, who, with good reason, doubted Army assurances that it was not seeking its own air force.[99] Within a fortnight of taking office, Ironside had taken up the fight with energy and bombast, 'disgusted with the way in which the RAF treat cooperation of the Air Force with the Army',[100] castigating his predecessors – 'Each successive CIGS has funked tackling the Air Ministry' – and declaring his own hand: 'I have told them that we are at war now and there can be no delay.'[101]

The RAF's position on the issue of support to the other services was strictly in line with the doctrine of its founder Lord Trenchard – still, in the late 1930s, an *eminence grise*. The Trenchard doctrine, popularised by Baldwin's assertion in 1932 that 'the bomber will always get through. ... The only defence is offence',[102] held that the air forces should be used for long-range 'strategic' bombing and that other roles were a dangerous distraction and a misuse of air power. The RAF's senior officers in 1939 spoke in unison with the voice of true disciples, and Newall, according to his Secretary of State Samuel Hoare (in 1940), 'never wavered in his defence of the true faith'.[103] Indeed, Newall had declared close air support to ground troops to be 'a gross misuse of air forces'.[104] Evidence of the success of such support in the Spanish Civil War, and later, in German success in Poland may have caused some to have private doubts, but it did not shake their publicly declared faith. The reason was simple. If the Army was allowed to have control of its own air support, it was but a small step to the formation of its equivalent of the Fleet Air Arm and thus the dismemberment and death-knell of the RAF. Feelings ran high. Air Chief Marshal Sir Arthur Harris was later to recall, '[F]or twenty years, I watched the army and navy, both singly and in concert, engineer one deliberate attempt after another to destroy the Royal Air Force. Time after time they were within a hair-breadth of success; time after time Trenchard, and Tren-chard alone, saved us.'[105] For the RAF, the major existential threat seemed to be not the Luftwaffe, but the other two British services. Thus, when in March 1939 the Army produced a report on its 'Require-ments from the RAF for the Field Force' which demanded, amongst other things, no less than thirty-nine army cooperation squadrons, twenty-four direct support squadrons and six long-range reconnais-sance squadrons, it opened old wounds in the Air Ministry, causing the Director of Plans to warn Newall.

There is a regrettable revival of the old idea, which there has been some reason to think dead, that when the soldier talks about cooperation between the Air Force and the Army he really means the subordination of the Air Force to the Army.

It should be strenuously resisted ...The War Office disclaim ... any idea of an Army Air Arm, and then go on to propose an organization in which the responsibility of the Air Force is entirely confined to the production, supply and technical training. In fact, the Royal Air Force are to be manufacturers, garage proprietors and chauffeurs for the Army.[106]

In summary, there were considerable tensions between the service Chiefs in September 1939 – tensions that were set to get worse.

There was, thus, a hierarchy of four levels of strategic decision-making: the Supreme War Council, the War Cabinet, the Military Coordination Committee and the Chiefs of Staff Committee. But below the latter was another important part of the process: the Joint Planning Sub-Committee, or 'Joint Planners'. Advice to the Military Coordination Committee and War Cabinet from the Chiefs of Staff came in the form of written reports. The Chiefs did not, of course, write these reports themselves. As anyone who worked in the service ministries – or has worked in today's Ministry of Defence – knows, reports signed by the great men are actually written by staff officers, following direction – sometimes only very broad direction - from the Chiefs, who may then call for amendments to be made to the draft. The staff officers concerned with providing the most important policy advice are always, and for obvious reasons, very carefully selected and are invariably 'high-flyers' within their own service. This was indeed the case in late 1939 for the three officers – the Directors of Plans of each service – who made up the Joint Planners, which was the group whose function it was to write the reports or 'appreciations of the situation'. These officers were Royal Navy Captain Victor Danckwerts, an officer of 'excellent brains',[107] succeeded in March by Captain Charles Daniel (who would rise to the rank of full admiral); Air Commodore John Slessor (a future Chief of the Air Staff);[108] and Brigadier John Kennedy (later to become Assistant CIGS), succeeded in January by Brigadier Ian Playfair (later to be one of the official historians of the war).[109] The Joint Planners' role was to be a highly significant one. Their title, though, was something of a misnomer. As has been seen, their task was to produce reports and 'appreciations', not to produce joint operational plans. Remarkably, no organisation existed to produce the latter.

One of the first wartime tests for the strategy makers was to be posed by British policy towards Norway.

2   'A Legitimate Side-Show'

Norway had featured in British strategic planning well before the Second World War and did so increasingly from the war's outbreak. On 4 September, following a proposal by Halifax that an attack on Norway (except by air) should be treated as tantamount to an attack on Britain, the Chiefs of Staff had provided the War Cabinet with a paper which considered the possibility of German military action in the event that Norway restricted the export of iron ore to Germany. The Chiefs recommended that in such circumstances 'it would be in our own interests to come to Norway's assistance'.[1] The War Cabinet agreed and commitment to that support was duly communicated to the Norwegian government. But the Chiefs' paper also contained a deeply flawed planning assumption which reflected Admiralty thinking at the time – an assumption which had become an article of faith and which remained unchallenged until the moment it was dramatically proved to be disastrous. Having assessed that '[a] seaborne invasion [by Germany] in the face of superior British naval forces would be attended by very serious risks', it concluded that '[a]ny such operation directed against Norway's western seaboard can be dismissed as impracticable for this reason.'[2] No one in the Cabinet challenged this. As the editor of the official history of the Second World War, J. R. M. Butler, observed, the assumption 'turned out to be a miscalculation of critical importance'.[3]

The commitment to come to Norway's assistance was made within a grand strategy for the conduct of the war that was a complex mix of various strands of policy – diplomatic, military, political and economic. Among the most fundamental principles were two which had traditionally guided British foreign policy: seeking to prevent an adverse balance of power within Europe and seeking to safeguard the Empire. More specifically in September 1939 was acknowledgement that there was no realistic prospect of early victory, but rather a perception (in particular, that of Chamberlain) of the possibility of 'convinc[ing] the Germans that they cannot win',[4] leading to the overthrow of Hitler and a negotiated settlement. A further fundamental principle was the need to build an alliance against Germany. In addition to preserving the partnership with France, it was necessary to attract more allies, notably large ones, such as the United States, but also smaller ones, such as the Scandinavian states. At the same time there was the need to discourage other countries, notably Italy, from joining Germany, as, in effect, the Soviet Union had done following the Molotov-Ribbentrop pact of 23 August. Maintaining the moral high ground, abiding by international law and supporting vulnerable neutrals were also held to be enduring principles by some members of the War Cabinet, although for others it was the appearance of doing these things that was rather more important. The deeply felt desire to avoid the bloody attrition of the Western Front in the previous war was undisputed. As Michael Howard has pointed out, '"[n]ever again" was not just an epitaph; it had become a guiding principle of strategy.'[5]

Of particular significance was the long-war policy.[6] Having started the war with relatively weak armed forces, it was held that the Allies' stronger economies could outperform Germany's and thereby improve their military strength and readiness faster than Germany could: 'time was emphatically on our side'.[7] A war of three years' duration was anticipated from the outset.[8] Belief in the efficacy of the long-war policy was, however, far from unanimous within the War Cabinet. Indeed, it is difficult to know where personal opinion lay. Chamberlain and Halifax appear to have subscribed to it.[9] Simon, though, was concerned about Britain's financial 'staying power' in a war,[10] and there were increasing concerns about its effect on civilian morale. For his part, Churchill was impatient with the long-war policy and favoured getting to grips with the enemy at the earliest opportunity. As J. R. M. Butler diplomatically put it, 'It soon became clear that he was not content with the prevailing tempo in the conduct of the war.'[11] Soon after his return to the Admiralty, Churchill was telling his staff, 'the search for a naval offensive must be incessant'.[12] His fear was that without active measures to recover the initiative, Britain would relapse 'into a defensive naval strategy and habit of mind'.[13] Although there was no contradiction between a long-war policy and some offensive action within it, Churchill found it hard to curb the ambition of his offensive schemes. Others, also, saw good reason for some form of limited offensive military action and even more reason to be seen taking it. With regard to the long-war policy, there were divisions, too, within the British military. The policy was favoured by the Joint Planners but not, wholeheartedly, by the Chiefs of Staff. In their draft report in mid-September on 'The Possible Future Course of the War', the Joint Planners recommended that '[w]e should concentrate our initial efforts on securing our positions, particularly in the west, while building up our strength and ensuring the maximum degree of economic pressure. We adhere to our previous view that time is on our side', adding that the chances of Germany getting a quick decision in the west were 'most unlikely'.[14] But when the Chiefs sent the report to the War Cabinet, these sentences had been removed.[15] The reason is unclear. It may have been because the Chiefs fundamentally disagreed with the statements, possibly influenced by increasing scepticism within the French military,[16] but more likely by the Chiefs' instinctive dislike of passivity and their desire not to give the War Cabinet the impression that money was not urgently needed for the armed forces. To a certain extent, they were playing tactics. Indeed, at the War Cabinet meeting, Ironside reported that the French Chief of National Defence, General Maurice Gamelin, anticipated the possibility of a major decision on the Western Front 'within the next few weeks'.[17] He recorded in his diary, 'I had a great day at the War [Cabinet]. They were havering at the number of divisions they would make and I told them that Gamelin was terrified of a German attack. ... It was electrifying. We got our orders to make fifty-five divisions. Personally, I do not believe the Germans will attack this winter.'[18] It is difficult to judge whether his personal view had changed or whether he was still playing the 'imminent attack' card when, the following week, he told the Chiefs that '[t]o attack us in France is the only method of getting a quick decision and I think they will do it'.[19]

Many in the armed services shared Churchill's impatience to take action. For the military, the long-war policy contradicted all that they had been taught about the paramount need to seize and hold the initiative. Ironside was already ruminating on this point within the first week of the War: 'We are now sitting and wondering what Hitler will do next and doing nothing ourselves.'[20] There was also political impatience, reflecting a perception of public restlessness. Chamberlain, himself, remarked that 'this war twilight is trying people's nerves'.[21]

Finally, the desire to take the initiative, but to do so somewhere other than on the Western Front, chimed not just with the French but also with ideas popularised by the influential military historian, theorist and polemicist Basil Liddell Hart. He strongly advocated an 'indirect approach' to warfare, seeking ways around a head-on confrontation with the enemy's main strength and returning to what he called 'The British Way in Warfare' - avoiding continental military entanglements and using superior British sea power, including the use of a blockade, to attack the enemy. (He was later to counsel in opposition to operations in Scandinavia.)[22]

Against this background, the prospect of a relatively painless shortcut to victory through interdiction, as suggested by the newly created Ministry of Economic Warfare, looked highly attractive. In September

1939 the Ministry drew attention to two potential targets for action: Germany's supply of oil from Roumania and its import of iron ore from Scandinavia. The Chiefs of Staff were wary of involvement in the Balkans. The French were advocating action there amongst a number of proposed *projets* – a word that was to become synonymous in Whitehall with wild, impractical schemes.[23] Interdiction of the iron ore traffic was deemed to be a much more feasible possibility, and one that deserved further study. An additional factor drawing eyes to the north was the prospect of a possible invasion of Finland and Scandinavia by Russia. In October the Chiefs suggested that the British Army might have a role to play in Scandinavia. 'A small British force, say a Brigade Group, based on the Narvik-Boden [in Sweden] railway and operating in support of the Norwegians and Swedes, might have an effect out of all proportion to its size. Although campaigning conditions in Scandinavia would be extremely arduous, the despatch of a small expedition would be a practical proposition'.[24] But the Chiefs were most reluctant – and with good reason – to take on further commitments.

We could, however, afford no assistance to Finland against Russian aggression. ... In our view, we and France are at present in no position to undertake additional burdens and we cannot, therefore, from a military point of view, recommend that we should declare war on Russia. On the contrary, we should endeavour to postpone the issue until we are stronger, and we should try to avoid any action likely to consolidate the alliance between Germany and Russia.[25]

When the paper was discussed in the Chiefs of Staff committee, Ironside was explicit, opposing land operations in Norway 'in any circumstances'.[26]

At the end of November, two events caused eyes to turn again to the north. First, word came from Norway that the iron ore traffic had resumed at a high level, and the Ministry of Economic Warfare assessed that its stoppage would have a serious impact on Germany's ability to continue the war. Indeed, the Ministry's prediction was that 'a complete stoppage of Swedish exports of iron ore to Germany would ... end the war in a few months.'[27] Churchill seized on this and ordered Admiralty plans for intervention to be advanced. When he brought the subject to the War Cabinet, he sought to reassure its members that only 'a few small minefields, each perhaps three or four miles square, would be enough for the purpose.'[28] Not for the first time, nor, indeed, the last, Halifax argued for circumspection. He expressed concern, not least at the legal and ethical aspects of the violation of Norwegian neutrality (no doubt mindful of the effect on world opinion), and called for a study of the subject. Along with this, the War Cabinet commissioned a report from the Chiefs, examining the military problems involved, including possible German retaliation.[29]

The second event was the Russian invasion of Finland on 29 November. It quickly became apparent that public opinion, as expressed in the media, was strongly supportive of the 'Gallant Finns'[30] and that the government wished to do something to support them, or at least to be seen doing so. Halifax expressed the view that 'it would be to our advantage to help Finland as much as possible', and Hoare favoured 'a more forward policy'.[31] But unsurprisingly, it was Churchill who pressed most strongly for greater aid for the Finns, although his motives were, as his memoirs reveal, not entirely altruistic. 'I sympathised ardently with the Finns and supported all proposals for their aid; and I welcomed this new and favourable breeze as a means of achieving the major strategic advantage of cutting off the vital iron ore supplies of Germany.'[32] The Chiefs, however, continued to be wary of any dissipation of resources, agreeing only reluctantly to the provision of a small quantity of equipment, including some semi-obsolete aircraft, and telling the War Cabinet that 'we were not in a position to provide any effective support'.[33] Ironside noted in his diary, 'Our front line is in France and we must fight in France. We cannot escape that', adding, 'I am wondering if we have big enough men in the Government to make the proper decisions as to strategy? If so, I haven't met them yet.'[34]

Sensing his moment, Churchill pressed for direct and immediate action. In a memorandum of 16 December to Cabinet colleagues, he argued forcefully for stoppage of the iron ore supply, painting an enticing picture: 'No other measure is open to us for many months to come which gives so good a chance of abridging the waste and destruction of the conflict, or of perhaps preventing the vast slaughters which will attend the grapple of the main armies.' Action of some sort would, of course, also be required at Luleå, the ore export port in the Gulf of Bothnia, and at Oxelösund, the export port for the much smaller ore field in central Sweden. In the case of the former, Churchill suggested 'the laying of a declared minefield ... by British submarines would be one way. There are others.' In the case of the latter, he alluded to 'methods which are neither diplomatic nor military' – code for a Secret Intelligence Service sabotage operation already in the planning stage.[35] Action at Narvik, he argued, was required immediately. 'If Germany can be cut off from all Swedish ore supplies from now onwards till the end of 1940, a blow will have been struck at her war-making capacity equal to a first-class victory in the field or from the air, and without any serious sacrifice of life. It might, indeed, be immediately decisive.' Finally, knowing that many around the Cabinet table would be horrified at the proposed violation of Scandinavian neutrality, he argued that infringement of international law was justified and necessary: 'The letter of the law must not in supreme emergency obstruct those who are charged with its protection and enforcement. ... Humanity, rather than legality, must be our guide.'[36]

At the War Cabinet on 18 December, Churchill took the argument a stage further. Echoing Francis Bacon ('He that commands the sea is at great liberty, and may take as much and as little of the war as he will'[37]), he now declared that 'we had everything to gain by the war spreading to those countries [Norway and Sweden] so long as we retained our command of the sea. ... It would give us the opportunity to take what we wanted, and this, with our sea power, we could do.'[38] Whatever they may have thought about this highly dubious assertion (our sea power, for example, did not extend to the Baltic), no one around the table challenged it. Ministers had a greater concern: the potential reaction, particularly in the United States, to the violation of Scandinavian neutrality which Churchill's proposal entailed. In reply, however, Halifax was emollient, remarking that '[a]t this stage he was not, perhaps, prepared to go the whole way with the First Lord in believing that it would be to our benefit to involve Norway and Sweden in the war at once, though he entirely agreed with his estimate of the advantages which we would derive if the war should happen to extend to those areas.'[39] He proposed, and the Cabinet agreed, that the subject should be referred for further study to the Military Coordination Committee and the Chiefs of Staff.

Two days later the Military Coordination Committee met to consider the matter. Alongside Churchill's memorandum of 16 December were short papers by Halifax and the Ministry of Economic Warfare as well as the long-awaited Chiefs of Staff report, called for on 30 November. What is remarkable about this meeting is that almost no time was spent discussing the concerns raised in the Chiefs' report about the implications of stopping the iron ore traffic. The report contained a number of warnings, raised by the Joint Planners, that Germany might invade and establish coastal bases from Oslo to Stavanger, their initial forces might be flown in and, since Britain could not effectively interrupt sea communications through the Kattegat to Oslo, further reinforcements could speedily follow. Furthermore, the weak Norwegian Army could not be expected to mount much resistance, so the Germans would require no more than two or three divisions to occupy all of Norway, south of Trondheim. The paper also warned that British Army formations were unsuitable for operating in the difficult terrain of southern Scandinavia at any time of year, although it suggested that 'a force on skis might be organised with Dominion (e.g., Canadian) assistance'.[40] The paper mentioned, but did not recommend, a much bigger project: an expedition from Narvik to Gällivare or Luleå to sabotage or seize the ore fields or railway.

Ironside's enthusiasm appears to have got the better of him. When he spoke, it was not to represent these concerns, but to be positively upbeat about the feasibility of sending a force overland from Narvik to Gällivare. While admitting that the northern ore fields were inaccessible and it would be very difficult to operate large forces in the area, he declared that

large forces would not be required for this purpose ... it would be better to use a force of three or four thousand men, especially equipped to move on skis or snowshoes. The French had Alpine troops trained in the use of skis, and we could pick special troops from the British army and from the Canadians who would be well fitted to operate under the difficult conditions prevailing in the minefield area.[41]

Ironside noted in his diary, 'I told them that if the iron-ore was vital to Germany, then a small expedition to Northern Sweden would be more than desirable. It was quite possible and could be of limited scope. ... I told them that here was a legitimate side-show.'[42] There was clearly the alarming possibility of this sideshow setting off war with Russia, but Churchill stepped in to offer reassurance that 'it would not make war with Russia inevitable', and urged that '[p]lans for the despatch of a military force to Scandinavia should be put in hand at once'.[43]

Ironside's change of view had been both dramatic and swift. Only a month previously he had resolutely declared his opposition to land operations in Norway 'in any circumstances'.[44] Just three days before the Committee meeting, he had written in his diary 'we shall have no side-shows – if I can prevent the starting of them'.[45] And he had signed up to the Chiefs' report which was full of reservations about intervention in Scandinavia. His head seems to have been turned by Churchill's persuasive exposition of his proposal at the War Cabinet on 18 December. That night, he recorded in his diary, somewhat wide-eyed, 'Winston Churchill is pushing for us to occupy Narvik in Norway and prevent all the iron-ore going to Germany. All his ideas are big if they are nothing else. He talks about occupying the islands and controlling the coast.'[46] Here at last, for Ironside, was an opportunity to take the initiative and an attractive alternative to what he called the French 'usual mad excursions'.[47] At the Supreme War Council in Paris the following day, the CIGS had publicly committed himself to the proposal. At the meeting, the French Prime Minister, Edouard Daladier, had made great play of a private memorandum by an exiled German steel magnate, Fritz Thyssen. In Thyssen's opinion, Germany's dependence on Swedish iron ore was so great that if the Allies gained control of it, Germany's powers of resistance would soon be broken.[48] Ironside recorded in his diary, 'I said that if the iron ore is vital, then we ought to go all out to stop it.'[49] This had been the moment for strategic circumspection, not bravado, but Ironside had unfortunately (as it turned out) chosen the latter. Why? There may be truth in the suggestion that he was in some way beholden to Churchill, to whom, in part, he owed his selection as CIGS and that, as historian Wesley Wark put it, 'Scandinavia acted as a temptation on a grand scale [to him] ... in the first instance because it was an imaginative project mooted by Churchill, his main backer ... [and that] he could not hold on to the scepticism and caution which had initially informed his judgment on Scandinavian plans.'[50]

The scene was set for the War Cabinet on 22 December. Churchill knew he had to allay his colleagues' concerns about a number of issues: the violation of international law, the impact on neutral countries, the subsequent threat to Norway and Sweden, the threat of war with Russia and the awkward fact that, according to the Ministry of Economic Warfare, 'the stoppage of the Narvik exports alone would produce only a limited effect – perhaps an embarrassment for a period of a few weeks by about May 1940.'[51] He set out to do this with a bravura display of his dialectical skills. Persuading Chamberlain to read out extracts from the Thyssen memorandum, Churchill then emphasised the potential prize and described the steps, diplomatic and military, which would be needed to win it. He was supported by Hoare, Hankey and Ironside. Hoare had been caught up in the enthusiasm, writing to Chamberlain two days previously, 'I am more than convinced that Scandinavia is the key place of the war.'[52] Ironside played down the threat of German intervention in southern Norway and Sweden, opining that 'Germany was inexperienced in combined operations. An invasion of southern Scandinavia would be an enormous commitment for her.'[53] The main opposition came from Halifax who argued that the complete stoppage of the iron ore was key, that a clearer picture was required of the military action needed to achieve it and that '[i]t would be unwise to prejudice our success in the larger project by action at Narvik which would only have a limited effect.' Instead, he recommended a diplomatic initiative, proposed by the French, to encourage Norway and Sweden to provide assistance to their Finnish neighbour, with a hint that Britain and France might come to their aid if Germany took action against them. In Halifax's corner were Chatfield and Wood;[54] Churchill was short of supporters. Chamberlain, unhappily faced with adjudicating, said there could be no doubt that the decision to be taken was of the utmost importance: 'It might be one of the turning points of the war.' But while he was, he said, greatly impressed by the statements contained in the Thyssen memorandum, and it certainly seemed as if there was a chance of dealing a mortal blow to Germany, he sided with Halifax's proposal. Despite Churchill playing a last-minute card that reports had been received that the Russians were preparing ships to seize Narvik, the War Cabinet agreed to delay a decision on military action and follow the diplomatic route, albeit with a warning of the intention to prevent the export of iron ore to Germany. It also called for a report from the Chiefs on all of the military implications of the plan, on the technical and material support assistance that could be given to Finland and on the assistance that could be offered to Norway and Sweden in the face of a German threat to them.

Irritating though the decision may have been to Churchill, it was a wise precaution.

3 Deciding to Decide

Christmas intervened. The Chiefs' report was not due until the end of the year, but the War Cabinet met again on 27 December to discuss its policy towards Scandinavia. Churchill, clearly aware that the possible expedition to Gällivare posed a threat, or at least a delay, to his treasured scheme for naval action, now adjusted his argument accordingly. Despite having urged the Military Coordination Committee that '[p]lans for the despatch of a military force to Scandinavia should be put in hand at once',[1] he now declared that he had 'not contemplated that we should land troops at Narvik or send an expedition to the Swedish ore fields at the present stage'. And he asserted that his proposed naval action, far from jeopardising the larger project, actually facilitated it: 'As soon as Germany saw that we were laying our hands on the iron ore from Narvik she would take action against southern Scandinavia which would give us full justification for the larger operation.' Thus, the German invasion of southern Scandinavia, which the Chiefs had told the War Cabinet would cause Britain such a problem and pose such a threat, was now to be welcomed as a positive blessing. No one challenged this assertion. The Admiralty, said Churchill, was ready to send a force of destroyers to intercept the traffic as soon as the War Cabinet authorised it. Halifax intervened to say, with some justification, that he 'was reluctant to appear to pledge us to action in Scandinavia until we were satisfied that it was feasible. This would presumably be for the Chiefs of Staff to say.' Chamberlain, however, allowed discussion to move on to consider the content and timing of the diplomatic *démarches* giving assurance to Norway and Sweden of Franco-British military support in the event of German action against them and also warning them of the proposed naval action in Norwegian waters. But among the Cabinet's conclusions was a presumption that all that held up the naval action was a satisfactory response to these *démarches*: '[N]o final decision should be taken to order Naval vessels to enter Norwegian territorial waters for the purpose of stopping coastwise traffic from Norwegian ports to Germany until we had learnt how the communication [with Norway and Sweden] was received.'[2] The forthcoming Chiefs of Staff report on the feasibility of military action seemed to be taken for granted. Whether they realised it or not, the War Cabinet had just taken a further half step towards military action.

Churchill was also preparing the ground carefully for the Cabinet meeting scheduled for 2 January at which the Chiefs' report was to be discussed and decisions taken. Sensing his need for more allies, and that the CIGS, a potentially influential voice, was sympathetic to his cause, Churchill invited him (behind Hore-Belisha's back) for an evening discussion on 27 December to enlist his support. Ironside's diary shows that he, like Churchill, was becoming both increasingly frustrated with the passivity of the long-war policy and attracted to the idea of operations in Scandinavia. Despite, in the previous month, having ridiculed 'civilian strategists' for 'grasping at any mad idea in the hopes of that they have discovered a golden road to victory',[3] he now came close to believing that he had discovered one himself. In the week after Christmas he wrote: 'I believe that we have "stumbled" on a means of upsetting the enemy';[4] 'It is the opportunity to make Germany answer to our movement';[5] and 'we must not sit supine, hoping something in our favour will come to pass. We cannot "convince the Germans they cannot win"... by doing nothing.'[6] Ironside was starting to get carried away by his own impatience and enthusiasm. In a memorandum on 'The Position in Northern Europe', he wrote, 'All we send will be at the expense of France and the BEF. But I feel that the effect of action will be electric. All German eyes will be directed that way. We have a brilliant opportunity for making a diversion at small expense, though at the effect of transferring the war to Scandinavia.'[7] And in a draft paper on 'Our War Strategy', he wrote, 'I think the moment has arrived for some plan which will upset the German calculations, cause them to disperse their forces, confuse their curious leader, and escape from our position of passive waiting with all its alarms and doubtful advantages of increasing strength.'[8] But it was far from clear in strategic terms whether Ironside was arguing for a change from a long-war policy to a short-war one, and whether 'transferring the war to Scandinavia' meant just a diversion or a complete change of main effort.

Ironside was blowing hot and cold almost simultaneously, as increasingly became the case. For all the confidence he appeared to show in the Scandinavian operation, he was also becoming anxious, as well he might be, that the Scandinavian strategy was getting out of control. He shared his anxiety with the Chiefs at their meeting of 28 December. As the minutes recorded,

Every day the scope of the problem was expanding, and he was apprehensive lest we should embark on a course of action without having foreseen to the full the results which might follow. He understood that it was proposed to take action against the Narvik trade quite soon, unless the Norwegian and Swedish reaction was very unfavourable. This might lead to a sudden demand for a force to be sent to Narvik, with the eventual object of seizing the Swedish mines. The German reaction might take the form of an invasion of Scandinavia. Before setting in motion a train of events so important in its results, it was essential to make quite certain that we were ready to carry our policy through to the end, and that such forces as might be required were available, and fully equipped.[9]

Far from reining back their ambitions, however, the Chiefs, in their report which came to the War Cabinet on 2 January, recommended a substantially larger and more complex expedition than had hitherto been envisaged. The operation from Narvik to Gällivare would require an initial force of up to two brigades – the possibility of employing French and Canadian mountain troops was mentioned – and two further divisions might be required shortly after as a follow-up force. But this was nothing compared to what was envisaged further south. To open up a proper line of communication to the troops at Gällivare, and to obtain Norwegian and Swedish cooperation, which was quite rightly regarded as an essential prerequisite, it was deemed necessary be able to provide them 'substantial military support' in the event of German aggression, or the threat of it. Additionally, it was assessed that if the Germans gained a foothold in southern Scandinavia, they could seriously interfere with both the operations in northern Scandinavia and sea communications in the North Sea. This military support would indeed be substantial: it was envisaged that four to six Allied divisions would be required, 'which could be made available only at the cost of the front in France'. The lines of communication for the force would operate through the port of Trondheim, and possibly other smaller ports nearby. Nor was this a short-term operation; since the troops occupying Gällivare might have to remain there for up to a year, so would the troops in the south. Moreover, in addition to the forces for Gällivare and Sweden, a third force of about a brigade would be required to secure the southern Norwegian ports. Furthermore, the naval commitment would require up to forty destroyers, a quarter of Britain's total operational strength. However, the Chiefs maintained that, apart from the main objective of stopping the iron ore, the plan had a further attractive selling point. 'By employing some five to six Allied divisions in Scandinavia, we may expect to compel Germany to divert perhaps twenty divisions to that area.' This dispersion of her effort, they asserted, 'would finally rule out the possibility of a successful German offensive in the West'.[10] Thus, it was argued, the plan would actually buy the Allies security on the Western Front.

The report, however, contained a number of serious reservations, raised by the Joint Planners.[11] First, there were those concerns included in their previous report about the inability to prevent Germany from establishing air and naval bases in southern Norway or interdicting reinforcement, adding that '[t]he establishment of German Air and Naval bases in Southern Norway would entirely alter the situation in the North Sea greatly to our disadvantage'. Secondly, there was acknowledgement that as a result of the action recommended 'we may ... become involved in war with Russia'.

Next was the air threat. It was acknowledged that the Narvik-Boden railway line, the vital link for the Gällivare force, was highly vulnerable to air attack, that the Germans could mount air attacks which could seriously threaten the railway link and the base at Narvik, and that 'we could provide little effective fighter or bomber support for the force'. In the south, the position was even worse. It was assessed that the whole of southern Norway and Sweden was within effective bombing range of the German air force operating from bases in Germany and that even Trondheim was within the extreme range of German bombers. The report concluded that if the Germans were to establish air bases in southern Norway or Sweden, the threat to the lines of communication of British forces might become 'precarious'; 'the allocation of fighter squadrons for operations in Sweden would be a particularly serious commitment', to which the Chiefs had added, 'and we could in fact not afford more than a token protection to the land force'.[12]

A further challenge was timing. The Chiefs had concluded that British intervention in northern Scandinavia was 'very likely' to provoke a German attack on southern Norway, that they considered it 'essential' both that the Germans be denied bases on the Norwegian coast and that British forces should forestall them. Thus, if the naval action – what they termed 'the minor project' – went ahead immediately, it was very likely that the force to deny the bases would be required in short order. Indeed, the report emphasised that all three operations (northern Norway, southern Sweden and southern Norway) were complementary to the success of 'the major project' – the full-scale deployment – and that the forces for each should be prepared to carry out their tasks concurrently.[13] But in a second paper, submitted at the same meeting, on the balance of advantage between the major and minor projects, the Chiefs had reiterated in a single sentence the key point made on 20 December about the readiness, or lack, of British forces: 'We cannot be prepared for such operations before March.'[14] This was a potential showstopper to immediate execution of the minor project.

There were, thus, a large number of high risks – risks that had both a high likelihood of materialising and a high impact if they did so. Taken together, the compound risk of the plan was very high indeed. The Chiefs, however, chose not to make this point in their report. On the contrary, their overall risk assessment was minimalist in the extreme: 'The policy under review ... must involve some risk. Nevertheless, in view of the possibility of obtaining decisive results we think the risk can be accepted.'[15] And with this, the Chiefs firmly recommended their plan. But it was a recommendation unsupported by the body of the report; it had been reached in spite of the evidence, not as a result of it. In strategic terms, the ends, ways and means were nowhere near in balance. True, the Chiefs underlined the fact that their recommendation was entirely based on the assumption, given to them, that the stoppage of the exports of iron ore to Germany would be decisive, but the prize appears to have been so glittering as to have been worth almost any cost. At the Cabinet meeting Ironside warned that the cooperation of the Scandinavians would be required, since without it this would be 'a very hazardous affair',[16] although this implied that providing such cooperation was gained, the venture would not be very hazardous.

The Chiefs also rejected proceeding with the minor project on the grounds that it would prejudice the major one, and it was on this issue – and not the viability of the major project – that discussion focused at the War Cabinet meeting on 2 January. Churchill pressed his case strongly, reiterating his argument that the naval action might provoke a German invasion which would justify British occupation of the ore fields. The German invasion, he declared, would be vexatious but would be in no way decisive. As for the suggestion that the Narvik-Boden railway would be cut, he declared loftily, the Germans could not carry out sabotage in northern Scandinavia, and 'it was well known that the effects of air attack on a railway line were negligible.'[17] No one challenged these sweeping assertions. He then made an impassioned plea for action. All preparations had been made, he said, and the Navy's ships were standing by for immediate action. In an attempt to discourage further examination of where the consequences might lead, he declared that 'it was impossible in any operation of war to see a way clear through all the objections that could be raised to any particular course of action. It was right that all the difficulties should be fully examined, but we should not be deterred from action simply because there were certain objections.' The War Cabinet, however, was, unsurprisingly, not wholly convinced by this, inviting the Chiefs to return the following day, having given yet further examination to the military implications of a German occupation of southern Norway.[18]

When they did so, the Chiefs found themselves under pressure. Much revolved around the likelihood of a German invasion, but they were effectively silenced on the subject by the War Cabinet agreeing that such an assessment was 'a political matter which was for the War Cabinet to deal with, and which did not lie within the province of the Chiefs of Staff'. This was a highly disputable statement. Although the final judgment was indeed a political matter, providing their own assessment by way of advice was very much within the province of the Chiefs of Staff. But the Chiefs did not contest this. A number of Cabinet members, including Chamberlain, considered that a German invasion was unlikely. Halifax, whose stance had somewhat weakened, said that the Narvik project by itself would not be worth the risk, but he was ambivalent as to whether it would prejudice or improve the chances of the major project. Churchill, moving with the mood of the meeting, expressed his conviction that the Germans would not invade southern Norway in retaliation for the stoppage of the iron ore from Narvik. 'On the other hand, if they did invade Norway, he would be glad. They would become involved in a serious commitment, and, if they tried to secure control of the Swedish iron ore by conquest, they would certainly ruin their chances of obtaining a large quantity in 1940.' The whole of the larger project, he argued, was not necessary at this stage, so long as the Norwegian west coast ports could be occupied in the event of an invasion. 'There was no reason why this small diversion should develop into a large commitment unless we wished it to', he said. Throwing down the gauntlet, he added that if the War Office were unable to find the troops for these detachments, he would use Marines.

There was much that needed to be said by the Chiefs in response, not least to reiterate their advice that it was essential to forestall the Germans; that Britain could not prevent a German invasion of Norway; that our troops were neither equipped nor trained for operations there; that, in such circumstances, a German invasion might be welcome politically but was certainly not so militarily; and that there were huge risks involved. But none of the Chiefs made these points, nor did they speak with a united voice. Newall commented that even if Germany was confined to the far south of Norway, their bombers based there would, when the snows melted, pose a 'very serious threat' to our shipping. Ironside had confided in his diary the previous night with some passion:

Lord knows what the consequences may be and we are not ready in the Army for any hurried action. We have warned the Cabinet against this half-cocked scheme in Scandinavia. It is like putting a stick inside a hornets' nest without having provided yourself with a proper veil. It is the Dardanelles over again ... we are in fact seeking to extend the theatre of war to Scandinavia without being ready to do so.[19]

But when he now spoke in Cabinet, there was no hint of these concerns. Instead, he made light of the problems: the Germans might have a project to invade Norway later in the year, he said, but 'at the present time the weather would make operations in the country very difficult indeed'; the main delay to our readiness was [just] the provision of warm clothing for the troops; the force for each of the three ports could soon be found; and it was recognised that the troops at Bergen might have to occupy the mountains, come the spring, and hold on indefinitely. Pound remained silent. It was Hore-Belisha who registered unease with the proposal, saying that 'a much more careful examination of the possible developments in Norway, and the eventual size of the forces which might be required, should be undertaken before we launched these expeditions'. But this was out of step with the Chiefs. Chamberlain ignored Hore-Belisha's intervention and allowed discussion to move on to other subjects. The War Cabinet thus approved Churchill's project, subject to a satisfactory response from consultations with Norway and Sweden, and from sounding out the degree of support from the Dominions.[20] In the face of opposition, the Chiefs had favoured discretion as the better part of valour – and, in doing so, were failing in their duty.

Over the two days, however, the Cabinet had failed to focus on the plan in the context of overall policy. This had been spelt out in the Chiefs' reports: 'It must be realised that to embark on an offensive in Scandinavia in the Spring of 1940 represents a fundamental change of policy. Up to date the policy has been to remain on the defensive on land and in the air while our armaments are increased.'[21] The reports also stated that

[i]t must be clearly understood that the forces for the major operation to stop the supply of ore can only be found at the expense of the British Expeditionary Force and Air Defence of Great Britain. Once the operation has begun, it must be pursued with the greatest tenacity of purpose. It must, in fact, be regarded as the main and decisive objective; and all our efforts should be concentrated on attaining it. All other operations involving detachments of force will have to be considered strictly in the light of their relations to this main objective.[22]

It was clear that what was being proposed went way beyond just another blockade in the economic warfare policy; combat on a large scale might result. What was unclear was whether the War Cabinet had consciously endorsed a fundamental change in policy – away from that which avoided a major offensive until military strength had been built-up – or whether it viewed the operation in Scandinavia merely as a diversion within the existing policy. Nor was it clear whether the highest priority was to be the Western Front or Scandinavia.

Ministers had also endorsed a plan which was highly questionable. Its impracticality can be seen in the military preparations which were then set in motion. On 6 January the War Office issued a warning order to its senior commanders to

hold certain units in readiness for the possibility of immediate operations in Scandinavia. These measures entail the preparation of units for embarkation with special scales of equipment; and to preserve secrecy they will be permitted to believe that their ostensible destination is France, although their commanders will have been told the true story and sworn to secrecy at the conference on Monday [8 January]. It is thought that the earliest time and date of embarkation will be noon on 17 January.[23]

This must have been received with amazement bordering on incredulity. To expect a cobbled-together force of troops, many of whom were semi-trained Territorials, to be ready to deploy on operations in eleven days' time from a standing start, with unfamiliar equipment, into or close to the Arctic Circle was out of touch with reality and a recipe for disaster. The fact that the Chiefs had not made this point also misled ministers into believing that this sort of short-notice operation was feasible – a misapprehension that all concerned would, in due course, come to regret.

The prospect of imminent operations in northern Norway was viewed with concern in a number of quarters. John Colville, one of Chamberlain's private secretaries, thought it 'dangerously reminiscent of the Gallipoli plan', commenting that 'it would be dangerous and might involve disaster or withdrawal and the consequent blow to our prestige'.[24] He was not alone in the reference to Gallipoli. The Chief of Staff of the BEF, the notably acerbic Lieutenant General Henry Pownall, denigrated the plan as 'the brainchild of those master strategists Winston and Ironside ... its inception smacks alarmingly of Gallipoli'.[25] The developing views of Halifax and Chamberlain were also becoming apparent. Sir Alexander Cadogan, Halifax's Permanent Under Secretary at the Foreign Office, commented in his diary:

Fact is, this Narvik business is silly – as I knew it would be, I continue to think we *can* do it – if Winston insists – but (a) it won't be very effective in itself, and (b) it *must* prejudice the 'larger scheme'. H [Halifax] saw PM about it and finds latter is of same view more or less. ... We must now persuade Winston – if we can – that we must climb down as gracefully as we can.[emphases in original][26]

The matter came to a head at the War Cabinet on 12 January. In the previous week, reports of the Norwegian and Swedish reactions to the proposed action had come in and had been actively hostile to the British approach, fearing the possible German reaction.[27] The Norwegian response included a letter from King Haakon VII to his nephew, King George VI, asking him to use his influence to effect a change of policy.[28] Churchill had then attempted to hustle the War Cabinet into immediate action, arguing that 'every week the prize was melting'. It was to our advantage, he had reiterated, that 'the Scandinavian countries should be embroiled with Germany and the war extended to Scandinavia'. Furthermore, he said, 'We should have to make them more frightened of us than they were of Germany.'[29] On 11 January Churchill, 'straining at the leash',[30] had again been thwarted by Halifax's refusal to agree to the Narvik project and showed his frustration by urging that 'whatever course was decided upon, it was essential that we should now act decisively'.[31] That evening Cadogan, recorded in his diary, 'H[alifax] now convinced that WSC[hurchill] is on the wrong tack. ... Heard later PM shares his view. Fear this will produce something of a Cabinet split.'[32]

Cadogan's fear was well founded. The War Cabinet meeting the next morning was, at times, stormy. Halifax opened by saying he had been much influenced by a senior visiting Swedish diplomat, Marcus Wallenberg, who had emphasised the potentially adverse effect on Swedish public opinion of precipitate British action. This, said Halifax, had 'definitely weighted the balance of his judgment against the Narvik project', which, additionally, would prejudice the larger plan. Invited to give their views, the Chiefs of Staff did not speak with one voice. Newall gave what he said were their views: they doubted the value of the Narvik project and believed it might militate against the major project and cause the Germans to sabotage the all-important railway. In addition, he said, the operation might develop into a very large commitment which might divert Allied forces away from the 'decisive' Western Front; 'generally speaking, [they] felt some apprehension at the prospect of forcible action against the Narvik traffic'. The CIGS, however, was at pains to distance himself from such apprehension. General Gamelin, he said, accepted that a Scandinavian deployment might delay the despatch of additional British troops to France and was already preparing Alpine troops for the operation. Ironside declared that 'his own personal view was that a diversion in Scandinavia would be sound strategically, and would probably rule out the possibility of offensives elsewhere on any scale by either the Germans or the Russians.' Churchill now gave his much awaited view, making an impassioned plea for immediate action and doubting that the Swedes would ever agree to the major project. Of course, he said, he was not 'impatient merely for action's sake' but wanted to take the 'fine chance of forcing Germany into a situation which she had not foreseen, and of seizing the initiative'.[33] Further reasons for delay were produced, including a newly arrived telegramme from the Prime Minister of Australia advocating consultation with the Dominions before any decision was taken. Churchill became increasingly angry and 'an acrimonious tone entered the discussion'.[34] But with the mood of the meeting clearly against him, Churchill bowed to the inevitable, and said – no doubt through gritted teeth – that he 'did not propose to pursue the matter further'.[35] The War Cabinet decided to drop the minor project 'for the time being'.[36] The forces which had been stood to for the operation just one week previously were stood down.[37] And many members of the War Cabinet must have heaved a large sigh of relief.

4   Warning Signs

The government's strategic decision-making machine had faced its first major test of the war. If anyone had had the time and inclination to review its performance to date, they might have concluded that there were grounds for considerable unease.

The War Cabinet, itself, was showing some significant weaknesses. Firstly, it appeared to have a very limited understanding of strategy or to have an overall guiding policy for the conduct of the war, and its attention was increasingly being distracted from high-level, long-term strategy and policy by the attraction of short-term projects. This left many important questions unanswered. For example, was the action planned for Scandinavia to reinforce the economic blockade in pursuance of the long-war policy? Or, was it an acceptance of a change of strategy and therefore intended as an immediate and decisive action in pursuance of a short-war policy? What was the policy now? Did a successful outcome depend on military victory (as Churchill claimed) or could it be delivered through a collapse on the German home front (as Chamberlain and Halifax seemed to believe)? These fundamental elements of grand strategy were left undebated in the War Cabinet.

Secondly, the War Cabinet had yet to shake off its peacetime mentality or transition to a proper war footing. The nature of the Phoney War had meant that there had been no electric shock to jolt the War Cabinet into doing so. Major General Hastings Ismay, Deputy Secretary of the War Cabinet, later recalled, 'It is hardly going too far to say that "business as usual" seemed to be the prevailing mood'.[1] Certainly, for many, it was a case of peacetime hours of work, and Chamberlain 'retired to the peace of Chequers for two weekends out of three'.[2] The Admiralty switchboard closed down completely for the weekend at noon on Saturdays,[3] and, according to Ironside's military assistant, in the War Office '[t]he civilian staff "downed pens" punctually at 5pm whatever work had to be done'.[4] One historian has observed, 'This government continued to insist on carrying on a war, as it had in preparing for it, on gentlemanly terms', citing as an example the response to a proposal made in the House of

Commons that incendiary bombs should be dropped on the Black Forest, a concealment area for millions of tons of munitions. The Air Secretary, Kingsley Wood, had replied, 'Are you aware it is private property? Why, you will be asking me to bomb Essen next.'[5]

Thirdly was a lack of leadership. Chamberlain was not relishing his role and was showing an unfamiliarity with the military issues which increasingly represented the main business. His performance was not helped by the fact that he had been suffering from a number of ailments – influenza, nettlerash and gout, the latter so serious that, according to Colville, he was 'worried at the prospect of not being able to carry on if these attacks increase in number and violence'.[6] The government was, as A. J. P. Taylor observed, 'still moving into war backwards, with their eyes tightly closed'.[7] And as he also observed, there was one exception: Churchill, 'a cuckoo in the nest'.[8] Churchill was dominating the Cabinet, although his considerable powers of advocacy were often not matched by the strength of his case. Churchill had an aura about him. His military experience included fighting in India, the Sudan and South Africa and commanding a battalion (albeit briefly) on the Western Front in the previous war. He had also been First Lord of the Admiralty in that war, and his political experience included time as Secretary of State for War and Air, and Minister for Munitions, as well as Chancellor of the Exchequer and Home Secretary. Even if highly dubious, his views could not easily be dismissed as the voice of inexperience. Chamberlain must have been continually aware of this. Moreover, far from confining himself to naval matters, Churchill was busy 'firing off a barrage of minutes about other departments, some of which were extremely blunt',[9] cross-examining ministers and chiefs of staff and speaking with some authority, not only from his previous experience but also from the battery of statistics provided by his special adviser 'Prof' Lindemann.[10] In addition, he let it be known to his War Cabinet colleagues that he was on personal terms with the President of the United States who had told him, so Churchill said, that he would be 'glad at any time to receive a personal message from the First Lord on any matter which the latter wished to bring to his notice'.[11] Such a revelation did Churchill's status no harm in the eyes of his colleagues. Chamberlain knew he had to manage Churchill carefully and keep him within the Cabinet, however jealous he might be of his popularity with parliament and public. The Prime Minister's main concern appears to have been to maintain harmony within a Cabinet that was often divided and, thus, avoid contentious issues and postpone difficult decisions. Nowhere was this more important than on the subject of the long-war policy. He would have been aware of Churchill's scepticism of, and impatience with, this policy and his

Figure 4.1 A key relationship: Churchill and Chamberlain
(Getty Images)

pent-up frustration at the perceived passivity of his Cabinet colleagues (and, indeed, Churchill's lingering suspicion that many of them might not be averse to the notion of a compromise peace). Yet despite the fact that the grand strategy underpinning the long-war policy was clearly a valid subject for debate – indeed, arguably none was more important – Chamberlain avoided discussion of it in Cabinet; so did Churchill, probably for fear that his view might not prevail. Thus, without whole-hearted agreement as to the overall policy, Cabinet members tended to view military plans on their tactical merits, rather than on their contribution to strategic objectives.

To add to its problems, the War Cabinet was often erratic in its treatment of the military advice it was receiving, particularly that from the Chiefs of Staff, sometimes overruling their advice for little logical reason, at other times failing to challenge questionable advice, possibly because their knowledge was insufficient to know the right questions to ask. According to Ironside, the relationship between Chiefs and Cabinet was not one of mutual respect:

> They look on the Chiefs of Staff as a clog upon their energies. They are bitterly jealous of their constitutional power to run the strategy of the war, though their knowledge of war is nothing, and their ignorance of the administrative questions involved is still less, if that were possible ... they grasp at any mad idea in the hopes that they have discovered a golden road to victory.[12]

For his part, Chamberlain, in the words of one historian, 'gradually came to regard the COS as obtuse, unimaginative professionals whose advice could be safely ignored'.[13] Indeed, the level of mistrust is reminiscent of that between the 'frocks' (frock-coated ministers) and 'brass hats' (military leaders) in the First World War.

There were organisational factors, too, which were contributing to erratic strategy in Cabinet. Military advice came formally to the War Cabinet from three different sources. One was the Military Coordination Committee, which discussed most of the Chiefs of Staffs' reports before they came to Cabinet and on which the committee's chairman, Chatfield, commented at Cabinet meetings. The second source was the advice given by service ministers at Cabinet. Their membership, though, came at a price in terms of coordination. Churchill recognised the disadvantage and later observed, 'The decision to bring in the three Service ministers profoundly affected Lord Chatfield's authority as Minister for Coordination of Defence.'[14] The main source of military advice, however, was the Chiefs of Staff themselves, either in the form of written reports or of oral advice at Cabinet meetings. All these sources made for diverse and frequently conflicting advice. Furthermore, the Chiefs' advice was often uncertain and full of inconsistencies. The dominant voice among them was Ironside's. Hore-Belisha had apparently drawn some satisfaction from this, telling Kennedy, with more than a little indiscretion, 'Ironside is doing very well; he dominates the Chiefs of Staff. ... Look at his opposite numbers – nonentities!'[15] He may have been the dominant voice, but there were reasons to doubt both the intellectual rigour that lay behind that voice and the degree to which the other Chiefs fully agreed with the analysis, or were just prepared to go along with it. Their predisposition to stick to their own subjects made it difficult to tell. It was also clear that the Chiefs were keen for Britain to seize the initiative and to take the war into Scandinavia to stop the iron ore export, but less clear were the lengths that they were prepared to go to pursue this agenda and the risks they were prepared to take in doing so. Their advice was not the result of a careful and objective balancing of ends, ways and means, less still clarity of thought as to the overall policy context. Nor was it realised, outside a close military circle, that their key advisers – the Joint Planners – had considerable reservations which the Chiefs were not representing fully to the Cabinet because they believed they knew better and for fear that the Cabinet would have cold feet about their military plan.

The Chiefs were not helped by the system in which they found themselves – a system that was bureaucratic to a fault. The Military Coordination Committee had seemed like a logical construct at the outset but was proving to be of limited practical value. Even at this relatively peaceful stage of the war, it was apparent that it was not working well and that it would be quite unsuited to fast-moving events. Ismay, its secretary, later recalled:

The Chiefs of Staff, after considerable discussion of a problem, would report their conclusions or differences, to the Ministerial [sic] Co-ordination Committee. There the whole ground would have to be gone over again, and perhaps a new set of conclusions or differences would be reached. The matter would then go to the War Cabinet, and once more the process of explanation or disputation would have to be repeated. I believe that most of us, whether Ministers or officials who were cogs in the machine, felt that it would fail to secure the necessary speed of decision once the war started in earnest.[16]

Churchill was beginning to dominate the Committee even more than he was the War Cabinet. As a member of the secretariat later recalled, '[he] was so much larger in every way than his colleagues on this committee that it ran like a coach with one wheel twice the size of the other three, and achieved very little with much friction.'[17]

The existence of the Committee also contributed to one of the greatest sources of dysfunctionality for the Chiefs: the demands on their time and the amount of time they spent in meetings. Even without the Military Coordination Committee, this was debilitating. In October, Ironside recorded:

One of the worst days we have had. I had two hours in the morning with the War Cabinet and the Chiefs of Staff. And then we had four and a half hours in the afternoon with the Army Council and the Air Conference. And then I had two hours with the Secretary of State from 11 till 1, having had from 9 till 11 with my own people. That is ten hours of talking and arguing and thinking.[18]

Again in January, he recorded, 'A long day. Actually eight and a half hours in Conference and Meetings. You cannot make war like that.'[19] His Director of Military Operations recorded, 'Tiny himself is on endless conferences, which irritates him, as he feels so many are a waste of time, and leave him little time to do his work in the War Office.'[20] This was set to get worse.

Further pressure on the Chiefs – although to an extent self-generated – and a source of increasingly bitter dispute between them was the ongoing battle over the role, control and allocation of air power. This became obvious even to outsiders. At the Foreign Office, Halifax's Principal Private Secretary, Oliver Harvey, noted in early November, 'A great row has broken out between the Air Ministry and the War Office over the provision and control of aircraft for the BEF.'[21] By the end of November, Ironside was recording, 'This damned struggle with the Air Ministry . . . gets worse and worse.'[22] The Admiralty, too, was in competition with the RAF for control of Coastal Command, and by January, Churchill was planning a takeover bid 'to relieve them of the whole coastal work in home waters'.[23] Two years later, one admiral was to write, 'Our fight with the Air Ministry becomes more and more fierce as the war proceeds. It is much more savage than our war with the Huns.'[24] Meanwhile, the RAF was lobbying hard for the initiation of the strategic bombing campaign against Germany. Lord Trenchard sent to Churchill and others on 2 January a paper on 'The Advantage of an Early Air Offensive' urging 'a campaign of attack by air on Germany with as little delay as possible'.[25] Not only were these inter-service disputes time-consuming, energy-sapping and a source of acrimony but also the excessive tribalism they represented was a distraction from focus on the enemy and the strategy for defeating him.

Less obvious than the battles between the services, but equally dysfunctional, were the internal tensions in all three service ministries. In the War Office the honeymoon between Ironside and Hore-Belisha, if it ever existed, was short-lived. Within a week, Ironside was writing, 'I have a Secretary of State who knows nothing about military matters whatever . . . [he] cannot take anything from reading it. He will not even begin to pick up the contents after having read it several times.'[26] In October, Ironside was remarking, 'He knows nothing and cares nothing of what is happening strategically.'[27] For his part, Hore-Belisha may have resented the CIGS's patronising tone. Ironside, a fluent French linguist, boasted to one of his staff of having reprimanded Hore-Belisha for speaking French in discussions with Gamelin: 'I told him his French was Le Touquet French – all right for talking to Mademoiselle X on the *plage*, but no good for military conversations.'[28] Relations deteriorated over various spats, culminating in a row about pillboxes in the BEF and criticism of the army in a Cabinet meeting after Ironside had left it.[29] The Pillbox affair also soured the relationship between Ironside and Gort and severely undermined the confidence of the army in its secretary of state, as well as consuming huge amounts of time and energy on the part of commanders and staffs. After a covert campaign by senior officers,[30] Chamberlain sacked Hore-Belisha on 5 January.[31]

At the Admiralty, the problem was rather different. Churchill dominated the place from the moment he walked back through the door.[32]
This posed considerable challenges for Pound. Where should the Minister's business end and the service Chief's begin? Churchill would
hardly have recognised the question. 'Any German raider or blockade
runner reported to Churchill brought him to his map room. ... There
he would work out what force and dispositions were needed to bring
about the destruction or capture of the enemy ship.'[33] On the day that
the pocket battleship *Graf Spee* sought refuge in Montevideo harbour,
'Churchill hardly left the first lord's map room. It was the centre of
action, with the first lord, first sea lord, and operations division chiefs all
sitting round the table watching the charts being plotted. Churchill was
in terrific form.'[34] Pound's solution was entirely pragmatic. He knew
Churchill, and he knew himself, well enough to know that he could not
oppose Churchill outright and that the best he could achieve was an
approach of consent and evade. So he would not argue the case, but,
having left the map room, make his own decisions, and was ready to
face explaining any discrepancy to Churchill.[35] This did not, however,
cover the circumstances when Pound or his deputy was not present.
Apart from the vast amount of staff time that it wasted, 'consent and
evade' worked well for Churchillian schemes such as Operation
Catherine – his proposal for forcing a passage into the Baltic, which
he believed to be 'the supreme naval offensive open to the Royal
Navy'[36] and 'a short cut to victory'.[37] Pound did not attempt to stop
what was a clearly impractical idea but instead told Churchill that the
staff would examine the proposal and produce a report, telling his staff,
'Don't worry. It will never take place.'[38] Churchill, perhaps sensing that
the staff might be less than fulsome in support of his scheme, brought in
a feisty retired Admiral of the Fleet, the Earl of Cork and Orerry, to take
over the planning, with a view to command the operation.[39] Pound
acquiesced in this. (Pound eventually persuaded Churchill to drop
Catherine in mid-January).[40] When Churchill proposed mining the
Norwegian waters, Pound, similarly, passed it to the planning staff.
But the Director of Plans, Captain Danckwerts, (also a member of the
Joint Planning Staff), gave it short shrift which 'marked the beginning of
an intermittent conflict between the First Lord and Plans Division'[41]
and certainly marked Danckwert's card in Churchill's eyes. It was
clearly difficult for Pound to express his own opinion if it disagreed
with Churchill's, in Cabinet or, indeed, in the Chiefs of Staff Committee. Thus it is difficult to know from the minutes of either, when Pound
was silent, whether he was in agreement, disagreement or, as his
detractors would have it, asleep.[42] But, according to his biographer, it

became very obvious by early 1940 that Pound was 'driving himself into the ground' and that (writing of 1943, but probably equally true of 1940) 'he had to fight Hitler by day and Churchill by night'.[43] Although opinion is divided about the extent to which (if at all) Churchill dominated Pound,[44] few would dispute that an unhealthy amount of dysfunctionality reigned at the Admiralty.

There were tensions, too, within the Air Ministry where Newall was under constant and conflicting pressure from his two most senior CinCs, both of whom were strong, uncompromising characters. Ludlow-Hewitt of Bomber Command was urging greater expenditure on equipping, manning and training his command. Dowding, at Fighter Command, was doing the same, insisting that the safety of the home base was the first prerequisite and that 'in any clash of interests Fighter Command must be given priority'.[45]

An analysis of top-level decision-making over the period might have concluded that the organisations concerned were logical and appropriate. Such a conclusion, though, would have missed the point that these organisations were also organisms – groups of human beings – and how well or badly the organisations worked in practice was in large part the result of the competence of those human beings, both individually and as groups, which in turn resulted in large part from the personal chemistry of their interaction, one with another. It was in these latter areas that fissures were appearing.

In summary, by the second week in January, four months into the war, national strategy making was facing a number of challenges: political leadership and direction were weak; neither the War Cabinet nor the Chiefs of Staff were thinking strategically; the War Cabinet was having difficulty coming to logical decisions or reaching agreement; the policy-making machine was overly bureaucratic; military advice was disparate and often flawed; the Chiefs appeared to be wedded to their plan, come what may; and internal tensions were limiting the effectiveness of all three service ministries. With hindsight it is easy to see these things. Whether any or all of them were warning signs which could have and should have been recognised at the time is a different matter. Once planning for a campaign is under way, events tend to move fast and time is short. It is, therefore, often easier in theory than in practice to carry out a quick review during a campaign in a detached and objective way. The benefits of carrying one out may, however, hugely outweigh all the effort involved.

5   'The Major Project'

The result of the War Cabinet's rejection of the 'minor' project –
Churchill's Narvik plan – on 12 January meant that the 'major' project,
the Chiefs' three-part plan for a full expedition, which had been accepted
at the beginning of the month with little critical scrutiny, was now very
much back on the table and the subject of detailed planning.

The first part of the plan was an operation, code-named Avonmouth,
for an Anglo-French force of, initially, one or two brigades 'specially
equipped for rapid movement and winter conditions',[1] including a newly
raised British ski battalion,[2] to land at Narvik and travel up the railway to
occupy Gällivare and possibly Luleå. A further echelon of up to two
divisions might follow. In a second operation, code-named Stratford, a
force of around brigade strength would occupy the Norwegian ports of
Trondheim, Bergen and Stavanger. The third operation, code-named
Plymouth, envisaged a large force of four to six Allied divisions landing at
the ports, primarily Trondheim, and moving into southern Sweden to
assist the Swedes in defence against German attack.[3]

The first indication of the eye-watering scale of the force required for
the whole expedition came to the War Cabinet on 19 January. If the
Chiefs were having any lingering doubts about the wisdom of the major
project, they were not showing them, perhaps because, having so firmly
recommended it, it would require considerable moral courage now to
admit to having second thoughts. They reported that for the operation in
southern Sweden, Plymouth, the initial force alone would number
around 80,000 men with 10,000 vehicles and would take 12 liners and
39 store ships 60 days to land them, or half that time if a second port and
twice the number of ships were available. A corps headquarters and two
divisions destined for France would be retained for Scandinavia, and a
number of completely new units would have to be raised for supporting
troops. The force, they said, would be ready by April providing that a
decision was made by 2 February. The exact size and shape of the
second-echelon force was yet to be worked out, but, it was revealed,
all the base and line-of-communications units would need to be raised

from scratch. For the vital air support, two squadrons of bombers, two of fighters and an army cooperation flight had been earmarked, with advanced bases for further four bomber squadrons. But, the report admitted, '[L]ack of suitable aerodromes and facilities is likely ... to prevent us providing even this scale of air assistance.'[4] This represented a serious deficiency, recognised in the Air Ministry and emphasised in discussion by Wood; but in reply to a question as to whether the land and air forces were adequate, Ironside merely said that an appreciation of the numbers required could not be determined without staff talks with the Swedish General Staff. Anyway, he said, the force for southern Sweden might not be required till later, 'say in May'. Chamberlain pointed out the obvious flaw: that if we sent an expedition in March, the Germans might well take immediate action and not wait till May before invading. Remarkably, he did not demand an explanation from Ironside and allowed discussion to move on to more politically interesting matters: the game plan for the forthcoming meeting of the Supreme War Council.[5]

Nor was the absence of staff talks a trivial issue; there was further risk involved here. But without Scandinavian agreement, such talks could not take place. Additionally, the report said, of the two brigades needed for the first echelon of Avonmouth – the Narvik/Gällivare force – one would be French, one British, and would be ready to move by the end of February. Unmentioned was the fact that the British brigade was, as yet, utterly unprepared for this role, despite the previous stipulation that 'our initial force must be trained and equipped for movement on snow'.[6]

For its part, the War Cabinet did not give the Chiefs' plan serious critical examination. It was sceptical that it would ever be put into operation. Chamberlain commented that 'it was necessary to make full preparations for sending forces to Scandinavia, but that their chief value might well be as a bargaining counter with the Swedes. He was anxious, he said, not to divert too much effort and money to the preparation of forces which might not be used after all.'[7]

Throughout the latter part of January, Scandinavia remained the subject of attention in the War Cabinet and of contentious debate, with Churchill and Halifax usually in opposing corners. On 17 January 'the fur flew' in Cabinet as Churchill advocated putting strong pressure on the Norwegian and Swedish governments to take action themselves over iron ore exports.[8] 'Winston was most emphatic over this ore question,' recorded Ironside.[9] Relations between Churchill and Halifax deteriorated further as a result of a stirring broadcast three days later in which

Churchill was highly critical of neutral states: 'Each one hopes that if he feeds the crocodile enough, the crocodile will eat him last.'[10] Churchill may have irritated jealous colleagues by another rousing speech the following week which sounded positively prime ministerial: 'Come then: let us to the task, to the battle, to the toil – each to our part, each to our station.'[11]

Differences of opinion over the whole Scandinavian policy were now becoming evident between, on the one hand, the Chiefs, especially Ironside, and on the other, the Joint Planners. In draft reports the Joint Planners voiced their concerns about Germany's capability to forestall the Allies.

There are possibly 6–7 Divisions on the Pomeranian coast, and in North-East Germany which have been given some training in combined operations. There are doubtless other formations in Germany which have had similar experience and these could be concentrated quickly on the coast, as could the three Mountain Divisions (trained in snow warfare). ... There is believed to be a total of at least 1,000 [troop-carrying] aircraft which could be concentrated quickly. Germany also has a minimum of 4,000 parachute troops and 6,000 air-landing troops.[12]

In a further paper, they registered an even more fundamental concern about Plymouth, the operations in southern Sweden.

These operations ... considered in themselves are not militarily sound, nor are the land and air forces we can make available adequate for the protection for Sweden ... we have advised acceptance of the military disadvantages of the southern operation at grave risk to the forces engaged there, if by that means alone we can secure the Scandinavian cooperation which will make possible the stoppage of export of the ore to Germany.[13]

Neither of these concerns, which would have set alarm bells ringing, were included by the Chiefs in the final report that they sent to the War Cabinet,[14] perhaps because they – or, at least, Ironside and Pound – did not want to give the War Cabinet reason to question the proposed policy or to withdraw their support from it.

Although the leading protagonist for that policy amongst the Chiefs was Ironside, within the War Office he was not alone in his enthusiasm for it. His deputy, Major General Hugh Massy, also pressed for it in a paper written at the end of December, even arguing that 'should Germany forestall us by attacking on the Western Front ... we should still attempt to carry out the Scandinavian project with the object of wresting the initiative from him.'[15] Ironside drew heavily on Massy's views to express his own related preoccupation in a paper for the Chiefs of Staff in late January. Entitled 'The Major Strategy of the War', it also expressed his frustration with an essentially passive, long-war policy. His conclusions were instinctive, rather than supported by the rambling argument of the paper. Amongst them was the suggestion that 'the most effective aid we can give Finland is by attacking Russia', although a week later he was already having second thoughts, confiding in his diary his concern about the prospect of war with Russia 'with all its complications'.[16] His main conclusion, however, was that, while ensuring adequate security at home and on the Western Front, Britain should take military action to seize the initiative and that the best way of doing it was to stop the supply of Swedish iron ore to Germany.[17] What the paper did not consider, though, was whether Britain had the ways and means of achieving this end; it was, therefore, bereft of strategy. Indeed, in commenting on it in his diary, Ironside demonstrated both the extent to which his 'strategy' was a gamble and the fact that herein lay one of its major weaknesses: 'I feel that now is the moment, however ill-prepared we are in trained troops.'[18]

Part of Ironside's apparent confidence in the Scandinavian venture was his low opinion of Germany's senior military officers. This was based not on intelligence assessments but on his own beliefs and instinct. He had visited Germany in 1937 to observe the German Army manoeuvres, had briefly met Hitler and felt that he had a more personal knowledge and, therefore, a better understanding of the German officer corps and its ethos than anyone else. 'He said he knew a lot of these German generals personally; they were alright at drawing up and carrying through a carefully prearranged plan, but if anything went wrong to upset their calculations they were far too rigid and inflexible.'[19] Ironside reiterated this view in his diary, welcoming an opportunity to 'upset the German's plans' and 'prevent Germany from carrying out her preconceived plan and cause her to improvise, an art in which she does not excel'. [20] It was a very personal view and a caricature that was already outdated in 1918, let alone 1937. Ironside's view also, by implication, over-elevated the supposed British strength of improvisation, which, in practice, was often just an excuse for the absence of sound planning and a reliance on muddling through.

That Ironside did not hold the German Army in higher regard is surprising, given the evidence of the campaign in Poland. Many reports came in after the fall of Poland detailing the, literally, devastating performance of the German armed forces – the remarkable combination of air force and army, the impact of all-arms cooperation, the high standard of training and the effectiveness of German doctrine.[21] Ironside had noted many of these attributes during his 1937 visit, expressing considerable admiration of the German Army in his diary.

I think that the German Army had developed in a marvellous way. It is madly enthusiastic and very efficient. ... Everybody watching this effort is terrified, and I am sure nothing will stand up to it when the moment comes. ... The German Army, Navy and Air Force are all united and are working for one thing together. They have one direction and as far as I could see no jealousies. They have no watertight compartments. They have thus a great advantage over us.[22]

Yet he seems to have remembered only what he chose to remember, despite continuing intelligence reports of the high standard of training and equipment of the German Army. For example, an intelligence assessment in January drew attention to the newly raised and largely reservist Landwehr divisions: 'Whilst their military value may be lower than that of Regular divisions, it should not be under-estimated since the men are now for the most part experienced, well trained and equipped.'[23] The same could not be said of the Territorial Army in Britain. Another assessment predicted, 'Whatever action Germany decides to take, the preparation for it will be thorough and her execution efficient and ruthless.'[24] Also apparently overlooked by Ironside was the fact that Germany had no less than three divisions of specialised mountain troops, some of whom, it might be expected, would be used in the snows of Scandinavia.

Ironside's confidence in the Scandinavian venture was not unanimously shared by his fellow Chiefs. The Air Ministry, in particular, was not keen on the operation on principle. At the Chiefs of Staff meeting on 24 January, the CIGS's enthusiasm about the strength of Britain's likely position in Sweden, and the difficulty the Germans would have in attacking it, was questioned by implication by the Deputy Chief of the Air Staff, Air Vice Marshal Peirse, standing in for Newall. Peirse reiterated concerns about the inadequacy of the air support that could be spared for Scandinavia and returned to the RAF's preferred policy – bombing the Ruhr, by which, he said, Britain could upset Germany's industrial capacity just as well, and perhaps more quickly, than by a campaign to stop the iron ore. Ironside's response was that 'the operation of seizing the Gällivare ore fields was not difficult, and we could be sure of the effect'.[25] At the Chiefs' meeting two days later, Ironside again found it necessary to make the case for the Scandinavian operation as 'the only opening likely to be available in the near future which might lead to decisive results'. [26] However, he, too, was sceptical of it actually taking place, confiding in his diary that 'I am afraid that we shall never get a chance of carrying it out. Our diplomats show no signs of preparing the situation.'[27] Two days later he reiterated this, 'Personally, I give ourselves practically no hope of getting Scandinavia with us.'[28]

The Chiefs' report on the plans and implications of intervention in Scandinavia was one of two that came to the War Cabinet on 2 February. It shows much of Ironside's influence, repeating his well-worn arguments, particularly in its conclusion that 'Speaking generally, we feel that the enterprise offers us a chance of wresting the initiative from the Germans and upsetting their plans, forcing them to improvise (which is their weak point) and to disperse their forces and, indeed, of shortening the war.' The Chiefs' report was much more upbeat than the Joint Planners' draft. Not only did they omit the Joint Planners' candid warning that 'these operations ... considered in themselves are not militarily sound', but they added a conclusion that was breezily dismissive of the risks. Having acknowledged that '[t]he difficulties and consequences of the enterprise are considerable', it went on, 'We do not, however, consider that undue weight should be given to the inherent difficulties of the enterprise. The stakes are high, but the prize of success is great.'[29] This was gamblers' logic, except that it gave scant regard to the odds.

Again the War Cabinet did not give the Chiefs' paper critical examination, but instead focused on the second report, which concerned French proposals for intervention in Scandinavia, and on the impending meeting of the Supreme War Council. Throughout January, the French government had been urging the British towards action in Scandinavia. French public and media attention had been increasingly concentrated on the plight of the Finns, and the French government had been putting pressure on the British government to join it in taking action beyond the supply of weapons and equipment. In part, this was a reflection of growing scepticism within the government of the validity of the long-war policy, in part a continuation of a French desire to move the war into a theatre well away from France. It was also motivated by the desire for military action against the iron ore export from Narvik. But the most pressing concern was the desire to be seen to be providing support for the Finns; Daladier was being sharply criticised for inaction. Enthusiastically advocated by the French to the British was a *projet* to seize the northern Finnish port of Petsamo, held by the Russians, and to send a force of 30,000–40,000 men, ostensibly 'volunteers', to fight alongside the Finns. The occupation of Petsamo, the French argued, would also provoke a German response which the Allies could then exploit. The plan, which had a number of obvious practical flaws as well as the alarming prospect of war with Russia, was firmly opposed by the Chiefs. Ironside described it in his diary as 'a military gamble without any political prize',[30] a judgement with which the War Cabinet was in full agreement. But the Cabinet was attracted to the idea of sending forces to Finland. Firstly, it could apply the necessary pressure for Norwegian and Swedish cooperation, whilst also providing the cover for an expeditionary force from Narvik to Boden, whose main purpose was to seize the Gällivare ore fields. Second, the Cabinet had an unashamedly political point: 'Finland had at present the sympathy of the whole world, and if she collapsed, the blame would be laid at the doors of ourselves and the French. It was, therefore, essential to show to the world that we were ready to do our part, and to shift the onus on to Norway and Sweden.' This, it noted, could be achieved without having to go anywhere near Petsamo; it could be achieved through Narvik. But the War Cabinet went well beyond this. Support to the Finns, far from being merely a means to an end, suddenly became an end in itself: 'It was of the utmost importance', it agreed, 'to prevent Finland being overrun by Russia ... and that this could only be done by considerable forces of trained men entering Finland from or via Norway and Sweden.' Remarkably, the military implications of this added commitment, let alone war with Russia, were not discussed. The Cabinet merely noted, with probably unconscious understatement, that '[t]he despatch of forces to assist Finland would involve preparations on a rather larger scale than those envisaged [in the Chiefs' paper].'[31]

At the Supreme War Council meeting in Paris on 5 February the main objective for Chamberlain was to find a way to facilitate occupation of the ore fields, to further the war against Germany; for Daladier, it was to gain a British commitment to join forces in support of Finland in a war against Russia. Daladier opened proceedings with an impassioned declaration that 'Finland must not be allowed to disappear off the map of Europe' and strongly advocated the Petsamo plan. Unstated was his desire to appease those right-wing French politicians who were keen to take-on Bolshevism. Chamberlain skilfully brought the discussion round to the British plan – part of which was now an expedition from Narvik to both Gällivare and Finland – and won Daladier over with a proposal to make immediate and complete preparations for the despatch of the expeditionary force. A division would be withdrawn from the BEF and two divisions about to join it held back, which Daladier clearly thought was a fair price to pay. Both leaders agreed that the plan, preceded by a Finnish appeal for help, was the best chance of winning Swedish and Norwegian acquiescence and, in Chamberlain's words, of 'killing two birds with one stone'. Chamberlain accepted Daladier's proposal that the force should be under British command, and they both agreed a face-saver that the rejected Petsamo *projet* 'could be borne in mind' in future military discussions.[32] Both Chamberlain and Daladier had got what they wanted. The meeting ended in harmony and self-congratulation: 'Everybody purring with pleasure', according to Ironside.[33] But as J. R. M. Butler pointed out, 'an air of unreality pervades the proceedings of this conference'.[34] In their eagerness to arrive at this highly agreeable outcome and avoid any unpleasantness, the leaders had failed to confront the tough questions of strategy – of considering ends, ways and means and establishing priorities – and instead, indulged in considerable amounts of wishful thinking. There was no consideration of the impact of depriving the Western Front of much needed resources, let alone of the consequences of war with Russia. The probability of failing to gain Norwegian and Swedish cooperation was dismissed in cavalier fashion – and contrary to the evidence – as 'a very remote contingency'.[35] Lastly, there was a naive acceptance of a military plan which even a layman could see carried with it alarming amounts of risk. But as an exercise in diplomacy, the meeting had been a huge success. Cadogan's verdict was probably shared by many of those present: 'Rode French off their silly Petsamo scheme, and got them to accept our idea. ... Everything agreed and merry as a marriage bell.'[36] Ironside, however, recognised that things were in danger of spinning out of control, confiding in his diary the risk assessment he had chosen not to voice to his political masters: 'One is almost frightened by the boldness of the plan, knowing what slender means one has at the moment to carry it out.'[37]

6   'Hare-Brained'

In the aftermath of the Supreme War Council meeting, a number of concerns were raised about the viability of the military plan on which the policy rested. The very next day, the Joint Planners warned the Chiefs that '[t]he Germans probably already suspected that the Allies have it in mind to intervene in Scandinavia.'[1] A week later they again warned that plans for the southern operations – Plymouth and Stratford – 'must allow for frequent attacks by German air forces on shipping, ports of disembarkation and communications from the outset of operations ... [and that] adequate air defence is not possible'.[2] The War Office staff was concerned about some of the optimistic statements which the CIGS had made in Paris. At the Supreme War Council he had said that the division removed from the BEF could leave its equipment behind and be re-equipped in Britain. The Military Operations staff commented, 'This suggestion by CIGS hardly seems to be practical: even if trained personnel were brought back and replaced in France, the fresh equipment for re-equipping the trained personnel does not in fact exist.'[3] The CIGS had also said at the Chiefs of Staff meeting with the French high command that, in addition to the first two reinforcement divisions, 'two further divisions would be ready by the end of May'. In fact, the staff warned, the first two divisions would not be ready till early June or July, with the other two in July or August.[4]

In addition, as might be expected, there was 'soreness at [BEF] GHQ'[5] over the implications for the BEF and the fact that there had been no consultation over the removal of major assets. Ironside's visit to explain the new policy met with a cool reception. Lieutenant General Sir Alan Brooke, who was to become CIGS in 1941, wrote in his diary, 'The proposed plans fill me with gloom. ... We seem to be falling into all the errors that we committed in the last war by starting subsidiary theatres and frittering away our strength.'[6] Pownall was scathing: 'CIGS [says] "in our opinion it would prevent the Germans attacking in the West, or the Balkans for the matter of that. It will upset the tenor of their development." (Oh God, what does that mean?)'[7] According to Pownall, two members of the Army Council – the Adjutant General (General Gordon-Finlayson) and the Quartermaster General (General Venning) – were so concerned about the administrative inadequacies of the plan that they 'formed up and told CIGS that they were very unhappy about the whole business – but got no change by doing so'.[8] These are probably the two senior officers referred to in Ironside's diary; according to the historian Wesley Wark, Ironside 'dismissed their concerns as a product of "terror" and lack of imagination. He thought they "should be able to realise the vital show this is."'[9] Ironside's mind was already dangerously closed on the subject.

Then there was the issue of air defence. The Military Operations staff warned that the chances of effective protection by fighter aircraft in Scandinavia were remote and that the base locations, lines of communication and forward troops would have to rely on anti-aircraft artillery. But the allocation required in Scandinavia would leave the Air Defence of Great Britain and that of the BEF in France dangerously exposed.[10] Concern about air defence was also the subject of a Joint Planners' report to the Chiefs. It drew attention to the vulnerability of Trondheim, the key base and port, and the likelihood of it becoming the target of large-scale enemy air attack. The Joint Planners did not mince their words:

[T]he fact must be faced that the scale of air attack which we must be prepared to endure will be very heavy indeed. It must be borne in mind that in the initial stages we shall be able to present no opposition whatever – except such air defence as the Norwegians and Swedes may be able to afford with their very limited resources on the assumption that they are actively engaged on our side.

They added a stark warning: '[W]e feel bound to represent the situation to the Chiefs of Staff. If we have underrated the possible effects of enemy air action the result may, in the worst case, be a local disaster. It is even possible that the forces may not get ashore at all.' Their report concluded that this 'must effectively dispose of any idea that we could send strong reinforcements to southern Sweden and build up a battle front, held by Allied land and air forces, sufficient to withstand indefinitely the scale of land and air attack that Germany could bring against it'.[11] The Director of Military Operations represented further concerns to the CIGS about the air defence of Trondheim, together with a warning: anti-aircraft artillery would not arrive there until fifteen days after the first troops landed; barrage balloons would take thirty-five days to arrive, and aircraft could arrive only when the airfield became secure and useable.[12] The Chiefs, however, were dismissive of the Joint Planners' advice. After a short discussion they agreed that although the air threat was serious, 'the risks involved were part of the price we might have to pay for seizing the ore fields and hastening the end of the war'. They also decided not to forward the Joint Planners' report to the War Cabinet – effectively suppressing it – and instead agreed that their chairman would report the situation orally during the next progress report to the War Cabinet.[13] When, the following day, Newall did so, he took the line that the Chiefs' were concerned about the air situation and that a major attack on Trondheim would almost certainly materialise, but that they 'were prepared to pay the heavy price'. No one sought to ask for an estimate of the price – no doubt relieved that the Chiefs had accepted, and thus taken ownership of, the risk.[14]

The same day, 16 February, an event occurred which was to have a major impact on both Allied and German plans for intervention in Norway – what became known as the *Altmark* incident. *Altmark* was a supply ship to the German pocket battleship *Admiral Graf Spee* which had been scuttled off Montevideo in December 1939. *Altmark* had been hiding in the North Atlantic and was returning to Germany with 299 British prisoners on board. Spotted off the coast of Norway by aircraft, she was boarded in Norwegian territorial waters, on Churchill's personal orders, by sailors from *HMS Cossack*. After a brief skirmish, in which four Germans were killed, the prisoners were released to cries of 'the Navy's here!' This was a small tactical-level action with immense strategic-level impact. The Norwegian government immediately protested at the violation of its territorial waters, a protest somewhat undermined by the fact that a Norwegian navy ship had told *Cossack* that *Altmark* had already been inspected and cleared. In Britain, the incident was welcomed by a public badly in need of a morale boost and was given full and unrestrained coverage by the press: the *News Chronicle* likened it to Sir Richard Grenville's stirring action in the Azores in 1591;[15] the *Times* paid tribute to '[t]he daring rescue of the prisoners is a story of the kind to delight the authors of *Treasure Island* and *Westward Ho! ...* Just such a sequel was required to complete national pride and satisfaction in the victory of the River Plate';[16] 'Well done!' trumpeted the *Daily Mail*, 'the courageous efficiency with which the Royal Navy carried out a difficult operation, and the boldness of Mr Winston Churchill in carrying it out. Let us praise him highly for a resolute and realistic course of action.'[17]

Churchill's hand was hugely strengthened, and he wasted no time in making capital out of it, arguing in Cabinet for a speedy return to his Narvik project which, deliberately downplaying its scale, he now christened 'Wilfred' (the smallest of three characters in a popular strip cartoon). 'No opportunity so good as the present one might recur', he asserted. And in an attempt to bypass the obvious obstacle of Norwegian and Swedish non-cooperation, he took the line that '[h]e was not convinced that we could not reach Gällivare from Narvik, even in the teeth of Scandinavian opposition. The railway from Narvik might be sabotaged, but a small force under a determined leader might overcome the difficulties.' The Chiefs had previously reported that this was out of the question. Newall merely replied that it was 'very doubtful'.[18]

Further risks were emerging. The degree to which the plan depended on secrecy had been emphasised from the outset, but there was now evidence of 'large-scale leakage' in Paris.[19] 'The whole project must be well known by this time,' Ironside wrote in his diary, '[Germany] must be watching us like a cat does a mouse.'[20] The air defence situation had worsened: the Deputy Chiefs of Staff reported that production figures for anti-aircraft guns had fallen and there was no prospect of any considerable improvement.[21] Additionally, an intelligence assessment suggested that the number of German divisions on the Western Front had increased to 147, of which 100 were concentrated close up to the Front;[22] a diversion of effort to Norway would therefore increase risk on the Western Front. The Joint Intelligence Committee (JIC) warned that any German expedition to Sweden 'could be assembled and loaded into ships without our having any definite warning', noting that Germany had some 1,200 troop-carrying aircraft and a parachute capability, with cover provided by fighter aircraft based in Germany.[23] The War Office staff added that without military staff talks with the Scandinavians, there could only be assumptions about the availability of administrative support on which the expedition depended.[24]

Finally, there was the question of timing. Although much effort had been devoted to working out what the British could deliver and by when to Norway and what the Germans could deliver and by when to Sweden, little attention was paid to what the Germans could deliver and by when to Norway. The question was not put to the JIC. The complacent assumption prevailed that Norway's relative proximity to Britain would prevent surprise and allow interdiction by both sea and air. Moreover, the plan depended on nothing short of perfection in the synchronisation of diplomatic and military activity. For the Allies to avoid being forestalled, the Finns needed to make their appeal for help just one day before the troops were ready to sail, which was not before 15 March at the earliest.[25] Ironside admitted in his diary that he was 'terrified at our timing in this Scandinavian show being upset. If it comes off, the various parts all hang together, and any false advance may upset the whole scheme.'[26]

Even taken individually, these risks were a cause for concern. Taken together, and when added to all the other risks which had previously been notified, the degree of risk was nothing short of a gamble. The Chiefs may not have recognised this, or they may have recognised it, but chosen not to bring it to the attention of the War Cabinet. Either way, it is difficult to escape the conclusion that they were failing in their duty.

Serious questions were first raised about the plan's viability at the War Cabinet on 18 February. Significantly, they were asked by service ministers, perhaps showing – unless their questions had been planted by their service Chiefs – a certain lack of ministerial confidence in the men in uniform.

First, Wood asked whether the Chiefs of Staff were satisfied that the possible scale of German air attack on Trondheim would not endanger the security of the forces. He was informed that Trondheim was in range of 1,400 German aircraft which might drop up to 100 tons of bombs each day on the port and that this weight of attack might be increased if the Germans seized airports in southern Sweden. Now was Newall's chance to express his concerns. But while agreeing that a considerable risk was involved, he merely repeated the mantra about the risk being worth the advantage of securing the ore fields and added that, since the risk would be even worse if the enemy had use of Stavanger airfield, it would be important to forestall them there. The Cabinet agreed that Wood's point should be investigated as a matter of urgency.

Then Oliver Stanley, Hore-Belisha's replacement as Secretary for War, made one of his rare interventions in Cabinet. It deserved more attention than it got. He doubted, he said, whether the Cabinet realised all the implications of the proposed plan. First, of the four and a half divisions which would go to Scandinavia, only one was a Regular division, and the others 'were not at present in a very advanced state of training'; for example, the last Territorial division to go to the BEF was considered by the CinC to be unfit for mobile operations. Second, the danger of air attack to which Wood had referred was a serious limiting factor. Third, the Swedish General Staff, knowing the challenges the British would face in operating in Scandinavia, might well doubt that they could make good their offer to protect Sweden. (Just the previous day, the Swedish government had made a public announcement 'to the effect that they would not in any circumstances permit the passage of foreign troops across Swedish soil to aid Finland'.)[27] Finally, he noted, the British commitment in southern Scandinavia had grown from two divisions to three and a half. 'The whole affair', he concluded, 'was in danger of becoming an unmanageable commitment', adding that 'if we undertook a new commitment on this scale, we should not be able to send any more troops to France until well on into the summer.' Chamberlain's only comment was that these doubts as to the quality of the

Territorial troops were a new and somewhat disturbing feature, which had not before been brought to the notice of the War Cabinet. He made no comment, however, on Stanley's conclusion, or the fundamental point about strategic priorities that it raised, and allowed discussion to drift on to other subjects.[28] Perhaps Chamberlain did not notice the point; perhaps Stanley's conclusion was simply too awful to contemplate; perhaps Stanley's status in Cabinet merely counted for little. Perhaps all three.

Having agreed that all preparations necessary for the laying of the minefield off Narvik could be made, the War Cabinet spent the last ten days of February vacillating about taking action. The messages from Finland were mixed as to how well the Finns were doing and whether they could hold, and if so, for how long. Diplomats were busy trying to ascertain the Finnish requests in detail and to gain Norwegian and Swedish acceptance to the transit of an Allied force.[29] The War Cabinet found itself the object of conflicting pressures: on the one hand, holding good on the commitment made at the Supreme War Council (recently reinforced by further French pressure for action) and wishing to avoid the opprobrium of having failed to support Finland; on the other, increasing doubts about the wisdom of potential war with Russia, the feasibility of the military campaign in Finland and the likelihood of it taking place. Indeed, on 22 February it concluded that the likelihood 'must now be considered as extremely dubious'.[30] But within a week the situation had changed, and with it the increasing realisation that a difficult decision might very soon be required – something which, in principle, Chamberlain was always keen to avoid.

Churchill continued to vent his frustration, repeating all the arguments with which ministers were now wearily familiar, and with all his powers of advocacy, one moment 'plead[ing] earnestly',[31] the next 'in somewhat tigerish mood',[32] urging the Cabinet to 'strike while the iron is hot!'[33] Where pragmatism called for it, however, he was happy to adjust his case to the mood of the court, now arguing against landing in the face of Norwegian opposition.[34] His colleagues, for the most part, continued to favour caution. Halifax had considerable reservations about the effect on neutral opinion (particularly in the United States[35]), on British imports from Scandinavia and on the 'major project'. The Attorney General was concerned about the breach of international law. Stanley again voiced his concern about the deleterious impact on the BEF.[36] Advice from the Chiefs continued to be divided. For example, when Newall rightly voiced concern about the possibility of the Germans forestalling the Allies at the key airfield of Stavanger with an airborne operation, he was immediately rebuffed by Ironside, who declared that many of Stavanger's inhabitants were trained as volunteers and even very small forces could resist an airborne operation of this nature'.[37] The Joint Planners continued to express their scepticism, and they were uncompromising about the prospects for a force attempting to operate through the port of Trondheim: '[I]t certainly could not progress in the face of opposition from German air and land forces.'[38]

Ironside's own staff also voiced increasing reservations about the strategy. The Director of Military Operations and Plans, Major General Richard Dewing, was worried about the impact of the growing Scandinavian commitment: '[T]he basis of our strategy is the security of the United Kingdom and of France, and we ought not to cut our resources below the level necessary for the security of these areas, as defeat in either would mean the loss of the war.'[39] The Scandinavian operation, he noted, would require the raising of some forty-five new Lines of Communications units, and the diversion of around forty others from the second and third contingents of the BEF.[40] He also pointed out that the force was not ready and that 'assistance can only be *immediate* after 12 March' [emphasis in original], warning that, without staff talks, the adjustments critical to the force 'would require so much time as to make the operation virtually impossible'.[41] Ironside continued to be sceptical as to whether the Scandinavian operation would ever actually take place. In early February, he told Gort that he did not think there was 'the slightest chance', not least because the Foreign Office was very halfhearted.[42] A fortnight later, Dewing was already contingency planning – 'agreed by DCIGS [Deputy Chief of the Imperial General Staff]' – for the dispersal arrangements for the force in the event of the operation not materialising.[43]

The Chiefs continued to be upbeat in their reports to the War Cabinet. On 29 February they confidently advised that '[a]ll arrangements are proceeding according to plan'. The shipping was all ready; the loading of stores would commence the following day; Force Stratford (for Trondheim, Bergen and Stavanger) had been ready to move for three days; the principal staff officers for all three operations had visited the War Office and been given detailed briefings; an aircraft carrier with aircraft would deploy; and there would even be a portable runway provided for use at Boden.[44]

After much deliberation, Chamberlain now arrived at a decision: 'My own mind varied as fresh considerations were brought to my attention. Finally, I decided – against Winston – and told one or two colleagues who showed considerable anxiety about the discussion in Cabinet.'[45]

Any anxiety was quickly dispelled. The Prime Minister's decision 'not to proceed, for the time being, with the measures proposed'[46] was accepted with scarcely a murmur by Churchill (Chamberlain had briefed him privately before the meeting). Chamberlain was clearly relieved and also hugely pleased with his own performance, reporting to his sister, 'Simon whispered to me, "Splendid! You are a *real* Prime Minister"' [emphasis in original].[47] According to the Cabinet Secretary, at the end of the meeting Chamberlain was 'like a schoolboy on the first day of the holidays'.[48] The Prime Minister's decision had nothing to do with the questionable viability of the military plan; he feared prejudicing Scandinavian cooperation for the larger operation, the probable reaction in the United States and the likelihood of Norwegian reprisals (for example, cancellation of the shipping agreement).[49] But the latest Chiefs' report left the impression that they had every confidence in their plan, which could no doubt be implemented at short notice, if required. It was an unfortunate impression to leave.

If Chamberlain thought that there was some finality to his decision, events over the next few days quickly proved him wrong. The very next morning, Daladier, applying a little blackmail, let it be known through his ambassador in London that he 'felt that he could not maintain his position if effective steps were not taken to help Finland',[50] warning that his successor would probably pursue 'another policy' – a dark hint that he might, at best, be a less accommodating partner or, considerably worse, seek a compromise peace with Germany.[51] This caused an alarmed War Cabinet to reopen the whole debate. Ministers produced various off-the-cuff suggestions, including sending an expedition to Narvik and, in the event of Norwegian opposition, either forcing a way through or returning, or if the latter, sending material aid. The Cabinet could not decide which course to adopt beyond requesting cooperation from the Norwegian and Swedish governments and assuring them of British support if hostilities with Germany resulted. If the request was rejected, the Cabinet had, at least, the benefit that the Scandinavians would have to 'take the blame before world opinion'.[52] An evening meeting of the War Cabinet was interrupted by news that Daladier, without further consultation, had publicly announced his agreement to all the support requested by the Finns. This 'bad example of lack of cooperation' – more colourful language may actually have been used – would, as the Cabinet immediately recognised, 'allow the French to bluff, knowing that they could throw on us the whole blame for the failure to redeem their promise'. Ministers agreed that the French should be told that 'it was not possible for the Allies to fulfil the offer which M Daladier had made'.[53] Nevertheless, confidence in the decision to take no action was shaken.

Wishful thinking about the Scandinavians 'seeing sense' and letting the Allies through should have been short-lived: rejection of the diplomatic approaches swiftly followed. But the mood of baseless optimism and the avoidance of awkward facts continued. The urgency of support for the Finns was building momentum, with increasing pressure from public opinion and in the press. With little other action to report, the national newspapers had, for the past month, been giving considerable and dramatic coverage to the Winter War: 'Help in Time. Finland Is in Grave Peril';[54] 'the world is filled with admiration';[55] 'Allied Troops For Finland. MPs' Demand';[56] and 'Fighting On. They must get more help.'[57] Further articles were now appearing, along the lines of 'the whole sentiment of this country demands that Finland should not be allowed to fall',[58] and high-profile public meetings, including one at the Mansion House in the City of London, were being held to rally support for 'The Champions of Freedom'.[59]

One minister was resisting this temptation. On 4 March, Hankey sent Chamberlain, 'for his eyes only', a paper which reviewed the relative advantages and disadvantages of deploying forces to Scandinavia to help the Finns. The paper was an exercise in strategy – weighing up the ends, ways and means. It argued logically towards its conclusion that '[t]he fact is that we are not yet ready for a diversion on this scale' and that it might 'result in a humiliating retreat and great loss of prestige'.[60] Chamberlain was sufficiently impressed by the paper to write, 'This is a formidable case.'[61] Hankey sent a similar paper to Halifax and received the reply that '[my] own mind has moved in much the same way'.[62] Ismay shared Hankey's view; Colville recorded, 'Personally, Ismay can see no point in all these risky proposals and thinks we should do better to stick to our original thesis that we can win a long-drawn-out siege by outstaying Germany.'[63] Strategy, however, was increasingly being dominated by internal Cabinet dynamics, political considerations and political pressure.

Such pressure was becoming intense. In the first week in March, the minimum help acceptable to the War Cabinet appeared to be further material support, albeit with the stakes raised to fifty bombers which was said to be the Finns' 'crying need'.[64] But, as the Chiefs pointed out, that, by itself, would not achieve 'our primary object'[65] – getting to Gällivare and stopping the ore trade. Since the latter required the Finnish appeal for help, together with Norwegian and Swedish cooperation, the provision of the bombers should only be offered as a quid pro quo for the appeal, which in turn might unlock Norwegian and Swedish cooperation on which, they reiterated, success depended. But it was becoming increasingly apparent that the chances of gaining that cooperation were minimal. As far back as 20 February, Ironside had told Gort that the potential operation was 'nebulous and improbable' and that 'neither S of S [the Secretary of State – Stanley] nor I consider there is much chance of getting into

Scandinavia'.[66] Chamberlain was of the same opinion, telling the War Cabinet on 8 March that 'he did not feel there was much chance of our Scandinavian expedition coming off'. Churchill's way round this was to argue that '[i]t would be a mistake to cancel the expedition altogether merely because the Swedes *said* they ... would not co-operate' (emphasis in original). The arrival of the expedition might change the atmosphere altogether, he suggested, triggering the cooperation of the Scandinavian peoples, despite what their governments had declared. He thought that the Norwegians would not seriously oppose the landing, and the force could succeed with a mixture of 'persuasion and cajolery'. He was supported by Chatfield, who suggested that 'test forces' should be sent to the Norwegian ports, and if they were successful in getting ashore, the remainder of the expedition could follow.[67]

Despite the commitment of the War Office staff, planning was still very broad-brush – unsurprisingly for hard-pressed staffs working at the military-strategic level. As late as 8 March, the designated tactical-level commander of Avonmouth, Major General Pierse Mackesy, made representations to the Director of Military Operations about serious planning deficiencies – including the loading plan, the slow rate of build-up of forces, the lack of air defence and the paucity of logistical support – concluding, with some justification, 'It is my considered opinion that the plan as it now stands may well result in a dangerous if not disastrous situation if and when the force arrives at its destination.'[68] With no commander and staff between the military-strategic and tactical levels, there was a planning lacuna.

At the Cabinet meeting on 11 March, Chamberlain took up with gusto Churchill's and Chatfield's suggestions (shared by the French) about test landings, not for reasons of military feasibility, but because, if the expedition was abandoned as a result of a diplomatic refusal to a demand for passage, '[i]t would be said that we had never meant business at all and that our offer of assistance had been a mere sham.' There still remained the argument that the progress of the expedition up the railway beyond Narvik depended on the goodwill and cooperation of the Norwegian and Swedish governments and people. There was thus the prospect of the British action failing both diplomatically and militarily – violating Norwegian neutrality and being ignominiously stuck in Narvik. Churchill's response was that having a force ashore at Narvik was 'a valuable prize' in itself, whether or not further progress was possible.[69] (He had told Pound, 'Having got to Narvik, we have got our foot in the door.'[70]) He also questioned whether landings at the southern Norwegian ports were required until the outcome at Narvik was known. The Chiefs were invited to report on these matters the following day and to prepare instructions for the landing commanders.[71] It was evident that a landing, at Narvik at least, was about to be ordered. Ironside appeared to be happy with the outcome, envisaging a landing which was not seriously opposed: 'I can see our great big Scots Guards shouldering the sleepy Norwegians out of the way at 5 a.m. in the morning.'[72] Disregarded were the warnings of his staff that, without the active cooperation of the Norwegians (and Swedes), operations in Scandinavia were 'a dangerous detachment'.[73]

Differences of opinion between the Chiefs again became evident at their meeting that afternoon. Among those present was Admiral Sir Edward Evans, a dashing figure – participant in Captain Scott's Antarctic expedition and much decorated First World War hero – who was an acknowledged expert on Norway and married to a Norwegian. A late arrival was Brigadier John Kennedy, the former Joint Planner, who had been nominated as the senior staff officer of the land force. As Kennedy arrived, Evans was 'holding forth with immense enthusiasm ... although he thought the plans as they stood were half-hearted'. According to Kennedy, Ironside was 'almost as keen as Evans ... but the meeting was far from unanimous. As we walked out Newall said to me, "I think the whole thing is hare-brained." Ismay agreed with him. So did I.'[74] Where Pound stood on the matter is not recorded, but it is highly unlikely that Newall would have caved in to Ironside had Pound voiced strong objection to the plan.

The discussion at the War Cabinet the next day (12 March), led by Chamberlain, quickly descended to the tactical level, examining the precise defences at the ports and the best way of defeating them. Ironside summed up the meeting as 'dreadful'.

The Prime Minister began peering at a chart of Narvik, and when he had finished he asked me what scale it was on. He asked what effect an 8-inch shell would have on a transport and finished up by saying that he was prepared to risk a 4-inch shell, but not an 8-inch. He then asked what the weight of the shells were. ... The Cabinet presented the picture of a bewildered flock of sheep faced by a problem they have consistently refused to consider. Their favourite formula is that the case is hypothetical and then shy off a decision. I came away disgusted with them all.[75]

Part of Ironside's disgust may have been due to the fact that the War Cabinet rejected most of the Chiefs' recommendations. Churchill, probably sensing that his Narvik project was jeopardised by the inclusion of the Trondheim, Bergen and Stavanger operations, managed to get the Trondheim operation made conditional on success at Narvik. He rejected the necessity for landings at Stavanger and Bergen, neither of which, he observed caustically, 'were on the way to Finland'. Newall pointed out rather lamely that the occupation of the Stavanger aerodrome was 'most desirable', but the War Cabinet rejected his advice, declaring that the forces for Bergen and Stavanger should be held in readiness but need not be despatched. Newall did not rejoin, as he should have done, that this would unhinge the whole plan, the success of which relied on the simultaneous implementation of all of its elements. The War Cabinet had finally decided that the Narvik operation should go ahead.[76]

Ministers met again that evening to approve the instructions for commanders. Also present, along with the Chiefs of Staff, were Evans, Mackesy and Kennedy. The latter recalled, 'The meeting began with Evans giving an enthusiastic exposé of the whole plan, with all the details. The Prime Minster looked tired and lugubrious enough when he began; but as Evans warmed to his subject, Mr Chamberlain looked more and more horrified.'[77] The meeting then considered in detail the orders for the commanders – including, bizarrely, those for platoon commanders – line by line. These had been drafted during the afternoon by Kennedy, directed by Ironside, 'exhorting them to use bluff and good humoured determination as a substitute for force. If force had to be used, it must be the minimum necessary for the safety of the troops. If we could not get through to Norway and Sweden without fighting, then the whole business would be called off.'[78] The Prime Minister emphasised that in no circumstances should the Norwegians or Swedes suffer casualties. The orders for the military force commander were then examined and amended. 'By the time the instructions had come through the mangle they were extremely detailed, and gave the commander little discretion.' The only note of dissent came from Halifax who remarked, 'Well, if we can't get in except at the cost of a lot of Norwegian lives, I'm not for it – ore or no ore. The meeting came to an end. The Prime Minister shook hands with us as we filed out of the room, saying "Good-bye, and good luck to you – if you go."' Outside, Kennedy and the others discussed the likelihood of the operation taking place and 'resorted to betting ... Bridges [Cabinet Secretary] said he thought the chances were against it; Newall was laying three to one against; Mackesy a hundred. There were no takers, as usual.'[79]

Later that night Finland surrendered. The operation was off. The troops, who were already embarking, were halted. Within three days the whole force was dispersed and the specially formed units, including the ski battalion, disbanded.

7 Taking Stock

If after 12 January – when the War Cabinet had last come close to immediate intervention in Norway – it might have been useful and timely to review, even briefly, the government's higher direction of the war, a similar exercise after 12 March would have been even more revealing.

The strong sense of relief that the operation had been cancelled was widely shared. Chamberlain was well aware of the many 'possibilities of disaster' which it had entailed.[1] Halifax had 'some feeling of thankfulness' that the government had narrowly avoided sending an expedition which would be 'bogged down where it could not be maintained'.[2] Gort believed that it 'might prove a Gallipoli'[3] and told Stanley of his 'relief after 12 March, ... [having had] qualms about [the force's] readiness for battle.'[4] Cadogan was 'secretly relieved. Our plan was amateurish and half-hatched by a half-baked staff.'[5] Bridges, the Cabinet Secretary, recalled that as the final orders were being signed, notification was starting to come in to the effect that Russia and Finland had come to terms. 'I am bound to say', he wrote, 'that a good many of us felt so little real confidence in the Expedition that we could not avoid the feeling that perhaps it would be as well if this proved to be the way out.'[6]

Government policy had had a 'near miss'. The War Cabinet had approved a plan that, even at the time, let alone with the benefit of hindsight, obviously contained so many high risks that it amounted to a gamble with very high stakes at very long odds. And, with the troops already embarking to carry it out, it had come within a hair's breadth of implementation. In the light of the widespread awareness of this, even a brief exercise in reflection, let alone inquiry, might have commended itself as a sensible course of action to prevent a recurrence.

It would have been clear to an observer that Churchill's strength of personality and formidable powers of advocacy, together with his restless energy and determination, were now making him the single greatest force in the formulation of policy. His strong instinct to take the fight to the enemy was becoming the basis of Cabinet strategy. As he had written, back in December, 'I could never be responsible for a naval strategy which excluded the offensive principle.'[7] In particular, his single-minded pursuit of action at Narvik to stop the ore trade, together with a desire to get 'our foot in the door' in Scandinavia, was driving much of the agenda in Cabinet. Unfortunately, his preoccupation with what he later called 'my pet ... my first love'[8] was becoming an obsession, blinding him to its relationship with overall policy.[9] Nor was anyone in the War Cabinet drawing attention to the fact that the Cabinet was consistently failing to give strategy more than a passing nod. Indeed, ministers seem to have completely lost sight of the overall war policy. Did this still rest on a long-war policy of avoiding major conflict while building up military strength? Or had this approach been rejected in favour of a short-war policy? Without an agreed strategy, proposed action leapt from one scheme to another – whichever happened to catch the eye on a given day – regardless of whether it led to the policy objective. Ironside despaired of the War Cabinet's predilection with tactical matters and their reluctance to focus on grand strategy.[10] François Kersaudy summed up the position succinctly: 'With the exception of Winston Churchill the War Cabinet ministers had not the slightest notion of strategy, and they knew it; as for Churchill's notions, they were highly imperfect – and he did not know it.'[11] Without framing discussion in the context of strategy, it tended constantly to return to the same subjects: according to A. J. P. Taylor, the War Cabinet 'continued to dither round the problems and debated it on sixty distinct occasions'.[12]

Arguably, the person primarily responsible for the War Cabinet's failure to focus on strategy was the Prime Minister. Over the past two months it had become even more apparent that Chamberlain's managerial style was unsuited for the job of Prime Minister in time of war. In particular, he too rarely showed leadership in Cabinet 'prid[ing] himself on summing up rather than leading discussion'.[13] A member of the Cabinet secretariat, Lieutenant Colonel Ian Jacob, shrewdly observed that Chamberlain 'presided efficiently over the Cabinet; business was managed in an orderly fashion; but nothing much happened ... he was a fine chairman of a board of directors [but] not the managing director necessary in war'.[14] Ironside put it succinctly: 'We need more drive at the top.'[15] Furthermore, Chamberlain seemed unaware of the tendency of ministers unfamiliar or uncomfortable with strategy to focus on short-term rather than long-term goals and to drag discussion away from strategy into the tactical weeds and 'what to do next', probably because he was as unfamiliar and uncomfortable with strategy as were they. If his justification for ministers poring over instructions for platoon commanders was that he did not trust his military advisers – as well it might have been – he should have sacked them long before.

Chamberlain was so ignorant of military matters that he did not know the right questions to ask, often failing to subject blatantly inconsistent military advice to cross-examination, and instead allowing discussion to drift on to ground more familiar to him. His Civil Service advisers share some of the blame here. There was - and is - no reason to suppose that a Prime Minister is familiar with military matters. In the circumstances, a special adviser might have been hugely useful.

Keeping the Cabinet together had increasingly become the priority for Chamberlain. In particular, Churchill's growing popularity in the country, resulting from his inspiring broadcasts, the reflected glory of the *Graf Spee* and *Altmark* incidents and the flattering articles and cartoons in the national press, meant that he could not afford Churchill's resignation and therefore had to handle him carefully. When Churchill was overruled in Cabinet, some form of titbit, however small, had to be given to him.

If the War Cabinet was suffering from the over-influence of one man with a preoccupation, and its failure to focus on strategy, so, increasingly, was the Chiefs of Staff Committee.

The influence of Ironside over the past two months had grown almost to the point of domination. The tendency of each Chief to stick to his service area of expertise and only rarely, if ever, to contribute or challenge outside it exacerbated this when, as became the case, the main subject under discussion was the land campaign. Newall, as chairman, exercised little leadership in the matter: partly because he continued to stick strictly to his remit as merely the spokesman for the Chiefs; partly, perhaps, because he became aware of his own lack of knowledge of the subjects under discussion; partly as a result of personal chemistry vis-a-vis Ironside. Furthermore, like Churchill, Ironside had strong views about the need to take the initiative, was wedded to a plan – which he saw as his plan – to achieve it, and was reluctant to accept, let alone admit to others, that his plan had flaws. By the first week in March he was even justifying the large force for Scandinavia on the grounds that 'the reduction of the BEF by three divisions is unlikely to influence decisively the outcome of the battle'.[16] Needless to say, Ironside's stock was not riding high in the upper echelons of the BEF. According to Pownall, his view of the CIGS was shared by Grigg: 'He at least is under no illusions about Ironside,' adding, 'We shall never get order out of chaos till he goes.'[17]

Many of the flaws in the feasibility of the expedition centred on the combat readiness of the Army, most obviously in its equipment, but, even more importantly, in its training. Even by the beginning of March 1940, the state of training in most Army formations was still very low, particularly in the Territorial Army, whose units formed the majority of the force earmarked for Scandinavia. The doubling of the size of the

Territorial Army from thirteen to twenty-six divisions ('equipped on the same scale as the Regular Army')[18] announced twelve months previously had been a neat piece of political showmanship but an administrative fiasco, putting huge strains on the existing organisation.[19] As J. R. M. Butler observed, '[H]owever valuable the decision to double the Territorial Army might be as a gesture, it was not accompanied by the necessary provision for training, or for constituting a properly balanced force, with its essential air component.'[20] Forming the new units, finding and adapting the necessary accommodation for them, and recruiting and training their commanders, had taken many months and, even at the outbreak of war, the process was far from complete. In addition, there remained 'an embarrassing and alarming deficiency in equipment, and an even greater shortage of instructors'.[21] Further strain was put on the military organisation by the introduction of limited conscription in April. In fact, between April and August 1939 there had been a marked *fall* in the efficiency of the Territorial Army.[22] 'Most battalions were split, each half forming the basis of a new battalion which was filled up with militia men. In each case, in place of one keen and fairly efficient unit, two untrained, ill-equipped and inefficient battalions were produced.'[23] The situation was exacerbated between September and December by what was called the 'combing out' of more than 11,000 Territorial soldiers to return to key posts in industry.[24] The level of experience and competence within the Territorial Army was very low. There was a formal assumption in place that, before any Territorial units were despatched overseas, they would have at least six months' intensive training;[25] but with competition for scarce training equipment and facilities, and the competing demands of Home Defence tasks, the training being undertaken in most units, even in early 1940, was still at a basic level.[26]

Ironside was well aware of these deficiencies. Indeed, in early March he 'talked about the prospect of sending low category divisions to the BEF to dig but not to fight',[27] and he reported to the Army Council that '55% of Territorial Army commanding officers had been found unfit to command in war'.[28] Yet the majority of the troops earmarked for Scandinavia were from the Territorial Army, although due to the need for secrecy they were unaware of it. Even in the Regular Army, training standards were a cause for concern. In early January, Ironside had described the BEF as 'largely untrained', adding, 'Politicians think because we have the men we have a trained army.'[29] In February he was observing that 'we ... have nothing left in England fit for fighting.'[30] The remainder of the troops for Norway were the forty or so Lines of Communications units being raised from scratch. Ironside must have known the challenges that awaited the wholly unprepared British force in Scandinavia and its inadequacy to meet them, but he chose not to advise the War Cabinet of this. The probable explanation, as well as an insight into his innermost thoughts, comes from a candid diary entry in January.

We have now a problem letting the people know the state of the Army. We have a shell, both in material and training. ... When it is discovered, there might be a row. The blame may well fall on the soldiers. ... Soldiers may fall with the government. I realized that fully when I consented to take over the duties of CIGS. I had no option but to take over.[31]

Even by April, things were little better, as Ironside confided in his diary: 'Nobody has dared to say that the Territorial Army is virtually untrained after seven months of training. It is untrained, and we don't seem to have made a very good show at it. There is a lack of leadership all through.'[32] As so often, Ironside was telling his diary what he should have been telling his political masters.

It is also surprising that Ironside did not focus attention on the training of those troops, Regular and Territorial, who were destined for demanding operations in Norway, many within the Arctic Circle. His yearlong service in Murmansk in 1918–1919 would have given him experience of the huge demands of warfare in Arctic conditions. Yet, apart from the specially raised ski battalion, there is no evidence that he gave any direction about the necessity for specialised or intensified training to take place, even though the unusually severe winter conditions in Britain lent themselves to such training.

It might also have occurred to Ironside to make enquiries about the readiness of the French Army's Chasseurs Alpins on whom so much depended in the plan. He would have found that they were not quite the elite ski troops he may have imagined: they were, in fact, 'new units which had recruited their rank and file in a hurry from the general run of *poilus* as much as from the villages of the Upper Savoy'.[33] There were also concerns about the Polish troops which were being formed into units in France: 'badly trained, ... armed and equipped, and would be useless as a fighting force', read one report.[34]

A further key deficiency greatly increased the risks which would have resulted from the planned expedition. Just a few days before the operation was authorised, the War Office staff had informed the Deputy Chiefs' committee of a crisis in anti-aircraft artillery. Production of Bofors (light anti-aircraft guns) had fallen so far behind target that only 388 of these guns had been produced, against a requirement of 3,194. The BEF had less than half its necessary allocation; the Air Defence of Great Britain, less than ten per cent. 'The danger of this', the Deputy

Chiefs were told, 'was impossible to exaggerate, and the facts of the situation should be represented most strongly at the highest level'.[35] The Chiefs duly reported to the Military Coordination Committee, underlining the fact that this was 'a weakness which might well lead to a disaster of the first magnitude'.[36] Thus, this was no time to be taking on new operational commitments.

This was, however, a rare example of the Chiefs not mincing their words in the strategic advice they gave ministers. Their readiness to do so on this occasion may not have been unconnected to the fact that they, themselves, could not be blamed – the fault lay with British industry and the Ministry of Supply. Too often, the Chiefs, in their consideration of strategy, glossed over the problems, not just in their advice to ministers but also apparently in their own minds, applying little intellectual rigour to their analysis and failing to draw logical conclusions about the feasibility of their plans. Moreover, they were positively cavalier in making a virtue of risk, using as their justification the rationale that the prize – stopping the ore trade and thus shortening the war – was so great that it was worth almost any cost: 'the stakes are high, but the prize of success is great'.[37] They made no effort to quantify the compound risk, perhaps because the result would have taken them to a conclusion they could not accept. They even convinced themselves that the risk to the security of the Western Front was minimal. Yet, they knew their plan was high risk. Even Ironside repeatedly acknowledged this in private: '[O]ne is almost frightened by the boldness of the plan, knowing what slender means one has at the moment to carry it out'[38]; 'terrified at the timing in this Scandinavian show'.[39] But they did not represent the full risk to the Cabinet and effectively suppressed the Joint Planners' report which did so, due, one can only surmise, partly to wishful thinking, partly because it was they who had recommended the plan in the first place, partly because they might appear fainthearted or defeatist, and partly for fear that the Cabinet might get cold feet and reject the plan. This was rash. Their plan had become detached from reality. As Slessor later observed, it was 'a triumph of wishful and entirely unpractical thinking – based on the most magnificent offensive intentions but almost unbelievably remote from the squalid facts of life'.[40]

The Chiefs' advice to the War Cabinet was causing considerable concern amongst their advisers – the Joint Planners and, in Ironside's case, his Military Operations staff. These advisers were constantly providing the Chiefs with warnings and cautionary advice which were either overruled or rejected and either not passed on to the War Cabinet or, in doing so, were watered down. To their great credit, the Joint Planners were consistent in their position, and at some risk to themselves. They were already in Churchill's sights as what he termed 'the forces of negation'.[41] Eventually, his patience snapped with the Admiralty's Plans division. Its director, Captain Victor Danckwerts, who had throughout been uncompromising in his advice, was summarily sacked in the first week of March, and his three most senior subordinates followed shortly afterwards.[42] The lesson would not have been lost on others in the Admiralty staff. Churchill was to repeat such action in April when Captain A. G. Talbot, Director of the Anti-Submarine Division, disputed his public exaggeration of the figures for destroyed U-boats.[43] He was sacked the same day.[44]

It would be surprising if a review at this time would not have asked some questions about the command and control arrangements for the expedition. What was in place was not a single command and control structure, but several. The naval operation at Narvik was to be commanded by an officer, Admiral Evans, who was appointed only on 12 March and who would 'fly his flag' from one of the deployed ships, reporting directly to the Admiralty. Naval operations in central Norway would be commanded by the CinC Home Fleet, Admiral Sir Charles Forbes. The joint British/French land operation at Narvik (Avonmouth) would be commanded by Major General Mackesy, reporting directly to the War Office. The operations at the three central Norwegian objectives of Trondheim, Bergen and Stavanger (Stratford) would, once ashore, be commanded by a brigade commander, and the expedition into southern Sweden (Plymouth) by a corps commander, both reporting to the War Office. Only when the Plymouth corps headquarters was established in Norway, scheduled to be around a month after the initial landings, would it take over responsibility for the Avonmouth and Stratford operations.[45] The air forces would support the land and sea commanders as applicable and report to the Air Ministry.

This highly unsatisfactory arrangement was the result not of a carefully constructed command and control master plan, but of incremental, ad hoc decisions as planning had progressed. The expedition was seen not as a single campaign – a campaign being a series of related operations within a given theatre – but as a number of independent, disjointed operations. It was indicative of an inherent weakness: no single hand or single body of commanders was designing and planning the expedition and one would not be commanding and controlling it; day-to-day coordination would take place in the Chiefs of Staff Committee and the Military Coordination Committee, with control being carried out by the staffs in the three service ministries. The military-strategic level in Whitehall, already overburdened by its existing duties and commitments, would, thus, deal direct with the tactical-level commanders deployed in

Theatre, with no intervening commander or headquarters. This arrangement might have been adequate for a simple, small, single-service operation. But for a combined operation of the scale, complexity and challenge of that which was planned for Scandinavia, it was a recipe for muddle and confusion – as events would show.

The existing doctrine, the *Manual for Combined Operations*, listed a number of alternative systems of overall command for combined operations, including 'Unified Command', in which authority over all participants was vested in a Combined C-in-C, and 'Command by One Service', in which authority was given to the commander of the service playing the chief part.[46] The Director of Military Operations, Dewing, advised Ironside to raise the matter in Cabinet, recommending the lead-service option for the planning stage, at least.[47] But Ironside did not do so; nor is there any record of the matter being discussed in the Chiefs of Staff Committee. It would undoubtedly have led to a row, most notably (although far from exclusively) over command and control of air forces. As Ismay later observed, 'It almost seemed as though the Air Staff would prefer to have their forces under Beelzebub rather than anyone connected with the Army. ... When one recalls the views which were then held by the General Staff on the employment of air power, one can scarcely blame them.'[48] Responsibility for each part of each operation thus remained with each service. This arrangement was messy, and of highly dubious practicality, but it probably suited the service ministries, since none would have to cede any precious authority to another or debate which service would be playing the leading role. None of the Chiefs of Staff appears to have raised the issue, and no minister appears to have questioned it. Besides, the single services at the most senior level paid scant attention to joint service (Combined) organisations and doctrine.

The demands of planning a venture on this scale were way beyond the resources available. The staffs within the service ministries, in particular the War Office, were simply not organised or manned to carry out the level of detailed planning required by what had been transformed from a minor sideshow to a full-scale campaign, and one of considerable complexity. Mackesy was told to carry out the detailed planning for the Avonmouth operation but was not given extra staff to assist him, whilst the Corps Headquarters for the Plymouth operation had not even been formed. The Joint Planners were already grossly overworked, writing appreciations and drafting reports at short notice on the whole gamut of military-strategic planning, and yet, six months into the war, it still totalled only six officers.[49] In mid-February, an Inter-Service Planning Staff had been formed; but this grand-sounding title belied the fact that it consisted of only three relatively junior officers, one from each of the service plans branches, together with an official from the Ministry of Shipping.[50] Their main task was low-level coordination work. Similarly, an Inter-Service Security Board and an Inter-Service Signal Board had been set up on a similar scale. This facade of integrated service planning may have provided reassurance to the War Cabinet, but it lacked substance.

Inquiry into the preparedness of the armed forces for amphibious operations might also have caused alarm bells to ring. Although no such operations were part of the plan for the Scandinavian expedition, it did not take much imagination to see that if things did not go strictly according to plan, some amphibious capability might be a distinct advantage, and the lack of it a distinct risk. Amphibious operations had not been entirely ignored by the services since the Great War. For example, the curriculum at the three service staff colleges included an annual four-week combined services module, culminating in a joint exercise at the Army Staff College at Camberley.[51] And the *Manual for Combined Operations*, which drew heavily on Great War experience, particularly Gallipoli,[52] had been updated as recently as 1938. At the top of the services and in the service ministries, however, interest in combined operations was decidedly limited. At a time of financial stringency, they viewed combined operations primarily as a drain on their budgets. 'No Service was anxious to pay for any specialist materials such as landing craft, so the matter was left in the hands of a Landing Craft Committee that "met once a year, had a yarn and went away again."'[53] The services could not even agree with each other on the likelihood of combined operations, or, indeed, the strategic need for them.[54] It was not until 1937 that they set up a committee to develop the combined operations capability, and not until 1938 that they agreed to establish an Inter-Service Training and Development Centre.[55] Even then, the centre consisted of only four officers and was closed down on the outbreak of war.[56] So poor was the amphibious capability that a report to the Deputy Chiefs of Staff in June 1939 concluded that 'it is impossible to stage any landing operation on a hostile shore, with a force of a brigade or more, sooner than six months from the time that the order is given'.[57] Plans were made to establish a Royal Marines brigade 'with the specific object that there should always be a force available for undertaking at short notice, offensive operations on an enemy coast',[58] but the Deputy Chiefs noted in February 1940 that it was still 'in the process of formation'. In March, no amphibious capability existed, although whether ministers were aware of this is not known.

As regards the Chiefs of Staff themselves, an observer would have noticed that the time pressure on them had further increased, leaving little opportunity for thinking. They had to spend far too long in committee. By March the Military Coordination Committee, of questionable utility in January, had shown that it was positively counterproductive, not least in wasting large amounts of time for very little added value. Ironside lamented, 'I get such a feeling of futility with all our committees. ... The Committee of the three Chiefs of Staff is slow enough in all conscience, but when all their efforts have to be re-examined by another Committee, the pace at which we work becomes funereal.'[59] One obvious solution was to give the Chiefs an additional and senior deputy. This happened, but not until late April, after Hankey had urged Chamberlain to adopt it, but by then the penalty for delay had, at least in part, already been exacted.[60] The Chiefs should, themselves, have pressed their case earlier.

The extent to which a brief survey of the government machinery for the higher direction of the war would, at this stage, have identified serious shortcomings in the intelligence system is harder to judge. None had become apparent. It is the fate of such systems that this only becomes obvious with catastrophic failure. But even a cursory glance at the Chiefs of Staff's plans shows that they were full of detail about what the Allies had in mind but rarely focused on German intentions and capabilities. The Chiefs did not seem as concerned as their advisers about the possibility of German pre-emptive action. The Joint Planners had warned of 'the possibility which must not be overlooked of Germany anticipating us in Scandinavia. In this event we might be forced to take action to ... prevent Germany seizing the west coast ports.'[61] In addition, the Allied Military Committee warned that if the Germans suspected that the Allies were about to threaten their iron ore supplies, Germany would 'almost certainly' invade Scandinavia.[62] When the Chiefs reported to the War Cabinet, they considered this was no more than 'likely'.[63] They would, thus, have been less concerned when the Joint Planners told them that '[t]he Germans probably already suspect that the Allies have it in mind to intervene in Scandinavia.'[64] Churchill came closest to considering this when he said to Halifax in the wake of the events of 12 March, 'Whether [the Germans] have some positive plan of their own which will open to us, I cannot tell. It would seem to me astonishing if they have not.'[65]

Intelligence about the countries into which this deployment was going to take place was also in short supply. Service attachés were the major sources for information on military matters in any country. And although there was a naval attaché based in Oslo, there was no military (army) attaché based there – cover for Norway was provided by the military attaché based in Sweden. With the best will in the world, he could not be expected to have the same contacts, knowledge and trust as one based in Oslo. A military attaché was not established in Norway as soon as operations there were mooted in November. As planning developed, it became more difficult to make good the deficit without indicating an increased interest in the country, and thus possible intent.

It is surprising that, following the cancellation of the expedition on 12 March and the widespread relief of so many decision takers and advisers, no one brought to the attention of the Cabinet just how narrowly it had averted a 'near miss' of strategic proportions. There were a number of reasons why this did not happen. First, the window of opportunity to do so was remarkably short; events soon began to move very quickly again. Second, throughout the past two months the whole business had the air of an academic exercise – 'our hypothetical plan',[66] 'nebulous and improbable'[67] – and thus wouldn't really happen and, therefore, need not be taken seriously. Many were guilty of complacency and wishful thinking. Others saw that the chance of Scandinavian cooperation – the sine qua non of the whole scheme – was negligible, but either continued to plan 'just in case' or saw an advanced plan as an important tool of diplomacy. And as the prospect of Finland's surrender became more likely, many saw the likelihood of intervention virtually disappear. As Ironside observed of the plan in late January: 'I am afraid we shall never get a chance of carrying it out.'[68] In mid-February the War Cabinet thought the expedition 'must now be considered as extremely dubious',[69] and Ironside was telling Gort, 'Neither the Secretary of State nor I consider that there is much chance of getting into Scandinavia.'[70] In early March Chamberlain told the Cabinet that 'he did not feel there was much chance of our Scandinavian expedition coming off', further conveying his doubt to the force commanders on 12 March with his valedictory, 'Good-bye, and good luck to you – if you go.'[71] This scepticism conveyed itself to the various staffs and down to the units who had been stood to and stood down twice in as many months, affecting their perception of the need for the operation to be taken seriously.

The main reason that the 'near miss' was not emphasised to the War Cabinet was that those whose duty it was to do so – the Chiefs of Staff – would have had to acknowledge to themselves, and admit to the War Cabinet, that compound risk in the operation had reached the point of recklessness. They were deeply divided on the matter. Newall, their chairman, considered the operation 'hare-brained' but had not said so openly. Ironside, to the very end, was expressing regret that the whole expedition, including the large deployment into southern Sweden, was being superseded by the limited operations at Narvik and the central

Norwegian ports. He told Kennedy on the afternoon of 12 March, 'I can't tell you how disappointed I am. They want to cut out the whole thing, except possibly Narvik; or at any rate to postpone the southern landings until we see how Narvik goes.'[72] And he subsequently showed his faith in the plan by pleading in Cabinet for the force to be kept in being and not dispersed.[73] He also, critically, failed to warn the Cabinet that there could be no question of the force being resurrected at short notice. His diary shows no hint of relief at the cancellation, only regret at seeing 'all our weeks of work come to nothing'.[74] Pound's view is not known, but his interest seems to have been restricted to the naval operations, where the prospect was brightest and the risk the least, even if, according to his biographer, the whole expedition was something 'the more sober members of his staff viewed with horror'.[75] Newall was, therefore, isolated, and it would have required greater resolve and strength of character than he possessed to act on his firmly held personal conviction.

8   Weserübung

On 10 October 1939 Grand Admiral Erich Raeder, head of the Kriegsmarine – the German Navy – paid a routine call on Adolf Hitler. Raeder used the opportunity to kindle Hitler's interest in the importance of Norway and its western seaboard to Germany's naval policy. The point had been emphasised by retired Admiral Wolfgang Wegener in his influential 1929 book, *Die Seestrategie des Weltkrieges*,[1] and Raeder had recently received a paper on the subject from one of his senior subordinates, Admiral Rolf Carls, warning of the possibility of the British establishing themselves on the Norwegian coast. The strategic impact would be considerable. In the words of historian Michael Epkenhans,

If the RAF could operate from airfields in Norway and the Royal navy [sic] from ports in the Skagerrak, the Baltic Sea would become a British lake and the inferior German navy would be systematically destroyed. Furthermore, British bombers would also dominate the industrial areas of Northern Germany. A British-occupied Norway would be a strategic disaster for Germany and must be avoided at all costs.[2]

Raeder recommended to Hitler that an operation should be planned to seize and occupy the key bases. Hitler said he would think about it. Two months later, on 11 December, Raeder received a visit from Vidkung Quisling, leader of the Norwegian proto-fascist National Unity Party. Quisling told Raeder that British landings in Norway were expected and that he and his supporters could help in 'placing the necessary bases at the disposal of the German armed forces'.[3] Raeder immediately reported this to Hitler, who agreed to meet him and Quisling on 14 December. Hitler was sufficiently impressed by Quisling to have a second meeting with him a few days later, after which he ordered the Oberkommando der Wehrmacht (OKW) – the Armed Forces High Command – to 'investigate how one can take possession of Norway',[4] stipulating that the study should be kept within OKW. Things moved quickly. The next day, the OKW Chief, General Wilhelm Keitel, met with his Chief of Operations, Major General Alfred Jodl, to make an assessment and assign initial tasks: Jodl would produce an initial report, to be called *Studie Nord,* by the end of the month; intelligence gathering was discussed, with special roles being considered for the air attaché in Oslo, the Abwehr (OKW Intelligence), and a special high-altitude Luftwaffe reconnaissance squadron. The Army Chief of Staff, General Frans Halder, learned that plans were afoot and immediately ordered Army intelligence to supply maps and information on Norway.

Raeder remained a key protagonist of the idea, calling on Hitler again at the end of December to reiterate the need to prevent Norway from falling into British hands. His own operations staff were decidedly unenthusiastic, but in mid-January they faced the fact that '[t]he Chief of the Naval Staff is still firmly convinced that England intends to occupy Norway in the near future in order to cut off completely all exports from the Norwegian-Swedish area to Germany and to prevent the latter from making use of Norwegian bases.'[5] Raeder's plan was to execute landings at major ports along the whole length of Norway's 1,000-mile coastline, from Oslo to Tromsø, an operation that was clearly entirely dependent on complete surprise. Later in January, for reasons of secrecy, Hitler ordered that *Studie Nord* be recalled and that all planning henceforth be conducted entirely by a special staff within OKW, under his personal guidance, for an operation to be code-named Weserübung ('Weser Exercise').[6] The special staff was remarkably small, comprising just one officer from each service, led by naval Captain Theodor Krancke. The single-service headquarters were so affronted at being effectively cut out of the planning that at the group's first meeting with Keitel on 5 February the Luftwaffe officer pointedly did not show up.[7] The Krancke Staff, as it was called, worked quickly and, within three weeks, had produced an outline plan for the invasion of Norway. The combined-services operation was to be executed by a corps, consisting of a mountain division, an airborne division, a motorised rifle brigade and six reinforced infantry regiments, with half the troops delivered by simultaneous landings at six ports from Oslo to Narvik and half delivered by air. Further waves of troops would follow by air and sea over the next four days. Little serious opposition was expected from the Norwegian armed forces.[8]

The Altmark incident on 16 February had a major impact on the place of Weserübung in German strategy. It convinced Hitler that Norway could not enforce its neutrality and that the British would no longer respect that neutrality. It also 'provided a further spur' to the operation[9] by confirming intelligence reports that the Allies were, themselves, planning an operation in Norway. At the first meeting of the Krancke Staff, Keitel had told the group that intelligence had been received 'from several sources' indicating that the British were planning such an

Figure 8.1 General Nikolaus von Falkenhorst
(Getty Images)

operation.[10] In the latter half of January, a report had been received from the Abwehr station in Hamburg that the Chasseurs Alpins were being withdrawn from the Metz sector for operations in northern Europe.[11] In addition signals intelligence was received – resulting from German Naval Intelligence's recently acquired ability to breach Royal Navy codes – reporting that Allied preparations for operations in Norway were intensifying.[12]

Three days after the Altmark incident, Hitler ordered that plans for Wesrübung should be speeded up. He also decided, following a suggestion from Jodl, that a corps commander should now be appointed for the operation and, significantly, that this commander and his staff should be brought in to take over the planning. On the advice of Keitel, the general nominated was fifty-four-year-old General der Infanterie Nikolaus von Falkenhorst, the commander of XXI Corps.

Falkenhorst was one of the few German generals of his rank with operational experience in the far north of Europe – he had been a divisional operations officer in the German intervention in Finland in 1918. He was summoned to the Reich Chancellery at noon the following day for what turned out to be a job interview. Hitler told him the objective of the operation, asked him how he would conduct it, and told him to come back at 5 P.M. with the answer.[13] A no doubt shell-shocked

Falkenhorst made straight for a bookshop to buy a Baedeker tourist guide to Norway 'to find out what Norway was like. . . . I had no idea; I wanted to know where the ports were and how many inhabitants Norway had, and what kind of country this was . . . I absolutely did not know what to expect.'[14] After a couple of hours work in his hotel room, he returned to present his ideas to the Führer. To what must have been his intense relief, Falkenhorst met with Hitler's approval.

The following Monday, Falkenhorst and his key staff from Headquarters XXI Corps started work in great secrecy at a nearby OKW building, taking the Krancke Staff under command. Three days later, the plan was presented to Hitler, who agreed two major changes. The first, proposed by Jodl, was that Weserübung and Fall Gelb – the plan for the invasion in the west – should be so constructed that they could be conducted independently of each other, in terms of both time and forces employed. The second, proposed by Falkenhorst, was that, to enable success in Norway, Weserübung required the German occupation of northern Denmark. [15] Hitler, himself, made two further changes: the whole of Denmark should be occupied, and no attempt should be made to enlist Quisling's support for the operation.

Further intelligence was now received about Allied intentions. The German legation in Stockholm reported that 'a major operation' in Scandinavia by the Western powers was imminent.[16]

On 1 March the Führer directive for Weserübung was produced amid tight security, with only nine copies. It emphasised at the outset that '[t]he basic aim is to lend the operation the character of a *peaceful* occupation, designed to protect by force of arms the neutrality of the northern countries (emphasis in original); but if persuasion did not work, '[a]ny resistance which is nevertheless offered will be broken by all means available.' Falkenhorst would be responsible directly to Hitler, and the forces from the Luftwaffe would be under Falkenhorst's tactical command.[17] Additionally, two days later, Hitler directed that Weserübung would be carried out several days before the offensive in the west.[18]

The reactions of the three single services to the plan were very different. At Kriegsmarine Headquarters, Raeder remained wholly supportive, although some of his senior staff were most uneasy about the degree of risk to the Navy that it entailed.[19] Army Headquarters viewed the operation as a dangerous distraction from the main attack in the west and strongly objected to the allocation of Army assets being made by OKW. Moreover, Halder felt affronted at having not been consulted by Hitler, recording with some petulance, 'Not a single word has passed between the Führer and ObdH [CinC Army] on this matter; this must be put on record for the history of the war. I shall make a point of noting down the first time the subject is broached. Not until 2 March.'[20] This was as nothing compared to the Luftwaffe's reaction. Göring angrily confronted Hitler at a conference on 5 March, complaining of being kept in the dark, denouncing the planning as worthless, and demanding that he should retain command of all air force assets, including the deployment of parachute troops. 'The Feldmarschall vents his spleen', Jodl noted wearily in his diary, 'because he was not consulted beforehand.'[21] It was a measure of Göring's influence with Hitler, however, that his demands were met. Two days later, Falkenhorst went to Göring's country retreat, Karinhall, to present Weserübung and smooth ruffled feathers.[22]

With the change of command status, the Luftwaffe was not averse to the operation – indeed, the Chief of the Air Staff had proposed establishing air bases in Norway a month previously.[23] Both the Luftwaffe and the Army were now under instruction 'to operate in close cooperation with the Commander of Group XXI',[24] and there is no evidence to suggest that they had any intention of doing otherwise. Indeed, when the commander of the 10th Fliegerkorps, the air element for Weserübung, was briefed by Göring and his senior subordinates, the cooperation message was repeated, and he was given considerable additional assets. The commander threw himself wholeheartedly into the planning, establishing a special headquarters in Hamburg, taking over the top floor of the large Hotel Esplanade.[25]

On 3 March Hitler called for 'the greatest speed' in the preparations for Weserübung, with the forces to be ready at four days' notice from 10 March to launch the operation.[26] The plans were now well developed. Particular attention had been paid to intelligence on Norway. The German attachés – naval, army and air – in Norway had been active, providing detailed information about the Norwegian armed forces and their location,[27] with further information provided by Abwehr agents, including details of shipping movements in the main ports.[28] The high-level reconnaissance flights had provided topographical photographs of, amongst other things, all the Norwegian ports, navigation channels and serviceable airfields the length of Norway.[29]

In outline, the plan called for six divisions and a motorized rifle brigade to be allocated to the operation in Norway and two to Denmark. Almost the whole of the Kriegsmarine surface fleet would be involved in the operation to deliver the troops to the major Norwegian ports of Oslo, Kristiansand, Egersund, Bergen, Trondheim and Narvik, and to those in Denmark; 9,000 men would be aboard the ships with another 4,000 men aboard transports, along with 950 vehicles, 750 horses and 4 tanks, and

3,500 men would be landed by air. Parachute troops (a capability unused before in warfare) would seize the airbases at Oslo and Stavanger, and also the two key Danish airfields at Ålborg in northern Jutland. All of this would take place on day one. The plan called for a fast build-up of reinforcements, with 8,000 men being landed by sea and air in the next 3 days, and a further 17,000 the following week. The total force would amount to some 100,000 men.[30] The Luftwaffe would provide almost 1,000 aircraft. This was, thus, an operation on a big scale. Far from providing the bare minimum, and unlike the British, the planners were following the principle later to be made famous by General Heinz Guderian's much quoted aphorism, '*Klotzen, nicht Kleckern!*' (roughly, 'Clout, don't dribble!').[31] The possibility of Allied landings was considered, and units were told that if these were in greatly superior strength, they should avoid unnecessary losses by withdrawing inland until a counter-attack could be launched: a sensible tactic. The orders were detailed, with each formation being given its primary and subsidiary objectives.[32] The degree to which the plan depended on surprise was articulated by Raeder at a Führer Conference on 9 March at which he characterised Weserübung as 'contradicting all the principles of naval warfare ... but that success would be attained if surprise was achieved'.[33] Thus, by 12 March, German plans and preparations were well advanced. It was now a question of timing.

The German planning, unlike the British, had had the benefit of firm direction and the minimum of time spent in committee. It had been conducted within a highly centralised policy-making structure and had given due consideration to balancing ends, ways and means; it had also recognised where these were not in balance and the very high degree of risk that resulted. Again, unlike the British, initial campaign design had been conducted by a small, dedicated, full-time, tri-service team, with no other responsibilities or distractions. Then, with the appointment of Falkenhorst, campaign design and planning were delegated to a single, joint ('combined') commander and his headquarters who would also be responsible for implementation. This was what today would be called the operational level. Doing so was a key decision. OKW did not have the capacity for detailed planning, was not designed for it, and would have floundered as the campaign became more complex and intense. It required a dedicated subordinate commander and headquarters. The result, even by 12 March, was a highly sophisticated plan and, because OKW had planning authority over the single services, a high level of detailed preparation. It had not, however, all been easy-going with the single services, who resented – and, at times, actively contested – OKW's power and authority.[34] Finally, the plan had benefited from the effort put into intelligence and the result of a central intelligence organisation – the Abwehr (which reported to OKW) – even if the single services maintained some capabilities themselves.[35]

Weserübung was a highly impressive feat of staff planning, showing a sense of purpose, thoroughness and professionalism that makes the British approach look hopelessly amateur by comparison. But the plan had three obvious flaws. First, it lacked unity of command – that is, a single, unified, command structure. For what was a complex, combined-service operation – indeed, the first-ever such operation - where success depended on speed, agility and a high degree of coordination and synchronisation, this was a serious drawback. The plan, therefore, relied on unity of effort, but the experience so far suggested that the necessary cooperation between the services at all levels could not be assumed. Inter-service rivalry was not a purely British phenomenon and, in the German case, had been much exacerbated by the clash of big egos.

Second, Weserübung was a strictly military plan for an operation which was not a strictly military operation. Success, at least in part, was reliant on the political acquiescence of the Danish and Norwegian governments. Although Hitler laid great stress on this, insufficient attention was paid to the likelihood of achieving it, to the amount of diplomatic effort which would be required and to the coordination of diplomatic and military activity. For reasons of security, participation of civilian offices in the planning of Weserübung was prohibited, with political planning carried out by the National Defence Branch of OKW.[36] The German diplomatic service was largely kept in the dark until a very late stage.

The third and greatest flaw, by a considerable margin, was that, to be successful, the plan depended entirely on complete strategic and tactical surprise and simultaneity. If these were not achieved, the result was liable to be, not limited success, but catastrophic failure. Hitler recognised this and accepted – thus 'owning' – the risk. But there was clearly some nervousness among the staffs, including Falkenhorst's.[37] Raeder's words, '[S]uccess would be attained if surprise was achieved', appear to have been carefully chosen – it was a very big 'if'. Hitler was following his instinct in deciding to take the risk. To what extent his generals and admirals had quantified this risk can only be a matter of speculation. If they did so, they would have weighed up their chances of assembling 100,000 men, their equipment and stores, the shipping and aircraft to carry them, the orders and instructions required to do so and the act of transporting them from around Germany to their points of departure and, hence, to their destinations across the North Sea without the Allies spotting this activity, and come to the conclusion that those chances were very, very slim.[38] Perhaps it would not have been a career-enhancing move to air such a view in the Führer's presence – it brought into question his instinct and genius. But whatever the reason, the result was that the plan had one thing very much in common with its British counterpart: it was a gamble, although with even higher stakes and at even longer odds.

9   'Something Must Be Done'

If, following the Finnish surrender on 12 March, the first reaction of many in the British government and military had been one of relief, it was shortly followed by a widespread feeling of dejection. As J. R. M. Butler observed, 'In Whitehall, the prospect of seizing the initiative had been exhilarating, and the cancellation of the plan had a depressing effect.'[1] Many felt shame and impotence – questioning whether enough had been done for the Finns and how lack of support for them might be perceived around the world. Both Cadogan and the editor of the *Times*, Geoffrey Dawson, privately described the Finnish surrender as 'a black day'.[2] Harvey called it 'a defeat for democracy'[3] – a theme echoed in a number of national newspapers, for example, the *Sunday Pictorial*: 'Finland Was Betrayed!'[4] The *Times* reported reaction in neutral countries, including comment in a prominent Dutch newspaper that '[t]he credit of the Allies has suffered another shock.'[5]

It was a time for an immediate reassessment of grand strategy, but few at the grand-strategic level seemed to have recognised this. An exception was the Allied Military Committee, which had drawn attention to the fact that 'it was doubtful if anyone was really giving thought to our future grand strategy'. The British representatives believed 'that the "Appreciation of Possible German Action" was really only the first half of a full examination of how the war might be won, and fully ... expected that it would be followed at once by an "Appreciation of Allied Possible Course of Action in 1940."'[6] Sadly, their suggestion was not acted on in time.

Instead, attention was focused on rather more immediate problems. Pressure on the government to act came from a number of directions. Closest to home, it came from within the War Cabinet. After its meeting on 14 March, Ironside recorded, '[T]here was rather a feeling of deflatedness after the Scandinavian failure. Tempers ran fairly high. Winston particularly annoying.'[7] Churchill's appetite for action was clearly in no way diminished – 'straining at the leash' was how Hoare described it.[8] He still argued that the mining operation (Wilfred) should be carried out and that 'we might never get another opportunity of gaining a foothold in

Scandinavia.'[9] According to the Cabinet Secretary, it 'met, of course, with no support',[10] but Churchill left the impression that there might be other possibilities. Ironside noted, 'I can see that Winston wants to ginger people up into doing something. What, he doesn't quite know.'[11]

In fact, Churchill had three other schemes in mind. First, despite its rejection by the Admiralty staff, he had not given up on Operation Catherine, his plan (previously described to him by Pound as 'courting disaster')[12] to put up-armoured warships into the Baltic: 'I am doing everything in my power to nourish it', he wrote to Admiral Lord Cork on 20 March.[13] The second was a scheme for blocking the harbour at Luleå with torpedoes launched from planes flying from an aircraft carrier off the Norwegian coast.[14] The third was an operation, code-named Royal Marine, to drop fluvial mines into the Rhine.[15] This had received Cabinet approval in principle, and Churchill was now pressing the reluctant French to agree to it. Despite Churchill's protestations to the contrary, Colville was not far from the truth in his comment that 'Winston['s] ... policy is one of "action for action's sake."'[16] Ironside argued for the force for Scandinavia not to be dispersed, but the War Cabinet disagreed. Chamberlain responded that if Hitler got wind of it, it would give him an excuse to invade Scandinavia himself.[17] Chamberlain's real motivation may have been to kill off the expedition for good. The War Office staff, possibly in similar vein, were already advising Ironside that the BEF reinforcement divisions earmarked for Norway should be sent to France 'as soon as possible'[18] and, with almost indecent haste, were closing down the branch dedicated to planning for operations in Scandinavia.[19]

There was also political pressure on Chamberlain to act, both from within his party and from the opposition. His statement to the House of Commons on the Finnish surrender, according to one paper, 'left MPs uneasy', and some of them, notably the former War Secretary, Leslie Hore-Belisha, were quick with accusations of inaction.[20] Chamberlain faced criticism again in the House of Commons on 19 March in the debate on Scandinavia. Although he came out of it pretty well, and, according to 'Chips' Channon, one of his supporters, 'completely demolished the case against him',[21] some of his critics landed scoring punches. Harold Macmillan was uncomfortably close to the truth in his scathing comments on the government's indecision and feebleness.

It does throw a piercing light on the present machinery and method of government, the delay, the vacillation, changes of front, standing on one foot one day and on the other the next day before a decision is given ... these are patently clear to anyone. The moral of the history of these three months to be drawn for the future is, to use the phrase of Burke "a proof of the irresistible operation of feeble council."[22]

89

Other speakers put Chamberlain under pressure to take the initiative. For example, Sir Archibald Sinclair, Leader of the Liberals, probably touched a nerve with his intervention: 'We must seize the initiative, and hold it both militarily and diplomatically. It is time we stopped saying, "What is Hitler going to do? What is Mussolini going to do? What is Stalin going to do?" It is about time we asked, "What is Chamberlain going to do?"'[23]

Notable among the critics within Chamberlain's own party were those pressing for a more active and vigorous prosecution of the war who formed a 'watching committee' under the influential peer, Lord Salisbury, to hold the government to account.[24] Even some Chamberlain loyalists were becoming uneasy and impatient. One of these, the redoubtable Brigadier General Sir Henry Page Croft, wrote to Chamberlain (copied to Churchill) on 15 March: 'If time was our ally there is something to be said for politeness and turning the blind eye to enemy aid, but if we cannot afford a three-year war without irreparable ruin we must take the gloves off with neutrals and shorten the war by two years. We must act *now*. Take the initiative out of German hands' [emphasis in original]. Pound seems to have shared the sentiment; on Churchill's copy, he wrote, 'A very interesting paper.'[25]

Several newspapers expressed similar views: the *Daily Mirror* talked of the need for 'getting a little initiative out of the enemy's hands[26]; the *News Chronicle* asked, 'How much longer must we wait on the initiative of our enemies?'[27]; and the *Daily Mail* declared, 'The country is waiting for a lead – from real war leaders.'[28] Watching from the BEF, Pownall noted perceptively,

It seems that the public at home are all expecting ... Britain to *do* something, they are getting bored without it and feel they have kept patience during the winter long enough. Of course the public don't know *what* it is they want and have no idea anyway of what can or cannot be done. They just want *something*. But the War Cabinet are pretty foxed as to what that something should be. (Emphasis in original.)[29]

Strong pressure was also coming from the French, reflecting both escalating public impatience and the increasing perception of the French government that time was not on the side of the Allies.[30] On 15 March the French ambassador in London delivered a strongly worded message from Daladier, urging 'immediate and vigorous action'.[31] The French government, he said, 'considered it necessary, from the point of view of public opinion in neutral countries, that the Allies should do something to prove that they still had at their disposal the means of taking action'.[32] Specifically, action should now be taken against the Narvik iron ore traffic.

On 19 March the War Cabinet set its face against such action, favouring instead Operation Royal Marine.[33] Within twenty-four hours, though, the Cabinet was changing its mind, swayed by a further intervention by the French. Their ambassador told Halifax that information had been received from Herr Thyssen, the exiled German steel magnate, that the Ruhr steel plants were now shut down for three days a week due to a shortage of iron ore. Halifax advised the Cabinet that the information, if confirmed, was of great importance and any opportunity to interdict iron ore supplies should be seized.[34] (Thyssen was both right and wrong: right about the three-day week, wrong about the reason; in fact, the severe winter had frozen German canals.[35])

Further pressure for action resulted from an RAF raid the same day. The target was the German naval facility on the island of Sylt, off Schleswig-Holstein. The raid was neither very large nor very successful, but it was built up to be both by the government, keen to make the most of a rare military success. It worked a treat. When Chamberlain announced the raid to a packed House of Commons, '[c]heers broke out from every part of the House',[36] and next day the Air Secretary duly reported 'enormous damage' to further cheering. The press was unrestrained in its coverage: 'The smashing attack on Sylt was a day of rejoicing and praise for our brave RAF. ... The plight of Sylt today is a warning proof that we have the men, the machines and the fighting spirit essential to victory', trumpeted the *Daily Mirror*;[37] and 'Keep it up, Mr Chamberlain; keep it up' from the *News Chronicle*.[38] For Chamberlain, who, according to a biographer, 'read nearly the whole press every day',[39] the message could not have been clearer: military action was what the press and public wanted and what it increasingly expected from the government.

The building pressure, particularly that from France, was noted with some unease by the Chiefs, concerned that at the imminent meeting of the Supreme War Council, the French would come up with various *projets* to which they would try and gain British agreement. The Joint Planners were commissioned to produce a strategic appreciation covering the next phase of the war,[40] and at a meeting with the Chiefs on 18 March, some unusually clear strategic thinking emerged, showing that at least some of those present had been reflecting intelligently on recent events. The meeting was reminded of the fundamental policy, agreed at the outset of the war: remaining on the defensive while building up resources. 'Time was on our side', they agreed, 'but only if we are prepared to take full advantage of it. ... The first essential, therefore, was to pursue our present policy ... with the utmost vigour. It is important that facts should be put forward which will show Ministers that we are still in this phase of the war, and that we cannot organise for a long war and try and win a short one at the same time.' They noted that neither the Army nor the RAF was in a position to pass to the offensive, and agreed that '[w]e must therefore be careful to avoid being rushed by events or forced by uninformed public opinion into courses of action which would be unsound from the military point of view. In particular, we should not be led into any enterprise "for the sake of doing something."' If opportunities arose offering fruitful results at small expense, they agreed, these should be taken, 'always providing that they can be carried out with the resources at present available.'[41] The Chiefs agreed that a report on these lines should go to the War Cabinet.[42]

Before it did so, momentum for action started to build still further. As a result of sharp and prolonged criticism of Daladier's conduct of the war, and his perceived inaction over Finland, he was forced to resign, replaced on 21 March by Paul Reynaud. Reynaud had the reputation of a *belliciste* and man of action, but on the following day, he only just survived by a majority of one, a vote of confidence from a 'badly disunited and sceptical Chamber'.[43] Unsurprisingly, he was said to be 'casting about for some way of showing the country that something has changed with his arrival at the helm'.[44] A few days later, he sent Chamberlain a letter which sharply criticised the management of the war thus far and urged a policy to 'seize the initiative', with a more 'energetic and daring conduct of the war'. He also proposed that the Allies not only interrupt German shipping in Norwegian territorial waters but also launch 'decisive operations' in the Caspian and Black Sea areas to interdict the supply of oil to Germany.[45] When Chamberlain first read it, he 'went through the ceiling',[46] not least because he was implicated in the charge that the war was being managed with insufficient energy. Reynaud's note was having its desired effect.

Easter came early in 1940, and ministers and their staffs took full advantage of the four days' break. Ironside spent the time visiting the BEF. Chamberlain spent it pondering his widely anticipated Cabinet reshuffle, urged on by newspaper opinion. One unfortunate result of this leisure was that the Chiefs' report, drawing the War Cabinet's attention back to the overall policy and strategy of the war and warning against precipitate military action, did not come to Cabinet until 27 March, the day before the meeting of the Supreme War Council. At the Cabinet meeting, it quickly became apparent that the report was too late; it had been overtaken by events. The combined pressures for action had built up an unstoppable momentum. Indeed, the Chiefs' report was barely discussed, likewise a further report by Hankey which drew largely the same conclusions.[47] Newall warned against being 'stampeded into undertaking unprofitable military projects offering little prospect of decisive success, merely for the sake of doing something', but Chamberlain made it plain that doing nothing was no longer an option. 'The appetite of the public', he said, 'for spectacular operations remained, and this psychological factor could not be ignored. Any blow which we could deliver at Germany would encourage our own people and would be admirable for propaganda purposes.'[48] According to Ironside, 'Everybody expressed themselves in favour of a stronger policy, but nobody had the slightest idea of how this should be attained.'[49] Bridges noted, '[D]iscussion ranged from one subject to another, back again, and to and fro all over the place.'[50] Chamberlain favoured going ahead with Operation Royal Marine, but '[w]ith regard to the interruption of Germany's ore trade from Narvik, he felt that the laying of the mine-field was an operation which could be carried out at any time, and it was only a question of choosing the best moment.'[51] This statement should have caused the Chiefs to intervene. It had always been accepted that action against the ore export was likely to provoke a German invasion of Norway for which Britain had had a counter-operation planned. But, as all present knew, the plans had been shelved and the force dispersed or disbanded. Indeed, the Royal Navy's only modern aircraft carrier, *Ark Royal*, had been despatched to the eastern Mediterranean only five days previously to join another carrier, *Glorious*, exercising off Alexandria.[52] The operation in Norway could not possibly now be mounted in short order. The minutes, however, do not record any such intervention or anyone else raising this inconvenient point. The War Cabinet agreed that their line at the next day's Supreme War Council meeting would be to press the French for agreement to Operation Royal Marine – mining the Rhine – and, subject to that agreement, go ahead with Operation Wilfred – mining the sea off Norway. For Chamberlain, no doubt, a main attraction of both operations was that they offered the possibility of action without bloodshed, and therefore they would be relatively risk free.[53] One War Cabinet member, though, still had considerable misgivings. 'I am convinced that action for action's sake before we are able to strike effectively would be worse than useless,' noted Halifax later that day.[54] Unfortunately, he had not voiced his conviction.

That evening, the French delegation arrived in London, and Reynaud had a forthright message when he met Chamberlain and Halifax. 'I informed them that I would be unable to answer, before a parliamentary committee, the question of how we could win the war in the present circumstances, unless some action aimed at depriving the enemy of his supply of Swedish iron ore were undertaken.'[55] This message struck home. The two sets of Chiefs of Staff met at the same time. Gamelin warned Ironside that 'the politicians' had not studied the results and consequences of any of their proposals and asked him to see that the British impressed this upon Reynaud. In response, Ironside recorded, 'I told him they need have no fear, our Government would do nothing for the sake of doing it only.'[56] Ironside could not have been more wrong.

Apart from a grand resolution that the Allies would not separately come to terms with Germany, the Supreme War Council was, true to past form, less about strategy than about politics and tactics – in particular, what to do next. Reynaud wanted approval for one of the French *projets*, in particular minefields off Norway (Operation Wilfred), not least since this would be a British responsibility. Chamberlain wanted to avoid the wilder *projets*, such as those in the Caucasus and Balkans, and to gain French agreement to Operation Royal Marine before agreeing to Wilfred. Reynaud knew that Royal Marine would be difficult to sell back home but was happy to horse-trade, indicating that he would agree to it if the British would agree to Wilfred – although with a scarcely noticeable proviso that 'he thought' that his government would agree that effect should be given to Royal Marine at once. Chamberlain, knowing that Reynaud could not return to Paris and keep his job without agreement to the mining operation – 'French public opinion was demanding action without delay'[57] – also agreed to the horse-trade. The deal was done. As Hoare later noted, 'Wilfred and Royal Marine. We bartered one for the other.'[58] In all of this, almost no examination was made of the likely German reaction to the Wilfred mining operation, let alone to the available ways and means of dealing with that reaction; nor was any attention paid to what the Germans might, themselves, be planning. The Council was thus conducted in a highly agreeable manner with no unpleasantness but was detached from reality. The first session had lasted all morning, and only two people had spoken: Chamberlain and Reynaud. For some, no doubt, the highlight was the adjournment for lunch at the Carlton Restaurant, after which, two members of the French delegation dozed off.[59] The Council had, however, been nothing if not decisive: it had agreed that Wilfred would start on 5 April with, subject to the French War Committee's approval, Royal Marine commencing the day before.[60] The British government had just signed up to a high-risk operation – Wilfred – for which it was singularly unprepared and which, in any case, had little strategic benefit, to be seen to be doing something and to satisfy the demands of its alliance partner.

The fact that little thought had been given to the consequences of these decisions, and the extent to which the Chiefs of Staff found themselves wrong-footed by them, can be judged by the Chiefs' meeting the following morning. Some very basic questions were posed: What were the possible results of the Supreme War Council's decision to lay the minefield? What would be the mission of any landing at Narvik – would it be to get through to Luleå or merely to Gällivare? Should it be assumed that any landings would be opposed? Were the French Chasseurs Alpins still available? If so, when could they sail? It was agreed, rather obviously, that the Joint Planners would need 'to study the whole question as a matter of urgency'.[61]

The results of the study formed the basis of a Chiefs of Staff report, hastily produced over the next two days, which recommended the reconstitution, on a slightly reduced scale, of modified Avonmouth and Stratford plans. Thus, a British brigade and 'a French contingent' would be sent to Narvik, and a force of five British battalions would be sent to occupy the ports of Trondheim and Bergen and secure or destroy the airfield at Stavanger, but 'there could be no question of attempting a landing at any of these ports [in the face of] deliberate and determined opposition.'[62] The air plan, reflecting the RAF's lack of enthusiasm for the expedition and its dispersal of vital assets, was negligible: no air support would be deployed, nor any air defence except at Narvik. Flaws were already appearing in the Supreme War Council's decision that the operation should commence on 5 April: only one of the Stratford battalions would be ready to sail by that date. As to timing, the Chiefs recommended that '[t]he moment the Germans set foot on Norwegian soil, or there is clear evidence that they intend to do so', the Avonmouth and Stratford forces should be immediately despatched.[63] This, of course, relied entirely on intelligence being received and acted on faster than the Germans could act, and it was here that the plan was to fail catastrophically.

The attitude of the staffs at the Admiralty and the War Office to the prospect of imminent operations was very different. When, on the evening of the Supreme War Council meeting, two intelligence reports had been received at the Admiralty indicating that the Germans might be planning an operation against Norway, the Deputy Chief of the Naval Staff, Rear Admiral Tom Phillips, had advised Churchill that this was a golden opportunity to strike, regardless of the unpreparedness of the land force: 'If such an opportunity did occur', he wrote, 'I feel it would be absolutely vital to seize it immediately and to improvise the expedition with what we could make available in the time taken to load the ships and send them off at once.' He urged that any calls for 'proper organisation and preparation' should not be heeded, adding that the expedition 'starting at this late hour, would be a gambler's bid for a really vital stake which, if successful, might lead to the end of the war within a measurable period'.[64] This would have been music to Churchill's ears – indeed, it was, consciously or not, playing Churchill's tune back to him. It was also exactly the kind of reckless advice that encouraged Churchill's worst instincts.

At the War Office, where the branch responsible for operational planning for Scandinavia, disbanded a fortnight earlier, was now being hastily reconstituted,[65] the alarming prospect of remounting a flawed and complex operation at one week's notice from a standing start caused more sober counsels to prevail. The first official notification to the War Office staff of the imminent operation came in a warning order from the CIGS, 'Forces Stratford and Avonmouth are to be reconstituted at once',[66] and was passed on to an unsuspecting Army on Saturday, 30 March.[67] Bearing in mind that this was the third time in as many months that the earmarked units had been stood-to for the operations, only to be stood-down a few weeks later, 1 April was an unfortunate day for the news to be announced to the troops.[68] Bewilderment and cynicism must have accompanied the frenetic preparation, exacerbated by the fact that a fortnight earlier the War Office had directed that all secret planning documents for the operation be destroyed or disposed of.[69] The Director of Military Operations, Major General Dewing, had serious concerns: 'Some of the plans under discussion have as little relation to strategic and operational realities as to fill me with misgiving.'[70] Dewing probably spoke for all the staff involved when he voiced his concern to the Deputy CIGS: 'Avonmouth and Stratford plans have been reconstituted hurriedly, without thorough consideration of the consequences which may follow through implementation. This immediately becomes apparent when we start drawing up instructions for the commanders of the various forces.'[71] He pointed out other serious flaws: the lack of artillery and the fact that the airfield at Stavanger was nine miles from the port, but no transport would accompany the landing force.[72] The two brigades for Operation Stratford came from the 49th (West Riding) Division – a Territorial Army formation. Pownall's main concern was that '[t]he troops are untrained, and if they did get into a scrap with the Germans would surely get eaten,' adding resignedly, 'The perils of amateur strategy are all with us again.'[73] In the rush, and with no intermediate headquarters between the military-strategic and tactical levels, things that might seem trivial at the military-strategic level but would be vitally important at the tactical level got overlooked: for example, liaison officers, interpreters and proper mapping. Further issues were raised about the obvious delay in the arrival of the French half of the Avonmouth force – the demi-brigade of Chasseurs Alpins was still located in the Alps – and the inability of the weak Stratford force to counter a German invasion of Norway.

Ironside's solution was to resurrect the huge and cumbersome Plymouth operation, which would involve the mobilisation of the remainder of 49 Division and the withdrawal of up to three of the five Regular divisions from the BEF. In doing so, Ironside recognised that the Germans 'were militarily in a position to carry out an offensive without further concentration of troops and with little further preparation' and that the possibility of such an offensive was increased by the fact that 'Germany may well judge that a prior move on her part on the Western Front would be the best way of retaining the initiative.' He also accepted that 'there were strong military arguments against this plan, [and] that the Germans might achieve a decisive success on the Western Front'. Nevertheless, in a remarkable piece of logic and judgement, he justified his plan on the grounds that 'the reduction of the BEF by three divisions is very unlikely to govern the outcome on the Western Front.'[74] This overlooked the fact that the actual number of men which the Allies were now planning on sending to Scandinavia totalled 150,000. On 4 April the Chiefs duly endorsed Ironside's recommendation, while postponing the removal of the divisions from the BEF for the moment'.[75] Since most of the logistic units on which Plymouth depended did not exist and would have to be formed from scratch, this was probably just as well. Not for the first time, the Chiefs seemed to be detached from reality.

Amidst all the intensive planning which was taking place was an additional factor which was easy to overlook: the weather. The winter of 1939/1940 had been one of the coldest in living memory: the Thames had iced over ('Royal Swans Frozen In' reported the *News Chronicle*),[76] and even in late March there was no sign of spring. Similar conditions were affecting the continent of Europe – as members of the BEF could attest – and Scandinavia was by no means exempt. The prospect of carrying out a campaign in northern Norway with soldiers who were neither equipped nor trained for such conditions was an alarming one.

Over the last few days of March and the first few of April, the attention of ministers was distracted from Scandinavia by two events. First, on 30 March, Chamberlain chose to conduct his Cabinet reshuffle, swapping Wood and Hoare, dropping Chatfield, abolishing the post of Minister for Coordination of Defence and making Churchill chairman of the Military Coordination Committee. Without the necessary authority, the Minister for Coordination of Defence had contributed little – Chatfield, according to Ian Jacob, was 'totally ineffective'[77] – but Churchill was to impose his personality on the Military Coordination Committee to a far greater degree, if not always to better effect. Chamberlain's Cabinet changes were given a mixed reception. Of the eight London morning newspapers, only one was wholly satisfied, four others praised the particular appointments but add general reservations, while three were openly hostile.[78] The second distraction, the following day, was the French War Committee's rejection of Operation Royal Marine. Daladier, jealous of his successor, seized the opportunity to 'put a spoke in Reynaud's wheel'.[79] Chamberlain, irritated, made his views uncharacteristically plain to the French ambassador: 'I said "No mines – no Narvik."'[80] There followed intense negotiations to try to persuade the French to acquiesce.

Meanwhile, the national press, reflecting and influencing public impatience, was increasing pressure on the government for action. The *Daily Mirror* compared British inaction unfavourably with the French attitude: 'One or two sentences in M Paul Reynaud's broadcast to the French nation are worth the repeating for their refreshing realism, after much dope, "Our aim remains the same – to conquer the enemy." Just so. To conquer; and not to write essays about the future of Germany.'[81] The *News Chronicle* was specific: 'Now For Action. The best way to keep up our spirits is to show by deeds that the Allies mean to give teeth to the blockade.'[82]

This media pressure, together with that from Paris, was developing a momentum for action. The War Cabinet continued to vacillate over the three operations – Wilfred, Avonmouth and Stratford – now collectively referred to as R4, but minds were increasingly made up: it was a case not of 'if', but 'when'. At Cabinet on 3 April, Chamberlain appeared to sum up the mood: 'Matters had now gone too far for us not to take action.' Moreover, as Stanley emphasised, '[I]n view of the meeting of the French senate on Tuesday 9th April it was essential that action should be taken before that date, since otherwise the French Government would fall.' Discussion focused on timing, and the need to await the result of diplomatic pressure on the French to relent on Operation Royal Marine. The minelaying was postponed from 3 to 8 April.[83] Ironically, the decision to lay mines off Narvik had steadily become detached from the original reason for doing so – namely, to bring the war to an early end by depriving Germany of a vital raw material. With spring round the corner, and Luleå becoming ice-free, the Narvik route would shortly become irrelevant until the following winter. As the Minister of Economic Warfare put it, '[I]t would hardly be possible to choose a less useful moment for the carrying out of the operation.' Along with several other advisers, he considered that 'the disadvantages of the proposed operation, at the present time, greatly outweigh any possible advantage.'[84] This view was shared by the head of the Foreign Office's Northern department, Laurence Collier: the balance would be 'perhaps heavily to our disadvantage when the moral considerations are also taken into account'.[85] In retrospect, Hoare reflected that 'if we had not been influenced by the persistent demand for action of some kind, we should not have proceeded with the plan,' regretting '[our] failing to resist the outcry for action when waiting was the only wise course'.[86] According to Colville, Chamberlain was 'not over-enthusiastic', but felt that 'after the expectations aroused by the meeting of the SupremeWar Council … some effective action must be taken … [and] recognised the necessity of throwing occasional sops to public opinion'.[87] As for Halifax, Rab Butler observed that he 'had only agreed to [it] because of his loyalty to the PM'.[88] Something needed to be done, they agreed; the minelaying operation seemed to some to fit the bill nicely and to others to be the least-worst option. Not for the first time, the absence of rigorous strategy was leading to policy which was of dubious military practicality.

There was also considerable scepticism, shared by many in Whitehall, about whether Germany would react militarily. Churchill told the War Cabinet on 3 April that he 'personally doubted whether the Germans would land a force in Scandinavia'. At the same meeting, Halifax happily quoted 'Swedish authorities' who did not believe the Germans would react to the stopping of the iron ore traffic,[89] later reflecting, 'I have never been very keen on this myself as I believe its practical value is rather over rated, but psychologically – and this war seems to be largely one of psychology – it will make the Germans wonder a bit, and I hope will outweigh the other effects on Neutral minds.'[90] At the Foreign Office, Rab Butler thought that the Germans would not react forcibly because 'the German mind works like clockwork … and this activity on our part may, by destroying the clockwork precision of their plans, throw them into some confusion.'[91] There was also a feeling of optimism: at last the Allies would be taking the initiative, leaving behind the passivity of the long-war policy – although this was never formally debated. Hoare, dining with Churchill and Stanley on 3 April, noted that his guests were 'very optimistic' about the forthcoming venture.[92] It was as if the War Cabinet liked the cards in its own hand, without considering what cards its opponents might have in their hand. The following day, Chamberlain was almost jaunty. Delivering a morale-boosting address to a Conservative Party gathering, he told them, 'After seven months of war I feel ten times as confident of victory as I did at the beginning … I feel that during the seven months our relative position towards the enemy has become a great deal stronger than it was,' concluding that Hitler had 'missed the bus'.[93] As Churchill later commented, with studied understatement, the phrase was 'unlucky'.[94]

When the War Cabinet met on 5 April, Churchill was in Paris attempting to persuade the French to acquiesce with Operation Royal Marine. Daladier dug his heels in, demanding a postponement of at least three months.[95] Churchill was caught between a rock and a hard place and admitted defeat. In Gates' words, he was convinced that 'if they forced the French to fall in with their wishes on Royal Marine, in consequence of which French interests did in fact suffer serious damage, it might well be a mortal blow to the alliance; while contrarily, a failure to carry out the Norwegian operation would probably topple Reynaud.'[96] Not for the first time, the British government found its policy being driven by Alliance politics.

Churchill telephoned his findings while the Cabinet was in session, causing Chamberlain to crack a rare joke. Observing that Churchill had gone to Paris to convert the French but had ended up being himself converted, Chamberlain said it was 'like the story of the pious parrot which was bought to teach good language to the parrot which swore, but ended by itself learning to swear'.[97]

Amid this conviviality, the Chiefs provided their report on a key point – the ability to get sufficiently advanced warning of 'the moment the Germans set foot on Norwegian soil, or there is clear evidence that they intend to do so' to allow the Allies to forestall the Germans. 'Special arrangements', they assured the Cabinet, 'have been made for obtaining from Scandinavia, the earliest possible authentic information of a German move against Norway or Sweden. We have been informed of these arrangements and are satisfied that they should prove adequate.'[98] What exactly these arrangements were is unclear. The MI6 officer in the British embassy, Oslo, would have been one key source, but it would have been far from certain that he would get advance warning. A further source would have been four covert Military Intelligence (MI) officers sent to the four ports of disembarkation 'to prepare the way for the British invasion'.[99] But they would only be able to report the *arrival* of German ships and troops. The moment would be too late. Only advance warning could forestall them and that would be unlikely to be provided from Norway. According to the minutes, none of these points was raised. Discussion centred on other aspects closer to ministers' hearts, principally the media plan and press handling. The Chiefs' report was approved after only 'a short discussion'.[100] It was a fatal oversight. Part of the reason may have been the pervading optimism that these measures were largely academic: they were unlikely to be required. The result was complacency. Ironside had told the Chiefs that '[t]he Germans were ready mounted for an attack in the West. Any diversion to Scandinavia would be to their serious disadvantage and was therefore in his opinion most unlikely.'[101] Neither of the other Chiefs had demurred. That night, he recorded in his diary, nonchalantly, 'I personally don't think very much will happen.'[102]

10   The Jigsaw Puzzle

There had been no shortage of indicators that something was going to happen in Scandinavia. What is surprising is how much intelligence had been provided at this point and how little attention had been paid to it. Back in early February Allied plans had been leaked and German intelligence would have to have been very incompetent not to pick them up.[1] In early March, the military attaché in Stockholm had reported that German intelligence was setting up stations under the guise of 'travel agencies' in Oslo, Bergen and Stavanger.[2] On 26 March the assistant naval attaché reported a concentration of ships in Kiel, with a further fifty vessels passing through the Kiel Canal that day to join them.[3] The same day, the air attaché in Stockholm reported information from a source – thought to be reliable and known to the directors of both Military and Air Intelligence – that Swedish intelligence believed that the Germans were concentrating aircraft and shipping for the possible seizure of Norwegian airfields and ports.[4] This information, included in the JIC daily Secret Situation Report on 27 March,[5] was read the same day by Churchill [6] and, in the Foreign Office, by Laurence Collier. The latter annotated it: 'I wish I could believe this story. German intervention in Scandinavia is just what we want!'[7] On the same day, MI3 reported that the German Army had called up six different classes of Danish-speaking Germans and stopped all army leave.[8] On 29 March Admiral Phillips showed Churchill a report confirming the 27 March Secret Intelligence Report.[9] On 30 March the Director of Naval Intelligence informed the Naval staff about the activity of a German spy ship which, during the past few weeks, had been carrying out close observations in Norwegian territorial waters.[10]

As March turned to April, the flow of intelligence increased. On 3 April, at the Chiefs' meeting, Massy, representing Ironside, observed that 'the Germans were reported to be concentrating troops at Rostock, which might portend an invasion of Scandinavia.' The minutes record no comments on this from anyone else present.[11] Stanley reported in similar terms at that morning's meeting of the War Cabinet. Halifax commented that a telegram from the British Minister in Stockholm tended to confirm this report, adding that large troop concentrations had also been seen in the Baltic ports of Stettin and Swinemünde.[12] But, again, this does not appear to have sparked any further interest or enquiry, despite the fact that others present were receiving their own intelligence or briefings corroborating the increased threat of a German invasion of Norway. Indeed, Chamberlain had just received a memorandum from the Chairman of the JIC informing him that it was well known that troops and aircraft were being massed on Germany's north-west coast.[13]

Further information from many sources followed. On 4 April RAF reconnaissance reported sixty merchant ships at the mouth of the Elbe, steaming north. Two days later they photographed a big naval force, including the battleships *Scharnhorst* and *Gneisenau*, off Wilhelmshaven,[14] and that night reported 'intense shipping activity and brilliantly lit wharves' at Eckernförde, near Kiel, and a large German ship, possibly a battlecruiser, twenty miles north of Heligoland.[15] The same day, the British Minister in Copenhagen had reported that his American colleague had been told by a highly rated source that the Germans would be carrying out an invasion of Norway and Denmark, including a division to be landed at Narvik, but not Sweden, on 8 April.[16] The following morning, reconnaissance aircraft from Coastal Command reported what they took to be a cruiser force moving towards Norway,[17] and the Admiralty signalled to CinC Home Fleet that '[r]ecent reports suggest German expedition is being prepared. Hitler is reported from Copenhagen to have ordered unostentatious movement of one division in ten ships by night to land at Narvik with simultaneous occupation of Jutland, Sweden to be left alone. ... Date given for arrival at Narvik was 8 April.'[18] This information could have been decisive, but for the comment which had been added, with the approval of Phillips and possibly others: 'All these reports are of doubtful value and may well be only a further move in the war of nerves.'[19] The force mentioned in the signal was spotted and engaged by two bomber squadrons. Although unsuccessful, their report was crucial: the force consisted of a battleship, a pocket battleship, two or three cruisers and a large destroyer escort.[20] Something very big was afoot. The same afternoon, an analyst at Bletchley Park, the so-called Government Code and Cypher School (the forerunner of the Government Communications Headquarters [GCHQ]), told the Admiralty that there was a significant and most unusual increase in German naval radio traffic in the Baltic approaches,[21] and the naval attaché in Denmark reported that he, himself, had seen the *Gneisenau*, *Scharnhorst*, two cruisers and a destroyer escort off Langeland (in the Great Belt) heading north.[22]

In retrospect, it is scarcely believable that so many apparently obvious clues – one author lists thirty-three of them[23] – were missed. The resulting failure in intelligence was to have a catastrophic result in terms of the outcome of the campaign. How did it happen?

First, there was, at that time, no central direction of national intelligence. Thus, the three national agencies whose role it was to collect and analyse intelligence – the Secret Intelligence Service (MI6), the Security Service (MI5) and the Government Code and Cypher School – acted without regard for each other, and rarely, if ever, came together to coordinate their efforts or activity or to meet with other interested parties, such as the Ministry of Economic Warfare or the armed services. They were thus stove piped, poorly connected to their 'customers', and the whole was no greater than the sum of the parts. Unsurprisingly, the intelligence they produced was 'fragmentary and irregular' and the object of criticism, especially from the services.[24]

The central body for the collation and dissemination of intelligence – the JIC – was a very pale shadow of the organisation that today bears its name. Formed only three years before the war and reorganised in the summer of 1939, it was a sub-committee of the Chiefs of Staff Committee and comprised the Directors of Intelligence of the three services (in rank, brigadier and equivalent) and a Counsellor from the Foreign Office.[25] The attitude of the ministries involved is illustrated by the appointment of its chairman: '[T]he Services ... objected to a Service committee being chaired by the Foreign Office, and the Foreign Office raised difficulties of nominating a man of suitable seniority to a subordinate position.' As a result, it officially had no chairman, although in practice the Foreign Office member chaired the meetings.[26] Nor did it have any staff, apart from one secretary.[27] As is often the case with newly created joint service organisations (in the United Kingdom, at least), the single services viewed the JIC as a tedious irrelevance. In the opening months of the war, none of the service directors attended its meetings regularly. Indeed, not until February 1940 were all three present at the same meeting.[28] Its status in the eyes of the Chiefs of Staff is best illustrated by the fact that whereas the Joint Planners – the other main sub-committee of the Chiefs of Staff Committee – were required to be in a side room during the Chiefs' meetings and were often called in, there was no such requirement for the JIC, which, until May 1940, only ever attended a Chiefs' meeting once.[29] Furthermore, it was not until late March 1940 that service members of the JIC were systematically shown the Joint Planners' papers before these were sent to the Chiefs.[30] Nor did the JIC have the authority to coordinate or collate intelligence to be presented to its superiors.[31] In practice, intelligence analyses from the services often only came together for the first time, collated by the Joint Planners, at the Chiefs' meetings or even, in some cases, at the War Cabinet. In addition, the JIC at this time was purely reactive; it responded to requests for appreciations on given subjects. It was not until May, following a report by Ismay, that it was tasked with being proactive in choosing its own subjects. Lastly, to add to its challenges, the JIC was grossly overburdened, with much of its time being taken up by administration and with answering abstruse questions peripheral to intelligence.[32] As a result, the JIC's standing was weak[33] Senior officers were free with their criticism if they disagreed with its analysis. For example, in December 1939 Lieutenant General James Marshall-Cornwall, the British Army officer on the Allied Military Committee, told the Cabinet secretariat that the latest JIC report was '19 pages of journalese tripe'.[34]

Secondly, intelligence organisations in government departments had evolved in a very ad hoc, unsystematic way, resulting in many gaps and much overlap. A number of ministries had their own intelligence services and staffs. It may be a cliché that knowledge is power, but it is nevertheless a truism within a bureaucracy – like central government – where different organisations are competing for influence. Intelligence was central to acquiring and holding knowledge. Individual ministries opposed any centralisation that might undermine their independence. Thus, the Foreign Office was for some time reluctant to participate in the JIC,[35] and the service departments were disinclined to share assets or sources, let alone have a truly joint (inter-service) organisation.[36] Some government ministries, such as the Foreign Office, had more than one intelligence organisation, and departments within ministries often set up their own intelligence branch. Just as ministries were reluctant to share intelligence, so were individual branches. This state of affairs may have been satisfying for those involved, but it resulted in entirely counterproductive structures and practices. Hinsley gives a good flavour of the problem:

In the Admiralty, NID1 [Naval Intelligence Division 1], the geographical section dealing with Germany, was responsible for interpreting the SIS [Secret Intelligence Service] and diplomatic reports bearing on German intentions in Scandinavia, but the OIC [Operational Intelligence Centre], which was responsible for operational intelligence, including that of studying the movement of German ships and aircraft, received by no means all of the SIS and diplomatic information. To make matters worse, relations between NID1 and the OIC were not good, and NID 17 was not properly coordinating their output. In MI a similar situation prevailed. MI2a, responsible for interpreting reports received from Scandinavia about German intentions there, did not receive reports from Germany. The latter were studied by MI3, which did not see evidence from Scandinavia. Relations between the two sections were poor. More serious still, although MI2 was privy to plans for British intervention in Norway, MI3 was not.[37]

These problems were not restricted to the Admiralty and War Office. The Deputy Director of Air Intelligence recorded that in the Air Ministry there was a separate intelligence staff within the Plans Branch – a 'hidden-away, unofficial and unmentionably secret staff with no external resources of its own [which] was not admitted, even to me, as being in existence'.[38]

The fragmentation of the intelligence picture was not helped by the fact that the Chiefs of Staffs' daily and weekly intelligence résumés to the War Cabinet made no attempt to integrate the statements of the individual services, despite the obvious advantage of doing so.[39] The resulting product contributed to its suppliers' low reputation with their customers. As Hinsley points out, 'the outcome was a vicious circle.'[40] The intelligence from the agencies was not sufficiently geared to what the services wanted, the services' intelligence staffs were often insufficiently experienced or skilled, and their reputation for reliability suffered. In consequence, many senior officers, like Ironside, tended to prefer to trust their own instinct rather than the judgment of their intelligence staffs. Intelligence in the service ministries tended to be treated as a second-class trade,[41] and intelligence staffs 'did not have any great influence or impact on their departmental decision-makers'.[42] As the de facto JIC chairman, Victor Cavendish-Bentinck, later commented, 'I think that the reason for the mediocrity of the directors of intelligence was that officers who went into intelligence were not regarded as likely to command troops and rise to the top.'[43] He acknowledged that the Admiralty's intelligence director, Rear Admiral John Godfrey, was an exception to this rule, but he was 'a difficult character who did not get on with the other Directors of Intelligence'. Furthermore, the representative of the Ministry of Economic Warfare 'was rather touchy, and the military were inclined to snub him occasionally'.[44] Once again, it was not so much the effectiveness of the organisation that counted, as the effectiveness of the organism.

Economic intelligence was critical to strategy for the Norway campaign. The premise of the intervention was the Ministry of Economic Warfare's assertion that the complete stoppage of the Swedish iron ore trade would bring Germany to its knees. The assertion was well substantiated, but its veracity was undermined in the eyes of many in the War Cabinet by the fact that its main protagonist, the silver-tongued Desmond Morton, head of the Ministry's intelligence department, was a long-time ally and confidant of Churchill. Moreover, the service ministries had retained the right to provide their own economic intelligence directly to the JIC, but the JIC had no authority to adjudicate between them. Instead, in the field of economic intelligence, 'inter-departmental co-operation declined, rather than improved, on the outbreak of war.'[45] At the end of February 1940 the Joint Planners persuaded Chatfield to order a joint JIC/Ministry of

Economic Warfare review of Germany's industrial capacity, but it was not completed in time for the operation in Norway.[46]

Norway had been a very low priority for intelligence.[47] Thus there was, as has been seen, no military attaché resident there, and the main role of the SIS officer in the British Legation in Oslo, responsible for the whole of Scandinavia, was to focus on Germany, not Norway.[48] In order to establish the capacity of the main ports and railways, three MI officers were sent in January to carry out a quick, covert reconnaissance.[49]

Knowledge and understanding of the Norwegian armed forces was limited. Pre-war reports correctly noted their very small size, poor equipment and limited training time, but they were unduly disparaging and underestimated the latent capability, particularly in the army.[50] The accredited military attaché resident in Sweden, had visited a Norwegian Army training exercise in 1937 and remarked on the 'surprisingly good' standard achieved in a short period, noting that the troops had marched the thirty miles to and from the exercise area;[51] this would have been almost unheard of in the British Army. Moreover, a high proportion of Norwegian soldiers could ski, and with a large number of popular, state-sponsored shooting clubs all over the country, the standard of marksmanship was high.

The British also lacked topographical information. That which had been acquired had been poor, even for the areas most likely to be used for British deployment.[52] For other areas, many of which were where the campaign actually took place, there was little or nothing. In the absence of a level of command and control between the Chiefs of Staff and the tactical commanders, mundane details such as the quality of mapping tended to get overlooked. It is nevertheless striking that the Chiefs of Staff, with a campaign in Norway in prospect, did not ensure that their services were provided with the information and intelligence necessary for successful engagement.

In comparison, the German 'intelligence preparation of the battlefield' was much more professional. For example, mapping of Norway was ordered at an early stage; detailed reports were made of ports and airfields; agents were placed in ports to report Allied shipping movements; and merchant ships calling at Norwegian ports were allocated secret radio transmitters in case these were needed (as indeed they were on 9 April).[53] The headquarters responsible for Weserübung – Falkenhorst's Group XXI – coordinated intelligence specific for the operation. British doctrine laid down that, similarly, a Combined Intelligence Board should be established to coordinate operation-specific intelligence.[54] But no such board was set up for operations in Norway. As so often was the case, what British military doctrine prescribed and what actually happened were allowed to be two entirely different things. Theory and practice thus parted company.

An additional problem was the unfamiliarity of the intelligence staffs and their customers with the new technologies of intelligence, such as signals intelligence. Despite the fact that, in the First World War, Naval Intelligence had run a successful radio intercept and decryption operation from the Admiralty, the capability had been allowed to lapse, and apart from intelligence specialists, the three services' commanders and staffs treated signals intelligence with scepticism. When early in April the analyst at Bletchley Park had spotted the most unusual increase in German naval signals traffic in the Baltic, his telephone report to the Admiralty's Naval Operations Intelligence Centre was 'dismissed out of hand'.[55] The fact that he was a twenty-year-old civilian cannot have helped his cause. [56] Furthermore, it was one thing to have clever people at Bletchley who could decipher German 'Enigma' codes, which was increasingly the case from January 1940 (and for a period of a month from 15 April, entirely so with the Enigma Yellow Key code used by the German Army and air force in Norway),[57] but quite another to have the procedures and protocols in place to enable this information to be transmitted, analysed and disseminated in a speedy and secure way to those who could act on it. As a result, high-grade signals intelligence was not flowing regularly from the listeners to Whitehall until after the deployment to Norway, and even then not to commanders in the field[58] nor were signals intelligence detachments deployed.[59] This contrasted with the German use of signals intelligence in which intercept detachments were, from the outset, deployed forward on land and sea – including on the battlecruiser *Gneisenau* off Norway.

The Chiefs of Staff failed to place themselves in the mind of the enemy. This was and is a basic requirement of generalship taught at staff colleges the world over. The Chiefs are recorded as having done so together on only one occasion – at the outset of their report of 28 January. They addressed the subject of Germany's grand strategy as follows: 'In considering the Scandinavian problem, it is first necessary to place ourselves, figuratively speaking, in the minds of the German High Command, and to attempt to get at what they are now thinking and what they are likely to do in the next few months.' Their conclusion was at least partially correct: 'In our view, Germany is likely to decide to take action to ensure continuity of supplies of iron ore and oil ... before launching a heavy attack on the Western Front. In pursuance of this policy, Germany might well attempt to seize the Gällivare ore fields as soon as the Baltic becomes free of ice.'[60] The Chiefs are not recorded as having adopted the same approach until late April, when, at Slessor's suggestion,[61] they tasked the

JIC to do so weekly.[62] An attempt in the War Office to set up a small group to play the part of the enemy in portraying enemy intentions – what today would be called 'red-teaming' – proved brief. MI3 produced an appreciation of the situation in Norway 'by the German Commander'.[63] But the idea was disapproved of by traditionalists, and the Future Operations Enemy Section, as it was called, was short-lived.[64] Greater use of this approach during February and March might have corrected one flawed assumption that bedevilled intelligence analysis and strategic-level decision-making at the critical moment. Back in December, MI3 had stated that the number of divisions Germany would require for an invasion of Scandinavia was twenty-five to thirty.[65] But at the end of March and beginning of April, MI3 could only trace around six divisions in the North German area – around the normal number – and was therefore relatively relaxed about the prospect of imminent invasion. However, the twenty-five to thirty division assessment had been made for a successful invasion of both Norway and Sweden – only a fraction of which would be required for Norway alone. MI3 had seemingly not been told that now only Norway was the likely target. In December they had estimated that to occupy Norway south of Trondheim, the Germans would require no more than two to three divisions,[66] a fact that the Chiefs had clearly forgotten.

Moreover, little attention appears to have been paid to the effect on German strategic decision-making of known Allied security breaches and reports in British national newspapers. Allied security was known to be very lax. There had been leaks after the 5 February Supreme War Council.[67] Ironside had acknowledged that '[y]ou cannot keep anything secret'[68] and '[t]he whole project must be well known by this time.'[69] On 27 February the Inter-Service Security Board reported that 'as a result of considerable talk in high quarters, security was as good as compromised.'[70] Additionally, after the 28 March meeting of the Supreme War Council, Gamelin's copy of the meeting papers had been found behind a cushion at his London hotel.[71] The British press openly speculated that an operation was imminent. On 26 March national newspapers carried front page reports that 'Navy Acts to Cut Off Nazi Ore Supplies',[72] and 'Wait in the Skagerrak. Britain tightens grip on iron-ore route. ... It would be difficult for Germany to make any counter attack. She is hardly likely to risk sending warships into the North Sea where the British Navy is always active.'[73] At the end of March, the government apparently deliberately leaked its broad intentions to the press to assuage public opinion: both Hoare and Churchill told the editor of the *Manchester Guardian* that action would shortly be taken against the iron ore traffic.[74] Further headlines appeared, such as 'Tighter Blockade: Ore Will Be

Stopped',[75] and in Paris, *Le Temps* carried a similar story.[76] Yet scant attention seems to have been paid to the potential for a pre-emptive German move. The Chiefs seemed to have forgotten – or chosen not to recall – the advice from the Allied Military Committee that they had accepted back in January that 'if the Germans suspected action on the part of the Allies' in Scandinavia, it 'would almost certainly force Germany to secure her vital economic interests there'.[77]

The failure to build the jigsaw puzzle from its pieces sitting on the table suffered from two challenges which are easy to overlook. First, a lot of other pieces were sitting there as well. A mass of reports about possible German intentions and plans had come in over the previous few months which had proven to be wrong, spurious or even calculated deception by the enemy. For example, between the end of the Polish campaign and the end of March, some thirty reports had been received concerning the cancellation or reinstatement of German Army leave.[78] The problem, as so often is the case nowadays, was not the small quantity of potentially relevant information, but its surfeit. Second, some of those in positions of power refused to recognise what they saw for what it was. At the Admiralty, Churchill and those around him were wedded to, and immensely proud of, the assumption that Britannia ruled the waves and that the German fleet would not dare even to contemplate an amphibious operation on Norway's western coast. It had been included in the War Cabinet's strategic assumptions as far back as September. A mixture of 'group think' and the lack of any encouragement to think 'outside the box' had turned it into an article of faith. At the War Office, Ironside had similarly made up his mind that the Germans were simply incapable of carrying out a successful campaign in Norway and that they knew it. His low opinion of their generalship, of their capability to conduct amphibious operations, of their ability to adapt and improvise, all served to confirm his view.[79] If evidence was produced that supported his view, he would accommodate it; if it contradicted it, he would simply ignore it. As Pownall remarked, 'Tiny doesn't listen to advice.'[80] The impact of fixed minds – particularly in a strongly hierarchical organisation – on the corruption of intelligence was amply demonstrated. Some of those at both the Admiralty and the War Office disagreed with their bosses. But at the Admiralty, 'no intelligence section, until it was too late, dissented from the belief of Mr Churchill ... that a landing in Scandinavia was beyond Germany's power'.[81] And at the War Office, no one appears to have challenged Ironside's opinion: 'The CIGS supplied the framework of strategic vision into which the military intelligence people poured their findings. It was an arrangement that apparently suited both parties.'[82]

Ironically, in the spring of 1940 an enquiry, led by the Minister without Portfolio, Lord Hankey, was underway into the handling of intelligence, but it was not complete when he and the government of which he was part left office in May. An interim report was produced on 11 March, although it reached no momentous conclusions,[83] and it had little impact before the invasion of Norway.

In summary, intelligence was a critical weakness in Britain's military capability and a major factor in the failure of the British campaign in Norway. Hinsley sums up the underlying reason: '[T]here was ... no adequate machinery, within the departments or between them, for confronting prevailing opinions and lazy assumptions with rigorous and authoritative assessments of the massive but miscellaneous information about the enemy that was nevertheless available.'[84] As Churchill was to write in his draft of 'The Second World War' (although omitted from the published version), 'History will ask the question whether the British Government had any right to be surprised.'[85]

11   'Completely Outwitted'

On the morning of 1 April a most unusual event took place at the Reich Chancellery in Berlin. All the senior commanders for Weserübung from all three Services were assembled for a breakfast meeting with the Führer. The operational plans and preparations were complete, as Falkenhorst had confirmed to Hitler ten days earlier.[1] This remarkable gathering had a different purpose. Falkenhorst recalled that Hitler

> conferred with each one of the generals, and each one of the admirals. He cross examined every single general, who was to explain very precisely the nature of the task he was to carry out. He even discussed with the ship commanders whether they would land their men on the right or the left of a given objective. He left nothing to chance; it was his idea, it was his plan, it was his war.[2]

Finally, according to the German Naval Staff war diary, Hitler

> expressed his complete satisfaction with the way preparation had been made. He considered Operation Weserübung to be particularly daring – in fact one of the rashest undertakings in the history of modern warfare. Precisely that would ensure its success. ... He described the state of anxiety he would feel until the success of the operation as one of the strongest nervous tensions of his life. He had full confidence in the success of the undertaking. The whole history of warfare taught that carefully prepared operations usually succeeded with relatively insignificant losses. He pointed out that the strictest secrecy was vital to the success of the surprise attack.[3]

The commanders would have had no doubt that their Führer was depending on them individually to carry out a task of vital national importance in which he, himself, was personally involved, that they were a team and would be expected to work as a team, that his eye would be upon them, and that they were taking part in a high-risk but thoroughly planned operation. This strong motivation was to be reflected in the determination and unity of purpose of German commanders, and in the fighting power of their troops, throughout the campaign.

The next day, after a final conference on the weather and ice conditions, Hitler ordered the attack to begin on 9 April on all objectives

Map 11.1 Norway

simultaneously. Intelligence had played a key role in his decision. For some time, the Abwehr had been receiving important information from a member of the American Embassy staff in London, Taylor G. Kent. This information included transcripts of telephone conversations between

Churchill and Roosevelt.[4] Moreover, the Germans had learnt about the decisions taken at the Supreme War Council meeting of 28 March,[5] and on 30 March the Abwehr intercepted a Paris diplomat's report of a conversation with Reynaud in which the latter had said that operations in northern Europe would be launched in the next few days.[6] In addition, the Germans intercepted a report from the Swiss legation in Stockholm that both they and the British were about to invade Norway.[7] Increasingly, Berlin felt that 'Weserübung . . . is beginning to develop into a race between England and Germany for Scandinavia.'[8]

The attitude of the single services was very different. Whilst the Luftwaffe looked forward to the operation with some confidence, at the Kriegsmarine headquarters, assessments of the risks were sombre. Admiral Carls reckoned that unless particularly favourable conditions applied, fifty per cent losses were to be expected but that the operation was so important that it could be considered successful 'even if most of the German surface fleet were lost'.[9] At army headquarters, the senior generals remained pessimistic and kept the planning at arm's length till the end. The army chief, General von Brauchitsch, was notable by his absence from the final conference on 2 April. If the operation failed, the Army would be well placed to exploit the political consequences.

The final plans were in place. The invasion of Denmark and Norway would be simultaneous; a corps commander reporting to Falkenhorst would command the invasion of Denmark. For Norway, six divisions were allotted: an elite mountain division and five recently raised Landwehr divisions. Falkenhorst had asked for all three of the German Army's mountain divisions, but the other two were required for the invasion of France. The allotted divisions would be deployed as 'all-arms' formations – thus allocated their own artillery, engineers and, in some cases, reconnaissance troops. The first wave would consist of three divisions, many of the troops being delivered by air or warship. The warship echelon was divided into six groups, heading for the ports of Narvik, Trondheim, Bergen, Kristiansand, Oslo and Egersund. Nearly every surface ship in the Kriegsmarine would be participating in Weserübung. The air support was formidable: more than a thousand aircraft, including around five hundred transport aircraft. It was to be the first major tri-service operation in history.

For the landings to be made on 9 April, stores ships, transports and tankers sailed, some as early as 3 April, to get in position off their destinations. The tankers were critical since the German warships carried insufficient fuel for their return journey. On the afternoon of 6 April, troops started embarking. These initial moves were not without incident. On the morning of 8 April, the Polish submarine *Orzel* sank one of the troop-carrying merchant ships, the *Rio de Janeiro*, off the southern Norwegian coast. The survivors, most of them in army uniform, were picked up by Norwegian vessels and taken to Kristiansand. On questioning, some admitted to being part of a German force en route to Norway, the purpose of which, they said, was to help the Norwegians resist an Allied invasion.[10] This information was not, however, passed to the Allies.

That the *Orzel* had been in position to sink the *Rio de Janeiro* was due to the initiative of one man. The Vice Admiral Submarines, Sir Max Horton, was an officer who devoted much time and energy into out-thinking the enemy and would earn a reputation for what a subordinate described as 'an intuition of what the Hun would do, which was quite uncanny'.[11] Horton concluded that the minelaying operation would most certainly provoke a German response, probably an invasion of Norway.

On 29 March, with a Nelsonian disregard for the Admiralty's instructions, he ordered all his submarines to sea to take up positions off southern Norway. They were to sink transports as well as warships. By 8 April, nineteen submarines were in or near their patrol areas.[12] Over the next three weeks, they were to sink some seventeen German supply ships and transports.[13]

The final preparations for the minelaying force itself were efficiently carried out, and, after a postponement of two days, the force set sail, closely followed by an escort group which included the battleship *Renown*, under command of Vice Admiral William Whitworth.

The final preparations for the land forces for Operation R4 were less well ordered. In Churchill's retrospective view, 'It was easy to re-gather at short notice the small forces for a Narvik expedition which had been dispersed a few days earlier.'[14] This is disingenuous, but, since the Chiefs of Staff had not warned the War Cabinet to the contrary, it was probably a view widely held by ministers at the time. Not only had the units been dispersed (after the surrender of Finland on 12 March), some, for example the ski battalion, had been disbanded. The specialist stores and equipment had been withdrawn, and the War Office had issued strict instructions to units that all papers relating to Operations Avonmouth and Stratford were to be destroyed.[15] Most of the units had been on varying lengths of leave over Easter; some had been busy receiving new drafts of soldiers from basic training; two had been mounting guard at Buckingham Palace.[16] Following receipt of the warning order on 31 March – a Sunday – which specified a move just three days later, the units nominated for Avonmouth and Stratford rushed to ready themselves as best they could.[17] On 3 April the move was postponed by two days.[18] Only senior officers were allowed to know the destination or role. The troops came from two brigades of 49 Division – Territorial Army soldiers – plus the 24th Guards Brigade – Regulars. The total force numbered eight battalions, with a very small allocation of transport, supporting arms and logistics, and, initially, without air support.

The Avonmouth plan was for 24 Brigade to land at Narvik, secure the railway line to the Swedish border and await the arrival of the Chasseurs Alpins before moving to Gällivare (assuming Swedish cooperation). For Stratford, two battalions of 146th Infantry Brigade would occupy Bergen, and a third, Trondheim. Two battalions from 148th Infantry Brigade would secure Stavanger airfield. The troops would all be embarked in a mixture of warships and transports at Rosyth or on the Clyde, there to await the orders to sail 'the moment the Germans set foot on Norwegian soil, or there is clear evidence that they intend to do so'.[19] The remainder of 49 Division was being mobilised as a reserve, and plans were in hand to reconstitute Force Plymouth (the force to counter any German invasion of southern Scandinavia). The naval minelaying force would move into position on the night of 7 April. The Home Fleet would be poised at Scapa Flow in the Orkney Islands, ready to pounce on any move by the German Navy. On paper, and to the untrained eye, the plan looked straightforward, clear and plausible. What could possibly go wrong?

Admiral Sir Charles Forbes, CinC Home Fleet, was at Scapa Flow on 7 April when, at 1:30 P.M., he received from the Admiralty the intelligence report on which had been written the fateful words, "All these reports are of doubtful value and may well be only a further move in the war of nerves.'[20] Forbes wondered what the Germans were up to but did no more than place his ships at one hour's notice to raise steam. Four hours later, a further Admiralty signal reported a sighting by RAF planes of a large German naval force – a battlecruiser, two cruisers and ten destroyers – off the entrance to the Skagerrak, steering north-west. (The message had been inexplicably delayed in the Admiralty for several hours.)[21] Forbes now ordered the fleet to raise steam, but it was not until 8:15 P.M. that evening that the whole fleet was clear of Scapa.[22] The delay was critical. Unfortunately, Forbes saw no reason to take his aircraft carrier, HMS *Furious*, with him, even denuding it of 120 seamen to join the other ships as boarding parties.[23] He had concluded that the German fleet was not heading for Norway but rather breaking out into the Atlantic. According to one historian, 'This error ... sprang from traditionalism of outlook, for Forbes, too, shared the preoccupation with the majestic clash of heavy ships.'[24] As a result, he set a course north-east, well outside the course of the German fleet heading for Norway.

At the Admiralty, Churchill, Pound and Phillips shared this view and interpreted the latest intelligence as confirmation, relishing the opportunity of a great naval clash of arms. Not all the Admiralty staff agreed. At least one attempt was made to persuade them that the evidence pointed towards an invasion of Norway, but to no avail.[25] On the evening of Sunday 7 April, Pound, who had been away fishing, returned and ordered that the Army's R4 units aboard cruisers at Rosyth be disembarked to allow the cruisers to reinforce the fleet for the eagerly anticipated great naval battle. 'I argued madly for their retention on board,' wrote Captain Ralph Edwards,[26] the Admiralty's Director of Operations, 'and made myself a beastly nuisance in the eyes of authority.'[27] But in vain. The troops were disembarked the following morning in great haste and confusion, some of their equipment and stores remaining on board, and the cruisers set sail. Although Edwards believed that the decision was taken by Pound, not Churchill, it is scarcely conceivable that Pound would have acted without the approval of Churchill, who was present in the Admiralty at the time(even if he was, as Edwards noted, 'well dined').[28] Churchill's memoirs merely recounted that 'the ... movement was ... ordered',[29] (and that '[a]ll these decisive steps were concerted with the Commander-in-Chief' – which was manifestly not the case[30]). Inexplicably, Pound did not inform, let alone consult, the other Chiefs of Staff, and, according to the Deputy CIGS, when the War Office discovered what had happened the following morning, it 'came as a thunderbolt to us'.[31] It also came as something of a surprise to the War Cabinet that morning. Ian Jacob, the Assistant Cabinet Secretary, recalled that when Churchill announced that the cruisers had left the troops behind, 'He looked decidedly sheepish. The PM said "Oh", and there was a distinct silence.'[32] As well there might have been: the R4 plan had just been hijacked, and with it the whole basis of the campaign strategy.

The War Cabinet, though, had more dramatic news to take their minds off strategy. Earlier that morning a minelaying escort, HMS Glowworm, had reported that she was engaging an enemy destroyer off Trondheim. Her transmission had faded, and she had not been heard from since. In the Admiralty's view, '[I]t appeared that a German force was undoubtedly making towards Narvik.'[33]

The fate of the Glowworm was not revealed for some days. Shortly before 9:00 A.M. on 8 April, having become detached from Whitworth's screen during the night in search of a man lost overboard, she had encountered a destroyer from the Kriegsmarine's Trondheim group. As they exchanged fire they were joined by the heavy cruiser *Admiral Hipper*, which hit *Glowworm*'s bridge with her first salvo. Making smoke and firing torpedoes, *Glowworm* disappeared from *Hipper*'s view, emerging close enough to the German ship to ram her, ripping off 120 feet of her side armour plating, but breaking off her own bow in the process. At 10 o'clock, *Glowworm* blew up and sank.[34] For his courageous action, *Glowworm*'s captain, Lieutenant Commander Gerard Roope, was awarded a posthumous Victoria Cross – the first action of the war in which the medal was won.

A series of misjudgements now combined with uncertainty and chance to benefit the Germans. First, the Admiralty (according to Barnett, 'Churchill and Pound'[35]), by passing Forbes, ordered the minelaying force in Vestfiord, the sea approach to Narvik, to stand out to sea to join Whitworth who had been ordered to cut off any German ships which might be heading for Narvik. Perversely, this left the approach to Narvik completely unguarded.[36] Second, in response to a sighting by a British flying boat of a battlecruiser and four other ships off Trondheim heading west, Forbes altered course to the north-west, away from the Norwegian coast, with the aim of intercepting them. The German ships were the *Hipper* group, which were simply filling time before their scheduled arrival at Trondheim that night, and would shortly be reversing their course.[37] The result of this sighting was not only that the Home Fleet set off in the wrong direction but also that the approaches to Trondheim, too, were left unguarded.[38] Third, Whitworth assessed that with a north-westerly gale now increasing to a storm force 10, and with atrocious visibility, the Germans would not try to approach the coast in darkness, so he remained out to sea.[39] He had underestimated his opponents.

Back in London, the government appeared to be optimistic. When the Military Coordination Committee met in the late afternoon, it discussed numerous subjects – tank production, stick grenades, Operation Royal Marine, potential air targets on the Western Front – but did not consider Norway or what the Germans might be up to.[40] Later, Churchill was observed to be 'jubilant', believing that the German fleet was trapped and that 'if the Germans fly for home, they will leave their garrisons exposed to our expeditionary forces'.[41] He dined with Stanley and Hoare, the latter noting, 'Winston very optimistic, delighted with minelaying, and sure that he has scored off the Germans. He went off completely confident and happy at 1030.'[42]

The mood of optimism and complacency was about to receive a nasty shock.

Major General Ismay recalled,

In the very early hours of 9 April I was awakened out of a deep sleep by the telephone bell. It was the Duty Officer at the War Cabinet Office. I could not make head or tail of what he was saying, in spite of frequent requests for repetition; so, suspecting the trouble, I suggested that he should draw the black-out curtains, switch on the lights, find his false teeth and say it all over again. My diagnosis was evidently correct, because after a pause he started speaking again and was perfectly intelligible. His report was brutal in its simplicity. The Germans had seized Copenhagen, Oslo, and all the main ports of Norway. . . . As I hurried into my clothes I realised for the first time in my life, the devastating and demoralising effect of surprise.[43]

The Chiefs of Staff met at 6:00 A.M. The situation was far from clear. There were reports of German ships at Oslo, Stavanger, Bergen and Trondheim, but not at Narvik, although HMS Renown had reported a short action off the Vestfiord (it later transpired, with the Scharnhorst and Gneisenau). So, what to do? The Chiefs were perplexed. Dewing, the Director of Military Operations, later recalled, 'Newall, who was chairman, had no grip, and no-one had constructive proposals.'[44] Eventually it was agreed that the first object was to stop the Germans consolidating '1) at Bergen and 2) at Trondheim' – to both of which, warships would be sent - and secondly, 'to get to Narvik as soon as possible', for which 24 Brigade 'should leave at once'. It was also decided that RAF bombers would attack German ships at Bergen, and Trondheim, too, if it was in range; Newall, though Chief of the Air Staff, could not say.[45]

The War Cabinet met at 8:30 A.M., Churchill in his dressing gown.[46] Little further information had been received. Two critically misleading reports were made. Churchill reported that 'British destroyers were covering the mouth of the Vestfiord to stop enemy transports entering Narvik', but omitted to say that, since they had not been doing so through the night, the Germans might already be in Narvik. Ironside reported that 'our information was that the Germans were not in occupation there'.[47] The source of this information is unclear. There was an undercover MI officer in Narvik, from whom nothing had been heard (nor would be),[48] and Ironside may have assumed that the officer would have reported if the Germans had arrived there; in fact, the Germans had arrived, but the officer was unable to report.[49] Ironside's firm recommendation was that 'our first immediate action should be to go ahead with our plan for seizing Narvik' but that it was also most important to prevent the Germans from establishing themselves at Trondheim and Bergen. Although Churchill immediately supported this by saying that transports should be ready for the latter ports, he 'strongly advocated that we should proceed with the operation against Narvik'. Pound added that the Home Fleet had been ordered to destroy German ships at the two southern ports. The Cabinet agreed to proceed with the operations to recapture Bergen and Trondheim and to occupy Narvik, but the forces for these tasks should not move 'until the naval situation had been cleared up'.[50] There was, thus, no clear priority between Narvik and the other ports.

Later in the morning the Chiefs met, with the Joint Planners present. It is likely that the latter argued convincingly and successfully that a clear priority was required and that it should be Trondheim and Bergen, not Narvik – for that is what the meeting agreed. The Chiefs also agreed that ports should not be occupied before the naval situation was cleared up and proper reconnaissance carried out. The leading battalion should be forward-based at Scapa so that it could respond quickly. All of this was a triumph for clear thinking.[51] The political and strategic importance of Trondheim was obvious from a glance at the map and a quick read of a tourist guide. As Norway's second city and medieval capital, with an extensive harbour and well-developed port facilities, it was and is the transport hub linking the north and south of the country – the strategic key to Norway. The Joint Planners were sent away to produce an appreciation of the situation.[52]

The War Cabinet met again at midday. The intelligence picture was still hazy. Newall reported that, according to Oslo radio, a small German force had landed at Narvik. Churchill was delighted: '[W]e were in a far better position than we had been up to date. Our hands were now free, and we could apply our overwhelming sea power on the Norwegian coast. The German forces which had landed were commitments for them, but potential prizes for us.' He also informed his colleagues that orders had been given for naval forces to drive their way into Narvik and Bergen, with Trondheim being left for the time being 'until the situation had clarified'. This statement may have come as news to Pound, who might have expected to be consulted and who had come straight from the Chiefs' meeting which had agreed almost the opposite, but none of the Chiefs ventured to inform the War Cabinet of their conclusions.[53] Their failure to do so was to have far reaching consequences.

All of those involved wanted to find out what was actually happening, but the lack of a centrally directed intelligence organisation severely hindered them from doing so. The process of collating, analysing and disseminating the little intelligence that existed was far too slow, allowing a vacuum often filled by rumour. In addition, hard information was scarce. As the official historian observed, '[T]he British Government's information from Norway was little better than that of the newspaper reader.'[54] In mid-afternoon, some twelve hours after the Germans had made their landings, the Prime Minister was telling the House of Commons that it was 'very possible' to believe that the landing had not been made at Narvik, but rather at Larvik, a small port on the southern Norwegian coast.[55]

While this was going on the Joint Planners produced their appreciation of the situation. It emphasised that 'the immediate strategic object is ... to support Norwegian resistance to German invasion' and that Trondheim would be the key base to achieve this, and it strongly recommended that Trondheim be the top priority for action.[56]

Later in the afternoon, Reynaud, together with his War Minister, Daladier, arrived for an emergency meeting of the Supreme War Council, but it soon emerged that central Norway was not the primary focus of their attention. Daladier told the Council that the French had earmarked an entire division of Chasseurs Alpins, 15,000 strong, for operations in Scandinavia, the leading element of which was now en route to Brest. The first step, he said, should be to attack Narvik. Churchill, with the tantalising prospect of Narvik almost within his grasp, weighed in, saying, '[T]he actual operation of clearing any Germans out of Narvik should not present any difficulty.' Stanley questioned 'whether it would not be a mistake to concentrate too large a force on Narvik, and thus throw away the opportunity of recapturing Trondheim and Bergen', on which depended continuing Norwegian resistance. Both Daladier and Reynaud immediately rejected this suggestion. 'Narvik must', said Reynaud, 'be considered the most important place from the point of view of the Allies.' Chamberlain did not argue. The Council did not go as far as to prioritise Narvik but did agree that in considering future action 'the particular importance of securing Narvik ... should be borne in mind'.[57] Again, the importance of having an amicable meeting, rather than achieving the right outcome, seems to have been uppermost for some. Ironside noted: 'As usual, it went well.'[58]

There was one further meeting to be held. The Military Coordination Committee met at 9.30 P.M. with Churchill in the chair, clearly confident and, according to Ironside, 'behaving with monkeyish humour'.[59] There was not much further intelligence, but the latest reports now numbered the Germans in Narvik as six warships and 3,000 to 4,000 men. A destroyer flotilla, said Churchill, would attack at dawn, and he proposed that no action should be planned for Trondheim, although the possibility of gaining a foothold should be looked at. Namsos and Åndalsnes, two small ports to the north and south of Trondheim, were mentioned. Ironside backed up the principle that, with the forces available, the Allies should take on only one objective at a time. But contrary to the conclusions of the Chiefs of Staff Committee meeting and the recommendation of the Joint Planners, he now stated emphatically that 'we must concentrate our attack on Narvik and not until we had succeeded in capturing it should we attempt to expel the Germans from elsewhere'. Earlier agreement about the need to keep the Norwegians in the fight, and the central importance of Trondheim in achieving this, appeared to have been forgotten. Furthermore, since he said, rightly, that 'the success of the operation depended on the most careful preparation and would fail if it were rushed', the prospect of recapturing Trondheim in the short-term had all but vanished. Neither of the other two Chiefs elected to voice their views or refer to the conclusions they had agreed to earlier.[60]

During the course of the day the priority for action had swayed between Bergen, Bergen and Trondheim jointly, Bergen and Narvik jointly, before finally settling on Narvik. The War Cabinet and, indeed, the Chiefs (although not the Joint Planners) had lost sight of the key strategic issue – whether the immediate purpose was still to stop the iron ore trade or was now to bolster the Norwegians.

In seeking to explain this, one contributory factor was that Newall and Pound, as operational commanders, were both involved throughout the day in matters more pressing than the discussion of strategy. At 11.30 A.M. Forbes had ordered a detachment of four cruisers to attack the German warships spotted in Bergen. But the Admiralty was uneasy about the threat posed by enemy-held shore batteries, and in the early afternoon Pound and Churchill cancelled the attack.[61] (A pity, as it turned out: the shore batteries were not in service, and the German warships would have been caught in the harbour).[62] At the Air Ministry, Coastal Command gave notice that it was planning on attacking the airbase at Stavanger, now occupied by some forty German aircraft. But this was contrary to the existing policy regarding the bombing of land targets, so Newall cancelled the attack.[63] There were, thus, competing demands on the Chiefs' time. Churchill, too, faced such competing demands, many of his own choosing. He was observed to be in 'a high state of excitement in the map room'[64] as he involved himself in tactical decisions and dealt direct with flotilla commanders. It had also been a long, exhausting day for all concerned – some twenty-three hours, mostly taken up with meetings. As a no doubt weary Ironside recorded in his diary, '[T]he whole day gone and nothing but talk. You cannot make war like this. Sooner or later if we are to win the war we must have proper control.'[65]

By the following morning (10 April), although the situation was still far from clear, it had been established that German forces were in possession of Narvik, Trondheim, Bergen, Stavanger and Oslo. It was a sobering picture; the awful realisation dawned that, as Churchill put it in a memorandum to Pound, 'we have been completely outwitted.'[66] At the Chiefs' meeting, the Joint Planners' campaign strategy paper dealing with priorities was not even considered. It had, said Newall, been 'overtaken by events'.[67] The time for strategy appeared to be over; it was now time for planning and implementation. In accordance with the decision of the Military Coordination Committee, the Joint Planners were commissioned to produce a draft directive for a combined operation to capture Narvik, with detailed planning to be carried out by an ad hoc team: the commander selected for the combined operation, the Inter-Service Planning Staff and the staff of the Inter-Service Training and Development Centre – the experts in combined operations.[68] The Chiefs, notably Ironside, were losing touch with reality – as emerged at the Joint Planners' meeting to consider this task. Royal Navy Captain Loben Maund, the Centre's director, 'expressed the view, with some force, that we were in no position to undertake a combined operation involving an opposed landing. The equipment for such an operation did not exist.'[69] The proposal was also viewed with amazement by the Military Operations staff in the War Office. In the absence of equipment, trained troops, intelligence or suitable landing beaches and for an operation within the Arctic Circle facing an enemy force in prepared positions, their report was unequivocal in its conclusion: 'If ... the object is the immediate capture of Narvik, it is not considered that this is a feasible operation with the forces available.'[70] The report was taken to Ironside at 3 P.M. that afternoon by the Director of Military Operations, Major General Dewing, who recorded, 'I ... tried in vain to persuade him to support operations in the Trondheim area in preference to the Narvik project. ... [but] I couldn't move him.'[71] Ironside's mind was closed.

By the time the Military Coordination Committee met at 5 P.M., the latest intelligence estimate put the German strength at Narvik at around 3,000.[72] Ironside outlined the War Office plan: to establish a forward base 'somewhere in the vicinity of Narvik' where the expedition could be sorted out in preparation for the landing operation against the town itself. The force to be used would be 'the balance of Avonmouth and Stratford' (less the two battalions sent to establish the forward base), plus the Chasseurs Alpins, although the latter would not arrive before 23–25 April.[73]

The tactical actions of the first two days, on which the attention at Cabinet focused, had given grounds for satisfaction and optimism. A dawn attack on 10 April by five destroyers had caused 'very considerable damage' to a large German flotilla in Narvik Fiord, albeit for the loss of two of the five destroyers. In a chance encounter further out to sea, *Renown* had successfully engaged *Scharnhorst* and *Gneisenau*, causing the German ships to make a run for it. Both the RAF and the Fleet Air Arm had bombed German warships in Bergen harbour, the cruiser *Königsberg* being sunk by carrier-launched aircraft (the first-ever sinking of a capital ship by aircraft). The Fleet had survived a heavy air attack, albeit with the loss of one destroyer, and some minor damage to other ships from near misses. The Fleet had now been joined by the battleship *Warspite* and the aircraft carrier *Furious* (though, unhappily, without her fighter squadron).[74] Royal Navy submarines had sunk, it was believed, six German transports in the Skagerrak and Kattegat,[75] and, it was later reported, the submarines also sunk the cruiser *Karlsruhe* and severely damaged the pocket battleship *Lützow*. Details now emerged of the destroyer action at Narvik on 10 April. Under command of Captain Bernard Warburton-Lee, the destroyers, facing a far superior German force, had penetrated the harbour and in a fierce battle at short range had sunk two large German destroyers and six enemy supply ships, and badly damaged five further destroyers. Returning for a second attack, Warburton-Lee's ship, *HMS Hardy*, was hit, and he was killed.[76] He was awarded a posthumous Victoria Cross. A further British ship was sunk and another badly damaged. Controversy remains over the Admiralty's direct command of this operation, bypassing Vice Admiral Whitworth.[77]

But tactical matters apart, the strategy, particularly the priority given to the attack on Narvik – an operation now romantically christened Rupert (after Prince Rupert) by Churchill[78] – was still unresolved, and advice from the Chiefs of Staff remained divided. Ironside was a strong protagonist for priority being given to Narvik. Newall clearly had doubts. At the Military Coordination Committee on 11 April, he asked pointedly whether planning should be started for operations against Trondheim and Bergen. Churchill, obviously keen that nothing should get in the way of Rupert, said that a study could proceed for an operation in the Trondheim area – it would be called Maurice – but no action should be taken until it was seen what would be involved in Rupert. Newall did not choose to argue the point. Doubts about the wisdom of giving priority to Narvik were shared in both the War Office and Admiralty. Dewing recorded in his diary, 'Saw Tom Phillips and told him my view about Trondheim. He shares these views and says Naval Staff have been pushing them at CNS [Chief of the Naval Staff] as I have at CIGS.'[79] P. J. Grigg told the Cabinet office staff, 'We must get the PM to take a hand in this before Winston and Tiny go and bugger up the whole war.'[80]

The issue came to a head at a late meeting in the Admiralty. According to Captain Edwards, 'There was a long meeting with WSC [Churchill] in the evening. He was half-cocked as usual. Came to the conclusion about 2315 that they ought to attack Trondheim. It was decided to go and see Tiny.'[81] So it was that a small group crossed Whitehall from the

Admiralty to the War Office and, joined by Newall, paid a late night call on the CIGS. Ironside recorded in his diary:

I really cannot go to bed without putting down my last conference. Over came the First Lord [Churchill], Pound, and little Phillips ... with Newall and Joubert de la Ferté [the RAF liaison officer in the Admiralty]. They wanted me to divert part of my force from Narvik to Namsos, with a view to 'staking out a claim', as they put it, for Trondheim. I told them my reasons for not thinking it possible ... I am afraid I lost my temper and banged the table.[82]

Evidently Ironside was not the only one, nor the first, to lose his temper. Edwards recalled, 'The meeting was going well when Winston lost his temper and spoilt the whole show.'[83] Ironside had still not fully recovered the next day. 'Tiny very angry this morning,' recorded Dewing, 'having been invaded when in bed in his office at 1 am.'[84]

The key issue of where the priority lay, as between Narvik and Trondheim, continued to be debated throughout 12 April. Churchill updated the War Cabinet on the Narvik operation, and Ironside spoke enthusiastically about plans for the destruction of the Gällivare ore mines. Churchill acknowledged that 'the naval staff were keen to see Namsos occupied as soon as possible. The possibility of this was being studied,' he said, before adding quickly, '[I]t was not thought right to interrupt in any way the progress of the operations against Narvik. ...The recapture of Trondheim was an operation the difficulty of which should not be underrated.' Chamberlain made mention of the need to recapture Trondheim but did not go as far as to question priority remaining with Narvik. The War Cabinet duly acquiesced.[85]

Further pressure emerged at a second meeting of the War Cabinet in the afternoon. Halifax argued that 'operations at Narvik, however sound from the military point of view, would have very much less political effect than an attempt to clear the Germans out of the southern part of Norway.' The enemy, he said, was 'thrusting forward southward from Trondheim and northward from Oslo. If these two forces succeeded in joining hands, they would have the whole of southern Norway under their control.' Churchill, still obsessed with Narvik, countered that 'an opposed landing at Trondheim would be a very difficult operation, and if mounted without proper preparation might only lead to a bloody repulse' – an argument curiously absent from his advocacy of the assault at Narvik. Preparations for an expedition to Narvik, he said, were well advanced and the landing would be made within a few days. 'We could be reasonably sure of a success at that point, and a success would show that we should be able ultimately to clear the Germans out of all the ports in which they had obtained a foothold.' He received support from Stanley who observed that the assistance of French troops would be required for a landing at Trondheim, and the French had insisted that the Narvik operation should be carried out first. It was now that the Prime Minister needed to take a firm hand and demonstrate leadership. But he did not. In fact, there is no record of him speaking. The War Cabinet agreed that landings on the central Norway coast were 'desirable' but also that there should be no diversion of effort from the Narvik operation.[86]

A major clash between Churchill and Ironside occurred at a meeting at the Admiralty late that evening. The issue was the operations that would follow the capture of Narvik, an event now confidently anticipated by Churchill. As he explained in a note to the Joint Planning Staff, he had come to the conclusion that after capturing Narvik, the Allied force would not go on to Gällivare: 'If Sweden is hostile, they cannot. If Sweden is friendly they need not.' Instead, Operation Maurice would comprise a number of landings on the mid-Norwegian coast to inspire the Norwegians and, possibly, cause Sweden to favour the Allied cause. 'For this, major risks on a small scale may be run.' The operation would, he said, also have the purpose of a diversion – 'to give the impression of an attack on Trondheim'. Churchillian imagination was apparently boundless: '[W]e could be active on the whole coast from Namsos to Molde; cleansing the Leads[87] with cruisers and flotillas; using coastal motor boats to rouse the population and puzzle the enemy; we can make landings ... with forces incapable of serious action inland, which can be taken off if heavily attacked.' It was neither necessary nor possible, he added, to look beyond these minor operations. It might be that, if Trondheim had been heavily reinforced, Bergen could be attacked instead.[88] It is likely that Ironside brought the discussion down to earth, examining the military practicalities of some of these wild ideas. At any rate, the result was a rancorous atmosphere. According to Dewing, 'Winston was at his worst, baiting Tiny with no apparent purpose other than to wear down his endurance.'[89] Ironside summed it up as 'a dreadful meeting under Winston. I couldn't get him to draft the orders under which we were to operate. A meeting till midnight that could have been run in a few minutes if we had a man to give us our orders.'[90]

The following day (13 April) pressure for a change of priority – from stoppage of the iron ore to support for the Norwegian government – became intense. The British minister in Norway,[91] Sir Cecil Dormer, who had escaped from Oslo and moved north, maintaining links with the Norwegian government, had re-established contact with the Foreign Office and was clear where priorities lay. 'I venture to urge,' he wrote, 'that military assistance to Trondheim is the first necessity. Seizure of Narvik would be of little assistance to the Norwegian Government.'[92]

This was reinforced by a strong representation from the Allied Mission in Stockholm and the British and French ministers there. They stated unequivocally that it was essential and urgent to obtain a firm foothold at Trondheim if the Norwegians were to be prevented from surrendering: 'We realise that Trondheim stands high in the order of Allied objectives but we wish to emphasise most strongly that on both military and political grounds it should stand first and that time is of paramount importance.'[93] This advice was almost identical to that given by the Joint Planners to the Chiefs on the day of the invasion. In a memorandum to Halifax, the Foreign Office's Deputy Permanent Secretary, Sir Orme Sargent, summed up the situation bluntly: 'The issue as far as Norway is concerned will remain as unaffected by our capture of Narvik as by our occupation of the Faroes. For all practical purposes, Norway ends at Trondheim.'[94] At the War Cabinet, Halifax restated his position at the outset: '[T]he most important point was to secure Trondheim, and the railways leading from that port across the peninsula ... early action against Trondheim was imperative from the political view, while it seemed that, if necessary, the operation at Narvik could wait.' Chamberlain, too, said that he was 'impressed with the urgency of obtaining a firm foothold at Trondheim, particularly from the political point of view'. Churchill, predictably, countered strongly, arguing for the Narvik operation, the success of which, he said, could be expected soon, if, he added darkly, 'they were allowed to proceed without being tampered with'. This he compared with the 'much more speculative affair' at Trondheim. Careful consideration was being given to landings in the Trondheim area, he said, and a small landing at Namsos was due to take place that very afternoon. Ironside supported the 'Narvik first' argument. The chances of securing the town were good, he said, if the German forces numbered no more than 4,000.[95] Chamberlain was in a quandary and was not prepared to countermand Churchill. As a result, the War Cabinet made no alteration to the priority and agreed merely that reassuring telegrams should be sent to the Scandinavians that the British intended to re-capture both Narvik and Trondheim.[96]

The case for priority being given to Trondheim was further reinforced later in the day. First, the British ambassador in Paris told Halifax that the French had done a *volte-face* and now believed that 'Trondheim is ... the vital point and that Allied forces should be landed there as soon as possible. Narvik now seemed of less importance.'[97] Secondly, during the course of a meeting of the Military Coordination Committee, the first communication from the Norwegian CinC, Major General Otto Ruge, was received, addressed to the Prime Minister. In what was described as a 'desperate appeal for immediate assistance', Ruge declared that 'if he did not "get assistance at once, i.e. today or tomorrow" . . . the war would be ended in a very few days.' The Committee's response, however, was merely to 'send an encouraging reply' rather than to readdress the thorny strategic issue of priorities.[98] At a late night meeting of the Committee, strategic considerations were further complicated by reports that the German naval forces at Narvik had been destroyed, that German troops had retired from the town, and that it might be possible for Rupertforce to land in the town itself. Churchill was given authority to divert the second brigade of the Narvik force, 146 Brigade, to Namsos, if, in his opinion, an assault at Narvik would not be seriously opposed. Authority was also given for the staffs to study the possibility of landing part of the Namsos force at Trondheim itself. The atmosphere of the meeting became tense, with an argument again developing between Churchill and Ironside about the practicality of diverting 146 Brigade, with Ironside protesting that the brigade would have no orders, and the troops would have none of the correct maps.[99] Dewing recorded, somewhat wearily, 'Tiny again very sorely tried by Winston.'[100]

During the night, according to Ironside, in a recollection ten years later, he received a second nocturnal visit from Churchill, accompanied by Phillips.[101] The editors of Ironside's diary say that Churchill told him,

Tiny, we're going for the wrong place. We should go for Trondheim. The Navy will make a direct attack on it and I want a small force of good troops, well led, to follow up the naval attack. I also want landings made north and south of Trondheim at Namsos and Åndalsnes to cooperate with the assault when it comes off by a pincer movement on Trondheim.[102]

According to Ironside, Churchill 'ordered me to divert the rear half of the Narvik convoy to the Trondheim affair'. Ironside says that he 'protested violently, telling Winston that he of all people knew that a convoy packed for one place would not fit another'. He asked the First Lord of the Admiralty if he was acting as chairman of the Military Coordination Committee and was told "yes"'.[103] Curiously, unlike the previous midnight visit, Ironside made no mention of it in his diary, nor did Dewing in his, and it went unrecorded in the War Office Night Duty Officer's log,[104] although Macleod (his Military Assistant) claims that the CIGS discussed it with him the next day.[105] Whether or not the meeting took place, Ironside's view on the practicality of diverting 146 Brigade from Narvik to the Trondheim area changed completely within twenty-four hours. At the Chiefs meeting on 13 April, he and his colleagues had agreed that it would 'not be possible' to divert part of the Narvik expedition since ships had been loaded with the idea that the whole force would land at one place.[106] Yet, the following morning he told them that 'there was every indication that it would be possible' to do so, emphasising the need for an early decision in the matter, and that afternoon the Military Coordination Committee approved the plan to divert 146 Brigade to Namsos.[107] Also diverted was the demi-brigade (three battalions) of Chasseurs Alpins, complete with support weapons and transport.[108]

Attention in Whitehall was again focused on another great naval tactical success. The previous afternoon, Whitworth in *Warspite*, with nine destroyers and preceded by an attack by aircraft from the carrier *Furious*, entered Narvik Fiord and finished the job started by Warburton-Lee three days earlier. Eight large German destroyers and a U-boat were sunk, for the serious damage of only two Royal Navy destroyers. Whitworth considered the possibility of landing an assault force, improvised from his ships crews, but concluded that it would 'court disaster'.[109] Just how lucky his force had been only emerged later. The Germans had been expecting such an attack and had U-boats lying in wait. But although they fired numerous torpedoes, not a single one hit its target. Faulty fuses were to blame. According to one historian, 'The failure of these torpedoes, when it came to light, became one of the biggest scandals in the history of the German navy.'[110] For the British, though, the Royal Navy's spectacular success offered the prospect of an opportunity ripe for exploitation.

Before turning to this opportunity, it is worth standing back for a moment to consider the British high-level management of the first five days of the campaign. The first major strategic decision – to deploy the fleet for a great naval battle, rather than to the planned R4 operation – was a huge blunder from which the campaign never really recovered. The blame lay clearly with Churchill and Pound. The blunder is easy to see in retrospect, but even at the time, there were advisers in the Admiralty operations staff to whom this was apparent but to whom senior officers were not prepared to listen.

Next, the hugely debilitating impact of strategic shock was in evidence throughout 9 April. Many decision-makers and advisers were simply unable to think clearly and logically – the most obvious example being the Chiefs of Staff at their early morning meeting.

Following on, ministers and the Chiefs were over-focused on what to do next at the tactical level, rather than thinking strategically about what objectives needed to be met and their relative priorities. The Joint Planners, however, were thinking strategically and logically, and there is considerable irony in the fact that the Chiefs agreed to the Joint Planners' appreciation of the situation on 9 April, including the priority of Trondheim over Narvik, but were not prepared to argue the case with ministers. Instead, they bowed to Churchillian pressure for 'Narvik first' and saw their duty as implementing policy rather than also seeking to shape it with a balancing of ends, ways and means. Even when their staffs drew their attention to the dangers, as the War Office staff did to Ironside, this was to no avail. Ironside's deputy, Massy, had also voiced his concern. In a remarkably strongly worded memorandum to the CIGS, he criticised the Chiefs for their precipitate decision to favour Narvik over Trondheim as a 'serious strategical mistake' and urged changes in the machinery of the higher direction of the war to avert 'a similar or worse catastrophe in future'.[111] What the argument, vacillation and inconsistency about strategic priorities had most clearly illustrated, however, was the lack of clear thinking about strategy and the unwillingness of Chamberlain to overrule Churchill.

The establishment of clear priorities and logical decision-making had not been helped by the structure for the higher management of the war; in particular, the Military Coordination Committee, had, as many had predicted, become an encumbrance. With Churchill in the chair, it had become something for which it was not designed – a crisis-management, decision-making body. Widely known as the 'Crazy Gang',[112] it was apt to make ill-judged, impetuous, spur-of-the-moment decisions, often bypassing the staffs. As Ironside observed, in some desperation, 'You cannot make war by referring everything to Committees and sitting wobbling and havering.'[113] Somewhat ironically, Churchill was later to make the same point even more forcefully: 'One can hardly find a more perfect example of the impotence and fatuity of waging war by committee, or rather by groups of committees.'[114] In particular, the committee system tended to obscure where, precisely, authority and responsibility actually lay. It is also worth noting that enthusiasm for the evolving campaign was far from universally shared amongst the three services. At the Air Ministry, the prospect of an expanding commitment to the Norwegian campaign was already causing concern. As early as 12 April, the Plans Department was counselling prudence. Slessor forwarded to Newall a memorandum by the Deputy Director of Plans which advised, 'This may be the most important, and for that reason justifiably an intense phase in the Navy's operations. But this is by no means the case as regards the air war.' Germany had committed but a small proportion of its air striking force, and a full scale air offensive closer to home could be expected at any time. The memorandum concluded, 'I do not suggest that our current operations can be drastically curtailed but I do feel that we must view them in their proper perspective and do all we can to ensure that our effort is not unduly expended [in] advance of the decisive phase.' Slessor had added in his own hand, 'This is a very sound minute which I think you should keep by you for consideration when fresh demands for bomber action are made.'[115]

Indeed, this debate of immense grand-strategic consequence was not brought out into the open. Anything less than wholehearted support for the ongoing campaign would undoubtedly have been viewed in some quarters as pusillanimous and might have led to a spectacular row. The issue lay below the surface, colouring the attitude and commitment of the RAF to the campaign, causing resentment with the other services and contributing to flawed campaign strategy.

None of these shortcomings would have surprised anyone who had analysed the campaign-planning process and strategy after the cancellation of the operation on 12 March. But such analysis had not taken place. Instead, errors were repeated, and changes that could have been made were not. It would, however, be misleading to suggest that the muddle and confusion in strategic decision-making could have been totally predicted and prevented. The Germans had achieved complete strategic and tactical surprise. Much of this was due to excellent organisation, planning, preparation and judgment of risk. The Allies had, indeed, been 'completely outwitted'. But in the same vein, total surprise had been in large part the product of good luck. Hitler had believed that the Germans could conceal the buildup and movement of their forces and their intent to invade Norway. They had not done so. Only the mishandling of the myriad of intelligence indicators had allowed surprise to be achieved. And the poor British decision-making at both the strategic and tactical level had contributed to its impact. It is easy to underestimate the degree of uncertainty that existed at the strategic level. Much of British decision-making was based on uncertain information and guesswork, peering through the fog of war. As Clausewitz pointed out, 'War is the realm of uncertainty; three quarters of the factors on which action is based in war are wrapped in a fog of greater or lesser uncertainty', and 'War is the realm of chance. No other human activity gives it greater scope: no other has such incessant and varied dealings with this intruder. Chance makes everything more uncertain and interferes with the whole course of events.'[116] This was to be even more graphically illustrated as the campaign progressed.

The decisions, good or bad, had been taken on the basis of the information available at the time and of what the decision-makers thought had happened. What had actually happened was rather different. Chance had certainly played a large part in it.

At the same time on 7 April that Vice Admiral Whitworth's group had been moving to carry out its minelaying task off Narvik, the first of the

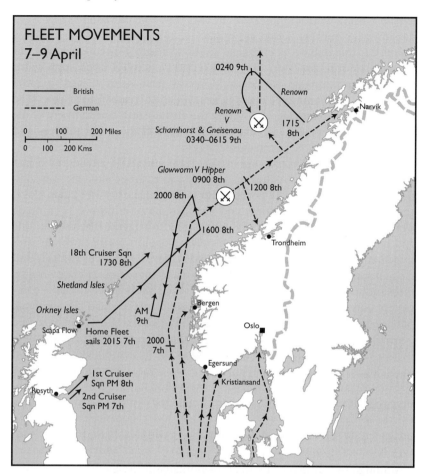

FLEET MOVEMENTS
7–9 April

—————— British

- - - - - - German

0   100   200 Miles

0   100   200 Kms

0240 9th

Renown

Narvik

Renown
V
Scharnhorst & Gneisenau
0340–0615 9th

1715
8th

Glowworm V Hipper
0900 8th

2000 8th

1200 8th

2000 8th

1600 8th

Trondheim

18th Cruiser Sqn
1730 8th

Shetland Isles

Orkney Isles

Bergen

Scapa Flow   Home Fleet
sails 2015 7th

AM
9th

2000
7th

Oslo

Egersund

1st Cruiser
Sqn PM 8th

Rosyth

2nd Cruiser
Sqn PM 7th

Kristiansand

Map 11.2 Fleet movements 7–9 April

six groups of the German invasion fleet for Norway had set sail from
Wilhelmshaven, followed over the next twenty-four hours by the other
groups, synchronising their arrival at their destinations for 4 A.M. on
9 April. To coincide with this, the supply ships and transports, disguised
as ordinary merchant vessels, had left their ports several days previously.
The weather had deteriorated rapidly and, by the night of 7 April, was
blowing a full gale, worsening still further the following day. Although
those on board the ships might not have appreciated it at the time, this
weather and atrocious visibility were a blessing for the German fleet in
helping it elude the Royal Navy and Royal Air Force and in achieving the
surprise on which the whole operation so heavily depended.

As has been seen, the British Home Fleet had set sail from Scapa Flow on the evening of 7 April amidst huge uncertainty not only as to where the German fleet was but also as to what it was doing. It was pure chance which had resulted in the interceptions that took place – *Glowworm* and *Hipper* off Trondheim on the morning of 8 April and *Renown* with *Scharnhorst* and *Gneisenau* (in which *Gneisenau* was severely damaged) the following day. And little did the German group making for Narvik know how close they came to being intercepted by Whitworth on the evening of 8 April.

What was not pure chance was the benefit that the Germans gained from the British deployment into the North Sea, chasing the assumed breakout into the North Atlantic. This had been anticipated by the German naval staff. In an astute piece of psychology, they had taken into account that early fleet movements might be detected and that '[i]t may ... be expected that the enemy will conclude it to be a break-through by Atlantic merchant raiders, and will concentrate his counter-measures in the area Iceland-Shetlands.' and thus away from the Norwegian coast.[117]

The other German task-force groups had reached their objectives but not without serious upset. As the group heading for Oslo made its way up the Oslo Fiord, it was engaged in the early hours of 9 April – on the sole initiative of a 64-year-old colonel, Birger Eriksen – by the guns and torpedoes of the forts some twenty miles south of the city.[118] Two cruisers, *Lützow* and *Blücher*, were hit. *Lützow* was able to withdraw, but *Blücher*, the Kriegsmarine's most modern ship, which was carrying a large number of troops including a divisional headquarters, was completely disabled, and some three hours later rolled over and sank. More than three hundred sailors and soldiers lost their lives.[119]

Although the British came to know of many of these events a few days after they took place, there was one important fact that was to remain unknown to them throughout the campaign: the Kriegsmarine's signals intelligence service, the B-Dienst, had partially cracked the Royal Navy cyphers and was reading over thirty per cent of the traffic it intercepted in the North Sea and Norwegian area.[120] Forbes later observed, 'It is most galling that the enemy should know just where our ships are, whereas we generally learn where his major forces are when they sink one or more of our ships.'[121]

What had been the Norwegian reaction to the invasion? Shortly before 1:30 A.M. on the morning of 9 April, King Haakon was woken by an aide-de-camp to be told, 'Majesty, we are at war!' The King replied, 'Against whom?'[122] It was a valid question. Following the violation of Norwegian neutrality by the British mining operation the previous day,

Figure 11.1 The heavy cruiser *Blücher* in Oslo Fijord, 9 April
(*Norwegian Armed Forces Museum*)

the Norwegian government had been discussing the possibility of finding itself at war with Britain.[123] Despite intelligence indicators that Germany might be mounting some sort of action against Norway – indicators which included the landing of the shipwrecked German soldiers from the *Rio de Janeiro* the previous morning – the invasion came almost as much of a strategic surprise as it had to the British, and a very much greater shock.

Nevertheless, the Norwegian government assembled in the early hours of the morning, decided to ask Great Britain for help and contacted the British Minister in Oslo, Sir Cecil Dormer. It also decided to mobilise the Norwegian armed forces, but, in the confusion, only a partial mobilisation was ordered and that, almost unbelievably, by post. The German minister in Oslo, Kurt Braüer, met with the Norwegian Foreign Minister, Halvdan Koht, and issued an ultimatum demanding unconditional Norwegian surrender. The ultimatum was summarily rejected and, by 7:30 in the morning, the Norwegian royal family and government had escaped the capital by special train to Hamar, a town eighty miles to the north. Two days later, having moved to a new location near Elverum, a further twenty miles to the north-east, the government decided to relieve the aged and defeatist CinC, General Laake, of his appointment, and in his stead promoted a dynamic subordinate, Otto Ruge.[124] The Norwegian fightback was about to get under way in earnest.

Also disturbed in Oslo in the early hours of 9 April had been a 27-year-old member of the British Legation, Margaret Reid. A graduate of Girton College, Cambridge, she had joined the Foreign Office the previous year and been appointed assistant to the Passport Control Officer at the British Legation, Frank Foley. In fact, he was the MI6 station chief. Foley telephoned her at 3 A.M., and dressed somewhat incongruously in her high-heeled shoes ('with rubber overshoes') and wearing 'my eccentric top hat and best coat, black with the Astrakhan border', she hailed a taxi and went to the legation to help burn the secret documents. They then hastily departed by car, following the Norwegian government to Hamar.[125] Critically, Foley had had the foresight to remove from the legation the SIS long-range radio set and emergency code books. From Hamar, they drove north-west, and with Margaret having now acquired the more suitable attire of a pair of plus fours ('cost: about fourteen shillings'), they eventually found their way to the headquarters of Major General Ruge and provided the vital radio link to London.[126]

For the Germans, Weserübung had, in many ways, succeeded beyond expectations. At 7 P.M. on 9 April, from his headquarters, significantly co-located with that of 10th Fliegerkorps in the Hotel Esplanade in Hamburg, Falkenhorst had signalled to OKW, 'The occupation of Norway and Denmark has been accomplished according to orders.'[127] Success in Denmark had been complete, and virtually bloodless. In Norway, the Germans were in possession of all their Day One military objectives – Oslo, Kristiansand, Egersund, Stavanger, Bergen, Trondheim and Narvik – with little resistance offered, and for the cost of only one capital ship. In Oslo, the main German force had entered the city marching as if on parade.

Politically, however, the failure to force Norwegian capitulation and to allow the escape of the king and government was critical. Hitler had specifically ordered that this was not to happen. Vidkun Quisling installed himself as head of a new government, but he was a far from popular figure. Leadership was provided by King Haakon who, in a stirring radio broadcast, rallied the country to resistance.[128]

In the days immediately following the invasion, Hitler had two additional major concerns. First was the very real possibility that the sea-borne reinforcement route across to Norway might be cut by British submarines. In an order dated 11 April, he designated the strengthening

Figure 11.2 German troops entering Oslo, 9 April
(Getty Images)

of the Skagerrak defences against this threat 'with all available means' as the main effort of the Kriegsmarine and Luftwaffe.[129] The other concern, which was to become a preoccupation for him in the coming days, and with some reason, was the situation at Narvik, and in this he was not alone.

12   'Boldness Is Required'

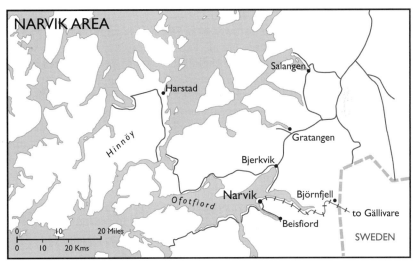

Map 12.1 Narvik Area

Major General Pierse 'Pat' Mackesy, commanding 49 Division, was on leave at his home in Suffolk, when, late at night on Saturday, 30 March, he was telephoned to be told that Operation Avonmouth, cancelled a fortnight earlier, was now being resurrected.[1] Since he had been highly sceptical of the likelihood of the operation taking place when he had attended the ministerial meeting at Downing Street on 12 March – offering odds of a hundred to one against – he must have been considerably surprised.[2] Knowing just how bad the planning had been for that operation, and given that all the nominated units had been either stood down or disbanded, the news that the plan was to be implemented at a week's notice must have also filled him with foreboding. Indeed, when he visited the War Office four days later, Dewing noted, 'Mackesy came in, less thrilled by his present prospect than he had been with his previous show.'[3]

Mackesy had been nominated in late January for command of Avonmouth, 'should the operation take place'.[4] As commander of the division from which came the majority of troops who would be operating in Scandinavia, he was the obvious candidate. As a Royal Engineer, Mackesy was an unusual choice as commander of an infantry division and had arrived in the job on merit. With a Distinguished Service Order (and bar) and a Military Cross from the First World War, he had then served with distinction in the British Military Mission in southern Russia in 1919–1920, held the prestigious job of instructor at the Staff College at Quetta, and commanded an infantry brigade in Palestine just before the war. He had a sharp mind and was a 'no-nonsense' commander.

The troops of 49 Division were all Territorials and the main job of the divisional commander and his very small staff was to train the troops to as high a standard as possible before they joined the BEF. The main planning for Force Avonmouth rested with the three-man Inter-Service Planning Staff and the various departments within the War Office dealing with plans, operations, manning and logistics. But since these departments were responsible for such functions for the whole of the Army, the amount of time they could devote to planning for Scandinavia, and thus the level of detail, was strictly limited. Moreover, since many believed that the operation would never actually happen, Scandinavia was not top of the agenda. A planning gap opened between, on the one hand, the broad-brush policy and planning guidelines of the War Office and Inter-Service Planning Staff, and, on the other, the detailed planning of the tactical-level commander and his tiny headquarters. This was exacerbated by the fact that the focus of Avonmouth planning was not on the landing at Narvik – with the assumption of Norwegian cooperation, this would merely amount to disembarkation alongside the quay – but on the multinational expedition to Gällivare, and in particular on the huge and complex logistic plan that would be required to support it. Indeed, of the 8,000 men who comprised the original force, almost half were logistics troops,[5] and the base would require several weeks' build-up before the expeditionary force could be fully supported.[6]

Mackesy's force was to be made up of two echelons: the first consisting of 24 Brigade; the second comprising the Chasseurs Alpins, together with other French and Polish troops. 24 Brigade was a newly created brigade, bringing together three Regular infantry battalions: 1st Battalion Scots Guards, 1st Battalion Irish Guards and 2nd Battalion The South Wales Borderers. The units had not trained together (the Guards battalions were based in London, the South Wales Borderers in County

Durham), and the brigade commander, Brigadier William Fraser, had arrived just two months previously. Indeed, he was not to meet the South Wales Borderers until they arrived in Norway[7]. By 7 April, and following the frenetic preparation referred to earlier, the units, along with 146 and 148 Brigades, destined for Trondheim, Bergen and Stavanger, were embarked on the Clyde and at Rosyth. Mackesy's initial orders, received on 6 April, were to secure the port of Narvik and the line of communication inland as far as the Swedish frontier and await the second-echelon troops who would move through to Gällivare and beyond. Two constraints were emphasised. Landings were not to take place in the face of serious Norwegian opposition, and there was to be no bombardment of the civilian population.[8] But on the evening of 9 April, in the wake of the German invasion, came new instructions. The Hallamshire battalion of 146 Brigade, embarked for Trondheim, was to sail for Narvik; Mackesy and 24 Brigade were to sail to an unnamed base to secure it 'after the port has been cleared by the Royal Navy'[9] – code for Trondheim.

The convoy departed on 10 April, but when it called in to Scapa the next day, Mackesy was met by Brigadier Lund, Deputy Director of Military Operations, who handed him yet another set of orders. The objective for Mackesy and 24 Brigade, as well as for 146 Brigade, was, after all, Narvik. They were first to establish a base at Harstad, a small fishing port in the Lofoten Islands about thirty-five miles north-west of Narvik, to make contact with Norwegian forces, plan further operations and receive reinforcements. The orders, signed by the CIGS, instructed, 'It is not intended that you should land in the face of opposition.' They also told Mackesy that he would be joined by two Territorial Army brigades between 16 and 18 April, the leading echelon of the Chasseurs Alpins between 21 and 25 April, and the remainder of 49 Division on 27 April.[10] In addition, there was a handwritten note from Ironside which was not a model of clarity. It began, 'Owing to naval difficulties in escorting we have decided to send four battalions together, the whole arriving 30 hours before the arrival of the other two battalions with a week's interval before the arrival of the other two battalions.'[11] According to Mackesy, 'This cryptic sentence could not be explained by Brigadier Lund at all.'[12] The note went on, 'Latest information is that there are some 3,000 Germans in Narvik. They must have been knocked about by naval action.' The note also included some bizarrely extraneous detail which showed what was on the CIGS's mind: 'There should be a considerable number of ponies in the village and neighbouring ones. Let no question of paying trouble you. Issue payment vouchers and we will see that you get a paymaster as soon as possible. Don't allow any haggling over prices.' This sentence was immediately followed by something more important: 'You may have a chance of taking advantage of naval action and you should do so if you can. Boldness is required.'[13] Brigadier Lund delivered some additional oral instructions which, according to Mackesy, included direction that '[t]he first thing was to get in touch with [the Norwegians] to prevent them throwing their hand in. It was realised that it would probably take me "some weeks" to make a plan.'[14] Mackesy was, thus, not short of instructions, only of coherent ones.

During the afternoon of 11 April, Mackesy and his two leading companies commenced transfer to *HMS Southampton*, but the operation was suspended for the night and continued the next morning. It was not until one o'clock that afternoon that naval preparations were complete and *Southampton* sailed for Harstad.[15] The delay was critical, but there appears to have been little sense of urgency or understanding that, in warfare, time is precious and irretrievable. Accompanying Mackesy were the brigade commander, Brigadier Fraser, and Captain Maund, Royal Navy, head of the Inter-Service Training and Development Centre, who had been appointed chief of staff to the Naval Force Commander who was himself en route for Harstad from Rosyth in *HMS Aurora*.[16] Also heading for Narvik was the convoy comprising the main party of 24 Brigade and the whole of 146 Brigade. On the evening of 14 April, the convoy commander suddenly received orders from the Admiralty to split the convoy, diverting 146 Brigade to Namsos. The first echelon of Rupertforce had just been halved.

When Mackesy had left London, the Naval Force Commander had been Admiral Sir Edward Evans, who had been the naval commander appointed for the aborted expedition in March. The two men had met and discussed the operation, had established a cordial relationship and would probably have made a good team. Evans, however, because of his strong Norwegian connections, had been chosen for a diplomatic mission on 10 April. As his replacement, Churchill had selected Admiral of the Fleet Sir William Boyle, 12th Earl of Cork and Orrery, an old favourite and fellow spirit, whom he had re-called the previous September to take forward Operation Catherine – the scheme to put up-armoured warships into the Baltic.[17] Mackesy had never met Cork and, apart from the fact that both were strong characters, the two men could scarcely have been more different. For while Mackesy was a circumspect, methodical Royal Engineer, 'Ginger' Boyle was well known throughout the Navy as a pugnacious and irascible fire-eater. Aged sixty-six, the earl was very senior in every way: a former CinC Home Fleet, he had been a full admiral when Mackesy was still a colonel. Furthermore, the two men had completely different instructions for the capture of

Narvik. Almost unbelievably, Cork had been given no written orders. As the official historian puts it, with considerable diplomacy, Cork 'had been orally briefed on 10 and 11 April with varying degrees of informality by the First Sea Lord, by a meeting of the Military Coordination Committee, and by Mr Churchill in his car travelling from the Admiralty to the House [of Commons]'[18] – a distance of a few hundred yards. Cork recalled, 'My impression on leaving London was quite clear that it was desired by HM [His Majesty's] Government to turn the enemy out of Narvik at the earliest possible moment and that I was to act with all promptitude in order to attain that result.[19] Thus a joint service (combined) amphibious operation was in prospect which flouted almost all the doctrinal guidance for such operations:[20] no overall commander was appointed; there was no centralised control or intelligence; the orders issued to the commanders were contradictory (or as Churchill put it in his memoirs, 'somewhat different in tone and emphasis');[21] there had been no liaison between the service Chiefs; and no regard whatsoever had been paid to the compatibility of the service commanders (despite this being both common sense and an important factor laid down in combined operations doctrine).[22] Moreover, the troops were untrained for such operations, no proper reconnaissance had taken place or rehearsals conducted; indeed, no planning had taken place. All of this was amateur in the extreme. In addition, fragmented command and control was exacerbated by the command of naval forces being split between the CinC Home Fleet (Forbes) and the Flag Officer Narvik (Cork) who, incidentally, outranked Forbes, with both of them reporting direct to the Admiralty which, itself, had a penchant for interference in tactical details.[23] Adding a final touch of dysfunctionality, Churchill established a private line of communication with Cork which bypassed all the Admiralty staff, including the First Sea Lord.[24]

As Cork in *Aurora* approached the Norwegian coast on 14 April, he received a signal from Whitworth, following the *Warspite* attack on Narvik, saying that, although it was understood that there were 1,500–2,000 troops in the town, he was 'convinced that Narvik can be taken by direct assault now without fear of meeting serious opposition on landing'.[25] Cork immediately signalled *Southampton* to meet on the approach to Narvik and suggested to Mackesy an assault landing at Narvik, supported by naval forces, at daylight the next day.[26] The signal, however, was not received until much later that day and after *Southampton* had landed its troops as planned at Salangen, on the mainland north-east of Harstad and thirty miles overland from Narvik.[27] (Unreliable communications in and around Norway were to remain a feature throughout the campaign.) Mackesy was unimpressed by Cork's

Figure 12.1 Major General Pierse Mackesy
(National Portrait Gallery)

Figure 12.2 Admiral of the Fleet the Earl of Cork and Orrery
(www.admirals.org.uk)

scheme, all the more so having received War Office intelligence reporting that German troops at Narvik possibly included an infantry regiment of three battalions, and that thirty long-range German bombers were operating as far north as the town.[28] He replied to Cork, casting doubt on the feasibility of the plan but saying that more troops would be available with the arrival of the advance party the following day.[29] Cork also received a signal from the Admiralty telling him, 'We think it imperative that you and the General should be together and act together and that no attack should be made except in concert.'[30] Cork, therefore, made for Harstad, arriving the next morning.

The first meeting of Cork and Mackesy was witnessed by a number of onlookers. One recalled, 'I remember the General climbing up the companion way to the quarter deck, where he and the Admiral saluted each other, and simultaneously fitted their monocles to their eyes and took a look at each other for the first time. It was clearly a dramatic moment, and someone turned to me and in a half whisper said, "15 all!"'[31] The meeting was not a cordial one. Cork was 'astonished to hear that not only was his force embarked for a peaceful landing and consequently unready for immediate operations, but that the orders he had received just prior to sailing, ruled out any idea of attempting an opposed landing. Thus the general and I left the UK with diametrically opposed views as to what was required.'[32] Mackesy now explained the other limitations. His troops were untrained in amphibious operations or for operations in very cold climates; they had very limited small arms and mortar ammunition, and no vehicles, radios or maps, let alone field artillery, air defence guns or landing craft.[33] To Cork, this must have sounded like a litany of negativity, but there was more. The snow was lying three to four feet deep down to the shoreline, off-road movement without skis was impossible, and there were very few civilian trucks.[34] Mackesy's chief of staff had met his opposite number in the Norwegian divisional headquarters and learnt from him that the Germans had captured intact the pillboxes and defensive positions in Narvik; a signal from London had confirmed that the Germans were 'strongly entrenched'.[35] Although the Norwegian forces in north Norway, the 6th Division under Major General Carl Gustav Fleischer, had been partially mobilised for some months as part of Norway's 'neutrality watch', the remainder were still in the process of mobilisation and were already engaged with the German mountain troops to the north and east of the town.

Cork seems to have accepted these arguments and Mackesy's plan because the next day (16 April) he signalled to the Admiralty that 'German defences are known to be strong and the possibility of assault is ruled out.' He also ruled out operations on any scale across country 'until snow melts at the end of April', stating that his intention was to advance on German positions to the west of Bjerkvik and await the arrival of the Chasseurs Alpins to operate against the Germans around Gratangen.[36]

Churchill received this signal late that evening – clearly with some anger, because he immediately drafted a proposed reply for War Cabinet approval which, with minor amendment, was despatched after the Cabinet meeting the next morning (17 April). It reflected not only the disappointed expectations in London about the imminent fall of Narvik but also the growing concerns about operations further south. Success at Narvik was becoming critical, politically as well as militarily. The signal read:

> Your proposals involve damaging deadlock at Narvik and the neutralization of one of our best brigades. We cannot send you the Chasseurs Alpins. The Warspite will be needed elsewhere, in two or three days. Full consideration should be given by you to assault upon Narvik covered by the Warspite and the destroyers. . . . The capture of the port and town would be an important success. Send us your appreciation and act at once if you consider right. Matter most urgent.[37]

Cork responded the next day to Churchill reporting that Mackesy and his senior subordinates were strongly opposed to an assault, adding, 'I have urged assault but feel obliged to accept soldiers' views, which seem unanimous, at least until snow disappears ... short of a direct order, soldiers refuse to entertain the idea of assault.'[38] However, probably reflecting that this was unlikely to satisfy his political master, he convened a conference that evening to try and achieve a more rapid solution. The conference, attended by the staffs, did not begin well for Cork. Mackesy strongly demurred from his proposal for an amphibious assault from open boats, describing the plan in emotive language as 'sheer bloody murder'. He said that he would only carry out the assault if given a direct order, in which case he would do so loyally and energetically, 'though he deprecated the snows of Narvik being turned into another version of the mud of Passchendaele'.[39] An alternative, he said, was a heavy naval bombardment which might demoralise the enemy and allow a landing by a force poised offshore. But, with a large civilian population in the town, he questioned whether the Admiralty's instructions allowed such a bombardment, because the Army's did not. Cork dodged this key question, but seized on the proposal, declaring that 'the bombardment is certain to be effective', although agreeing that an assault was impractical.[40]

Back in London, the CIGS had initially been supportive of Mackesy, concerned that he was having pressure put on him by Cork and Churchill. On 15 April he visited Pound 'to get him to understand that it was fatal to start monkeying about from here with the general on the spot'.[41] But three days later, Ironside's confidence in Mackesy was fast fading: Mackesy was becoming a liability, not least in Ironside's relationship with Churchill. Having dined with Churchill and been clearly influenced by him – indeed, this may have been the purpose behind the dinner invitation – Ironside recorded in his diary, 'I have come to the conclusion that I must send up another officer to investigate and if necessary take over from both Mackesy and Fraser.'[42] As so often, however, what Ironside confided in his diary and what he actually did were two very different things. His instinct for quick and decisive action was the correct one. But it was to be ten days before a general was nominated to go to Harstad, and a further fortnight before he was despatched.[43] The delay is remarkable and does not reflect well on the CIGS's decisiveness or effectiveness. In the meantime, the impasse between Cork and Mackesy continued, with Mackesy receiving no indication of support from the War Office.

Mackesy's increasing frustration shows in his signal to the CIGS on 19 April: 'I must point out that I have not even one field gun and I have not even one anti-aircraft gun. I have practically no mortar ammunition. My force is probably inferior to the enemy.' He added that more troops were required and that he would be unable to undertake offensive operations 'for some weeks',[44] receiving the dismissive reply, 'The War Office fully realises [the] state of your forces.'[45] For Mackesy, there were other competing challenges. Unloading stores was proving a long and somewhat chaotic process, with transports having to anchor many miles off Narvik, their loads being transferred onto destroyers or, more often, the local Norwegian paraffin-engine fishing boats which the British christened Puffers. The situation was further exacerbated by air attack and the absence of any air defence. This brought an unwelcome, but not entirely surprising, change of attitude in the local population who 'now regard our presence a liability rather than an asset'.[46]

In the meantime, Churchill, having clearly been poring over a large-scale map of Narvik, indulged his fascination with tactics, telling Cork,

I thought that the tongue of land, especially its tip occupied by Narvik port and town could certainly be dominated by the fire of warships, and that the houses could be occupied with the forces you possess. .... As I see it, once you have got the Narvik tip, and are ensconced in the houses and wrecked pill-boxes, all his detachments in the country are ruined, and can be reduced at leisure. Now if you can get this tongue-tip, all is well, and the snow is only the enemy's trouble.[47]

Figure 12.3 Narvik from the north-west
(Imperial War Museum)

At the time, Mackesy was conducting a reconnaissance of Narvik in *Aurora* and, on his return, again signalled the CIGS. In summary, he considered:

My original opinion that the conditions essential for a successful opposed landing do not at present exist is fully confirmed. ... Owing to the nature of the ground, flat trajectory of naval guns, and impossibility of locating the concealed machine guns, I am convinced that the naval bombardment cannot be militarily effective, and that a landing from open boats in the above conditions must be ruled out absolutely. Any attempt of the sort would involve not the neutralisation [the term Churchill had used], but the destruction of the 24th (Guards) Brigade.[48]

Churchill now gained the War Cabinet's agreement for Cork to become CinC Narvik, thus bringing Mackesy directly under his authority.[49] This, of course, should have been the arrangement recommended by the Chiefs of Staff at the outset. Mackesy accepted the new arrangement, telling Cork,

[a]ny order you give me will be carried out to the best of my ability. ... I realise that you must know that my appreciation of the military situation is contrary to that which you have expressed. Should you desire my removal and replacement by some other officer I will entirely understand, and no personal feelings whatever will enter into the matter.[50]

Cork, however, seems to have been as reluctant to use his new powers as Mackesy was to see them used. According to the latter, he was approached by Captain Maund and the naval liaison officer, Commander Hubbacks,[51] about the morality of bombarding a town full of civilians, following which he made a further protest to his new boss, asking that 'these views may be represented to His Majesty's Government'.[52]

Before proposed action against Narvik commences I have the honour to inform you that I feel it my duty to represent to you that I am convinced that there is not one Officer or man under my command who will not feel shame for himself and his country if thousands of Norwegian men, women and children in Narvik are subject to bombardment proposed.

Whatever Cork's view, he was not prepared to give it, delphically annotating the message, 'I have no remarks.'[53] In doing so, Cork was acting less like a Commander-in-Chief and more like a post office.

When the signal was received in London just after midnight, Churchill, 'angered almost beyond endurance',[54] clearly believed that Mackesy was a malign influence, and the next day his dramatic reply was on its way back to Cork: 'If this officer appears to be spreading a bad spirit, do not hesitate to relieve him or place him under arrest.'[55] Although he was happy to cajole others into issuing orders for the bombardment, Churchill was not prepared to give the direct order and nor was Cork. Instead, Churchill suggested to Cork that he inform the German commander that all civilians must leave the town and that he would be held responsible if he obstructed their departure. He also suggested that the population should be removed by ship or that Cork promise to leave the railway line unmolested for six hours to encourage the population to leave.[56] This was clutching at straws.

Prospects at Narvik had not been improved by several days of continuous, heavy snowfall. Cork had ventured ashore to test conditions for himself but ended up waist-deep and angry, having to be extricated by his escorting Marines.[57] He had also flown a reconnaissance over Narvik, showing his buccaneering spirit by daring the crew to shoot down the swastika flying above the town.[58] Pressure from London required that an assault should at least be attempted. Cork and Mackesy met to try to agree on a plan. Cork's chief of staff, Captain Maund, recalled, 'The meeting was painful, but agreement was reached.'[59] A naval force would approach Narvik with a military force embarked and conduct a naval bombardment, now restricted to military objectives only.[60] If the bombardment was effective – which Cork defined as white flags appearing onshore – the embarked force would be landed.[61] With considerable irony, the date chosen for this dubious operation was 24 April, eve of the anniversary of the landings at Gallipoli. The day dawned to a blizzard. This had the welcome advantage of preventing interference from the Luftwaffe, whose aircraft, based in Trondheim, had been bombing Harstad whenever weather permitted. But the falling snow also had the predictable disadvantage, which became obvious at the end of the bombardment, that it was impossible to see any flags, let alone white ones. The operation was aborted and the flotilla returned to Harstad. In fact, the bombardment caused no vital damage and not a single German fatality.[62] Following a British-inspired announcement from the Norwegian radio at Tromsø that all civilians should leave the town, the Germans were expecting an assault, and the commander had moved non-essential military personnel out of Narvik.[63] The next day Cork informed the Admiralty of his judgement that 'under existing conditions any direct attack upon Narvik is impracticable' and reported that he intended to work towards Narvik overland from either side of the Ofotfiord[64] (Mackesy's plan). It would take over a month for Narvik to fall.

Was this a missed opportunity? Would a coup de main, amphibious assault have succeeded? These questions are intriguing, because had Narvik fallen within the first few days of the initial landing, the outcome of the whole campaign might have been very different. With all the resources and effort free to be concentrated further south, the Germans might have been dislodged from Trondheim. Politically, too, the fall of Narvik and the destruction of the German forces there could have had far-reaching consequences in Berlin where Hitler had accepted the whole responsibility. From another perspective, had the assault gone ahead and ended in a Gallipoli-style disaster, with the deaths of hundreds of soldiers (and Norwegian civilians), it would probably have ended the political career of the operation's main protagonist – Winston Churchill.

The questions have been the subject of much controversy, both at the time and since. Churchill was quick to suggest that the fault for a missed strategic opportunity lay with Mackesy – who was sacked the following month. But for Mackesy, he suggested, Narvik would have been taken at an early stage, but the general had 'continued to use every argument, and there was no shortage of them, to prevent drastic action'.[65] Some authors have agreed, one stating that 'the facts must speak for themselves' in that the eventual capture of Narvik was achieved by 'relatively small forces at low cost', although failing to point out the wholly different circumstances.[66] A number of commentators have taken the view that an 'opportunity [was] offered on the 13th ... remaining open perhaps a couple of days thereafter' for a practicable assault[67] or that 'a landing during the first days [up to 16 April] would have had a good chance of success'.[68] Captain

Louis Hamilton, of *Aurora*, endorsed this view, writing in late May 1940, 'I still think, with Lord Cork, that the soldiers underestimated the shattering effect of close naval bombardment, and that if they had gone bald-headed for it that there was a good chance of success.'[69] Others are more dubious.[70] Most, including the Norwegian divisional chief of staff, consider that an attack after about 16 April would probably have failed, at least until several weeks later when the thaw came, resources had been built up and local tactical successes achieved.[71] Although most agree that the best chance of success was on 13 April following the *Warspite* attack, not all agree that that chance would have been very high. Mackesy's naval liaison officer, Captain Hubbacks, 'doubted the statement that we could almost certainly have won Narvik on 13 April'.[72] Captain Maund, Cork's chief of staff (who had been head of the Inter-Service [amphibious] Training and Development Centre), told Derry, 'Lord Cork's first proposal to land a few hundred men in ships' boats ... against an unknown garrison and to propose an advance over un-reconnoitred ground under deep snow was so silly that it cannot be defended.'[73] A more comprehensive and well-argued assertion that an amphibious assault would have failed at any stage was made by Mackesy's son – an eminent historian, but hardly an unbiased judge.[74] Derry ultimately was ambivalent: '[I]t must be left an open question whether Lord Cork's instinct for the offensive, while it involved grave risk of heavy loss, might not have justified itself in the event.'[75]

One person who firmly believed that Narvik was lost to the Germans was Adolf Hitler. The Führer had been deeply disappointed that Weserübung had failed in one of its key objectives: the capitulation of Norway and with it the surrender of the Norwegian armed forces. This was of particular concern at Narvik, because, unlike the other divisions in the Norwegian Army, the 6th Division, centred on Narvik, was partially mobilised and had five battalions on active duty at the time of the German invasion, all of them equipped for winter warfare. The immediate counter-attack by the Royal Navy on 10 April made the position of the German forces look precarious. Hitler had ordered that his forces in Narvik, commanded by Major General Eduard Dietl, be resupplied by air. This began on 12 April, but the Führer's confidence was shaken. At a strategy conference the same day, he made it plain that, as Halder noted in his diary, 'If things turn ugly up North, we won't force the issue, but turn to the West! In eight or ten days.'[76] On the evening of 13 April, following news of the second British naval attack, the mood at the Kriegsmarine headquarters in Berlin was 'serious and depressed', with talk of Narvik having 'become a mousetrap for our forces'.[77] The following afternoon the head of the Army, General von Brauchitsch, returned from a meeting with Hitler to tell Halder that '[h]opes have been abandoned to hold Narvik.[78] It was clear to those around him that Hitler's confidence was shaken. Jodl noted, 'Nervousness has now reached fever pitch ... Führer wants Dietl to make his way south. I come out against such an unthinkable project.'[79] Jodl's deputy recalled seeing Hitler 'hunched in a chair in the corner, unnoticed and staring in front of him, a picture of brooding gloom. He appeared to be waiting for some new piece of news that would save the situation.'[80] The next day, 15 April, Hitler declared that the German forces at Narvik should either be ordered to withdraw into Sweden or be evacuated by air – both proposals opposed by Jodl. Two days later, Hitler signed an order giving Dietl discretionary authority to withdraw his force into Sweden and be interned. Jodl delayed its transmission long enough to persuade Hitler that all was not lost and instead to sign an order telling Dietl to hold Narvik for as long as possible.[81] By the next morning, Jodl noted, 'The Führer is calm again.'[82]

To what extent had Hitler's crisis of confidence been justified? What was the position on the ground at Narvik?

The German military force that arrived at Narvik in the early hours of 9 April was the 139th Regiment of the 3rd Mountain Division. Its peacetime location was Graz in southern Austria, and the majority of its soldiers were Austrian. They were highly trained mountain warfare specialists – Gebirgsjäger - and had combat experience from the Polish campaign, fighting in the Carpathian mountains. They were among the best troops in the German Army. The 139th Regiment comprised three battalions reinforced by a company of naval artillery and one of engineers, plus additional signals and intelligence personnel. The force numbered about 2,000 men.[83] With it came the divisional commander, Major General Eduard Dietl.

Dietl, aged forty-nine, was born in Bavaria and had served throughout the First World War in the 5th Bavarian Regiment, including fighting as a company commander at the Somme, Arras and in Flanders. After the war, he had joined the Freikorps Epp, a paramilitary bunch of ultra-right wing thugs, responsible for the murderous suppression of their political opponents in Bavaria. As an early Nazi, he became closely acquainted with Hitler, and his Reichswehr company was on standby to assist in the Beer Hall Putsch of 1923. After a job instructing in tactics at the Munich Infantry School, Dietl commanded a battalion in the Bavarian Infantry and later a mountain regiment. He was also an accomplished skier and mountaineer, had attended a two-month winter-warfare course (ironically at the Norwegian Infantry Winter School) and was a pioneer of mountain warfare in the German Army. For all his faults, he was tough, professional and charismatic. An ardent Nazi, he was also one of Hitler's

Figure 12.4 Major General Eduard Dietl
(Getty Images)

favourite generals. For the divisional commander to accompany just
one of his regiments – the rest of the division was at Trondheim – was
unusual, but it demonstrates the importance and scale of the task with
which this regiment was faced, and the faith that Hitler had in Dietl to
deliver the goods.

Now isolated, with the nearest German support some 500 miles away
at Trondheim, Dietl's powers of leadership were to be put to the test.[84]
His troops, most of whom had never seen the sea before, arrived in
Narvik after two nights and a day without sleep, in ships which had been
heading at speed into a severe gale. There had been many broken limbs
below deck. At least ten men had been swept overboard, as had a large
amount of heavy weapons, ammunition, communications, equipment
and stores.[85] On the approaches to Narvik, the Kriegsmarine ships had
been challenged by two Norwegian coastal defence vessels, *Eidsvold* and
Norge, which they had sunk. Dietl's first task, to seize and secure Narvik,
was, however, relatively simple, aided by the Norwegian garrison commander, Colonel Sundlo, a long-time member of Quisling's political
party, who immediately surrendered the town.[86] But Dietl knew that
serious resistance could be expected from the Norwegian troops to the

north and east of Narvik and that an attack by the British could be expected. He immediately secured the surrounding area, sending forces up the road to the north and along the railway line towards Bjørnfjell and the Swedish border. He also seized the Norwegian military depot, thereby obtaining a large amount of weapons, including 8,000 rifles and, significantly, 300 light machine guns and 15 heavy machine guns, together with large quantities of ammunition.[87] Also gained from the depot was much needed equipment and clothing. The latter was important: the German troops had arrived without much of their specialist winter-warfare clothing.[88] Indeed, none of the three assigned stores ships had made it to Narvik. Dietl received some resupply by air on 12 April and again a day later, more important this time as it brought an artillery battery with its four 75 mm guns.[89] Over the next few days, further minor resupply was to arrive by air. In addition, he had supplemented his harbour defences by stripping the wrecked destroyers of those guns that could be removed, including ten 105 mm guns taken from the five British armed merchant ships which had been involved in the attack on 10 April.[90] However, the threat from the north and east of Narvik required two of the three battalions, leaving only one for the defence of the town from seaborne attack, supplemented by some of the crews of the two ships sunk on 10 April. These crews, who, like all Kriegsmarine sailors, had undergone basic small-arms training, were clothed, armed and equipped from the captured supply depot, and organised into companies, although by the time of the *Warspite* attack on 13 April this process had only just begun.

The *Warspite* attack was not entirely unexpected; B-Dienst had warned the previous day that a British attack was likely on 13 April.[91] The attack undoubtedly – and unsurprisingly – caused panic amongst some of the defenders. One witness records the sight of 'soldiers and sailors scrambling along the railway line or into the mountains to escape the expected British landing'.[92] The Mayor of Narvik claimed to have observed a collapse in morale that evening, but a quick recovery next day.[93] The undercover British Military Intelligence officer at Narvik, Captain Torrance, in a hideout above the town, corroborated this: 'That evening the whole mountain was swarming with German soldiers some of whom were throwing away their rifles ... many of them sailors from destroyers that had been sunk and wearing Norwegian uniforms ... their morale was badly shaken. ... The following morning they returned to the village, others were looking out for their rifles in the snow.'[94] There are reasons to suggest, though, that if there was panic, it was not widespread. First, although almost 300 German sailors lost their lives, not a single German on land was killed that day,[95] nor did Dietl see the need to call up any reserves to assist.[96] German sources, which draw attention to panic at other times, do not mention it on this occasion.[97] It is particularly unlikely that panic extended to the more seasoned of the Gebirgsjäger, who knew that they were under the eagle eye of their redoubtable divisional commander. It would have taken very few of them to seriously disrupt a disembarkation from Whitworth's ships coming alongside the quay on 13 April, and it is known that a reserve of one company was in position above the town ready to counter-attack against any landing. Even if *Southampton*, with its two companies of Guardsmen, had been present, and even if they had been armed, equipped and prepared, it is highly questionable as to whether an assault would have been successful. Nevertheless, the German defenders believed that the British 'had let slip their big opportunity' of taking Narvik.[98] What chances there were rapidly receded. During the following day, discipline would have been restored, certainly amongst the Gebirgsjäger battalion and progressively amongst the shell-shocked sailors who had fled their destroyed ships. These sailors, like those from the ships wrecked in the 10 April destroyer attack, were then organised, reclothed, equipped, armed and formed into companies. Ironically, the British naval successes had resulted in the size of Dietl's force being more than doubled, from some 2,000 men to around 4,500.[99] Although the sailors' combat capability was limited, it is unlikely that Narvik could have been held without them. In addition, their technical support was considered to be 'exceptionally valuable'.[100]

Thereafter, the firepower at the German's disposal, including four mountain guns, six heavy mortars, guns taken off the sunken ships and ten heavy machine guns – in prepared positions, many of which were defiladed from low trajectory naval gunfire – made Narvik a very hard nut to crack with what the British had at hand. The chance of a successful frontal assault in daylight – and at that time of year there was no complete darkness – by a few hundred infantrymen from open rowing boats would have been very low. Indeed, it is probable that most of the boats would not even have reached the shore. Had those troops managed to gain a foothold on land, they would have been hard pressed to hold their position for long against a determined German counter-attack. German air superiority, with Narvik in range of the Luftwaffe bombers based at Trondheim, would have made the operation even more hazardous whenever conditions allowed flying. Finally, since the troops would have been most unlikely to have got ashore dry-shod, they would all have suffered from frostbite as soon as the sun set. Even as a peacetime exercise, the result would probably have been a shambles. Yet Dietl, with his troops increasingly thinly stretched – much more so than Mackesy believed – was far from optimistic; the Germans were mystified by the British failure

Gebirgsjäger und Matrofen in Stellung

Figure 12.5 A German machine gun post overlooking Narvik harbour
(*Bundearchiv*)

to launch an amphibious assault.[101] Both Dietl and Mackesy overesti-
mated their own vulnerabilities in comparison to each other's.

It is impossible to say with complete certainty that the operation
proposed by Cork could not have succeeded – only that, with the benefit
of hindsight, its chances of success were very low. With the information
available at the time, Cork's plan looks to have been, as he himself
described it, 'a gamble'[102] – and a reckless one at that, particularly
around the period 17–24 April, when he was under greatest pressure
from London to act. It seems that Cork, himself, came to recognise just
how high the risk was. Having been appointed CinC on 20 April, he had
the authority to order Mackesy to carry out the frontal attack – and the
latter had said he would do it, if given a direct order; but, for the
moment, Cork chose not to give that order. As he later commented,
'by this time the chance of a coup de main had passed.'[103]

The initial operations had shown both the strengths and weaknesses of
the British capacity for making war. Many accounts, as well as popular
folk memory, tend to concentrate on the former. The performance of
the captains and crews of individual ships of the Royal Navy, such as
those of *Glowworm* and *Hardy*, had been superb and inspiring. Many

other aspects had not been. The despatch of the Army and Navy commanders with separate and contradictory orders, which had such unfortunate consequences, also illustrated the level of amateurism and incompetence in the British higher direction of the war and the failure to learn lessons of the past. As Ismay later commented,

the worst shortcomings of the First World War, as exemplified by the Dardanelles campaign, were faithfully repeated. The Chief of the Naval Staff and the Chief of the Imperial General Staff acted with sturdy independence. They appointed their respective commanders without consultation with each other; and, worse still, they gave directives to those commanders without harmonising them. Thereafter they continued to issue separate orders to them. Thus confusion was worse compounded.[104]

The failure to consider the compatibility of the two deployed commanders had the most serious consequences. It was clearly not a consideration for Churchill when he selected his old friend, Cork, and Pound was either not consulted or raised no objection. Either way, the result was a dysfunctional command. At the first sniff of trouble, Ironside should have sent out a senior officer to report back.

The rapid and confusing changes to the deployment plan were symptomatic of an unclear and wavering strategy and the lack of firm direction at the top. Nor were responsibility and authority clearly defined. At first, Cork was constrained to act only in consultation with Mackesy. Even when he was made the sole authority, Cork failed to exercise that authority, instead referring decisions to London. This failure was not just, or indeed primarily, a personality issue. Cork lacked the necessary knowledge or experience to overrule his Army subordinates, and had no Army adviser on his staff. Nor was anyone in authority in London prepared to remind Cork that, as CinC, he and he alone, was responsible for giving orders 'in theatre'. Here again, the Chiefs of Staff should have been giving advice to ministers – and direction to Cork.

The Chiefs of Staff also failed to follow the doctrinal guidance given in the *Manual for Combined Operations*, produced only two years earlier. There may have been a number of contributory factors. First, doctrine of any sort in all three services was generally treated with some disdain as the enemy of improvisation and initiative. Second, the doctrine had been largely produced by one service – the War Office – which may have undermined its validity with the other two. Third, such was the perceived place of doctrine, the Chiefs may not even have known that the doctrine existed, or if they did, thought that they knew better.

Finally, Mackesy chose to have almost nothing to do with the Norwegian Army, in whom he had 'not much confidence'.[105] His view was unchanged when he later wrote, 'Taken as a whole I regarded them as being utterly untrustworthy, perhaps 50%, or more, were in sympathy with, and a large number actively assisted, the Germans.'[106] The basis of this allegation is unclear. One Norwegian historian asserts that right up to the invasion the Norwegian armed forces were 'rich in Nazi sympathisers and members of Quisling's political party' and its general staff 'crammed with officers sympathetic to Hitler and Germany'. But closer inspection would have shown Mackesy that Major General Fleischer and his soldiers fought the Germans with wholehearted commitment, passion and self-sacrifice. As a result of Mackesy's view – a view widely shared within his force – British and Norwegian efforts around Narvik were uncoordinated, and all the weaker for it.[107]

13   'An Even Greater Prize'

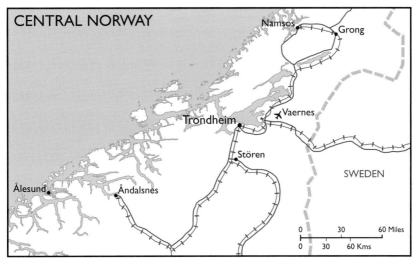

Map 13.1 Central Norway

If the War Cabinet had found campaign strategy for Narvik challenging, it was about to find the strategy further south even more so.

The fog of uncertainty which had shrouded the picture of what was actually happening in Norway at the time of the invasion was slow to lift, and by 14 April, when the decision was taken to divert 146 Brigade to Namsos, the picture was only a little clearer. A major source of information was the SIS officer, Frank Foley, who had hurriedly left Oslo with Margaret Reid on 9 April and managed to locate the Norwegian military headquarters in the Gudbrandsdal valley, north of Lillehammer. Foley had with him his long-range wireless telegraph set that was capable, albeit intermittently, of contacting London.

The decision to divert 146 Brigade had followed optimism about the imminent capture of Narvik after the successful *Warspite* attack, the growing pressure on and within the War Cabinet to recognise the importance of propping up Norwegian resistance and the requirement for the speedy capture of Trondheim. A late addition to this pressure was the personal appeal for help from General Ruge to Chamberlain.[1] The Prime Minister had replied, 'We are coming as fast as possible and in great strength.'[2]

Churchill had anticipated the formal decision to divert 146 Brigade, informing the Military Coordination Committee the previous evening that, 'in any event', the Admiralty had ordered warships to land a small party of marines at Namsos that very night or the following morning, with a similar landing planned for Ålesund, a small port south of Trondheim, a few days later. In addition, the Committee had directed the Chiefs to study the possibility of a direct landing at Trondheim itself. It was, however, unclear as to the purpose of the landings at Namsos and Ålesund. Was their rationale, as Churchill now suggested, that they 'would tend to attract the Germans away from Trondheim itself and lead to their dispersal',[3] or was it still, as he had suggested only twenty-four hours previously, 'to give the impression of an attack on Trondheim'?[4] Or were they to provide support for the main landing at Trondheim, if it took place? Or, if the landing at Trondheim proved unfeasible, were Namsos and Ålesund to become the main entry points for an overland attack on Trondheim? None of the Chiefs sought clarification or questioned the suitability of these little ports as points of entry for a large military force. It was, however, pointed out that 146 Brigade was a Territorial Army brigade 'whose training was not yet advanced' – a gross understatement – but there was no alternative immediately available. Furthermore, the threat to these operations that came from the Luftwaffe based at Stavanger was recognised, but the meeting was told that it would be taken care of by RAF attacks on the airbase and, 'it was hoped', by naval bombardment.[5] Events would show this optimism to be misplaced.

Churchill had come to accept the vital importance of Trondheim, describing it in a letter to King George on 15 April as 'an even greater prize than Narvik'.[6] The dazzling success of the *Warspite* attack and the prospect of the imminent capture of Narvik encouraged Churchill to hope for a repeat performance at Trondheim. In his memoirs he claimed to be a somewhat reluctant convert.

Left to myself, I would have stuck to my first love, Narvik; but serving a loyal chief and friendly Cabinet, I now looked forward to this exciting enterprise to which so many staid and cautious Ministers had given their strong adherence, and which seemed to find much favour with the Naval Staff and indeed among all our experts. Such was the position on the 17th.[7]

In fact, Churchill quickly became the chief protagonist for a direct attack on Trondheim. As early as 13 April a signal had gone from the Admiralty to the CinC Home Fleet, Forbes, which, in Churchill's euphemistic words, 'raised with him in a positive manner the question of whether the Home Fleet should not force a passage'.[8] Pound was optimistic: 'The naval staff anticipated no difficulty in silencing the shore batteries at Trondheim.'[9]

Forbes's response to the Admiralty, however, was decidedly unenthusiastic:

Shore batteries could no doubt be destroyed or dominated by battleship in daylight [...] if she had high-explosive bombardment shells for main armament, but none in Home Fleet have. This, however, is only the minor part of the task. The main difficulties are (1) Surprise having been lost, to protect troopships from a heavy scale air attack for over 30 miles in narrow waters, and (2) then to carry out an opposed landing of which ample warning has been given, under continuous air attack. [...]For foregoing reasons, I do not consider operation feasible, unless you are prepared to face very heavy losses in troops and transports.[10]

Forbes's fear of air attack must have sounded oddly pessimistic to those who – like Churchill, Pound and Phillips – had not experienced it and had yet to recognise the way that air power had changed warfare. The early results of German air attack had not been dramatic and had lulled some into a false sense of security. The Military Coordination Committee on 15 April noted with satisfaction that 'German air attacks on our shipping had practically ceased ... their losses had no doubt been considerable.'[11] Two days later, Ironside was remarking on 'enemy bombing all along the Norwegian coast, but most ineffective. At Harstad ... nine planes bombed for five hours and hit no ship or even the town. No casualties. ... At Lillesjona and Namsos some two hours with five planes on [one ship] without result.'[12] The perspective of those who had been on the receiving end of the Luftwaffe's attention was somewhat different. As Admiral Whitworth noted, on 9 April one ship, *HMS Gurkha* had been sunk, two others had had been damaged by near misses and, despite orders to conserve anti-aircraft ammunition, 40 per cent of heavy AA ammunition stocks had been expended in a single day.[13] Elsewhere, another battleship (*Rodney*) had had a lucky escape – hit by a large bomb which failed to explode and a further three ships were damaged by near misses. Faced with this scale of threat, the prospect of continued operations was clearly alarming. Forbes had pulled his ships away from the Norwegian coast (in doing so, forfeiting the opportunity of their destroying the German ships returning home)[14] and concluded that his surface fleet would have to confine its activity to the northern area.[15]

The Admiralty's reply addressed Forbes's stated concerns: the Fleet would be provided with high-explosive shells; the airfields at Stavanger and Trondheim would be bombed and, in the case of Stavanger, also bombarded from the sea, immediately before the attack; and the operation would not take place for seven days, which would be devoted to careful preparation. The message ended in characteristic Churchillian style, 'Pray, therefore, please reconsider this important project further.'[16] Forbes reiterated his concern about air attack, in particular his concern about long-range German bombers from airbases further afield, but got on with planning the operation.[17]

The Joint Planners, as requested, had considered the proposal and reported back on 15 April. Their findings, however, were resolutely opposed to the scheme:

To capture the port and aerodrome of Trondheim a full scale combined operation involving an opposed landing would be necessary:

a) Troops would have to be properly trained and equipped.
b) Most careful detailed planning by commanders and staffs would be required.
c) Even if the long delay involved were accepted, the heavy scale of air attack would still have to be faced.
d) Such an operation would not afford the immediate support which the Norwegians require.
e) This operation could not possibly be carried out by Force 'Maurice'. That force is not big enough nor is it at present organised for an opposed landing.[18]

Their conclusion was succinct. 'A direct attack upon Trondheim would be costly in execution and would be unlikely to result in the capture of Trondheim.'[19]

These findings were most unwelcome to the Chiefs of Staff when they considered the report that evening. They set out their position at the start: '[I]t was essential on political, as well as military, grounds, to recapture this port from the Germans.' The Chiefs then received a prophetic warning about the potential impact of air power on the operation.

Air Commodore Slessor drew attention to the risks involved from air attack in relation to the importance of the object. While realising the political necessity for an attempt on Trondheim he considered that this port could not subsequently be used to maintain large forces to keep Norway in the war for long, or to supply Sweden. He felt that the Chiefs of staff should be aware of the scale of air attack to which Trondheim is liable, in order that they could assess the risks involved, especially to capital ships and destroyers, in a combined operation in the Trondheim Fiord. Previously, before the Germans had seized Stavanger and Denmark, it had been assessed that an average of 100 tons a day, on a conservative estimate, could be directed against Trondheim. This could now be very much increased.[20]

This argument did not, however, persuade the CIGS. His response to Slessor is revealing about his perception of strategy and the Chiefs' role in it: not as that of ensuring that the ends, ways and means were in balance, but purely as the implementers of policy. 'I told him that he had argued the wrong way', Ironside recorded in his diary. 'We were considering how to attack it, not whether we should or not. That politically we had been ordered to attack it and that it was the only way to save Norway.' Ironside's subsequent comments also reveal his domination of the other Chiefs: 'We went on to make the plan: two landings north and south and a dash up the fiord with a battleship as at Narvik. ... I was pretty forceful in what I said and I forced the committee to continue planning. We are now at a critical moment of the war from a morale point of view and we must expect to suffer casualties.'[21]

The Chiefs rejected the Joint Planners' advice and ordered that preparations for a direct attack upon Trondheim should be put in hand forthwith. As to Slessor's warning, 'Experience would show', they said, dismissively and with apparent disregard for the consequences, 'whether or not substantial forces could be maintained in the face of air attack.'[22]

The atmosphere at meetings of the Military Coordination Committee had become strained and acrimonious under Churchill's chairmanship – and a long way from his claim in his memoirs that '[l]oyalty and goodwill were forthcoming from all concerned.' [23] On 14 April Ironside recorded,

[o]ne of the fallacies that Winston seems to have got into his head is that we can make improvised decisions to carry on the war by meeting at 5 p.m. each day. It is regardless of the enemy and decisions which have to be made at all hours of the day as the enemy reacts. The S[ecretary] of S[tate] is going to see the Prime Minister to-day to tell him that the war cannot be run by the Staffs sitting round a table arguing. We cannot have a man trying to supervise all military arrangements as if he were a company commander running a small operation to cross a bridge. How I have kept my temper do far I don't know.[24]

Ismay believed that the situation could erupt. At the Chiefs' meeting on 16 April he 'cleared the room ... and implored the Chiefs of Staff to exercise the most rigid self-control over themselves and at all costs to keep their tempers. He told them that, if there was a row at the meeting, he was afraid of a first-class political crisis.'[25] Churchill, sensing trouble, had already moved to invite the Prime Minister to chair future important meetings of the Military Coordination Committee, so the latter was in the chair that morning when the Chiefs reported–back on plans for the direct attack on Trondheim – what was to become known as Operation Hammer.[26]

In accordance with the discussion the previous evening, the report was presented, not as an appreciation of the feasibility or wisdom of conducting the operation, but as a plan. There was, thus, no consideration of strategy – of whether the ways and means were adequate to achieve the goal, and whether its achievement would lead to a strategic objective. The Prime Minister certainly did not question this. As Ironside outlined the plan, Chamberlain's only concern was 'the need for carrying out the main operation on Trondheim with the least possible delay'. Consideration of risk gave way to wishful thinking, and it seemed to be infectious. Churchill described Hammer as 'a hazardous and, if it was successful . . . a brilliant operation'. Ironside said that the force at Namsos 'should' be ready to begin active operations on 21 April, omitting any concerns about the capability of an unsupported, semi-trained Territorial Brigade to engage in a manoeuvre battle against the Germans. He 'hoped' to have available for the operation two battalions of Guards [from Narvik] and two of the French Foreign Legion. When information arrived at the meeting that the latter would not be available before 25 April, Ironside said that he would 'do his best' to expedite their arrival. When he said that he 'thought' the Regular Brigade (15th Infantry Brigade from the BEF) – which the meeting members had agreed was essential for the operation – 'could' be made available in under a week, Chamberlain intervened to say that planning should proceed on the assumption that it 'would' be available. Pound, the only other person to speak at the meeting, also succumbed to the mood. On the key issue of the air threat to the operation, he merely said that the Germans would 'probably' not obtain more than two hours warning that the landing was about to take place, and it therefore 'seemed unlikely' that they could reach the area before the troops had landed. Awkward subjects, such as whether there would be sufficient time to organise and prepare an amphibious operation and what the likely strength and capability of the German forces at Trondheim might be when it took place, were simply not mentioned.[27] It was as if to do so would have been in bad taste.

Hardly had the plan been ratified by the War Cabinet the next day than its impracticalities started to surface. At a meeting of the Chiefs of Staff, attended by the nominated commander for Operation Hammer, Major General Hotblack, it was uncertain how the troops would be landed; Hotblack wanted eight landing craft for the task. It was accepted that the single battery of anti-aircraft guns allocated would be totally inadequate and that further batteries would have to be withdrawn from the BEF and from Great Britain. Some of the warships would have to remain behind to provide artillery support for the troops on land. And it was recognised that the policy which prevented bombardment of towns would need to be changed. Outside the meeting it was also recognised that extra forces would be required, and approaches were hastily made to the Canadians to provide two of their battalions, based in Britain.[28] The planning was further affected by a series of misfortunes. That evening Hotblack was found unconscious, having suffered a stroke. The operation was postponed. A successor, Brigadier Berney-Ficklin, was hastily appointed, briefed and despatched with his staff to Scapa, but his aircraft crashed on landing, seriously injuring all occupants. The operation was again postponed, while the third (and final) commander, Major General Paget, was nominated and briefed.

Meanwhile, in the Air Ministry, Slessor was working assiduously to undermine the plan. Writing on 17 April to Air Marshal Joubert de la Ferté, who had been put in charge of a special planning staff at the Admiralty for the assault on Trondheim, he told him that 'regarded as a military operation in a purely professional sense, this operation is entirely fantastic' and likely to fail, so,

> for pity's sake keep your stakes as low as you can. Don't push in three battleships if you can do with one; and don't push in more destroyers or troopships than you can possibly avoid – especially the former. Don't let's kid ourselves that the capture of Trondheim is going to win this war. And – let us remember – that after Trondheim we've got to go on fighting a long war – possibly with Italy as an enemy.[29]

Further serious doubts about the plan's feasibility were shortly to follow. On 18 April reports came in about the cruiser *HMS Suffolk* which had carried out a bombardment of Stavanger airbase the previous day. Heading back out to sea, *Suffolk* had been caught by the Luftwaffe and, without the expected fighter escort,[30] had been subjected to some seven hours of bombing. Her eight four-inch anti-aircraft guns caused no hits on her attackers, and, worryingly, even after the appearance of Fleet Air Arm fighters, the attacks continued unabated, with a number of near misses so close that they caused further damage. She barely escaped, limping back to Scapa where she arrived with her quarterdeck awash, thirty-two of her crew dead and thirty-eight wounded.[31] One historian later observed, it was 'the first visible evidence to the fleet that a new era had dawned in naval operations'.[32] However, the fact that, despite thirty-three separate attacks over seven hours, mostly against a crippled ship, the Luftwaffe had failed to sink her seemed to be overlooked. The

Admiralty had already been concerned by the impact of the Luftwaffe on the landings at Namsos, in particular, the number of near misses and the alarming rate at which anti-aircraft ammunition was being expended. With practically every available warship being committed to Operation Hammer, little imagination was required as to the possible outcome in the confined waters of the Trondheim Fiord. Forbes was now informed that the Royal Navy's remaining stock of anti-aircraft ammunition was no more than 7,000 rounds, information that he considered so sensitive to morale that he did not pass it on.[33] With Forbes still 'bitterly opposing the operation',[34] and others in the Admiralty having severe doubts,[35] Pound began to get cold feet.

Although there is a suggestion that he met with Ironside that evening and persuaded him that Hammer should be cancelled,[36] Ironside makes no mention of it in his diary, noting only a dinner with Churchill, discussing Narvik.[37] Pound formally raised the Admiralty's concerns the following day (19 April) at a hastily convened meeting of the Chiefs of Staff.[38] Ironside did not attend – he appears to have been busy with tactical-level affairs concerning the ongoing deployments; Massy went in his place. Churchill, unusually, was also present for part of the time. Pound set out a radical alternative plan. Based on the success of the landings at Namsos and Åndalsnes (which had been preferred over nearby Ålesund), he proposed that, in place of a direct amphibious assault, Trondheim should be 'invested' (surrounded and besieged) by a pincer movement of land forces from these ports. On paper, this must have looked quite promising: there would be almost 13,000 Allied troops ashore to the north and south of Trondheim and only an estimated 3,000 German troops. The new plan, they concluded, 'should be perfectly possible' and avoided 'an operation which had always been recognised as of a very hazardous nature'. It was acknowledged that this might mean a delay in the capture of Trondheim, but it provided, so it was said, 'a greater certainty of success'.[39] In his memoirs, Churchill claimed, 'When I became aware of this right-about-turn I was indignant, and questioned searchingly the officers concerned. It was soon plain to me that all professional opinion was now adverse to the operation which only a few days before it had spontaneously espoused.'[40] It is, however, inconceivable that Pound would have proposed this change without first consulting Churchill. And it was far from true that 'all professional opinion' was adverse to the operation; the CIGS's view had not been sought, nor had the staffs been consulted about the feasibility of the new plan. According to Chamberlain, Churchill convened the meeting (it was held, most unusually, at the Admiralty) and 'O. Stanley ... declared to me that W. bullied the staff into agreement with a course which they disapproved.'[41] Furthermore, the Chiefs' conclusions that 'subject to the approval of the War Cabinet the proposed alterations in the plans for the capture of Trondheim should be accepted' contained a most important caveat: 'provided the scale of air attack could be competed with'.[42] This inconvenient caveat was quickly forgotten. By the end of the afternoon, Churchill, acting with precipitate speed, and perhaps not unmindful of Gallipoli, had obtained an immediate decision from the Prime Minister to cancel Hammer.[43]

Only now were the staffs involved, and serious doubts about the new plan emerged. First were concerns about the capacity of the port of Namsos. A report had been received from one of the destroyer captains earlier that week: 'Facilities for landing and accommodating large numbers of troops at Namsos very inadequate. Consider it impossible to deal with more than one transport at a time and consider that there is a grave risk to town and transport unless command of air is certain.'[44] The Military Operations staff were most unhappy about the new proposal – 'palpable nonsense' was how Dewing later described it.[45] Their appreciation raised a number of serious concerns. The first concern was the size of the enemy force in the Trondheim area: 'say, 3,000 to 5,000, liable to be reinforced by air up to a total of say, 8,000'. The second concern was the large Allied force needed to combat the expected German link-up operation from Oslo: '[A]s the Germans advance, we may well need a division'. The next concern was the anticipated increase in air attack. Last , they were concerned about the warnings that the facilities for the development of a base at both Namsos and Åndalsnes were 'meagre in the extreme', limiting the force size which could be maintained, and that ships approaching these ports would be vulnerable to air attack: '[I]t follows that the hasty despatch of troops through these bases entails risk of administrative breakdown.' The appreciation concluded:

It is therefore clear that for some weeks, it would be out of the question to provide any appreciable force to advance on Trondheim from the south. It is probably true that our pincer movement could not be developed within a month. The capture of Trondheim could therefore only be effective before this date by an advance from Namsos.[46]

At ten o'clock that night Ironside attended the Military Coordination Committee meeting and gave a summary of the General Staff appreciation. It must either have been a much watered-down version or presented unconvincingly, because while the Committee acknowledged that there was a possibility of the Namsos force meeting difficulties, 'it was felt that these would not be insuperable, and that there was no reason to feel undue anxiety regarding the position of the troops both in the course of disembarkation and subsequent land operations.' Nor did any of the Chiefs raise the vital caveat that they had agreed, 'provided the scale of air attack could be competed with'. Churchill was hardly likely to go back to Chamberlain saying he had been overhasty and made a mistake. The Committee duly gave formal endorsement to the cancellation.[47] Fatigue had finally caught up with the Chiefs. Slessor recalled, 'I've never seen three men more exhausted and therefore less fit to consider objectively a military problem on which so much depended. Ironside could hardly keep awake.'[48] They were, said Slessor, 'exhausted men, ready to succumb to Winston's pressure'. [49]

Some of the major practical challenges to the new plan were raised at the War Cabinet the next morning (20 April), not by the CIGS, but by his minister who had clearly picked up on the comments of the War Office staff. Stanley warned of the risks of putting large forces through the small ports of Namsos and Åndalsnes, commenting that '[t]he new plan was indeed little less hazardous than that of a direct attack on Trondheim.' The description of a pincer movement was, he suggested, something of an illusion: the southern force would be preoccupied with the Germans advancing northwards, and it might well be a month before any serious move could be made against Trondheim from the south. Having agreed to the plan the previous evening, Ironside now found himself in a difficult position, and his advice was self-contradictory. He said that 'the troops at Dombas had no guns or transport and were therefore not in any condition to fight a serious action', but that '[t]hey should, however, be able to hold a defensive position.' No one chose to question why a defensive position might not qualify as a serious action. Churchill intervened to say that Massy, the newly appointed CinC of the Central Norway land operation, was signed up to the plan and had said that as far as Hammer was concerned, 'the stake was disproportionate to the result, particularly as the latter could be obtained by other methods.'[50] This was very much paraphrasing Massy, but the War Cabinet was persuaded: Operation Hammer was abandoned.

Would it have succeeded?

Churchill certainly thought so, both at the time and in retrospect. 'On the knowledge that we had in the middle of April,' he wrote, 'I remain of the opinion that having gone so far, we ought to have persisted in carrying out Operation Hammer.' He blamed himself for listening to his advisers.[51] But as with an assessment of the proposed coup de main landing at Narvik, it is necessary to look at the enemy position.

The force that landed at Trondheim in the early hours of 9 April was the 138th Mountain Regiment, from Dietl's 3rd Mountain Division. It consisted of three slightly under-strength battalions, with two companies of naval coastal artillery, a troop of mountain artillery and a company of engineers – a total of about 1,700 men.[52] They took over the town while it slept, and by the following day, the forts at the entrance to the fiord, the main supply depot (including twenty-eight artillery pieces) and the airfield at Vaernes, twenty miles to the east, were all in German hands.[53] The task was eased by the Norwegian divisional commander, Major General Jacob Laurantzon, who left the city and 'adopted a rather passive attitude towards the German invasion'.[54] However, the Germans were worried about the naval position and their supplies. The warships which had brought the garrison were damaged and their fuel situation critical;[55] of scarcely less concern, only one of the stores ships had made it.[56] They wasted no time in putting things right. With the help of local civilians, 'drawn by good money, cigarettes and alcohol',[57] work was immediately started to improve the surface of the airfield, and within a few days it was operational.[58] About half of the force was retained in or near the town, ready for the expected British seaborne counter-attack, but companies were also deployed up the railway line to the Swedish border, to the north to keep the Norwegian military at arm's length and as a guard force to the south. Reinforcements arrived steadily by sea and air. By 13 April, the garrison had been increased by two troops of anti-aircraft guns, a troop of medium artillery and seven dive bombers based at Vaernes. In the next few days, around 120 tons of ammunition were delivered by submarine.[59] On 14 April, a further battalion of infantry (less one company) arrived by air and was complete by 18 April. Two days later, another battalion and a further troop of mountain artillery arrived, accompanied by Major General Kurt Woytasch, commander of 181st Infantry Division from which the troops – recently raised, apart from the Gebirgsjäger – came. By 21 April, the German force in the Trondheim area comprised five-and-a-half battalions of infantry, elements of two batteries of mountain artillery and a company of engineers. This totalled around 5,000 men, just under half of which (about two battalions) was guarding the town, airfield and entrances to the fiord.[60]

British estimates of the German strength at Trondheim on 11 April were of a force of around 3,000,[61] corroborated by Norwegian reports on 14 April.[62] Two days later it was believed that Vaernes was defended by anti-aircraft guns, with a number of bombers on the ground.[63] On 21 April, significant reinforcements, including artillery, were noted,[64] and the estimated strength for the Trondheim area was put at 6,000 'of which

2,000 – 2,500 are probably concentrated for defence of the town itself.'[65] British estimates were, therefore, on the high side throughout.

The German perception was that Trondheim was not nearly as secure as the British imagined. Keitel wrote to Falkenhorst on 23 April, 'The Führer's one great pressing anxiety is the situation at Trondheim', detailing the landings at Namsos and Åndalsnes as particular concerns and urging reinforcement by air.[66] Two days previously, Hitler had ordered 2nd Mountain Division to Norway and initiated plans for it to be reinforced by 1st Mountain Division. On 22 April Raeder succeeded in talking Hitler out of a desperate measure to send a division to Trondheim in two ocean liners.[67]

For the British, Trondheim was a less challenging objective for an amphibious landing than Narvik. Unlike Narvik, the terrain and climate did not overwhelmingly favour the defender. With comparatively little snow at sea level, there was no need to land at the town itself. There were a number of possible landing places nearby. There was also the potential threat to the defenders from Allied landings to the north and south, with support from two aircraft carriers. Furthermore, the fiord forts were far from formidable[68] and were thought vulnerable to land attack (although their defences had actually been somewhat strengthened).

The prospects for a direct attack somewhere in the Trondheim fiord were, therefore, not nearly as daunting as at Narvik. Indeed, the official historian ventured the opinion that 'it is difficult to resist the conclusion that sufficient promptness of action, even with relatively small forces, could have won back the port'.[69] Others also believed it eminently achievable. Notable among them was 67-year-old Admiral of the Fleet Sir Roger Keyes, champion of forcing the Dardanelles in 1915 and hero of the daring raid on Zeebrugge in 1918, now a Member of Parliament. He argued the case vociferously and pressed Churchill to allow him to command the attack, 'reminding me', wrote Churchill, tellingly, 'of the Dardanelles and how easily the straits could have been forced if we had not been stopped by timid obstructionists'.[70]

The opportunity for a direct assault at Trondheim was, however, fleeting. A good rule of thumb – and one that holds good in this case – is that attackers are at their most vulnerable to counter-attack when they are still reorganising on their objective. Had the Chiefs of Staff pressed their initial belief that Trondheim, not Narvik, should be the point of main effort, and had all resources – British and French – been devoted to securing it, there might have been some chance of success, even with a force untrained in amphibious operations. But thereafter that chance faded rapidly. Indeed, a retrospective German assessment concluded that 'a direct attack on Trondheim would only have been possible in the first days of the German operations'.[71] By the time that Hammer was approved on 16 April, it was accepted, quite reasonably, that a ten-day delay would be required before the two Regular brigades from the BEF could be moved and prepared for the task against a prepared defence.[72] By that time, the German garrison, unless heavily pressed from north and south, would have been much better placed to resist an attack, particularly with German air superiority, to which the British fleet in the confined waters of the fiord would have been highly vulnerable. With such a high proportion of capital warships involved – for example, forty-five out of the Fleet's available sixty-three destroyers were earmarked for the operation – the stakes were high.[73] Some may have speculated that just as it was said that Admiral Jellicoe at Jutland could have lost the war in an afternoon, so Admiral Forbes at Trondheim could come uncomfortably close to doing the same thing. Forbes, himself, remained sceptical of success, believing that the operation would have been 'a gamble which might have succeeded, but probably would not'.[74]

Whatever the chances of Hammer's success, the focus of the decision makers on the chances of a successful battle missed the real strategic point. As the Joint Planners had emphasised all along, the important issue was not the capture of the town, but whether it could be held and used to achieve campaign objectives at acceptable cost in resources and casualties. And here the official historian was rightly unequivocal: '[I]t seems quite clear that if we had captured Trondheim we could not have held on to it indefinitely.'[75] Ismay put it more graphically: '[W]e should have been bled white in trying to maintain ourselves there.'[76] At the time, though, such judgments were far less clear.

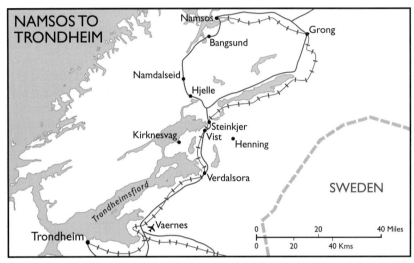

Map 14.1 Namsos to Trondheim

A lot was now riding on the operation at Namsos – Operation Maurice. On 19 April Churchill had reported to the War Cabinet that the force had landed successfully and had already made good progress inland;[1] indeed, the situation map would have shown them at a point almost halfway to Trondheim. The next day he reported that the first convoy carrying the Chasseurs Alpins had arrived and completed disembarkation, and that the second convoy was ready to sail.[2] The Military Coordination Committee had concluded that the difficulties the force might meet 'would not be insuperable, and that there was no reason to feel undue anxiety regarding the position of the troops both in the course of disembarkation and subsequent land operations'.[3] The southern force at Åndalsnes might take some time before it could turn its attention

northwards towards Trondheim, but the force at Namsos had no such
distraction and was due to be reinforced by a further demi-brigade of
Chasseurs Alpins. The Chiefs appeared to be reinforcing success after
the 'highly successful' landing at Namsos.[4] Ironside was confident, or at
least optimistic, writing in his diary, 'We ought to get a definite success
here with luck.'[5] On paper, optimism seemed well justified. The reality
was somewhat different.

146 Brigade consisted of three Territorial battalions – the 1st/4th
Battalion of the Lincolnshire Regiment, the 1st/4th Battalion of the
Kings Own Yorkshire Light Infantry and the Hallamshire Battalion of
the York and Lancaster Regiment. Like those of 24 Brigade, the battalions had been stood to for operations in Scandinavia twice before: in
early January (only to be stood down a week later) and in early February
(only to be stood down after the Finnish surrender in mid-March). On
30 March they received their third set of mobilisation orders, and the
following day their commander, Brigadier Charles Phillips, was briefed at
the War Office. The brigade's destination would be similar to that for
which it had been destined before 12 March, namely, Trondheim and
Bergen as part of Force Stratford. However, there followed a bewildering
sequence of 'order, counter-order and disorder'. On 6 April the battalions moved by rail to Scotland to embark – the Hallams at Gourock, on
the Clyde, the remainder of the brigade at Rosyth. On 8 April, those who
had embarked at Rosyth were hastily disembarked (as the Fleet proceeded to sea), although much of their equipment had remained on
board. The following day they were re-embarked on other ships and told
that they would now be going to Narvik as part of Force Avonmouth.

On 14 April, as their convoy headed north, 146 Brigade's ships were
diverted to Namsos. Unbeknown to the British, they were expected: two
days earlier, Kriegsmarine B-Dienst had intercepted a Royal Navy message ordering a reconnaissance of the port with a view to a landing there.[6]
A party of Royal Marines and sailors who arrived to secure the port were
duly visited by the Luftwaffe on 15 April.[7] 146 Brigade was landed over
the following two nights. As the troopships carrying them approached the
area, the troops were hastily transferred – some in darkness, others under
air attack – to destroyers to take them into Namsos. Some were transferred more than once. There was insufficient time to unload all their
stores, and 170 tons were left in the hold of one ship.[8] Inevitably, in the
chaotic circumstances, some of their weapons, ammunition and equipment were also mislaid. Indeed, 'transferring ship' is a misleadingly
orderly title for what was, under the circumstances, a far from orderly
activity: 'Two chutes were lowered to the deck of the destroyer and down
them hurtled kitbags, ammunition boxes, food, and all the paraphernalia

of the battalion. Some kit fell into the sea, some got left on the *Empress of Australia* in the blackout, and some more was left on the destroyers.'[9] Unloading at the Namsos quay was much the same: 'The many kit bags were simply thrown over the ship's side and it was not possible to keep them sorted by battalions much less by companies. In addition, the quay was already littered with other units' equipment.[10]

The reality was, therefore, a long way from the neat situation report being given in London that '[a]ll stores of Brigadier Phillips brigade have been unloaded.'[11] Moreover, on arrival at Namsos they discovered that the brigade commander and his chief of staff, who were travelling in a different ship, had been taken on to Narvik – as had the brigade's transport.[12] If the soldiers were uneasy that they were on an operation, the planning of which fell someway short of perfection, they had good reason to be. Their morale would, however, have been lifted by the general who was there to meet them.

Major General Adrian Carton de Wiart was a legendary fighting soldier. One-armed, one-eyed and 'outrageously brave',[13] he had been wounded eight times as a result of service in the Boer War, Somaliland and the First World War and had won the Victoria Cross in temporary command of a brigade at the Battle of the Somme. 'With his empty sleeve and black eye patch he looked like an elegant pirate'[14] and was, indeed, the inspiration for Evelyn Waugh's character Brigadier Ritchie-Hook in the *Sword of Honour* trilogy.[15] After the First World War, Carton de Wiart had gone to live in Poland, indulging his passion for duck shooting in the Pripet Marshes. When Poland was invaded, he was appointed as head of the British Military Mission to the Polish government and, on the fall of Poland, returned to Britain where he was given command of a Territorial Division. On 12 April he was suddenly summoned to the War Office and given his orders as commander of Mauriceforce. Three days later, accompanied by only one staff officer, he was flown to Namsos in a flying boat which was machine gunned from the air on landing, seriously wounding the staff officer who was evacuated home. After a chance meeting with two enterprising young captains – the author, Peter Fleming, and the polar explorer, Martin Lindsay, both members of Military Intelligence (Research), a clandestine branch within the War Office[16] – the general, in his own words, 'there and then appropriated them' as his staff, 'and a better pair never existed'.[17]

All of this is, of course, wildly romantic, but it glosses over the fact that command and control of Mauriceforce were completely inadequate. The commander had no proper staff to plan and execute his orders, almost no usable radio communications, or the ability to find collect, analyse and disseminate intelligence or to coordinate and synchronise the activity of

Figure 14.1 Major General Adrian Carton de Wiart at Namsos
(Imperial War Museums)

his formations, let alone organise logistics or liaise with the Norwegians.[18] He had never even met his brigade and battalion commanders. He could, and did, provide an inspiring example, standing out in the open, nonchalantly smoking his pipe as bombs burst around him,[19] but there is a limit to which courage and charisma can substitute for proper command and control of a military formation in war.

Carton de Wiart had been told that he was to be the commander of all Allied forces which were being despatched to central Norway and that his command would be of considerable size. Joining 146 Brigade within a week would be the other two brigades of 49 Division – 147 and 148

Brigades – artillery and support troops, and a démi-brigade of Chasseurs Alpins. 'A second landing should be carried out about Trondheim', he was told, although it was unclear who would be responsible for this.[20] The immediate challenges facing him were considerable. Namsos may have looked a good prospect to those sitting in London, but reality was different. First, it was immediately evident that this small timber port was a most unsuitable point of entry and base for a military force; its facilities were, just as the Military Operations staff had told Ironside, 'meagre in the extreme'. Not only was the harbour too small for the transport ships, and equipped with only one stone quay and two wooden wharves, but also the town was small, with a population of less than 4,000 and very limited support infrastructure or provisions. Secondly – a point again made by the staff – its approaches were particularly vulnerable to air attack, and the town, like most coastal settlements in Norway, consisted largely of equally vulnerable wooden buildings. Thirdly, with only about three hours of darkness each night, German air superiority became even more of a threat and greatly limited the time available to disembark stores and troops. Added to this, the snow was lying between two and four feet deep, but deeper in drifts and on high ground, and his troops had no snowshoes, let alone skis.[21]

Also of concern to Carton de Wiart was the state of his force. Under the original plan for Stratford, prior to 12 March, 146 Brigade was a garrison force, not a manoeuvre formation. It was thus not structured, trained or qualified for the role that now confronted it. An entirely Territorial formation, its troops' basic training was far from complete. As the general shrewdly observed, very few of them 'really knew the Bren [gun]',[22] and 'it was soon evident that the officers had little experience in handling men.'[23] In addition, apart from a section of Royal Engineers, the force consisted solely of infantry, with no artillery or air defence. The maps were of the Narvik area. The battalions had no mortars, signalling equipment or transport and, as we have seen, had lost much of their equipment in transit. But, perversely, they were grossly overburdened by the clothing with which they had been issued. Each man had three kitbags full, including special Arctic clothing such as a fur coat, but, as Carton de Wiart observed, 'if they wore all these things they were scarcely able to move at all, and looked like paralysed bears.'[24]

The general received further instructions from the CIGS, but these were vague: the plan was clearly still being formed. 'Capture of Trondheim considered essential', it read, 'Propose you should exploit from Namsos, while force from Åndalsnes will also threaten Trondheim in conjunction with Norwegian forces. Meanwhile, combined operation for direct attack on Trondheim will be developed to take advantage of your pressure.'[25] As a result of all that he had seen and heard, Carton de Wiart was uneasy: 'I felt in my bones that the campaign was unlikely to be either long or successful.'[26]

The British general now met with the Norwegian divisional commander, Major General Laurantzon, but seems to have been unimpressed, not just by Laurantzon, who was soon after to be 'invalided out', but also with the Norwegian military capability. At least in part, this was probably due to Carton de Wiart's preconceptions about the Norwegian Army. Like Mackesy and many other British commanders, he seems to have been briefed, or just taken the view, that the Norwegian military – like most foreigners – were generally ineffective, poorly trained, unreliable and incapable of keeping a secret, and, in the case of the Norwegians, actively infiltrated by Quislings – the latter, a belief fuelled by contemporary newspaper reports based on little evidence from an American journalist in Oslo.[27] The conclusion seems to have been that it was better to fight a British campaign with some artisan Norwegian support, rather than a joint campaign. Not only was the caricature inaccurate but also the conclusion was to cost the British dear, not least because local knowledge was at a premium. The disparaging view of the Norwegian military was reinforced when Brigadier Phillips, happily reunited with his brigade, met with the Norwegian Army's local brigade commander, Colonel Getz, whom, Phillips reported, described his own troops as 'inexperienced militia' and very short of ammunition (of particular concern since Norwegian and British weapons were of different calibres).[28] Getz, who proved to be a tough and resourceful commander, offered to provide whatever help the British wanted, but the British seemed to have been happy with ski detachments and lorries, rather than joint planning and combined operations. The British did not, for example, inform their allies of the overall plan. 'The Norwegians are hopeless,' Carton de Wiart reported to the CIGS. '[T]hey promise anything you like but there the matter ends.'[29] Even in retrospect, Carton de Wiart's view was unchanged. In his final report he said that he lacked confidence in them and that they were 'of little fighting value, continually sending erroneous reports and wild rumours'.[30] His view was not shared by some who had actually witnessed the Norwegian soldiers in combat. The British liaison officer with Getz's brigade, Lieutenant Sneddon, reported that 'morale has been under-rated. They are very keen. Some of the wilder elements have to be held back. They have undoubtedly got guts ... they are very bitter against the Germans.'[31] In passing, the fact that Carton de Wiart's liaison officer was a mere lieutenant says much about the perceived importance of the Norwegian military.

To be ready to synchronise his attack with the Navy's move on the fiord, Carton de Wiart knew he needed to be poised close to Trondheim.

He therefore wasted no time in sending troops south in Norwegian trucks and by rail, although in the haste, at least one battalion was separated from its kitbags and stores.[32] By the afternoon of 17 April, they had reached Steinkjer, and two days later, leading elements were seventeen miles further south at the head of the Trondheim Fiord and only sixty miles from the town itself. Their advance had been unopposed. Further instructions from London informed Carton de Wiart of the new plan for Operation Hammer and about the further landing south of Trondheim at Åndalsnes – Operation Sickle. The campaign looked to be taking shape, particularly with the imminent arrival of the elite troops, the Chasseurs Alpins, 4,000 strong, trebling the size of Mauriceforce and providing it with the key ability to manoeuvre off-road.

The first echelon of the Chasseurs Alpins duly arrived that night, together with their brigade commander, Brigadier General Antoine Béthouart, and the divisional commander, Major General Gérard Audet. Like 146 Brigade, they had been diverted en route to Narvik, and the loading of their ships had also been 'a shambles'.[33] The troops disembarked hurriedly and were dispersed into the woods around the town, but there was no time to move from the quayside the stores that had been unloaded. These now stood out in the open for all to see. It did not take long for the price to be paid. Early the following morning (20 April), a Luftwaffe reconnaissance aircraft appeared punctually (as was to happen throughout the campaign), and at ten o'clock – ironically, almost the exact time that the War Cabinet was meeting in London to cancel Hammer and put its faith in Maurice and Sickle – the first German bombers arrived over Namsos. For the next four and a half hours, Carton de Wiart recorded, 'they had the time of their lives with no opposition whatsoever.'[34] The result was, literally, devastating. When the destroyer *Nubian* arrived that night, 'the whole place was a mass of flames from end to end'.[35] The wooden houses, railhead, rolling stock, and much of the wooden wharves and the superstructure of the quay were destroyed, along with the water and electricity supplies. Although casualties were not heavy, those killed included a number of key French HQ staff officers, and the wounded included General Audet.[36] That night, Carton de Wiart reported the destruction of Namsos to the War Office with a stark warning: 'At present impossible to land more men or material. ... I see little chance of carrying out decisive or indeed any operation unless enemy air activity is considerably restricted.'[37]

Carton de Wiart's plans were to be further frustrated. His key mobile troops, the Chasseurs Alpins were unable to move. 'I wanted the French troops to push on,' he recounted, 'but they felt they could not do so without their transport – and they had practically none at this stage.'[38]

Figure 14.2 British troops search the ruins of Namsos
(Getty Images)

Furthermore, when he suggested that their ski troops might move forward, it was found that, although they had their skis, they did not have the bindings. Events were to conspire against Carton de Wiart still further. It was found that the French troopship, *Ville d'Alger*, with the remainder of the Chasseurs Alpins and all their stores, was too big to berth at the quay. Although the majority of personnel and some light stores were landed, the ship left for Scapa with the heavy stores, including the anti-aircraft guns and all the transport, still on board. It was almost a week before they were landed at Namsos. The resulting absence from the front line of the Chasseurs Alpins was quickly to prove critical.

On 21 April Norwegian and British troops sixty miles to the south at Verdalsøra came under attack from the German forces from Trondheim. In the eleven days since the Germans had landed there, they had been considerably reinforced and now included the commander of 181 Infantry Division, Major General Kurt Woytasch. Far from remaining on the defensive, Woytasch initiated a rapid offensive to the north, using a mixed force of a battalion, two companies of mountain troops with artillery and air support. Colonel Getz had warned Phillips that, with the Trondheim Fiord thawing, there was a seaborne threat to the Allies (Churchill, too, claims to have warned 'the staffs' about this[39]). Phillips had made plans to guard against this threat, but too late. In the early hours of 21 April, in a bold amphibious manoeuvre up the Trondheim Fiord, Woytasch moved two companies of mountain troops by destroyer to Kirknesvag and a company of infantry by motor torpedo boat to Verdalsøra, landing behind the Allied front line.[40] Simultaneously, he moved a link-up force of a reinforced infantry company and an artillery troop by road and rail to Verdalsøra, taking the town, which was held by Norwegian dragoons, during the morning.[41] The result was considerable confusion, particularly as the British troops were spread out over about fifty miles and were operating in a largely uncoordinated way with Norwegian forces. The German leading elements quickly reached Vist, held by the Lincolns, but were not joined by their main force until evening.[42] During the day, the town of Steinkjer, where the brigade headquarters and administrative units were located, was subjected to heavy air attack, and by evening it was 'reduced to a flaming mass of ruins', its road bridge destroyed and railway bridge rendered useless.[43] To the south of Vist, the KOYLI who were spread out over about fifteen miles, now cut off from the remainder of the brigade, infiltrated by ski troops and uncertain of the situation to their north, withdrew on foot across country, half during the night and half the next day, to the village of Henning, five miles to the east of Vist. Without transport, any weapons or equipment that could not be carried had to be abandoned.[44]

The following day (22 April) the Lincoln's position at Vist came under severe pressure. According to Phillips, the position was being 'shelled from the land, from destroyers from the sea and machine gunned from the air'.[45] One company, under considerable pressure, was ordered to retire by the battalion second-in-command, the commander on the spot. This, said Phillips, 'caused a certain amount of confusion' – as, indeed, it would have done. Neighbouring companies would have been left exposed and, being without radios (and thus with their communication dependent on runners, who might or might not get through), could not be confident that a general retreat had not been ordered and that they were about to be isolated. Uncertain of the position of the KOYLI, the battalion second-in-command, contrary to instruction from his commanding officer, gave orders for the other companies to withdraw.[46] It was three hours before the order reached all the troops, and the withdrawal was far from coordinated. During the move back they were subjected to 'continual bombing and machine gunning from the air'.[47] The situation can be imagined from the words of the official historian: 'The commanding officer tried to organise a further stand halfway to Steinkjer, but "the withdrawal once commenced was impossible to check."'[48]

It was to take more than two days for the Lincolns and KOYLI to pass through the rear-guard position, held by the Hallams at Hjelle, fifteen miles north of Steinkjer. The Lincolns, split into company groups, made their way, mostly on foot; the KOYLI moved cross-country from Henning in single file, 'strung out over a couple of miles'.[49] With deep soft snow under a frozen crust, these forced marches over distances of about fifty miles were extremely arduous, and both battalions arrived at the new position at Namdalseid completely exhausted[50] and 'without any kit other than what they stood up in'.[51] They were in no fit state to resist an attack, but fortuitously for them, the Germans chose to halt their advance, apart from probing attacks north-eastward towards Grong. German progress there was slowed and then brought to a halt by a stout defence conducted by Norwegian ski troops. In his report to the CIGS, Carton de Wiart reflected, '[T]he German attack . . . was poor, but good enough to scatter the young Territorials. The guns from the destroyers started them off . . . their casualties are not heavy – their morale, however, is very shaken. I am putting the two battalions who suffered, in the back area where there is a lot of fatigue work to be done.'[52]

As early as the night of 21 April, Carton de Wiart had been pessimistic about the prospects for Operation Maurice and was already contemplating failure and withdrawal, telling the War Office that 'if you decide evacuation send ships not larger than 5,000 tons max, and fear it may take two nights to embark.'[53] Two days later, he was signalling to the War Office: 'May be no alternative to evacuation through Namsos or Bangsund.'[54] This was underlined later in the afternoon by a further signal: 'Phillips' brigade roughly handled by skiing troops, artillery and aircraft. Retiring on French bridgehead at Bangsund.'[55] Carton de Wiart was still expecting to be told at any moment the date for the main thrust, Operation Hammer. At least his force was providing a threat to Trondheim, even if the threat was somewhat less than the Germans might imagine. Due to an embarrassing oversight in the War Office, however, Carton de Wiart had not been informed that Hammer had already been cancelled.

Over the following few days, Carton de Wiart's position apparently improved in a number of ways, but none of them not quite as good as they looked on paper. On 24 April a stores ship disembarked ammunition, rations and vehicles, but the vehicles were without drivers.[56] On the same day aircraft carriers came within range for the first time, and on the next, Fleet Air Arm planes attacked Vaernes airbase at Trondheim, establishing local air superiority over Namsos.[57] But their presence could not be sustained.[58] On 27 and 28 April, ships arrived with the remainder of the brigade's transport (fifteen lorries), a Bofors (light anti-aircraft) battery, a Royal Marine light howitzer battery and the divisional staff.[59] But, typical of the campaign's mal-administration and hasty improvisation, the lorries had no chains, spare wheels or toolkits, the Bofors anti-aircraft guns came without their predictor sights or spare barrels, and the light howitzers arrived with untrained gunners and without ammunition.[60] In any case, it was all too late to make a difference.

Early on 28 April, Carton de Wiart received notification from Massy in London that evacuation of Mauriceforce had been decided in principle.[61] The following day he was told to send a detachment by sea to Mosjøen, ninety miles to the north, and to conduct a fighting withdrawal north from Namsos overland, but following a reconnaissance by Captain Fleming, he declared that the withdrawal could not be undertaken because the roads were impassable. Despite pressure from Massy, Carton de Wiart was not to be moved, nor was Audet, whose troops would be conducting the operation.[62] Carton de Wiart's disdain for the opinion of his Norwegian allies prevented him seeking their opinion; a pity as they would have told him that the route was far from impassable – as the Germans would shortly demonstrate. This error was to have far-reaching consequences and was to be neither forgotten nor forgiven by Massy in his official despatch.[63] Carton de Wiart's orders also instructed him not to inform the Norwegians, and he obeyed them to the letter.[64] It was not until 10:30 on the evening of 2 May, as the ships were loading, that he and Audet told Colonel Getz what was happening. The Norwegians had every reason to feel aggrieved. Getz saw no alternative but to surrender a few days later.

The final evacuation of Mauriceforce was completed in one night – a considerable feat – although attempts to maintain secrecy were spoilt by the Prime Minister's statement, broadcast on the afternoon of 2 May, announcing the completion of the evacuation at Åndalsnes.[65] The operation was aided by thick fog, but at 8:45 the following morning, the Luftwaffe found the ships at sea off Namsos and subjected them to continuous attack for seven hours.[66] Remarkably, only two ships (*HMS Afridi* and the French destroyer, *Bison*) were sunk. The human cost, however, was more than 250 lives.

After 22 April 146 Brigade was not involved in any further fighting in Norway. Its war had lasted one week from when it landed, or three days from the time it came under ground attack. It had ended in defeat and hasty withdrawal. Yet the brigade had suffered remarkably few casualties – a total of nineteen killed, forty-two wounded and ninety-six missing (almost all of whom were captured), out of a total strength of 2,000.[67] Indeed, in the fighting south of Vist only six men had been killed and nineteen wounded.[68] Its troops had not been involved in a prolonged battle, and it had been defeated by a much smaller force. How is this to be explained?

Quite simply, the British military had been outclassed in every way. First, 146 Brigade had been the victim of 'mission creep' – the process in which a mission is gradually and almost imperceptibly extended, ending up a long way from its original intent. Under the original Operation Stratford, the brigade's mission had been that of a static defensive force, bolstering indigenous forces, to deter and, if necessary face, attack – a role for which it was, in any case, inadequately trained. It was then given a more demanding mission – that of supporting a Regular Brigade in an attack at Narvik. Next its mission was to hold a port in an enemy occupied country, to be reinforced by Regular troops. It ended up as a manoeuvre brigade, a task for which it was utterly unprepared, even if it had had the necessary supporting arms and services – artillery, engineers, air defence and logistics – which it did not. The lack of this support was critical, particularly when facing some of the best troops in the German Army – the Gebirgsjäger of 138 Mountain Regiment – who had the benefit of all these things in addition to air superiority.

Second, the Allies had not worked together. The British had fought Maurice, not as a combined operation with the Norwegians but as one which held the Norwegians at arm's length, disdainful of what they could possibly contribute. Moreover, 146 Brigade fought without the support of the Chasseurs Alpins. Had the latter been able to fight alongside the brigade, the outcome might have been very different.

Third, the brigade had been caught spread-out in penny packets along the route towards Trondheim. This was not entirely the fault of Carton de Wiart and Phillips, whose task was to be poised for the imminent amphibious assault on the town. The War Office had failed to inform them that the assault had been cancelled.

Fourth, the primary cause of the decision to evacuate Mauriceforce was the inability to defend and protect Namsos from air attack. It was believed that key points could be guarded by land-based or ship-based 'point air defence' and thus that the guns of the Royal Navy's anti-aircraft cruisers and the Army's shore-based guns would protect Namsos. Not only were the numbers deployed insufficient but also the mountainous country rendered point air defence inadequate. The anti-aircraft sloop *HMS Bittern* and three armed trawlers were sunk. Another armed trawler, *HMS Arab*, recorded thirty-one air attacks on her in five days, her captain, Lieutenant Commander Richard Stannard, winning the Royal Navy's third Victoria Cross of the campaign. There was, however, no substitute for achieving at least local air parity, which the British achieved only rarely and briefly. For the rest of the time, the Luftwaffe ruled the skies above Namsos. In a period of less than three weeks, it launched 330 sorties against the port.[69]

Last, the sudden and violent bombardment by artillery and from the air, synchronised with fast and aggressive ground attack by troops able to move off-roads, and combined with the surprise seaborne outflanking man-oeuvre, had resulted in shock so severe that it had caused many of the defenders to retreat in confusion. The tactic had been seen in Poland and would shortly be seen again in France. Woytasch's attack had accomplished the immediate mission given to him by Hitler – to secure Steinkjer – but more importantly he had relieved the threat to Trondheim from the north by giving the Allies 'a bloody nose', keeping them at a safe distance and putting them on the defensive. The Luftwaffe would do the rest, by destroying the Allies' line of communications and base at Namsos. Woytasch's attack was greatly facilitated by a number of factors: It did not face the whole of Mauriceforce. The most capable troops were left sitting back in Namsos, and the British troops were, as we have seen, overfaced by the challenge: poorly organised, trained and equipped; deficient in artillery, air defence, transport and logistics; and unprepared for the attack.

None of this was inevitable, and, in large part, all of it can be attributed to bad planning, bad judgment and bad management by the Allies, particularly the British, and good planning, judgment and management by the Germans. Also involved, however, was a large element of what Clausewitz called friction:

Everything in war is simple, but the simplest thing is difficult. The difficulties accumulate and end by producing a kind of friction that is inconceivable unless one has experienced war. ... Countless minor incidents – the kind you can never really foresee – combine to lower the general level of performance, so that one always falls far short of the intended goal. ... Friction is the only concept that more or less corresponds to the factors that distinguish real war from war on paper.[70]

The British plan for Operation Maurice – and not just for Operation Maurice – paid insufficient attention to the existence of friction and to the scope in warfare for minor errors to compound and have major consequences, for example, the lack of ski bindings ('all for the want of a horse-shoe nail'[71]). British decision-makers had come to regard real war and war on paper as the same thing. It was only when battle was joined that this expensive error was exposed in such dramatic form, and only then that the price was paid.

The bill was about to be presented again.

15   Sickle

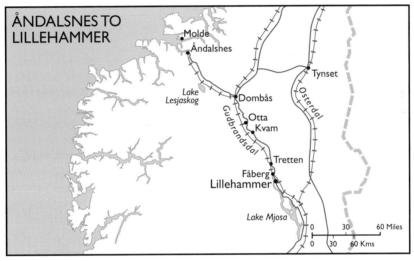

Map 15.1 Åndalsnes to Lillehammer

Like 24 Brigade and 146 Brigade, 148 Brigade had been stood to (for the third time) on 30 March for deployment the following week and, like them, had been involved in frenetic preparation. Their role was identical to that for which they had been warned for the operation before 12 March, as part of Force Stratford, to occupy Stavanger and secure or destroy the airfield. The brigade, a Territorial infantry formation, commanded by Brigadier Harold Morgan, consisted of just two, rather than the usual three, battalions: the 1st/5th Battalion of the Leicestershire Regiment and the 1st/8th Battalion of the Sherwood Foresters. They had been embarked on warships at Rosyth when, on 8 April, they, like 146 Brigade, were hastily disembarked. One officer recalled, 'The confusion and mixture of stores on the dock side is quite indescribable.'[1]

They were then told that they would be going to Namsos. Re-embarked on 14 April, they were ordered to trans-ship in the blackout and in a rush. Lieutenant Colonel Dudley Clarke, attached to the brigade headquarters, witnessed the scene.

The hatches were off now and the scene below decks had become a sort of Storeman's Inferno, with shadowy figures burrowing about in the semi-darkness of shaded lamps and torches. In the original haste to get off to a quick start goods of every kind had been packed into the holds in the order in which they arrived, with each following consignment piled on top. Now reserves of food and ammunition were mixed with unit equipment and skis for Norwegians; bicycles and sappers tools lay with medical panniers; while such things as long-range wireless equipment as often as not was split between two holds. There was never a chance of sorting all of this out in the dark and getting it into the right ships on time, so the plan was being adopted of skimming the top layers from every hold and loading them in turn into each warship as she came alongside.[2]

Among the critical items left behind were some of the brigade headquarters' radios, sights for the anti-aircraft guns, and all high explosive ammunition for the mortars.[3]

In the two-and-a-half days before they sailed – the delay was to prove critical – Brigadier Morgan received his fourth and fifth sets of orders, telling him he would be going to Åndalsnes, rather than Namsos, and that his role as Sickleforce would be to 'secure Dombås [a key road and rail junction, some sixty miles to the south-east] then operate northwards and take offensive action against Germans in Trondheim area'.[4] Like Mackesy and Carton de Wiart, he then received a personal instruction from the CIGS which served to confuse rather than elucidate. This instruction told him to 'prevent the Germans using railway to reinforce Trondheim', but also, 'You should make touch with Norwegian GHQ [General Headquarters], believed to be in area Lillehammer, and avoid isolating Norwegian forces operating towards Oslo.'[5] So, what was his priority? To operate northwards against the Germans in Trondheim or southwards in support of the Norwegians? Who could tell? Obviously, flexibility was at a premium. The two-battalion Territorial brigade, semi-trained and totally unprepared for all-arms manoeuvre operations, was like a village football team suddenly finding itself pitched into the premier league.

Åndalsnes, whither they were bound, had looked good on the War Cabinet map. Some 100 miles south-west of Trondheim, at the end of a long fiord, it provided a sheltered harbour and port, with railway access to the main Oslo-Trondheim line. But its practical suitability was even less than Namsos. As would have been obvious to Morgan on arrival, it was little more than a big village – a tourist destination in summer – totally inadequate as an entry point and base for a military expedition. Its docking facilities were limited to a concrete quay, 50 metres long of which only one side could be used for larger ships and a 20-metre-long wooden jetty with a single five-ton electric crane. Unloading several ships was, therefore, a long and painful process. In addition, with the thawing snow, the roads were effectively unusable by large trucks. The town's population was small, and its support facilities and infrastructure were very limited. It did not have much of anything to spare. This situation was a long way from what Morgan might have expected from reading the administrative instructions given to him at Rosyth.[6]

[T]he force will be entirely dependent on local authorities for transport, fresh supplies, accommodation, hospital and ambulance services ... no supplies of fuel and light are being provided except candles for emergency use. Supplies, including petrol for cookers, will be obtained locally ... no medical personnel other than the ADMS [senior medical staff officer] and SMO [senior medical officer] and personnel attached to battalions will accompany the force initially ... maps ... very old and mostly of pre-1900 date; they carry no grid and in most cases no contours [and were, of course, for Namsos] ... one infantry brigade signal set is provided to link up the three locations. Wireless and the civil telegraph system will be used.[7]

Most of the brigade – a total of around 1,000 men – arrived at Åndalsnes, some via the nearby port of Molde, on the evening of 18 April. The ports had been secured by a hastily assembled party of Royal Marines and sailors the previous night.[8] The remainder – two companies (effectively half the battalion) of Leicesters – together with the brigade's stores were in a later convoy which was not due for two days. With the standard organisation of four rifle companies per battalion, a brigade of three battalions would have a fighting strength of twelve rifle companies. 148 Brigade, without these two companies, had a fighting strength of half that. Moreover, the brigade had no artillery, high-explosive mortar ammunition, air defence,[9] explosives, radios or maps,[10] and much of its equipment, small arms ammunition, stores and vital winter clothing was missing.

Nevertheless, Morgan immediately ordered a company to go by rail to secure Dombås, 2,000 feet up at the head of the pass into the Gudbrandsdal valley. He accompanied them to ascertain the position for himself. Before doing so, he signalled the War Office with a quick situation report, emphasising, 'No, repeat no local provisions available.'[11] The situation around Dombås was far from secure – a company of German parachutists had landed in the area – but Morgan met with, and was briefed by, a Norwegian colonel on the local situation. That afternoon (19 April) he was contacted by the newly appointed British military attaché, Lieutenant Colonel Edward King-Salter, recently arrived from Finland. King-Salter had made contact with the Norwegian

Figure 15.1 Major General Otto Ruge

CinC, Major General Ruge, and told Morgan that the Norwegian Army was in urgent need of assistance and that, unless this was forthcoming immediately, the Army would abandon all further resistance. 'He further stated that the War Office had sanctioned 148 Brigade coming under command of the Commander-in-Chief, Norwegian Army.'[12] This was completely untrue, and he knew it. But for better or worse, King-Salter pressed the point, later recalling, 'These instructions [to Morgan] conflicted with his previous orders; but he agreed, eventually, that he must come south.'[13] Morgan signalled the War Office for further instructions[14] and accompanied King-Salter to the Norwegian HQ, at Øyer just north of Lillehammer, arriving in the middle of the night.

For the past week, Major General Ruge had been organising the hastily and only partially mobilised Norwegian Army as best he could. As King-Salter explained to the War Office, 'These troops are the equivalent of only a few battalions and batteries. They are not really organised in regular formations or even units and consist of varied elements many of which are completely untrained or very incompletely mobilized. In some improvised units the officers and non-commissioned officers were created on the spot.'[15] Furthermore, the situation was confusing, and Ruge was out of communication with most of his force. His strategic plan relied on delaying the enemy long enough for the arrival of British and French forces which, Chamberlain told him personally, were arriving 'as fast as possible and in great strength'.[16] Ruge was forthright. Complaining, justifiably, that he was being kept in the dark about British planning and emphasising, equally justifiably, that his forces were exhausted, having been fighting and moving continuously for over a week, he declared that British plans for the recapture of Trondheim could wait; the priority was the southern front. He insisted that the British troops should be used to reinforce the Norwegian Army and come under the direct command of Norwegian commanders. Morgan 'felt he had no option but to comply'.[17]

When further guidance, requested by Morgan, came from the CIGS the following morning, it only partly vindicated his decision. While it directed that it was 'clearly necessary to prevent German advance from south-east in order to secure Dombås [and telling Morgan] you should if you can spare troops, [and] cooperate with Norwegian Commander-in-Chief', it also reiterated that 'you remain independent command under the War Office'.[18] When the question of command was raised at a conference with Ruge and his staff, the CinC produced a document which said that if the British detachment did not comply with his wishes, he would resign, and Norwegian resistance would come to an end.[19] King-Salter chose not to show Ruge a signal to the CinC from Ironside informing him that the British brigade remained under command of the War Office.[20] It also transpired that Morgan's troops were to be split between Norwegian commanders either side of the large Lake Mjøsa and used not to support the Norwegians but to take over their front-line positions. Morgan again acquiesced thus effectively forfeiting command of his brigade. While he can be criticised for poor judgement, he found himself in a highly invidious position and was undermined by the duplicitous, if well intentioned, King-Salter. Either way, 148 Brigade was about to be faced with a task well beyond its capability.

The battalions arrived at Lillehammer by train that morning (20 April). Here they were split up, half of the Sherwood Foresters and the half-battalion of Leicesters under command of the Norwegian divisional commander, Major General Hvinden-Haug, commanding the forces to the east of Lake Mjøsa; the other half of the Foresters under command of Colonel Dahl, who led an ad hoc group to the west of the lake. Hvinden-Haug gave orders for his British half-units to move up and take over front-line positions from the Norwegian troops to the east of the lake at 2:00 P.M. the following day. For Ruge and Hvinden-Haug, there was good reason for this: their troops were exhausted, and here were fresh reinforcements. But, despite protestations by Morgan, they seem to have had grossly over-optimistic expectations of the capability of the British troops.[21] For Morgan, things were about to get a lot worse. The freighter *Cedarbank* was torpedoed and sunk as it approached the Norwegian coast. It contained the brigade's four anti-aircraft guns and all its transport and stores, including its signals equipment, rations, explosives, mortar ammunition and reserves of small-arms ammunition.[22] 148 Brigade was in deep trouble.

The two groups of the brigade, still without maps or entrenching tools, duly moved into position that night: those to the west of the lake, to provide flank protection to Dahl Group; those to the east, in depth positions behind the Norwegians on and near the Lundehøgda Ridge, fifteen miles south-east of Lillehammer, ready to move forward.[23] Here it was discovered that that the signals equipment had also been split up: West Force had the field telephones; East Force had the cable.[24] Early the following morning (21 April), East Force moved forward to their positions and were met by withdrawing Norwegian troops who greeted them with, 'Good-morning, Tommy. Thank you, Tommy. Goodbye, Tommy.'[25] Very shortly after, by unhappy coincidence for the British, the Germans launched a strong attack with a composite brigade group of two-and-a-half battalions of infantry, a machine gun battalion, some Gebirgsjäger ski troops and an artillery battalion, supported by dive bombers.[26] These German forces were the leading elements of Group Pellengahr – a large part of the reinforced 196th Infantry Division (itself an all-arms divisional group) commanded by Major General Richard Pellengahr. Together with the remainder of 196 Division – Group Fischer - advancing up the parallel valley to the east (the Østerdal), their mission was to establish land contact with the garrison in Trondheim, a task now designated as the *Schwerpunkt* (point of main effort) of Group XXI.[27] Having left the Oslo area on 13 April, mainly in requisitioned civilian vehicles and horse-drawn transport, both groups had already met with, and overcome, delaying actions by hastily formed Norwegian units further south. The Norwegian units here at Lake Mjøsa had withdrawn following these engagements and were now in the process of being relieved by the British troops.

By evening, the German combination of fire and manoeuvre – both infiltrating and outflanking – caused the abandonment of East Force's position, which was held in insufficient strength. At about 4:00 P.M. Hvinden-Haug held a conference to issue instructions for a timed and coordinated withdrawal that night to Fåberg, just north of Lillehammer. But, without radio communications, the orders did not reach all of the force; indeed Morgan did not learn of them until several hours later.[28] Events took their own course. According to a regimental history of the Leicesters, one of their company commanders, 'sensing the hopelessness of the situation . . . ordered a withdrawal'.[29] According to a history of the Foresters, their companies saw the Leicesters withdrawing and themselves withdrew; 'No-one knew what the situation was . . . and there was no reliable information as to the exact location of the enemy.'[30] The retreat was at times chaotic. Only some of the promised Norwegian transport materialised, so that many in East Force had to abandon their equipment and make their way back on foot in platoon and section groups, pursued by the enemy.[31] As the Leicesters' War Diary recorded succinctly, 'The Germans caught up the battalion, and a great many of them were cut off.'[32] A number of these groups were taken prisoner, including one of five officers and fifty men from the Leicesters.[33] The Germans were soon in possession of Lillehammer, capturing British ammunition and stores and forcing the retreating troops to skirt the town across country.[34] One historian of the Leicesters summed it up, with apparently unconscious understatement, 'It had been a trying day.'[35]

The new position at Fåberg was situated above the village on the slopes of the Balbergkamp mountain. What remained of East Force arrived there during the early hours of 22 April, witnessed by Lieutenant Colonel Clarke: '[T]he tragic remnants of the men who had so confidently taken over the line on Lake Mjøsa the day before, now trickling back, wounded and lost, with the Stukas shooting up the road.'[36] The two battalions were 'completely intermingled' and amounted to no more than about three and a half rifle companies[37] equipped only with what they carried. They had no signals equipment and no means of digging a defensive position.[38] Cold, wet, without hot food for two days, exhausted and ill-equipped, they were in no fit state to deal with what followed. A lot can be read between the lines of King-Salter's single-sentence account of one air attack: 'Two sticks of four bombs fell right amongst us, and although there were not many casualties to men or vehicles, the effect on the already tired men was very serious.'[39] The situation deteriorated still further. Morgan, who had been given back command by Hvinden-Haug, appealed to Ruge for Norwegian ski troops as flank protection but was told that none were available.[40] Ruge probably came to regret that he did not do more to provide some; Morgan certainly did.

There was an awful inevitability about what followed. The position was heavily shelled and strafed during the morning, and in the afternoon German ski troops worked round the open eastern flank, cutting off the forward troops and causing Morgan to order his brigade headquarters to be abandoned and 'all ranks to make a run for it'.[41] 'For some hours the situation was utterly confused', recalled Clarke.[42] Another hasty withdrawal took place. For some, this may have been ordered by an officer;[43] for others, 'someone else [came] and said "Come on. We're pulling back."'[44] A few vehicles were available, with 'rations and other stores being jettisoned so as to pack all available transport with men.'[45] The remainder retired on foot in disarray, leaving, amongst other things, twenty-five machine guns and twelve Boyes anti-tank rifles on the position.[46] Some threw away their personal weapons. As soldiers later recalled, it was '[e]very man for himself.'[47] An intermediate position was hastily established at Øyer with the help of the two recently arrived companies of Leicesters, but in the face of the German onslaught, this was abandoned, and the troops retreated, mostly on foot, towards the designated fall-back position some ten miles further north at Tretten. Their journey was fraught: 'Caught up with by enemy aircraft which bombed and machine gunned them as they took cover in a wood'.[48] Those members of the two battalions that made it to Tretten arrived 'in several instalments' early on 23 April, utterly exhausted, having now been without food and sleep between thirty-six and forty-eight hours and without proper rest for a week.[49] ('I was drunk with lack of sleep', recalled one platoon commander, 'The mountains kept coming up and hitting me.')[50] They were joined by the two Foresters companies who had been attached to the Dahl Group on the west of Lake Mjøsa, fatigued and frozen after a long, circuitous journey in open trucks, and by the two relatively fresh companies of Leicesters. Also present were the remnants of three companies of Norwegian troops.

Tretten was a natural defensive position – a narrow defile – and had been partly prepared by the Norwegians with a few rudimentary sangars on either side of the river. But the absence of long-since-discarded entrenching tools meant that most of the British troops were lying out in the open.[51] Furthermore, Morgan no longer had the radio communications with which to command his brigade effectively: his rear link radio set had been captured in the Lillehammer area, and his forward link to his battalions had to be abandoned since there was no transport for it.[52] Communication forward, therefore, relied on despatch riders or liaison in person.

The first warning for many of the defenders of the impending German attack was in the early afternoon when, as Major Jefferis of the Royal Engineers observed, two platoons who had been in a forward outpost 'came running back into Tretten, having thrown away their arms, saying that the tanks had broken through on the road'.[53] The shock effect of the unexpected use of armour was considerable. For the British, '[i]t was the first intimation we had that they had anything heavier than troop-carrying track vehicles.'[54] There were only a few tanks, but only a few were needed since the only British anti-armour weapon possessed by 148 Brigade was the Boyes anti-tank rifle, which was of decidedly limited effectiveness and in which the British troops had no confidence.[55]

The attack down the road was combined with a heavy and prolonged artillery and mortar bombardment and air attacks, while ski troops out-flanked the position. The defenders, with no effective anti-aircraft or anti-tank weapons and no artillery, no high explosive ammunition for their mortars and low on rifle ammunition, held the position until early evening. A German contemporary account referred to 'strong enemy resistance [from] behind trees and rock barricades', but this resistance 'was broken by the combined fires of artillery, anti-tank guns and heavy mortars and by a bombing attack'.[56] Some groups of defenders were surrounded and surrendered; the remainder, according to the same German account, 'retreated in complete dissolution'.[57] The result was a rout. Some of the groups on foot were captured immediately; some headed east and made it to the Swedish border; some headed west and reached the coast. The remainder retreated north down the road to a temporary rearguard pos-ition formed by Norwegian troops, where some busses and trucks had been positioned.[58] As they moved off, they were 'closely attended by enemy aircraft with bombs and machine guns',[59] resulting in alarm and panic. Lieutenant Colonel Craufurd, Royal Engineers, witnessed the result: 'When I came down the main road the retreat lay before my eyes – on the road there was a regular stream of fugitive British soldiers on foot. Many had thrown away both weapons and equipment.'[60] Lunde quotes the description of a Danish officer serving with the Norwegian Army:

Truck after truck of hysterical British soldiers drove past me. When I reached Fåvang, there was wild confusion on the road. British officers had managed to stop the trucks and tried unsuccessfully to restore order. They refused to follow orders and drove on, yelling and screaming. It had a depressing effect on the Norwegian soldiers who witnessed the behaviour.[61]

The vehicles took them back to an assembly area forty-five miles to the rear in the relative safety of the Heidal valley, near Otta. When they arrived there and were joined by stragglers, they numbered no more than 9 officers and 300 men – little more than a quarter of their original strength.[62] Six days after arriving in Norway, 148 Brigade, as a fighting force, had ceased to exist.

As 148 Brigade was fighting its last battle at Tretten, the leading elements of a reinforcement brigade were starting to arrive at Åndalsnes.[63] 15th

Figure 15.2 Major General Bernard Paget

Infantry Brigade had been warned about a possible move to Norway one
week earlier.[64] Hastily withdrawn from the BEF, the brigade was originally destined for Operation Hammer but, on the operation's cancellation,
was assigned to Sickleforce. It consisted of three Regular infantry battalions: 1st Battalion, The Green Howards; 1st Battalion, The Kings Own
Yorkshire Light Infantry; and 1st Battalion, The York and Lancaster
Regiment. With it came its anti-tank company of nine 25-mm guns
(effective against German tanks) and a company of Royal Engineers.[65]
The brigade was now commanded by Brigadier Smyth, who had been
promoted from command of 1 KOYLI, when the brigade commander,
Brigadier Berney-Ficklin, had been taken for command of Hammer.

Also bound for Åndalsnes, as commander of Sickleforce, was Major General Bernard Paget. Aged fifty-two, Paget was a highly experienced and competent officer. He had spent most of his First World War service with his battalion or on the staff of a brigade. He had taken part in six major battles (including one where he and his commanding officer were the only officers in his battalion to survive) and had been wounded three times, finishing the war with a Distinguished Service Order, a Military Cross and four times Mentioned in Despatches.[66] Immediately prior to the Second World War he had been commandant of the Staff College, Camberley – a prestigious post. Paget was in command of a Territorial division based in Norfolk when, on the evening of 20 April, he was told to report to the War Office the following morning. Here he was informed that he was to command Sickleforce and was given a briefing on the operation which was already under way. His chief of staff, Lieutenant Colonel Nicholson, recalled,

[e]verything was in a state of improvisation; there were no maps – we had to tear them out of geography books and send the ADC [aide-de-camp] out to buy a Baedeker. From the Norwegian Embassy and a series of tourist agencies we gathered an armful of travel advertisement folders. From amongst them we unearthed one showing a picture with a bit of Åndalsnes in the background and other photographs of the valley between Åndalsnes and Dombås. These were the only clues as to what our prospective theatre of operations looked like.[67]

(There is, of course, the parallel with Falkenhorst, in a similar situation, rushing out to buy a Baedeker, but that was some six weeks before the operation, not after it had begun.)

The ADC, Captain Wilberforce, recalled,

Paget at once raised a number of points – no engineers – how were things loaded – which was to arrive first – how was the disembarkation to be managed – the stuff could not be left lying on the quay – how could it be got forward without MT [mechanical transport]? Each question revealed a complete absence of concrete planning. They had failed to think in terms of the man the other end at all.[68]

Nor had the War Office given much thought to a headquarters for Paget. Like Carton de Wiart, he had to start from scratch, collecting a staff as best he could.[69]

Paget and a staff of eleven left London two days later, along with the advance party of General Massy's corps headquarters – the senior logistics officer, Brigadier Hogg, and seven of his staff – and arrived at Åndalsnes (via Molde) on the evening of 25 April.[70] The town was in ruins, having been subjected to a series of heavy attacks by the Luftwaffe. Paget was met by Morgan, who reported the fate of his brigade. Before he left London, Paget had represented to Massy the urgent need for adequate air support and air defence,[71] a need he now reiterated in forthright terms in his first report to London: 'In view of the enemy advance, arrangements to evacuate should be prepared if aerial supremacy is not ensured forthwith.'[72] Paget's ability to command and control his force was strictly limited by the lack of communications. Of the four radio sets in his headquarters, two were broken and two had been sent without the battery acid necessary to make them work. As a result, he had to resort to the local telephone system, but its known insecurity compounded the difficulty of communication.[73]

Little did Paget know it, but almost exactly at the moment of his arrival, the British attempt to reverse the German domination of the air was lying in tatters just a few miles away. On 17 April the RAF had sent an officer to central Norway to find a suitable landing ground on which to establish an airbase. The Norwegians were affronted that he did not take their advice. Ruge commented, 'Here as in many other cases, the Allies often came with preconceived ideas, not willing to listen to us. Through this, valuable time was lost until they had to accept what we had suggested was best after all.'[74] The officer chose one of the only two sites deemed suitable – the frozen Lake Lesjaskog between Åndalsnes and Dombås. An advance party was sent there on 23 April in readiness for the squadron of Gladiators due to arrive there the following day. The idea was a good one, but its implementation epitomised the campaign as a whole. The stores had been so hastily loaded that none of the boxes were labelled, so all had to be laboriously opened at Åndalsnes to ascertain their contents; transport was only sufficient to take a proportion of them forward; only two refuelling troughs had been provided, but the starter trolley could not be used as the batteries were uncharged and no acid had been sent with them; and there was only one armourer for eighteen aircraft, (a total of seventy-two guns). Most important of all – and scarcely believable – was that although this was a key deployment of strategic importance and would clearly be a top priority target for the Luftwaffe, air defence for the site amounted to only two light anti-aircraft guns scrounged from the Royal Navy. The Gladiators duly arrived the following afternoon (24 April), but their crews had no experience of operating in sub-zero temperatures, and no Norwegian advisers had been provided (or requested). By morning the aircrafts' flying controls were frozen solid and the engines were difficult to start. The Luftwaffe, who had spotted activity at the lake the previous day, arrived in strength and caught the squadron on the ground. The ground crew, hastily assembled and untrained for the ordeal, took to the woods, leaving the officers and non-commissioned officers to refuel the planes. By mid-day, more than half the squadron's planes were destroyed; by

Figure 15.3 The remains of the attempt to establish an airfield at Lake Lesjaskog.
(Imperial War Museums)

mid-afternoon the runway was virtually unusable, as much of the ice had broken, and the remaining four aircraft left.[75] Had the operation been well planned and implemented, it might have had a significant impact on the success of Operation Sickle. As it was, it fell victim to rush, over-improvisation and muddle.

Paget would have passed Lesjaskog early the next morning (26 April) as he went by train to Dombås and thence to General Ruges headquarters. Ruge emphasised, as he had done to Morgan, that the Norwegian troops were exhausted and required relief. The two generals agreed that the British would be responsible for the Gudbrandsdal valley, with the support of Norwegian ski troops who would be under British command, while the Norwegians would be responsible for the Østerdal valley, to the east, where the Germans were also pressing hard.[76] Paget then moved forward to visit 15 Brigade, deployed in a succession of defensive positions in the Gudbrandsdal, south of Dombås and behind the Norwegian front line. The most southerly of the Brigade's positions, at the village of Kvam, had been occupied in the early hours of the previous day by the KOYLI, reinforced by its two 3-inch mortars, a company of the York and Lancasters and five of the Brigade anti-tank guns, but, critically, without artillery support or air defence.[77] Having driven the Norwegians back through Kvam, the Germans had attacked in late morning using the same tactics as they had at Tretten, but the KOYLI had prepared the position well. In the fierce battle that ensued, the Germans were rebuffed, and the KOYLI held firm throughout the day, despite losing most of one company.[78] Pellengahr had reported to Falkenhorst that 'his troops are making a determined defence'.[79] During the battle, however, the brigade commander, Brigadier Smyth, had received a serious shrapnel wound and had been replaced by the senior commanding officer, Lieutenant Colonel Kent-Lemon of the York and Lancasters. The latter was confident of the KOYLI's ability to hold for another day.

When Paget arrived at Kvam on 26 April, the KOYLI were coming under increased pressure. It was clear to him that until the arrival of some artillery support and air defence, the best that could be achieved by his force was a series of delaying positions.[80] He therefore ordered the KOYLI to withdraw that evening through the York and Lancaster's position at Kjørem, five miles behind, to take up a rearguard position just south of Dombås.[81] The British had lost some fifty men who were killed around Kvam. The withdrawal was achieved, though it was far from straightforward: the woods were set alight by incendiary shells, causing a precipitate withdrawal, and two companies never received the orders to withdraw and took to the hills on foot, subsequently rejoining the battalion after a long detour.[82] Fortunately for the British, the Germans, having received a hard knock, did not attempt a pursuit at night.

The following morning the German attack fell on the York and Lancasters, who, with a company of the Green Howards, held the position throughout the day. But with mounting casualties, and its position outflanked, the battalion was ordered to withdraw that night to reinforce the rear position, six miles further north at Otta, held by the Green Howards.[83] With the Germans holding a roadblock in the rear of the York and Lancasters' position, the retreat was, at times, chaotic. 'For several hours in the darkness ... platoons and often sections were forced to fight independent actions through the woods. In confused fighting, some lost their way and were cut off by the enemy.'[84] One group, led by the commanding officer, only made its escape by crossing over the border into Sweden. As a result, the York and Lancasters 'were not in a fit state to hold their sector of the Otta position',[85] which, though a natural defensive position and well prepared by the Green Howards, was now held in insufficient strength – particularly as the battalion was short of a company that was in reserve at Dombås. The usual early morning flight by a German reconnaissance plane was followed by bombers and, later in the morning, by a ground attack. The battalion held firm throughout the day, inflicting considerable losses on the enemy but, to

Figure 15.4 The German attack held up at Otta
(Bundesarchiv)

meet the evacuation plan, was ordered to withdraw that night. This they succeeded in doing, although, again, one company did not receive the executive order and had to improvise its escape over the mountains.[86] The Germans, clearly set back by the day's hard fighting, made no immediate attempt to follow-up, allowing the brigade to 'break clean' and make its way by train and truck back to Dombås, twenty-five miles to the north. Royal Engineers, using makeshift demolitions from sea mines and depth charges, blew the bridges behind them.[87]

It was during the battle at Otta that Paget received from Massy the order to evacuate. Paget's report on arrival at Åndalsnes on 26 April, urging air support, had been followed by one that night from Brigadier Hogg, head of the corps HQ advance party. Having been subjected to another day's continuous bombing, Hogg had reported 'severe damage in port area; Western wood jetty and vicinity completely burnt out' and opined that the base would 'become unworkable unless effective air support can be maintained continuously'.[88] The eight Royal Marine two-pounder anti-aircraft guns and Royal Navy anti-aircraft guard ship ('which inevitably ran out of ammo in half a day'[89]) had proved totally inadequate – indeed, two of the successive guard ships which had done duty at Åndalsnes had been hit and forced to limp home. The arrival of twelve Bofors light anti-aircraft guns between 18 and 24 April made little difference, and by the time eight heavy anti-aircraft guns arrived on 28 April, it was too late.[90] On 27 April, Hogg, who was out of communications with Paget, had told the War Office that evacuation was necessary and that he was planning it, starting on 1 May.[91] When Paget discovered this, he signalled the War Office, showing some irritation, but his advice was similar to Hogg's – just expressed in a positive form: evacuation was not necessary 'provided [that] more effective action can be taken to deal [with] enemy aircraft which at present operate with little hindrance and are systematically destroying base and communications'.[92] With no realistic prospect of this being achieved, minds in London were already made up: evacuation would take place on the nights of 30 April and 1 May.[93] The order instructed Paget not to inform Ruge – a reflection of British perception of Norwegian security and of ignorance of the central role being played by the Norwegian military in the campaign. Paget found this instruction both dishonourable and impractical and went straight to Ruge's headquarters.

I decided that the right course to take was to be perfectly frank. . . . I went in with considerable anxiety as to what his reaction would be; it was quite on the cards that he would refuse to play, as he already felt very sore about our not having sent more troops to assist him, and if he did so, there was little hope for Sickleforce, as we were entirely dependent on the Norwegians for road and rail transport, as well as for communications and medical services.[94]

Paget's anxiety was not totally unfounded, particularly since, at his previous meeting with Ruge, the British general had, according to the CinC's chief of staff, promised that 2,000 fresh troops would arrive at Åndalsnes each day.[95] However, Paget recalled, 'After an initial outburst in which he spoke of being betrayed, and declared that an Allied evacuation would totally destroy the morale of the Norwegian Army and people, he regained his composure, and promised to give what support he could.'[96] Ruge was to be as good as his word.

The challenges facing Paget in conducting the withdrawal to Åndalsnes were considerable. He needed to delay the enemy long enough both to allow his forces to move back and to protect the Norwegian forces' retreat from the Østerdal. There was a high risk of the enemy overrunning or outflanking him, and there was not nearly enough transport to lift his units back down from Dombås. The road was, in any case, in a chaotic state. Lieutenant Colonel Clarke, who had flown back to London to report in person, returned on 29 April and was shocked to find the road 'littered everywhere with stranded vehicles: hundreds of them, British and Norwegian; ditched, bombed, burnt-out, broken down – or just out of petrol. Scarcely any traffic was moving, and we passed little signs of life.'[97] The railway line was still intact but highly vulnerable to air attack.

The withdrawal and subsequent embarkation was, in contrast to much that had gone before, well organised and successful. It was also a close-run thing. A spirited rearguard action just south of Dombås fought by the KOYLI and a company of Green Howards, supported by four Norwegian field guns, successfully kept the enemy at bay just long enough for 15 Brigade's troops, together with those of 148 Brigade, to be put on trains for the port.[98] Their onward journey was not without incident – one of the trains crashed, causing a number of casualties, and many troops had to march seventeen miles to pick up the next train, hiding from air attack in a tunnel – before arriving at Åndalsnes. Others made it to the port on foot, some 'carrying their arms ... far from beaten yet',[99] some without their weapons,[100] some 'running like rabbits and the general stampede carried them on'.[101] Captain (later Brigadier) Mike Calvert remembered, 'It was a very sad sight, seeing the defeated British troops stream past us.'[102] On the nights of 30 April and 1 May they were embarked, 'dead beat and ravenously hungry', on Royal Navy warships.[103] Also evacuated (from Molde) were King Haakon, his family, the Norwegian government and General Ruge, all of whom, along with twenty-three tons of gold bullion – part of Norway's gold reserves - were taken to Tromsø. By 2 May, the evacuation was complete, and later that morning leading German units were in the ruins of Åndalsnes. Elements of Pellengahr's division had already made the vital link-up with the garrison at Trondheim. They had fought their way the 300 miles from Oslo in just 17 days.

Sickleforce had sustained heavy losses. In less than a week's fighting, 148 Brigade (two battalions) reported 706 men killed, wounded or missing;[104] a very high proportion of them, it turned out, were prisoners of war or interned in Sweden.[105] 15 Brigade (three battalions) had lost some 580 men. Both brigades had lost most of their equipment and heavy weapons.

For the Norwegian Army, the withdrawal and evacuation of the British was a disaster. The remainder of the Norwegian 2nd Division, which had at times put up what the Germans described as 'heavy resistance' in the Østerdal (thus protecting the British left flank), were trapped just northeast of Åndalsnes, and some 2,500 soldiers were taken prisoner.[106] The 2,000-strong Norwegian 4th Brigade in Valdres to the west of the Gudbrandsdal, having been involved in some of the fiercest fighting seen in Norway, were also ordered to surrender.[107] The capture of Namsos resulted in the surrender of a further 2,000 men of the Norwegian 5th Brigade. Later on 3 May, the Norwegian military signed the capitulation of all their forces south of Trondheim. There was, understandably, considerable bitterness that they had been abandoned by the British.

So, why had the British been so comprehensively defeated in the Gudbrandsdal?

Like the defeat of Mauriceforce, some of the reasons are obvious, some less so. It is not quite as simple as Moulton would have it, that '[t]here is really no great mystery why difficulties of terrain affected the Germans less than they did the British and Norwegians. It was that there were a great many more of them, and they had much better weapons.'[108] Certainly, numbers of men and quality of weapons were a major factor. The size of the German force meant that although the steep terrain often resulted in narrow attack frontages, with only one battalion group at a time able to attack, there were fresh battalions available to reinforce where required and to take over the lead after each attack. Such organisation also helped maintain momentum, pressure and the initiative. The comparative quality of weapons was, indeed, also a major factor, particularly as the Germans had bombing and strafing aircraft, artillery, tanks and mechanised infantry carriers, which the British did not; nor did the British units have anti-aircraft defence (nor, in the case of 148 Brigade, effective anti-tank defence). But over-focus on numbers and weapons obscures other, less glamorous but critically important contributors to fighting power, such as logistics and communications. German logistic support may have involved a considerable degree of improvisation, for example in resupply and transport, but at least it was a recognisable system. British logistic support, poorly planned from the outset, degenerated into chaos. In terms of communications, the British, reduced to reliance on despatch riders and runners, faced a force using radio.

In the same vein, over-focus on the physical element of fighting power obscures the other elements – conceptual and moral. Almost as important as the quality and quantity of weapons was the Germans' effectiveness in combining all these weapon systems with each other[109] and with the engineers, who so swiftly repaired blown bridges and removed obstacles. This efficient integration resulted from superior organisation and training and, less obviously, doctrine. As one historian noted, 'By insisting upon a clear, and well-understood doctrine, thoroughly instilled by training on uniform lines, they made it possible for units and even sub-units to settle down quickly in new groupings and under new commanders with the minimum of confusion. The British approach was quite dissimilar.'[110] And in line with their doctrine the Germans in the Gudbrandsdal (as elsewhere in Norway) were organised into all-arms battlegroups (*Kampf-gruppe*) and could quickly reorganise when the situation demanded. Additionally, cooperation between the different arms – for example, infantry, tanks, artillery and engineers – was an integral part of the German military ethos, as indeed was cooperation between the services, where the Luftwaffe supplied the Army with not only fire support but also vital intelligence.[111] Equally significant, in accordance with their doctrine and training, and unlike their British counterparts, German commanders at all levels were expected to use their initiative when an unexpected situation developed, and not wait for further orders.[112] Noteworthy, too, was the Germans' skilful combination of fire and manoeuvre. And often it was primarily manoeuvre that caused the British to withdraw - the fact that they were outflanked, or thought they had been or were about to be. Here it was not principally weapons that achieved this but the ability to move – notably using skis but also motor bikes (some of them half-track, mounting heavy machine guns), bicycles and on foot.

German Army doctrine and training focused on offensive operations and on the value of seizing and retaining the initiative through a combination of aggression, surprise and doing things – everything - faster than their opponents.[113] It placed high value on speed of decision and action, maintaining momentum and not allowing their enemy a moment's rest. Where they were held up, they were taught to outflank, and where this required, as it did in Norway climbing steep ground, they were physically fit enough to do so. Ski troops were often available to assist in outflank-ing. Keeping the Allies retreating was a major factor, particularly since, in the circumstances, every time the British fell back on foot, they had to leave behind equipment that could not be carried, including items of critical importance such as heavy machine guns, ammunition, food and cold-weather clothing. Pellengahr's division was far from being an elite Wehrmacht formation; it had only been raised towards the end of the previous year as part of the seventh wave of mobilisation, although many of its members had already undergone the standard eight weeks of basic training.[114] The Wehrmacht was not without its own problems with rapid expansion, including lack of accommodation, and shortage of weapons, personal equipment and qualified non-commissioned officers.[115] Nevertheless, the division had a leavening of experienced officers and non-commissioned officers and the advantage over its British opponents of being deployed as an all-arms divisional group, with organic combat and logistic support, and a functioning headquarters with proper communications. Apart from its attached Gebirgsjäger, its troops had had no special training – indeed, probably little collective training of any sort above unit level – but within these constraints, they had been remarkably thoroughly trained in the time available. For example, a British company commander noted that the Germans were 'using fire and movement tactics in copybook manner, with artillery'.[116] In Derry's assessment 'their superior mobility was chiefly as a result of superior fitness'.[117] Nor should this have come as a surprise. Military Intelligence had repeatedly commented on the 'impressive' physical fitness and stamina of German soldiers, that 'the most remarkable achievement of the German infantry was its ability to cover long distances without undue fatigue' and that this was 'not confined to Regular troops'.[118] For many German soldiers, this would have resulted, in part, from membership of paramilitary youth programmes and the six-month membership of the Reichsarbeitsdienst labour service, prior to enlistment. In terms of the moral component of fighting power – fighting spirit – the German forces, from the highest to the lowest ranks, were rarely found wanting.

Closer inspection of the British formations and units helps explain their deficiencies in comparison to their opponents. First, 148 Brigade's units, like those of 146 Brigade, had been the victims of 'mission creep', ending up in a role for which they were totally untrained. Indeed, their training was at such a basic level that they should not have been sent on deployed operations of any sort. Although they had in theory been training for the duration of the war, the units of 49 Division, to which both 146 and 148 brigades belonged, had been doing so for only ten weeks, and for only two of them with their full complement of equipment.[119] A number of factors combined to produce this result. One was the requirement to guard 'vulnerable points'. For example, the Leicesters had been involved in this commitment (and therefore not training) in part of September and December, had had their weapon training camp cancelled in November and were without forty per cent of their transport in the same month.[120] In at least one battalion, training in January was 'brought almost to a standstill', ironically due to the severe winter.[121] In one battalion, 'not every man ... was trained in the use of small arms', and hand grenades 'were of little or no use, as many, including some of the officers, did not know how to even prime [them]'.[122] In another battalion, 'none of us had ever fired the Boyes [anti-tank rifle]'.[123] Nor had the battalions had time to build up unit cohesion: the Leicesters came together as a battalion for the first time at Rosyth docks.[124] (It was to be a short meeting: the battalion was then split up between four ships for the journey to Norway.) The 1st/4th KOYLI had been formed in the summer of 1939 and had spent much of the time before Christmas guarding vulnerable points.[125] Not a single brigade exercise had been carried out by the time the battalions deployed.[126]

The original plan in 49 Division had been to complete brigade training by 21 May.[127] Norway came far too soon for them, although their training would have had little relevance: '[T]he commanders of the Territorial Divisions expected trench warfare and trained for it.'[128] Training in 49 Division was at such a low level that, as at 21 March, 'about 100 men in each battalion of 146 Brigade [and] about 650 men in 148 Brigade have still to fire the rifle and LMG [light machine gun] courses'.[129] In February the manpower establishment of Territorial battalions had increased by almost forty per cent, and 'thus even fully manned units had to cope with the disruption of absorbing and integrating large numbers of new people'.[130] For example, in the Leicesters, ten per cent of the battalion had only arrived in February and had immediately been sent on leave.[131] All of this turbulence had an adverse impact on unit cohesion. The Territorial Army also suffered from a low level of leadership training, with little built-in resilience. Whereas in the Regular Army, leaders were trained to act two ranks above their appointment, in the Territorial Army they were trained for their existing rank only.[132] Nor were Territorial Army commanding officers required to attend the Senior Officers Course prior to command.[133]

Almost as important as training, unit cohesion and trust in their commanders is the confidence of soldiers that the operation in which they are participating has been well planned and is well organised. Every experience of the soldiers of 148 Brigade since January, and increasingly since they deployed, was of an operation that, as old soldiers say, 'smelt bad': order, counter-order, disorder had been endemic; weapons, ammunition and equipment had been lost in transit; proper maps were non-existent; administration had been chaotic; the brigade, and even battalions, had been deployed split up and in a seemingly haphazard way. To many, it felt as if they were fighting with one hand tied behind their back. 'Bren guns

Figure 15.5 The fate of many: British prisoners being marched into
captivity
(Imperial War Museums)

against tanks', recalled one veteran later. 'Yer Boyes anti-tank bounces off
a tank. You can only stand so much.'[134] 'It was', recalled one company
commander, 'one colossal, chaotic muddle – I think we all thought
that'.[135] As the infantry training doctrine of the time stated, 'Men who
go into action harassed and hurried, feeling that adequate preparations
have been impossible, will lose much in morale.'[136] The importance of the
mission itself was also in question – it was far from obvious to many British
soldiers (in stark contrast to the Norwegians and, indeed the Germans) as
to why their mission in Norway was vital. In a most telling comment, the
regimental historian of one of the units in 146 Brigade wrote, 'There
was … no reason for the last man and the last round. … The criterion
of success therefore resolved itself into a reckoning of souls saved to fight
another day under more favourable conditions.'[137]

The soldier-historian General Sir David Fraser showed great insight in
his comments on the British performance in Central Norway:

Few men are born heroes. Few are incorrigible cowards. Most can be either; and
to help them towards the former rather than the latter state an army uses
leadership, discipline and training – a mix which produces confidence and

pride. The man well-led can believe there is a sense in what he is ordered to do, and that his commander both cares for him and knows his own job. The disciplined man knows that the habit of obedience and united action distinguishes a self-respecting body of soldiers from a mob. The trained man knows his profession enough to do what he has to do, and do it by instinct amidst great dangers. Without these characteristics in the body to which they belong soldiers cannot behave well in battle; and when they fail the fault is not theirs but lies in the system which has placed them there unprepared.[138]

As would be expected, 15 Brigade, a Regular brigade, with all its weapons and equipment, including the significant advantage of an anti-tank company, and with far greater experience and competence in its ranks, held much more successfully than did 148 Brigade and could have held longer had withdrawal and evacuation not been ordered. But even 15 Brigade, un-reinforced[139] – and without air support and with its lines of communications cut, it had little prospect of being reinforced – would have been overcome or out-manoeuvred before long by the all-arms and joint-service combination of the German armed forces.[140] Simply put, the German forces' fighting power – that combination of physical, moral and conceptual components that contribute to combat effectiveness – was significantly superior to that of their British opponents.[141]

The difference in fighting power between the two sides was exacerbated by the fact that the British and Norwegian allies were, in effect, fighting separate campaigns. The War Office had shown a remarkable lack of interest in the Norwegian Army, even when operations in Norway were being planned. A lot of store had been set on staff talks between the British and Norwegian militaries to discover what support could be expected from the Norwegians, but the talks never took place. The British military remained ignorant of the Norwegian military capability and plans, and of its senior officers. From the Chiefs of Staff downwards, the British military tended to look on the Norwegian armed forces as insignificant, unreliable and of little account.

Even after the German invasion, the British viewed the Norwegian military more as a potential obstacle than as vital partners. Liaison was established with the Norwegian CinC, but only by the service attachés. Admiral Evans, en route to Sweden on a diplomatic mission, called-in on Ruge but was badly briefed and no expert in land operations; he 'presumed that General Ruge, who was described as the best soldier in Norway, knew what he was doing'.[142] A senior officer should have been appointed as the Chiefs of Staff's liaison officer to co-locate immediately with Ruge and develop a common plan. Potentially, the British and Norwegian capabilities complemented each other well, but this potential was never realised.[143] The whole was never more than the sum of the parts.

If there was a single factor which contributed most to the outcome in central Norway, it was German air power. It influenced the result in two ways. First, Luftwaffe close air support was a major contributor to the fighting power of German ground troops. Second, and even more importantly, the failure of Sickle, like that of Maurice, was primarily due not to the defeat of the land manoeuvre forces but to the cutting of the lines of communications at the port of entry. This outcome was a triumph for air power and for the Luftwaffe.

16   'We Must Get Out'

It was not long after the decision was taken on 20 April to cancel Hammer and rely on Maurice and Sickle that there was cause for serious concern in London as to whether the right decision had been made. At first, there had been reason for optimism. The situation map showed the leading elements of Carton de Wiart's force to be south of Steinkjer – over halfway to Trondheim – and Morgan's brigade at Lillehammer – 150 miles south of Åndalsnes and less than 100 miles from Oslo. This situation, though, turned out to be as good as it got. By the evening, storm clouds were gathering. The Admiralty received warning from Namsos that 'unless some form of air protection or support is provided the situation will become untenable'.[1] Early the next morning, Carton de Wiart's report of the destruction of Namsos was received. Later came news of heavy bombing at Åndalsnes and the sinking of the stores ship, *Cedarbank*.

The seriousness of the situation started to dawn on the War Cabinet at their meeting late that afternoon. Suddenly talk of the new plan's 'greater certainty of success' was replaced by justification for what already had the look of an over-hasty decision. 'The position in Norway certainly gave rise to some anxiety', said Churchill, 'but was not by any means desperate. We had taken a risk with our eyes open, knowing that it was a very hazardous operation to throw lightly equipped forces ashore without proper maintenance facilities.'[2] Discussion descended into the details of what type of air defence should be provided, with even the Chancellor of the Exchequer offering his expert advice, suggesting that the answer was fitting aeroplanes with floats to land in the fiords. It was Stanley who, not for the first time, brought attention back up to the grand-strategic level and, in particular, to the important subject of priorities. 'He expressed the hope that we should not now switch our main efforts back on to Narvik. He felt that the correct policy would be to concentrate our efforts on the operations in central Norway and only allot to Narvik the forces which could not be made use of in that area.'[3] But Chamberlain, the consummate politician, was not interested in pursuing uncomfortable questions. He might have to adjudicate between Stanley and Churchill, who, just the previous day, had told Cabinet that ' it was of the utmost importance not to have our attention diverted by operations elsewhere from our principal objective, which had always from the very start been the control of the Gällivare ore-fields'.[4] Nor did any of the Chiefs of Staff consider the matter of sufficient importance to make an intervention. So discussion moved on, with unpleasantness neatly avoided, but the hard questions of strategy unaddressed.[5]

This inaction on the part of the Chiefs did not mean that none of them had a view on the subject. Ironside certainly did. In a paper circulated after the meeting, he said 'reinforcements [to Narvik] must not interfere with meeting the full requirements for operations in Central Norway', although warning that 'it appears that the capture of Trondheim is not now immediately possible.'[6] Churchill, clearly alarmed that the priority might be decided against Narvik, circumvented the Military Coordination Committee by penning a midnight note to Chamberlain urging 'a standstill both to the south and north of Trondheim' until a decision at Narvik had been reached.[7] The system that existed for the formulation of policy was fast unravelling.

Inadequacies not just in the formulation of policy but also in its implementation were also becoming apparent. Not until 19 April, three weeks after the mobilisation of the forces for Scandinavia and one week after planning commenced for mobile operations around Trondheim, was the issue of the command and control of the forces in central Norway belatedly addressed. Until then, an entirely ad hoc approach was adopted: as each new operation was planned and its force created, its commander was simply added to those under direct command of the War Office and the CIGS, a clearly unmanageable arrangement. For the original Operation Plymouth – the operation to send a large force into southern Norway and thence to Sweden – the command and control plan was for the appointment of a corps commander and establishment of a corps headquarters. No action, however, had been taken to set this in hand, and the plan had been shelved after the surrender of Finland on 12 March. The decision on 30 March to stand-to forces for Norway meant that a corps headquarters might be required, but as with the previous operation, it was not envisaged that it would be required initially. Furthermore, in the absence of an intermediary headquarters managing the campaign as a whole, the attention of the War Office staff was fully absorbed with the planning and preparation for the individual operations. So the establishment of a corps headquarters proceeded only slowly.[8] On 19 April all the operations in Norway, except at Narvik, were placed under the command of one CinC – CinC North West

Expeditionary Force – initially to be based in England. Massy was appointed and took command three days later.[9] He was intimately acquainted with the operational picture and was the more available since the appointment earlier in the week of General Sir John Dill to the new post of Vice CIGS. (Brooke wrote, 'I only hope that this may be a preliminary step to his replacing Tiny as CIGS. That would be the wisest step we had taken since the start of hostilities.')[10] However, the head-quarters to support Massy existed only in embryo. It would take many days just to accumulate the staff and the necessary infrastructure and weeks to organise them into a working headquarters that could be considered operational. Office furniture, stationery and vehicles were scrounged to form a corps HQ from scratch in a requisitioned building.[11] Unsurprisingly, the headquarters was quite incapable of commanding and controlling an ongoing, fast-moving, complex, overseas operation.

On 22 April the Chiefs of Staff received Carton de Wiart's signal that 'no more troops or stores should be landed in Namsos area unless there is a radical change in the air situation'[12] and came face to face with the possibility of withdrawal from central Norway. Pound and Ironside were absent, en route to Paris for a meeting of the Supreme War Council, and were represented by Phillips and Dill, the latter attending his first Chiefs' meeting. Phillips and Newall both seemed to be looking for reasons to justify a withdrawal. Phillips argued that the possibility of war with Italy meant that Britain would be better off investing its resources in the Mediterranean. Newall said that Narvik was the main objective in Norway, adding that 'a withdrawal from Central Norway would be unfortunate but that we would not lose the war thereby.' Dill retorted that 'our operations in Norway had hitherto been carried out in accordance with a policy which had made Trondheim our main objective.' Newall and Phillips did not respond.[13] Thus, twelve days into the campaign, the Chiefs of Staff were still undecided as to its main objective or the point of main effort and saw no reason to resolve the matter. As chairman, Newall has much to answer for in this respect. The Chiefs were, however, sufficiently concerned about the situation as to direct the staffs to 'consider the steps which a withdrawal from Namsos would involve'.[14]

These worries were not, at this time, shared by Ironside. Despite noting in his diary the loss of the *Cedarbank*, he talked to Gamelin about the difficulties of 'getting our people ashore at little ports of little importance', had 'a very cheery lunch in the [French] HQ Mess',[15] and told Harvey at the Embassy that 'we had landed 9,000 men in Scandinavia without a single loss, [and that] German aircraft [were] not very accurate or persistent'.[16] Critically, neither Carton de Wiart nor the French commander, Audet, had informed their superiors that the Chasseurs Alpins – the key component of Mauriceforce - were still immobile at Namsos.

The mood at the Supreme War Council that afternoon was also upbeat. Choosing not to inform the French of the War Cabinet's decision to cancel Hammer, Chamberlain, instead, focused on the positive. A considerable feat, he said, had been achieved in central Norway, landing 13,000 men without loss of life, and the forces had pushed forward further than expected. The operation at Namsos, he observed, had been 'rudely interrupted' by German air attack, but he expressed no concern about the future operation there: reinforcements would be required, but these, he said, were in plentiful supply, so much so that the limitation would not be the number of troops but the number that could be landed and maintained in-country. As for the capture of Narvik, he took it as a virtual fait accompli, focusing on subsequent operations there. Churchill emphasised some of the challenges and risks, but Reynaud was not for pursuing difficulties, instead encouraging maximum possible help to Norway and looking forward to continuing progress and success. On the subject of priorities (always a potentially contentious subject), a classic compromise was agreed. There would, in effect, be a joint-top priority: the capture of Trondheim and the capture of Narvik. On which note, the session adjourned.[17] As in previous meetings of the Council, both leaders had got what they wanted and avoided difficult subjects or any overt disagreement. Chamberlain had kept from the French the decision to cancel Hammer, avoided discussion of the lack of success of British troops and gained French agreement to deploy a proportion of French forces to the Narvik front. Reynaud had gained agreement to an overall increase of effort to a campaign well away from French borders. With the French supporting role, he was also personally well placed to claim his share of the credit for any success, while having someone else to blame for failure. As before, both sides thought the meeting a success. As before, both sides had been economical with the truth and avoided contentious issues of strategy. 'Complete agreement' and 'a successful conseil' was how Ironside described it.[18] A French admiral may have been closer to the truth in summing it up as having yielded nothing but 'academic resolutions amounting to a fine exercise in non-commitment, in the best parliamentary tradition.'[19]

According to Colville, back in London, '[t]he PM returned from France [on 23 April] and they all seemed rather elated. Here, on the other hand, gloom reigns.'[20] Across the road, Ironside returned 'to find Oliver Stanley and Dill sitting very glum in the War Office'.[21] News had come in of the bombing of Namsos and Steinkjer, the precarious position of 146 Brigade, and the withdrawal of 148 Brigade north of Lillehammer.[22] Dill had told the War Cabinet that '[a]t Namsos conditions were at their very worst, and in his view it was doubtful whether the force there would be able to hold on.' He had also warned of the possibility of 148 Brigade being cut off.[23] Stanley now told the CIGS that the situation at Namsos was 'desperate', but Ironside would not accept it.[24] Carton de Wiart had reported the previous day that Brigadier Phillips 'had the situation in hand',[25] but, significantly, had failed to mention that the Chasseurs Alpins remained stuck at Namsos. As the main manoeuvre troops of Mauriceforce, the operation was far from over if they were actively involved. As Ironside pointed out, 'There are more troops ashore at Namsos than there are Germans at Trondheim.'[26]

The issue came to a head late that night at a stormy meeting of the Military Coordination Committee, with the Prime Minister in the chair. The operational picture was not good. A report from Carton de Wiart of further bombing at Namsos and warning 'Fear [there] may be no alternative to evacuation ...'[27] had been followed by another report from him that 146 Brigade had been 'roughly handled' and had withdrawn to a bridgehead held by the French near Namsos.[28] The Chiefs shared Massy's view that 'everything possible should be done to enable us to hold on at Namsos', because '[t]o evacuate would have a very bad effect.' (This, of course, did not address whether the ways and means existed to achieve this end.) There was a report that 148 Brigade had retired to Tretten and – ominously, for those who could read between the lines – 'the German advance had not yet been brought to a standstill.'[29] Better news was that the Regular brigade from the BEF, 15 Brigade, would be arriving at Åndalsnes that night, and there were plans for their reinforcement by a further three brigades, two British, one French. In addition, to tackle the air situation, two aircraft carriers would be operating off Norway the following day, maintaining fighter patrols over both Namsos and Åndalsnes.[30] The members were also told that the new CinC, Massy, was examining the possibility of resurrecting Operation Hammer, or an adaption of it – a proposal that had emerged from the Assistant Chiefs of Staff earlier in the day.[31]

The row seems to have followed an intervention by Churchill, who was in a combative mood. In a diary entry that says much about strategic decision-making and interpersonal dynamics, Colville recorded:

Edward Bridges said afterwards that Winston was being maddening, declaring that we had failed at Namsos and making most unreasonable proposals. As for Oliver Stanley, Bridges said he hadn't an 'ounce of guts'. The PM is depressed – more by Winston's rampages than by the inherent strategical difficulties with which we are confronted in Norway.[32]

Churchill demanded that 15 Brigade, once landed, should immediately march on Trondheim.[33] Ironside, who was clearly under pressure explaining why this was not a good idea, was still fuming when he wrote in his diary, 'A really stupid wrangle about stupid little tactics. Every plan is torn to pieces by a lot of civilian amateurs. We simply cannot get on with the work at all. We are always explaining stupid detail. How can a staff function?'[34]

The root cause of this frustration was the quandary that faced the British strategists: to continue in central Norway, Trondheim must be taken quickly, but the chances of it being taken at all, let alone quickly, by the current plan of pincer attacks from Namsos and Åndalsnes were fading fast.

The search for a way out led to the idea of resurrecting Hammer. Churchill pursued it with Pound on 24 April and, at the War Cabinet, 'made an oration about the possibility of coming back to "frontal assault"'.[35] But by the time the Military Coordination Committee met that evening to consider Massy's plan, the situation had changed again: reports had been received of 148 Brigade's defeat at Tretten[36] and of 15 Brigade being under attack at Otta from the air and by armoured fighting vehicles.[37] Since any plan Massy might come up with for a direct attack on Trondheim (its feasibility was still being assessed) was predicated on the stabilisation of the southern front, it was becoming apparent that evacuation might be beckoning. Discussion turned to making the best of a bad job, and of how, if evacuation was required, this might be presented to the public. Churchill aired the view that 'if the worst came to the worst, and we were pushed right back in the south, we were intrinsically no worse than we thought we should be when the enemy made his first landing two weeks previously.' Chamberlain agreed. 'If we had to evacuate, there would be no reason for us to be ashamed or to regret the effort we had made. We must, however, face the fact that we should have incurred a psychological reverse and a blow to our prestige.'[38] There was also some clutching at straws. Earlier in the day, Chamberlain suggested that if only the Germans could be pushed across the Swedish border, the situation would be saved by Sweden's entry into the war.[39]

The Chiefs were confronted with strategic reality the following morning (25 April). An appreciation by the Joint Planners placed Norway in the context of the war as a whole – not as a campaign that must be won at any cost, but as one where the objective needed to be adjusted to the ways and means available. The appreciation began, 'We are threatened by a major attack in the West, and whether this will be delivered or whether it merely remains a threat, we must hold in readiness adequate forces to counter it. This must be our governing factor in our strategy in

Scandinavia.' The Joint Planners' logical conclusion was that, if Scandinavia became too great a commitment (for example, if Britain found itself at war with Italy), 'we should ... cut our losses [and] withdraw ... from southern Norway.' They continued, 'We appreciate the disadvantages which the abandonment of southern Norway would involve, but consider that we should have to accept them.'[40] These views may have been influenced by Ismay, who, the previous day, had pointed out to Colville that 'we have only a small stake near Trondheim and ... it does not much matter if we lose it', which, Colville commented, was 'a cold blooded military way of looking at things'.[41] But again, exhaustion was taking its toll on the Chiefs. Dewing recorded, 'Tiny, although very tired, is still doing nearly all the meetings. The most important brief this morning was entirely ignored!'[42]

Doubts about the wisdom of 'Hammer 2' grew during the day. Ismay was probably articulating what many in Whitehall were beginning to think when he told Halifax, 'We must get out.'[43] By the time of their meeting late that evening, the Chiefs were divided in their opinion. Doubts were raised about the feasibility of the operation if, as had been reported, the Germans had linked up with the garrison at Trondheim and would be able to 'pile reinforcements' into the town during the ten to fourteen days it would take to mount the operation. Ironside, however, was dismissive. Even if they had linked up, he said, they would be at the end of a very long line of communication, and we could synchronise our attack with an advance of our forces from Namsos. Another brigade, he added, could be immediately transported to Åndalsnes. The possibility of German reinforcement being conducted by air, which was exactly what took place, was disregarded. By 30 April the German garrison at Trondheim had doubled to 9,500 men.[44] Ironside's conclusions were at variance with those of Massy, who, in a paper considered at the meeting, had warned, 'Should it not be possible to interfere with his air force or to bring our own air force into play, the possibility of evacuation will have to be squarely faced. The time has certainly come when preparations must be made so that a withdrawal of troops in Norway can be effected at short notice.'[45] Newall must have known that there was little chance that Massy's criteria could be met, but he did not pursue the matter. Later, Churchill joined the meeting and, according to Ironside, announced that the Prime Minister 'had agreed that all preparations should be made' for the attack on Trondheim.[46] The Chiefs duly agreed to initiate preparations accordingly.[47] It had been, noted Ironside, 'another damnable evening'.[48]

When they met at nine o'clock the next morning (26 April), the Chiefs made an abrupt and complete 'about turn'. The catalyst was a report, produced overnight, by the Joint Planners on the military implications of establishing and maintaining a base at Trondheim. As in several previous reports on the subject, they were forthright: 'We must face the fact ... that the maintenance of this force may prove impossible.' They warned that the weight of air attack could exceed 100 tons per day – more now that the Luftwaffe was established in aerodromes in southern Scandinavia – and that only about one-tenth of the German bomber forces had so far been used in Norway. Furthermore, the air defences for Trondheim alone would, they said, require fifty heavy and eighty light anti-aircraft guns,[49] which, as the Chiefs observed, when added to the air defence requirements at Narvik, would commit practically all Britain's light anti-aircraft guns to Norway.[50] Additionally, the Joint Planners reminded the Chiefs that one of the main purposes of the operations in Norway was to cause Germany to divert far more troops from the Western Front to Norway than did the Allies; with the withdrawal of two further Regular brigades from the BEF being contemplated, the argument was looking threadbare. [51] The Chiefs were now face to face with reality and concluded that '[t]he logical deduction was that a modified operation "Hammer" should not be undertaken.'[52]

In addition, a number of grim overnight situation reports were filtering in, several telling of the debacle at Lake Lesjaskog. One of the first, from the RAF liaison officer with Sickleforce, advised, 'Essential to send two full strength Hurricane or Spitfire squadrons immediately, pending suitable land for aerodrome ... desperate situation. Army say unless more air support at once, cannot hold enemy.'[53] A trusted Military Operations officer who had been sent to Paget's headquarters to report on the situation emphasised the decisive impact of enemy air attacks and warned that if at least air parity could not be achieved 'a debacle may ensue'.[54] Also received that morning was Paget's signal advising preparation for evacuation 'if aerial superiority is not ensured forthwith'.[55]

At the Military Coordination Committee later in the morning, ministers accepted the Chiefs' advice and agreed to the cancellation of Hammer 2 and, in principle, to evacuation from central Norway. As Churchill was later to point out, with some irritation, 'Both claws of the feeble pincers were broken.'[56] Discussion focused on timing and presentation. Ministers favoured postponement, with Chamberlain suggesting that a force might be retained there to harass the Germans 'perhaps for quite a considerable time yet'. With an eye on public opinion, he further suggested carrying out the evacuation as slowly as possible before a speedy, final withdrawal. 'We should then', he said, 'be able to claim it as a strategical triumph and emphasise that it was all part of our plan for concentrating our efforts at Narvik.' This view was endorsed by Churchill who proposed withdrawal from the Trondheim area 'after giving the Germans as hard a knock as we could with the Regular troops' and concentration on Narvik.[57] The Committee agreed that evacuation should, if possible, be postponed until after the capture of Narvik. According to Ironside, 'There was no argument',[58] and by lunchtime the War Cabinet had endorsed the decision. A few ministers expressed dismay, but discussion centred on presentation not substance, in particular how the decision should be sold to the public and to the French government. The best line to take with the public might be that 'the landing of forces in central Norway had never been intended as more than a diversion'. [59] As for the French, Simon went as far as to suggest that they should not even be told of the intention to evacuate: '[I]t might prejudice secrecy'.[60] The subject of informing the Norwegians was not even considered.

The CIGS was tasked with breaking the news to Gamelin, who arrived in London that evening, telling Ironside that 'the British Government was mad to think of evacuation'.[61] At a subsequent meeting with British ministers, Gamelin argued in vain for a bridgehead to be maintained in central Norway and for guerrilla operations to be conducted against the enemy advancing north towards Narvik – '[T]he humiliation of defeat would thus be avoided'.[62] At a hastily convened meeting of the full Supreme War Council the following day (27 April), Chamberlain explained to a horrified Reynaud what was, in effect, a fait accompli.[63] There remained the question of timing, with both British and French ministers aiming for maximum postponement of an event almost too awful, politically, to contemplate. The matter was decided at a meeting of the Military Coordination Committee that evening. In attendance was Massy – remarkably, the only occasion on which he was invited to a meeting of the Committee. After a situation report of the dire position at both Åndalsnes and Namsos, he made it plain that 'unless we could overcome their air superiority we must withdraw, and must withdraw quickly.' His intention was, he said, to complete the evacuation from Åndalsnes by 1 May and from Namsos by 3 May.[64] Churchill now gave way, although earlier in the day he had argued at the War Cabinet meeting against immediate withdrawal and for 'leaving the troops now in Norway to put up the best fight they could, in conjunction with the Norwegians'[65] – a proposal which, if carried out, would probably have led to the capture (or death) of some 12,000 British and French soldiers. The Committee authorised Massy's plan.[66] Later that evening, the orders were issued. Only subsequently were the French informed.

The almost simultaneous evacuation of the Allied forces in central Norway from two separate locations, 150 miles apart, in the face of enemy pressure on the ground and under enemy air superiority was a complex operation and a daunting prospect. Its planning and conduct was given to Massy and his new, but still embryonic, headquarters, augmented for the task by the small Inter-Service Planning Staff. But since Massy's responsibility was not matched by authority – as a single-service commander, he could not give orders to the other services – and because this was an entirely new and untested way of operating, there was much duplication of effort. On 27 April the Military Coordination Committee agreed to the evacuation from both Åndalsnes and Namsos for the night of 30 April, with further evacuation at Namsos over the following night, and a third night, if necessary.[67] If security was to be maintained, speed was of the essence. The maritime operation was planned and conducted by the Royal Navy with great skill and efficiency. It was one of the most successful operations of the British campaign in Norway.

Over-focus on individual operations, battles and engagements – whether successes or failures – can, however, distract from the wider understanding of campaigns in the context of strategy. So, what does the experience in central Norway tell us about British strategy and about campaign planning and management at the time?

In short, they were inadequate in almost every conceivable way. First, the inability to address questions of strategic priority or decide on where the main effort should lie, the vacillation, the avoidance of uncomfortable decisions – all had been demonstrated to the full. Here, Chamberlain's unsuitability as a wartime leader was cruelly exposed. His lack of familiarity with the subject became a severe handicap. On 20 April, he wrote in his diary, 'The military keep saying that we are engaged in very hazardous operations, so I suppose we are.'[68] He also deferred too easily to Churchill's aura of strategic expertise – 'Well, he is the professional strategist', he recorded[69] – seemingly failing to understand that a strategist, whether professional or amateur, was not necessarily a good strategist. In addition, Chamberlain had a natural inclination to procrastinate and, above all, to attempt to preserve the calm equilibrium of his War Cabinet at all costs, at a time when making well-judged, timely decisions was what really counted.

Also exposed was the assumption that the campaign could be effectively planned from map and chart without an understanding of just how much neither map nor chart could portray. With it was a failure to understand that, in a fast moving campaign, the time taken to pass information meant that orders were often given on the basis of out-of-date information and overtaken by events before their receipt. It was for the Chiefs to bring these realities to decision-making, and to do so relentlessly, but any advice they may have given on this score made little impact.

The quality and timeliness of decision-making had also been impeded by the over-bureaucratic committee structure – quite inappropriate for crisis management in fast-moving circumstances. The decision-makers spent too much time in committee, so compounding the pressure. The effect became most evident in the Military Coordination Committee which, under Churchill's chairmanship, became over-involved in military details. Meetings became, in Ismay's words, 'at once more frequent, more controversial and ... more acrimonious'.[70] Colville recorded in his diary that when Churchill chaired the meetings, 'his verbosity and recklessness makes a great deal of unnecessary work, prevent any real practical planning from being done and generally cause friction'.[71] After his first meeting in the chair of the Committee, Chamberlain recorded, 'Winston's attitude was most difficult, challenging everything the Chiefs of Staff suggested and generally behaving like a spoiled & sulky child. This was the committee over which he is supposed to preside but which he had got into an almost mutinous condition.'[72] Churchill came to dominate the Committee's proceedings and fought his own battle of attrition with those who disagreed with him, most notably the Chiefs of Staff. His force of personality was too often not matched by the quality of his judgment, and his effect was debilitating for already tired people. Slessor's picture of 'Exhausted men, ready to succumb to Winston's pressure' tells much.[73]

Churchill's method of operating had further consequences. Ian Jacob recalled, '[H]e was always in touch with the situation personally ... [with] the operational telegrams brought direct to him, often while he was sitting in Cabinet'. Combined with his personality, however, '[t]he result was a series of ad hoc decisions'.[74] The outcome was often incoherent and chaotic, as the on-off decisions surrounding Operation Hammer showed. Churchill's almost complete ignorance of, and disregard for, logistics compounded the problem. 'Men like Winston never think of the tail, which whisks about so violently behind the head they push so gaily into new adventures', wrote Ironside wearily in his diary.[75] But he seems not to have recognised that it was his duty, not Churchill's, to bring the harsh logistic realities to the table. In addition, Churchill's notion of combat capability was out of touch with reality. As Jacob noted,

[h]e tended to think in terms of 'sabres and bayonets', the terms used by historians to measure the strength of the two forces engaged in battle in years gone by. ... He did not seem to understand that infantry on the Second [World] War battlefield had very little power unless properly organised in trained formations with good communications and a real command structure, and backed by artillery and anti-tank weapons as well as armour.[76]

Again, it was the CIGS's role and duty to disabuse Churchill.

Furthermore, Churchill was 'always in the [Admiralty] war room, to which he was irresistibly attracted',[77] and although his ever-loyal private secretary, Eric Seal, subsequently avowed that he 'took scrupulous care … not to force his view on any professional decision',[78] Churchill probably did not need to: his formidable presence, personality and comments sufficed.

The professional limitations of the Chiefs, individually and as a group, were further demonstrated starkly over this period. Conspicuous amongst these limitations were their apparent reluctance to address the obvious imbalance in ends, ways and means, and the resulting risk, and the failure of imagination, particularly on the part of Ironside, to envisage what was actually happening 'on the ground'. These were all significant contributors to the chaotic sequence of order, counter-order and disorder. Remarkable, too, was the unwillingness of the Chiefs to listen to the advice of their key advisers, in particular the Joint Planners, particularly apparent over the impact on the campaign of German air superiority about which the Joint Planners had been warning for months.[79] Moreover, each Chief was playing his own game. Newall was not in favour of dissipating precious air assets on the campaign and was slow to commit those necessary for the success of the land and sea operations. Likewise, in proposing the 'pincer' alternative to Hammer, Pound was influenced by the attraction of seeing the risk carried by the Army rather than by the fleet. In his turn, Ironside paid scant regard to the cost to the other services for the land operation to succeed. Unsurprisingly, they did not speak with one voice and generally fought their own corners, rather than work towards a coordinated and integrated solution. Indeed, according to Dewing, Ironside discussed with his fellow Chiefs the possibility of staging some form of protest that due account was not being taken of their advice, but that 'Tiny told me that neither Newall nor Pound would take any part in protest – so that was the end of that.'[80] In Slessor's retrospective view of Operation Hammer, 'The Chiefs of Staff were subjected to intense pressure (which perhaps they may be criticized for not resisting more strongly) to do something that we all knew was militarily impracticable.'[81] With two of the Chiefs still alive when he was writing, Slessor was pulling his punches.

When it came to the operations in central Norway, the strategic decision-makers and their advisers had a misplaced confidence that warfare could be controlled. They assumed that plans could and would be followed, that events could and would follow the plans, rather than conspire against them, and that the sort of big risks that might be considered unreasonable in peacetime could somehow be taken with impunity in warfare. There seemed to be no limit to the virtues of flexibility and improvisation, illustrated by de Lee's telling summary of the result of the deployment orders given to the two Territorial brigades:

'148 Brigade, bound for Stavanger, was diverted to Namsos, transshipped to Åndalsnes and ordered to attack Trondheim, ending up at Lillehammer. 146 Brigade was intended for Bergen and Trondheim but was diverted to Narvik and ended up at Namsos.'[82] Insufficient attention had been paid to practicality and 'the factors that distinguish real war from war on paper'. [83] It could not be expected that ministers would necessarily have much understanding of Clausewitzian friction. It could, however, be expected that their military advisers would do so and that they would ensure that it informed their advice with sufficient force.

17   The Third Dimension

Had the British analysed their enemy to identify what Clausewitz termed 'the centre of gravity ... the hub of all power and movement on which everything depends ... the point against which all our energies should be directed'[1] – they might have recognised that it was the German command of the air over Norway. Certainly air power, more than any other factor, had played the decisive role in the outcome of the campaign thus far. But how had this occurred? How was it that the German and not the British air force was dominating events on both land and sea? And what was the key to their success? The answer to these questions is essential to an understanding of the campaign in Norway.

Thinking about air power and its potential in future war had been much clearer in Germany than in Britain. Although the Versailles Treaty had prohibited a German air force, the visionary head of the German Army in 1919, General Hans von Seeckt, had formed a nucleus of highly talented officers to study the potential of air power. Seeckt ensured that air officers were not only well represented in the Reichswehr ministry but also integrated as an air staff throughout the chain of command. He also insisted that the third dimension was considered in all training and incorporated into operational doctrine.[2] When Hitler came to power in 1933, he, too, saw the potential of air power in warfare and in 1935 announced the formation of the Luftwaffe. He invested heavily in modern aircraft, specifically in aircraft for support to ground forces, rather than long-range bombers, and in the development of a transport fleet.[3] A Luftwaffe group, the Condor Legion, was sent to the Spanish Civil War from 1936 to 1938 and used as a test bed for concepts and tactics, with large numbers of pilots rotated through the force to gain precious combat experience.[4] A study of the lessons learnt resulted in even closer integration of air and ground forces into German training and doctrine. At the operational and tactical levels, more joint training led to a more joint culture. The Germans also learnt much about air-land cooperation in the Polish campaign, including the psychological impact of close air support; one report noted, 'The effect of the Stukas on the morale of the enemy was often decisive.'[5] The Spanish Civil War had also seen the formidable German air transport capability demonstrated; the Luftwaffe had airlifted some 12,000 of General Franco's troops from Morocco to Spain.[6] Lastly, by the outbreak of the Second World War the Luftwaffe was well equipped with modern aircraft, balanced between bombers, fighters and transport aircraft, and task-organised into Luftflotten – large groups which contained a mix of all these aircraft.

In Britain the picture was different in almost every way. Trenchard's doctrine held that the air force should be used for long-range 'strategic' bombing and that roles such as close air support were a dangerous distraction and a misuse of air power. Part of the reason for this doctrine was to thwart the other services in their desires and schemes to usurp the roles, and even challenge the existence of, the RAF. Minds were closed to evidence, such as that from the Spanish Civil War and Polish campaign, which might suggest that close air support was highly effective. A JIC study was commissioned in 1937 to report on the lessons from Spain, but its findings were corrupted by the determination of the individual services to include only those that furthered their own interests, in particular in the competition for resources in Whitehall. Thus, the CIGS of the day denigrated conclusions about the need for anti-aircraft defences for airfields ('the report had been drawn up on meagre evidence');[7] the First Sea Lord considered that although 'it would be useful to consider these reports ... no lessons of importance could be learned from them';[8] and the Chief of the Air Staff was careful that no lessons should be taken away that detracted from the Trenchard doctrine. Indeed, where the report drew attention to the effectiveness of close air support, concluding that 'the moral effect of air action against ground forces is out of all proportion to the material results achieved',[9] the Air Staff maintained the line that bombers should not be used on the battlefield except in exceptional circumstances: 'All experience of war', it declared, 'proves that such action is not only very costly in casualties, but is normally uneconomical and ineffective.'[10] Furthermore, the RAF officer who had chaired the study into the use of air power in Spain was discouraged by his superiors from including in his lectures any suggestion that the Luftwaffe might be used primarily for Army support and be subsidiary to the Army role.[11] These attitudes permeated doctrine and training. In the words of one air power historian, by 1939, RAF Staff College students 'had become receptacles for current wisdom, rather than contributors to it', with lessons learned 'selected to fit theory, rather than vice versa'.[12] Nor can it be claimed that the RAF staff college was entirely alone in this.[13]

With the need for strict prioritisation forced by the government's highly constrained funding for the armed services, the RAF chose to invest predominantly in heavy bombers, and it was not until 1937 that the Air Ministry was forced by the Cabinet 'in the teeth of stiff opposition'[14] to invest substantially in the fighter programme (though on economic and industrial, rather than tactical grounds).[15] Even so, in April 1940 Bomber Command possessed only 216 operational aircraft, barely a quarter the number of the Luftwaffe's bomber force, and all were outperformed by the German bombers.[16] Unsurprisingly, the Air Staff wished 'to avoid at all costs any action which would dissipate our air striking power unprofitably'.[17] Unlike the German armed forces, air force officers were not integrated in army formations and did not participate in army exercises; there was virtually no joint training (except at staff colleges) and no joint culture. The level of cooperation between the services was exemplified by the fact that the few Army Cooperation Flights of spotting aircraft were the lowest funding priority. Moreover, unlike the Luftwaffe with its organisation of multi-disciplinary Luftflotten, the RAF was organised into functional commands – fighter, bomber and coastal – a structure which had many benefits but did not easily lend itself to the deployment of an expeditionary air task force. Furthermore, control of air resources was divided between the RAF and the Royal Navy; the latter, after a bitter inter-service battle, regained ownership of the carrier-based aircraft – the Fleet Air Arm – in 1937, but not of the land-based maritime aircraft of Coastal Command. Following RAF priorities, the whole maritime capability had been poorly resourced throughout the 1930s, so that the carrier-based aircraft at the outbreak of the war were not just old, but obsolescent, and Coastal Command, according to its CinC, 'had no Striking Force whatever'.[18] Finally, for all practical purposes, the RAF possessed no transport aircraft.[19]

In terms of the campaign in Norway, the Germans had carefully task organised an air component, the 10th Air Corps (X Fliegerkorps), to match their campaign plan. In accordance with German doctrine, they thought in terms of a *Schwerpunkt* – a main effort – and were clear that Operation Weserübung would, temporarily, be the grand strategic main effort. It was accepted that this *Schwerpunkt* would shortly change to the Western Front for the invasion of the Low Countries and France, but the inherent flexibility of air power would allow this to be done quickly. Thus, the air task force for Norway could, and would, be immensely powerful, with more than 1,000 aircraft, and it was largely to facilitate the air campaign, through the use of Danish airbases, that, on Falkenhorst's recommendation, the invasion of Denmark was added to the plan by Hitler.

The British, by contrast, planned only a small air component for their campaign in Norway. This approach was due to four main factors. First, they had grossly underestimated the degree to which air power had changed warfare, particularly in the Royal Navy. Feelings on the subject ran high. When Phillips, Deputy Chief of the Naval Staff, had been one of the Joint Planners with Slessor, a close personal friend, they 'had a sort of pact not to discuss aircraft versus ships except when our duty made it inevitable in committee – when there was usually a row'.[20] The Royal Navy generally believed that sea-based air defence guns would provide the necessary protection against air attack; just as many in the Army believed that land-based air defence guns would. Second, the air component envisaged for Scandinavia – at one time six bomber squadrons and three each of fighter and Army cooperation squadrons[21] – was perceived as being both too small and too big: inadequate to face Germany's anticipated deployed air force, but a significant proportion of Britain's available air force, especially in fighters. It would take assets away from a much more important commitment – the air defence of Great Britain.[22] As a result, throughout the planning, the Air Ministry was consistent in its (at best) lukewarm support for the campaign. (This view was far from unanimous within the RAF. When an order came to RAF Scampton for three aircraft to attack Ålborg, Flying Officer Guy Gibson's response was, 'Why not the whole squadron?'[23]) Third, in further contrast to the Germans, there was no accepted concept of main effort, in this case one that could be switched rapidly if the need arose. There was, for example, no shared perception of the importance of the putative campaign in Norway relative to other commitments, such as the Mediterranean or the Middle East. Indeed, while the operations in Norway were being planned, the only modern aircraft carrier of the two in the Home Fleet was sent to the Mediterranean and did not deploy to duty off Norway until 23 April.[24] Last was the acceptance of risk. The War Cabinet had been told that there was considerable risk to the deployed force from air attack and, on the advice of the Chiefs, had accepted that risk.[25]

When the decision was made on 28 March to go ahead with the minefields off Narvik and to reconstitute the forces for the Avonmouth and Stratford operations, the Chiefs saw no need for air forces to accompany the initial deployment; Avonmouth was to be restricted to the occupation of Narvik, and Stratford to the occupation of Bergen, Trondheim and Stavanger. It was not expected that these forces would have to fight; if they did have to, it would only be to help the Norwegians defend these towns. As events proved, these assumptions were dangerously narrow.

The German air plan for Weserübung was imaginative and comprehensive. It included 330 bombers, 100 fighters, 70 reconnaissance planes and – an innovative masterstroke – 500 transport aircraft. The latter would facilitate coup de main operations on Day One, and allow the Germans to generate reinforcements and resupply extremely quickly, thus contributing to high tempo and retention of the initiative. The air transport plan was itself a hugely complicated logistic challenge, and the Germans turned to a professional to mastermind it: Colonel Freiherr von Gablenz, formerly a senior manager at Lufthansa. The 10th Air Corps' major Day One mission would be the protection of the naval operation, the seizure of important airbases – in Norway at Oslo and Stavanger and in Denmark at Ålborg. On 9 April, not everything went to plan – notably, a coup de main parachute drop on Oslo/Fornebu airport was called off at the last moment due to bad weather – but by the end of the day, the major objectives had been taken and transport aircraft were arriving.

By contrast, the British air plan was entirely reactive and improvised, and conducted not as a single air campaign but as separate and largely uncoordinated operations by the Royal Air Force and Royal Navy. The RAF's immediate response to news of the invasion was the despatch of aircraft to destroy the Kriegsmarine ships returning to Germany and then to close down the Norwegian airfields occupied by the Luftwaffe. The War Cabinet expected that it would succeed in doing so. Here, however, theory and practice parted company. For a start, 'no preparations had been made to operate over Norway ... it had been axiomatic that nothing would be done until the British and Norwegian staffs had conferred together, and that all the Norwegian aerodromes and air force stations should be at our disposal.'[26] The Air Staff were, therefore, planning from a standing start, and on the basis of very poor intelligence. The attempt to destroy the ships returning to Germany had only one success from the air: the Fleet Air Arm attack on the battleship *Königsberg* in Bergen harbour. The search at sea was unsuccessful despite the participation of no less than ninety-three bombers. Thereafter, the RAF switched its effort to attacking the German-occupied airfields in central and southern Norway, although not until 21 April did they attack the strategically important airfields at Ålborg – a critical error.[27] Initially, this operation was hamstrung by political restrictions on targeting. The Franco-British bombing policy permitted only machine gun attack, not bombing, on airfields in Norway, and this restriction was not lifted for two days.[28] In any case, many in the RAF continued to be less than enthusiastic about the operation, continuing to be concerned that it could drain resources from the anticipated 'decisive event' closer to home. Eventually (on 27 April), the Air Ministry directed the CinC Bomber Command, Air Chief

Marshal Sir Charles Portal, that 'it is no longer justifiable to hold back our heavy bomber force for operations on the Western Front'.[29]

According to one author, Portal had serious reservations about the policy of bombing 'distant airfields'.[30] First, navigation presented a significant challenge. Because no preparations had been made to operate over Norway, no reconnaissance of any kind had been carried out, nor had any maps of Norway been prepared for air navigation purposes. Thus, aircrew had to make do with 'a sheet from an exceedingly small-scale map, and a tracing of a town plan taken from "Baedeker's Guide to Norway [1912 edition]"'.[31] Second, for the British planes, operating at ranges of 300 to 500 miles from their bases and with no intermediate airfields for refuelling, time and space became a key limitation. Many of the British bombers either did not have the necessary range or were operating at their extreme range, with very limited 'time over target'. Since all but the closest targets were out of range of any British fighters, the bombers were for the most part operating unescorted and were highly vulnerable to the enemy's modern fighters, which had been deployed in large numbers very quickly. On 12 April a daylight raid by eighty-three aircraft on Stavanger airfield achieved little, but the heavy bombers on the raid took fifteen per cent casualties. Portal decided that such losses were unsustainable and that daylight raids by heavy bombers should cease. Such a change of policy was, according to Middlebrook and Everitt, 'undoubtedly the most important turning point in Bomber Command's war'.[32] The light bombers could fly by day, but only when there was sufficient cloud cover into which to escape. However, navigation was very difficult when the cloud cover was too great or at night. Third, at this time of year, the weather across the North Sea and over Norway was often adverse – particularly so in the late winter of 1940. Finally, although the German-occupied air bases offered a 'target rich environment' for the RAF – for example, it transpired that Stavanger had had 143 Luftwaffe aircraft on the ground on 24 April[33] – the Germans had quickly provided these airfields with anti-aircraft artillery, not in the penny packets which the British were wont to employ, but in mass. By 16 April the Germans had, or were looking to have, six heavy and four light batteries at Stavanger airfield, three heavy and two light batteries at the Oslo/Fornebu and Trondheim airfields and three heavy and one light battery at Bergen.[34] In addition, the Germans deployed their new radar installations to some of their airbases in Norway – notably Stavanger – giving them advance warning of incoming attacks.[35]

Unsurprisingly, the British success rate was very low: '[A] large proportion of raids that took off reached their target in reduced numbers, and . . . a fair proportion could not reach the target at all.'[36] For example,

Figure 17.1 A target-rich environment: Oslo's Fornebu airport
(Bundesarchiv)

in the first ten days of active operations following the lifting of restrictions, five sorties, involving thirty aircraft, returned after failing to find their targets, and a further three missions involving eighteen aircraft returned because of insufficient cloud cover.[37] Attacking such well-defended targets was hazardous. In late April, the Air Staff contemplated providing and maintaining standing patrols of fighters, six at a time, over the battlefield, but this idea was overtaken by events.[38] Only the makeshift Blenheim fighters, close to their range limit, could reach Åndalsnes but were unable to spend more than one hour overhead; Namsos was beyond their range.[39] The RAF was, therefore, unable to seriously challenge German air superiority. In the first month of the campaign, Bomber Command carried out over 900 sorties at a cost of thirty-six aircraft (3.9 per cent).[40] Many of these operations were laying magnetic mines at sea off the southern coast of Norway, although these only accounted for about a dozen German ships in the course of the campaign.[41] During that first month, Bomber Command carried out only twenty-eight raids in which bombs were dropped.[42] Despite optimistic reports at the time, the results were poor. The uncompromising verdict of one historian of the campaign (Air Commodore Maurice Harvey) was that 'it could not be claimed by even the most optimistic supporter of air bombardment that Bomber Command had any positive influence on the battle for Norway.'[43] This judgment is, perhaps, a little harsh. Not least, over the critical period of the evacuation from central Norway, Bomber Command succeeded in closing Stavanger airfield for all but emergency landings.

Coastal Command too played but a small role in the campaign. Very much the lowest priority in the eyes of the Air Ministry – not for nothing was it nicknamed the Cinderella Command – it had no purpose-built, modern anti-shipping aircraft and had to rely on obsolescent planes such as the Hampden.[44] There was optimism in some quarters that the Fleet Air Arm aircraft, flying off the carriers near Namsos and Åndalsnes, might redress the balance, but it was quickly shown that, despite some individual successes, their planes – also obsolescent – were no match for the modern German land-based aircraft and that the carriers were, themselves, highly vulnerable and prize targets. Indeed, Göring offered the Knight's Cross and 100,000 Reichmarks to any pilot who succeeded in sinking one.[45] Their perceived vulnerability forced the carriers out to sea, lengthening response times and limiting time over target. Fleet Air Arm aircraft could, thus, contest the air over Namsos and Åndalsnes only spasmodically, briefly and in very small numbers.[46] (According to Carton de Wiart, they appeared over Namsos on just two occasions, although when they did so 'the enemy planes cleared off at once.'[47]) In the interim, the Luftwaffe could operate unmolested. On 2 May the War Cabinet was told that '[i]t had been found that the aircraft carriers could not operate close enough to the shore to support our troops, and they were therefore returning to Scapa to refit.'[48] German air superiority in central Norway was, thus, never seriously challenged. From the outset, the Luftwaffe was able to conduct critically important offensive missions: destroying the Allied bases at Namsos and Åndalsnes, delivering resupply and reinforcements to Narvik and Trondheim, bombing Allied forces around Harstad and providing intelligence and close air support to the German ground forces in central Norway. It would only face a serious challenge in the final days of the campaign at Narvik.

The British were slow to recognise and respond to the need for airfields in Norway on which to base their own aircraft. As early as 15 April, General Ruge had suggested the occupation or denial of airfields in Norway, even providing a map of airfield sites north of Trondheim.[49] Such prompting, however, seems to have had little effect. This may, in part, have resulted from the reluctance of the Air Ministry, noted earlier, to get so involved and committed in the Norwegian campaign that it might be wrong-footed by the expected major attack closer to home. For

Figure 17.2 German reinforcements arriving by air
(Norwegan Armed Forces Museum)

whatever reason, the decision to find and establish an airfield in central Norway came too late to have an effect. The rush to establish the airfield at Lesjaskog was a brave attempt to rectify the situation, but it was an administrative fiasco which ended in disaster. Even if it had succeeded, it is unlikely that it would have altered the tactical situation for long. The old Gladiator bi-planes were no match for the modern German mono-planes. With a squadron of Hurricanes, success would have been greater, but probably only transitory. The real issue was the establishment and maintenance of air superiority, and the plain fact was that the Germans could apply more air power (bombers and fighters) than could the British and were operating on interior lines from other airbases such as Trondheim, Stavanger, Oslo and Ålborg, closer to the scene of action than the airbases in England and Scotland.

The failure to shut down the major German-held airbases in Norway and Denmark was serious, but even if it had succeeded, it would have required more, and better quality, aircraft than the British possessed to keep them closed. Having established themselves initially, the Germans were able to counter the challenges to their air superiority over southern and central Norway and to increase the airspace that they controlled as their ground forces advanced north, capturing or establishing more airfields as they did so. The result should have been unsurprising: the Air Staff and Joint Planners had been consistent in their warnings of what was likely to happen should the Germans gain a foothold in Scandinavia.

The achievement of air superiority by the Germans enabled three additional, significant contributions of German air power to campaign success. The first was their remarkable use of air transport. More than 29,000 men and 2,300 tons of supplies were moved from Germany to Norway by the 500 transport aircraft.[50] This was a logistical triumph.

The second was the impact of air attack, and the threat of air attack, on British maritime policy in the campaign. The impact was seen in the cancellation of Operation Hammer and the inability of the Royal Navy to dominate the Norwegian inshore waters. But it also resulted in the decision, following the Royal Navy's experience on 9 April, not to contest control of the sea off southern Norway with surface vessels, resulting in only minor disruption of the seaborne reinforcement on which the success of the German campaign depended. (British submarines accounted for less than two per cent of German sea reinforcement between 10 April and 13 May.)[51] Thus, Britain's command of the sea, on which the campaign strategy from the outset had rested, was shown not to extend to inshore waters dominated by Germany's command of the air.

The third contribution was the hugely effective German offensive air support to land operations. It was the Luftwaffe which cut the Allies lines of communication at the ports, thus unhinging their plan. It was the Luftwaffe which provided such effective close air support to their Army's operations. A large part of this success was due to communications.[52] Following the lessons of the close integration of air and land forces, and in particular the lessons learnt in Spain and later in Poland, the Luftwaffe invested heavily in communications. For Norway, it deployed no fewer than 3,000 signal troops, the equivalent of nine signal battalions.[53] Ground liaison officers with radios were deployed to formation headquarters and, on occasions, further forward, allowing relatively quick and timely targeting. German reconnaissance aircraft were highly active, and their customary, early morning reconnaissance flights, the harbinger of air attack, are noted in many British contemporary accounts and diaries.[54] These flights provided intelligence of not only where the Allied troops were located but also, equally importantly, where they were not, and thus how and where the positions could be outflanked. By contrast, the British forces in Norway had no such system of ground liaison. Without a theatre headquarters, Army requests for air support were referred back to the War Office where they were passed across to the Air Ministry; unsurprisingly, it was a ponderous and highly impractical process. On the rare occasions that British aircraft operated over British troops in Norway, ground forces could not communicate with them directly, and therefore there was little value, for example, in deploying bombers from Britain to hard-to-locate targets somewhere in the Gudbrandsdal.

Although the most obvious impact of German air power was physical – the destruction of the ports of Namsos and Åndalsnes[55] and the sinking of Allied warships – the psychological impact was less obvious, and therefore easy to underestimate. Bombing and strafing caused few casualties among British troops, but it did cause terror and panic. This effect was exacerbated by the lack of any means of striking back. For those on the receiving end, none of whom had had any training in the matter, it seemed that the enemy had a wonder weapon that was all-powerful and made resistance useless. For commanders back in London, none of whom had experienced air attack, it was difficult to imagine the psychological effect. Ironside later recalled, 'They showed us these dive bombers on the manoeuvres I attended in 1938. I pointed out then that infantry would be *impeded* if not *prevented* from firing at their ground targets if they were pestered by these dive bombers' [emphasis in original].[56] But no steps seem to have been taken to warn or 'inoculate' troops about the effects of a dive-bomber attack. Even in the 'Lessons Learnt from France and Flanders' report, dive-bombing attack was described as a 'new and unexpected development'.[57] The psychological effect of air attack was also seen at sea. Indeed, although the Luftwaffe's tally of ships sunk was substantial, and included a cruiser, six destroyers and sloops, a dozen smaller vessels and twenty-one merchantmen,[58] it is remarkable, given the number of air attacks, that many more ships were not sunk. Skilful evasive action and anti-aircraft gunnery played an important part in this. However, not only was the psychological effect on crews considerable, particularly those who endured continuous air attack for long periods, but also the fear of air attack played a significant role in strategic decisions.

There was also ignorance at the top of the British Army and Royal Navy of the principles and capabilities of air power. The heads of both services appeared to believe that the prime requirement was for a 'fire brigade' of aircraft capable of rapid response to calls for support over their key tactical activities. They seemed to have little understanding that, from a campaign perspective, the prime requirement was the establishment of air superiority, or at least air parity. The Army's doctrine went part of the way to recognise this, stating that 'the primary requirement [of an air force contingent with an army in the field] is to create and maintain an air situation which will enable the army and air force to work with the minimum of interference from enemy air action'.[59] However, the logic of this statement, if pursued, would have led to considerable investment in the air force's ability to achieve this situation – investment which would probably have been at the Army's expense. Ignorance of air capability was considerable. As late as 2 May the Secretary of State for War, Stanley, was still under the impression that Namsos was within range of British fighter aircraft.[60]

The German air campaign was by no means perfect. In particular, command and control were far from exemplary. Göring's insistence on retaining authority over Luftwaffe assets and operations had a detrimental effect on the speed and responsiveness of air operations. Although his insistence was primarily egotistical, it was not entirely misplaced: Falkenhorst's understanding of the application of air power was limited. On several occasions, for example at Narvik, he demanded close air support for ground troops when the better use of resources pointed towards air interdiction of land and sea targets. However, these inter-service disagreements were the exception rather than the rule, and, below the top level, cooperation between the services was, in general, excellent. Indeed, according to one historian, '[T]he Germans won the campaign largely because their services worked together much better than their Allied opponents'.[61]

In retrospect, German air power was the deciding factor in the military campaign in central Norway. The British had grossly underestimated the impact of the third dimension on the conduct of warfare, and the chances of retrieving the situation were slim from the moment on 9 April when the Luftwaffe established itself in Denmark and Norway. These things were, of course, far from clear at the time. The Germans had understood the potential impact of the third dimension on warfare, spotted the opportunity and exploited it. The British had failed to do so. Some of the blame for this can be laid at the door of successive governments who had failed to invest in air power. Some, however, rightly belongs to those at the top of the armed services – over a number of years – who underestimated the threat or, for various reasons, failed to address it. It was probably not only his fellow ministers whom Chamberlain had in mind when he wrote in his diary on 27 April, 'In particular, this brief campaign has taught our people, many of whom were much in need of teaching, the importance of the air factor.'[62]

18   'In the Name of God, Go!'

The hope expressed at the War Cabinet on 26 April that the evacuation from central Norway could be postponed until the capture of Narvik had been based not on strategic considerations but as a fig leaf to cover short-term political embarrassment. Neither in coming to their decision on 26 April, nor subsequently, had the War Cabinet given much thought as to what to do with Narvik once it had been captured. It was accepted, even by Churchill, that Swedish neutrality could not be breached by an expedition to Gällivare and Luleå, but he quickly came up with a scheme to 'turn Narvik into a miniature Scapa', with a garrison of up to 30,000 troops and eight squadrons of aircraft, 'so as to be ready to meet any German advance through Sweden and to take advantage of any opportunity to get to Lulea'.[1] The feasibility and wisdom of this scheme were not questioned by ministers, for whom the capture of Narvik held a much more immediate attraction. As Chamberlain had explained to the hastily convened Supreme War Council on 27 April, this was 'to . . . show that we were still active and powerful, and that we had a grip on the situation in the North'. If Chamberlain was preoccupied by presentation to the media and public, Reynaud, whose position in French domestic politics remained precarious, was doubly so. 'The Allies', he said, should 'take such measures as were possible to save appearances', suggesting that a force should be maintained in central Norway 'to wear out and harass the Germans, and to enable the Allies to show that they had not abandoned their aims in Norway'.[2] Gamelin had been uncomfortably close to the truth when, during a meeting the previous evening, he had commented that if measures such as this were adopted, 'the humiliation of defeat would thus be avoided'.[3]

The potential political consequences and the keen instinct for political survival were, with good reason, now clearly uppermost in the minds of members of the War Cabinet. Anthony Eden noted after the Cabinet meeting on 1 May, 'much of the time was spent by colleagues rehearsing their defence of our withdrawal from southern Norway'.[4] Similarly, the following day in the War Cabinet, '[f]urther discussion took place as to the points which should be made in the Debate in the ensuing week in the House of Commons on operations in Norway'.[5]

Suddenly there was much ministerial interest in the tactical plan to capture Narvik, as Ironside wearily noted on 30 April.

Once more, yesterday evening, I was astonished at the PM and Winston in the way they asked about the position of every company surrounding Narvik. What were they? To which regiment did they belong? Why did we think they were there? It seemed so futile and showed they were playing with futilities. I have no idea how we are to liberate ourselves from this. Perhaps, if the war becomes more general and when they are tired of playing with tin soldiers on a map, we may get on with our work.[6]

Strategy, on the other hand, was receiving less attention than it deserved. Thus, the starting point in adjusting the campaign plan to the new circumstances was not the consideration of what overall objective could be achieved with the ways and means now available. The starting point was the assumption that Narvik, once captured, would be retained. Churchill's scheme for a 'miniature Scapa' was taken forward without debate, and a 'Narvik Committee' set up to implement it.[7] As so often over the past six months, planning had developed a logic and momentum of its own. What was desirable in policy terms had not been subjected to the process of strategy. As Captain Edwards, the Admiralty's Director of Operations, observed, 'I am not clear why we want Narvik unless it is to walk into Sweden and seize the ore mines. We don't appear to have any national policy nor any naval policy and we just muddle along. It is too depressing for words.'[8]

It was not until 6 May that the War Cabinet addressed the question of what the new policy objective should be in the Norwegian theatre. When it did so, there was no mention of 'miniature Scapas'. The Chiefs of Staff had persuaded Churchill that the object of Operation Rupert was threefold:

To secure and maintain a base in Northern Norway from which we can

a) Deny iron ore supplies to Germany via Narvik.
b) Interfere so far as possible with iron ore supplies to Germany from Lulea.
c) Preserve a part of Norway as a seat for the Norwegian King and people.[9]

It was clear, though, from discussion in Cabinet that, although these were all plausible justifications, and that, in Churchill's words, it would allow us 'to mine Lulea and bomb the ore ships even if Sweden did not come in', that the main reason, presented by Chamberlain, was the potential impact on world opinion if we gave up Narvik: '[T]his would have a very bad political effect, not only on neutral Governments, but also on the French'.[10] Apparently ignored was the effect on opinion in the United States of a violation of

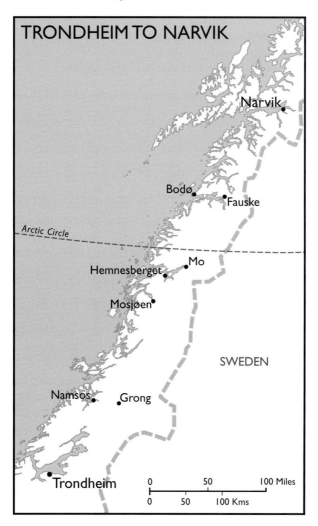

Map 18.1 Trondheim to Narvik

Sweden's neutrality at Luleå. What was also left unsaid, at least in the
minutes, was what must have been in the forefront of the minds of all
present, namely the political effect at home. Nor was there discussion of
whether the ways and means existed to achieve the stated policy objective.

It was not only the defence of Narvik itself for which resources would
be required. Linked to its retention were plans to prevent or hinder
further German advance northwards towards it. Massy's immediate

plan was to establish a firm base (including a harbour and aerodrome) somewhere between Namsos and Narvik and to deploy five recently raised 'Independent Companies' at Mosjøen (pronounced 'Morshern'), Mo-i-Rana and Bodø to conduct offensive, harrying operations.[11] As an interim measure, and to secure Mosjøen, he despatched a party of 100 Chasseurs Alpins and two anti-aircraft guns by sea from Namsos and ordered Carton de Wiart to conduct a fighting withdrawal overland to Mosjøen (which both Carton de Wiart and Audet had declined to do, the former citing impassable roads, the latter the shortage of skiers).[12] In the War Office, the Military Operations staff were alarmed at the prospect of establishing a firm base, warning that 'it is quite certain that we will be unable to provide, in the near future, the very considerable number of [anti-aircraft] guns which General Massy will require for this new project.'[13] Far from agreeing with his staff, Ironside, favoured the establishment of strong defensive positions, telling the Military Coordination Committee that action was being taken to establish a series of defensive lines between Namsos and Narvik, including light tanks, artillery and anti-aircraft guns – the latter to be provided, if necessary, at the expense of the Air Defence of Great Britain.[14]

It soon became apparent that these grand ideas for the retention of Narvik and the establishment of defensive lines and firm bases had not been thought through, let alone subjected to rigorous strategic examination. It was only now that proper consideration was given to the ways and means available to achieve the desired ends. First came the resource bill for the defence of Narvik which the Joint Planners estimated would require a large naval force, including three cruisers, ten destroyers and possibly a battleship, up to two divisions (which would have to come from the BEF), two Hurricane squadrons and a large amount of air defence, yet to be quantified.[15] The latter was estimated by the Vice Chiefs as a staggering 144 light and 144 heavy anti-aircraft guns, of which only sixty and forty-eight had been allocated. They concluded that to provide the required number of light guns was 'not in any way possible', recommending that no more than sixty should be sent. Even this level, they said, represented significant risk, not only at Narvik but also in the BEF and Great Britain. The BEF would be left with only fifty-seven per cent of its authorised scale of heavy guns, and thirty-eight per cent of its light ones. The Air Defence of Great Britain would be even harder hit: left with only forty per cent of its requirement for heavy guns and nine per cent of its requirement for light guns.[16] Next came the resource bill for the operations south of Narvik. Massy put this as a brigade of troops and a squadron each of fighters and bombers, with a single base requiring two regiments of anti-aircraft guns, one light and one heavy.[17] The Vice

Chiefs addressed this issue also, declaring that no air defence assets could be spared for this operation and that the commitment should be limited to the infiltration of small, self-contained parties to deny the ports and delay the enemy as best they could.[18]

Suddenly, the whole policy looked bankrupt: Narvik would be defended by only two thirds of the required number of anti-aircraft guns; the defensive operation to the south would be conducted by wholly inadequate forces which could do no more than delay the enemy; and both the BEF and Great Britain would be bereft of air defence.

These strategic contradictions presented a quandary to the Chiefs when they met to discuss the subject on 2 May. They decided that Massy's plan to establish a firm base was out of the question, that only light air defences could be spared for the small delaying detachments along the coast, and that the air defence risk should be spread, with light anti-aircraft guns for Narvik being limited to 60 (out of 144) and the heavy guns coming from the Air Defence of Great Britain.[19] The Chiefs also considered the abandonment of Narvik but, on balance, rejected it – although for a political, rather than military, reason: abandonment at this stage, they believed, would have a momentous political consequence, nationally and internationally.[20] But what the Chiefs had failed to address was the fact that, if the resources did not exist to do more than delay the enemy reaching Narvik, and if the Narvik defences were grossly inadequate, the probability was that Narvik would eventually have to be abandoned.

The Chiefs now came under pressure from a number of directions. From Paris, Gamelin was insistent that a front should be established at Mosjøen.[21] In the same vein, Churchill was horrified at the Chiefs' decision to rely on small detachments, instead of defensive positions and firm bases. He reminded them of the Military Coordination Committee's decision on 29 April that 'operations north of Trondheim with the object of preventing the further German advance should be conducted with the utmost vigour.' 'It would be a disgrace', he maintained, 'if the Germans made themselves masters of this stretch of the Norwegian coast with practically no opposition from us, and in the course of the next few weeks or even days.' A 'small sub-base' should be established at Mosjøen, he said, and the detachments there and at Mo should be reinforced with additional resources, including light tanks, where these could be landed, 'or at least tracked vehicles', and additional anti-aircraft guns.[22] Now Massy returned to the charge with his proposal for an aerodrome, at Bodø. Without it, he argued, fighter aircraft based at Bardufoss, fifty miles north of Narvik, would be too far away to influence events south of Bodø, and without air support, the small detachments of defenders would be quickly rolled up, one after the other. 'Eventually, Narvik itself will become untenable.'[23] The War Office staff viewed these representations with concern. Prior to the Chiefs' meeting on 5 May, Dewing advised Ironside, 'I feel that a firm policy is required with regard to our forces South of Narvik.' He was alarmed at the prospect of 'the opening of a new front with the consequent naval, air, army and anti-aircraft commitments which we are in no position to meet.'[24] The Chiefs, however, reversed the decision they had made just three days previously and now declared that 'it was desirable, and might prove practicable, to hold Bodo permanently'.[25]

Again, the Chiefs had vacillated between having their cake and eating it and ended up trying to do both. It was, however, difficult to disguise the fact that the strategy did not add up: the necessary ways and means simply did not exist. Even if air support could be provided by aircraft based at Bodø, the Independent Companies were capable only of delaying the German advance. Bodø would, therefore, eventually come under ground attack and would require substantial ground forces, in particular air defence, if it was to hold. But providing these resources from Narvik, already well below the number of anti-aircraft guns it needed, would leave the garrison located there critically short of air defence.

In the midst of these deliberations, Chamberlain had chosen to make a significant change in the machinery for the higher direction of the war. Following an ultimatum by Churchill a fortnight earlier that he would not take back the chairmanship of the Military Coordination Committee unless given the authority of a Deputy Prime Minister, Chamberlain informed the War Cabinet that Churchill would now have the powers to 'give guidance and direction' to the Chiefs of Staff Committee, including the authority to convene and preside over meetings. Furthermore, the Joint Planners would form a central staff working for Churchill through Ismay, and the latter, so often the voice of common sense, would, himself, become a member of the Chiefs of Staff Committee.[26] Chamberlain thus gave Churchill much added responsibility, although not matched by authority – Churchill still had to act in consultation with the other service ministers. Ismay was later to point out that this was unsatisfactory because Churchill 'had not the power to *give orders* to service Ministers or to the Chiefs of Staff' [emphasis in original].[27] This state of affairs may, of course, have suited Chamberlain nicely by keeping the highly popular Churchill visibly at his side while giving him responsibility and thus accountability, but without commensurate authority and thus, at least in theory, keeping him on a tight rein. 'Chips' Channon, Parliamentary Private Secretary to Rab Butler, certainly thought so. In his view, 'to gain time he [Chamberlain] has given Winston more rope, and made him what amounts to Director of Operations.'[28]

It was a time when, as events were to show, Chamberlain needed all the friends he could get.

———————

The concern of Members of Parliament in March about the government's conduct of the war, in particular in the debate after the surrender of Finland, had steadily grown during April. The vacillation and lack of military success had provided a focus for dissent, which the military reverses in late April served only to intensify. Harold Macmillan recalled, 'When, at the beginning of May, the news of the evacuation of Trondheim broke, the first reaction of MPs was one of incredulity. It was followed by a growing sense of indignation.'[29] For some, indignation was swiftly followed by a more disturbing conclusion. On 29 April, Lord Salisbury led a deputation of his 'Watching Committee' to express dissatisfaction to Halifax, leaving far from reassured. After a subsequent meeting of the group, one of its members, Harold Nicholson, recorded ominously, 'The general impression is that we may lose the war.'[30]

Genuine unease was, for others, mixed with a sense of opportunity. They cast about to see who should, or could, be saddled with the blame. According to Nicholson, 'The tapers and tadpoles are putting it about that it is all the fault of Winston.'[31] A number of insiders had their knives out for the Chiefs of Staff. Colville thought they were 'much to blame', recording that Butler, at the Foreign Office, 'agrees that [they] have an appalling lack of foresight', and that Grigg, at the War Office, thought Ironside to be 'the worst and most incompetent of men'.[32] Colville wrote, 'I feel it is most important to be rid of Ironside as CIGS and replace him by Dill.'[33] Others, though, had their sights set higher.

Chamberlain's brief announcement of the evacuation from Åndalsnes to a hushed House of Commons on 2 May had considerable and immediate reverberations, particularly in political circles and in the media. The high public expectation of success had suddenly been dashed. Almost every event in the campaign had, thus far, been met with wildly inaccurate, sensational and optimistic reports in the national newspapers: 'Gunfire was heard last night as a British fleet sailed up Oslo fiord' the *Daily Express* had trumpeted on 12 April;[34] 'Narvik Captured by British Troops' announced the *Daily Telegraph*, four days later;[35] 'Our Tanks Take Town Near Oslo' was the headline in the *Daily Mirror* on 22 April.[36] Many of these reports were fed by propaganda from the Ministry of Information and the service departments. As late as 1 May, as the evacuations began from Åndalsnes and Namsos, the *Daily Express* headline declared, 'British Halt Nazi Advance at Dombås. Heavy Enemy Losses at Steinkjer'.[37] It made the public's sense of shock, bewilderment, anger and humiliation all the greater and its eagerness to apportion blame all the keener. In retrospect, the evacuation from central Norway is eclipsed by the evacuation from Dunkirk only a month later. At the time, however, it was seen in a very different light.

Instead of coming clean and admitting that the Allies had suffered a defeat, Chamberlain tried, in his announcement of the evacuation to parliament, to put a positive spin on events. While promising details later, he said that he was 'satisfied that the balance of advantage lies up to the present with the Allied Forces. ... It is safe to say', he added, 'that if we have not achieved our objective, neither have the Germans achieved theirs, while their losses are far greater than ours.' [38] The statement did not convince the House, and the promised debate on 7 May was shaping up for a major confrontation. Channon recorded, 'The Westminster squall is blowing hard ... I am beginning reluctantly to realise that Neville's days are, after all, numbered.'[39] Ironside, too, noted, 'I hear that there is a first-class row commencing in the House and that there is a strong movement on foot to get rid of the PM.'[40] Reaction in the press was summed up by the *Manchester Guardian*,

No-one who studies the reactions of the British press, let alone those of neutral countries, can doubt the shock that the withdrawal from Mid-Norway has given. ... What makes the taste of the whole episode so much more bitter is that it follows so much shallow optimism, not to say boasting, from some Ministers ... [Mr Chamberlain's] capacity for self-delusion is a national danger, for it dampens the country's awareness of its peril and it almost certainly reflects a complacent handling of our conduct of the war.[41]

The House of Commons debate on 7 May was perhaps the most dramatic of the war. It was to be expected that opposition members would queue up, in the customary fashion, to berate the government over its perform-ance – and so they did. But two speeches, by members of Chamberlain's own party, raised the sense of drama. The first was by Admiral Keyes. Right up until the evacuation, Keyes had continued to badger Churchill and Chamberlain, criticising the conduct of the sea war as 'deplorably pusillanimous and short-sighted' and clearly piqued that his demand to lead the direct attack on Trondheim had received short shrift.[42] He had also been 'busy in the lobbies',[43] stirring discontent with the government. Now, dressed for the occasion in the full uniform of an Admiral of the Fleet 'with six rows of medals,'[44] he was bristling with indignation about perceived slurs ('a damned insult') on the Royal Navy's courage and claiming to be speaking 'for some officers and men of the fighting, sea-going Navy who are very unhappy'.[45] He denounced the government's failure to carry out the direct attack on Trondheim and its rejection of his demands to lead it. The conduct of operations had been, he said, 'a shocking story of ineptitude, which I assure the House ought never to have been allowed to happen'. He concluded in rousing fashion: 'There are hundreds of young officers who are waiting eagerly to seize Warburton-Lee's torch, or emulate the deeds of Vian of the "Cossack." One hundred and forty years ago, Nelson said, "I am of the opinion that the boldest measures are the safest," and that still holds good to-day.'[46] His speech lacked nothing in passion and drama, and it was received – unusually in the House of Commons – 'with thunderous applause'.[47] It paved the way for a further condemnation half an hour later by another Conservative and former minister, Leo Amery, which was to have a deadly effect. Amery was highly critical of the government's conduct 'throughout the whole of this lamentable affair', and his fire was concentrated in one direction. In a forty-minute speech of condemnation, he mentioned the Prime Minster no less than fifteen times and other ministers not once. As word spread of his ongoing invective, and Members crowded into the Chamber, Amery's rhetoric reached new bounds. Feeling himself 'swept forward',[48] he concluded by quoting Oliver Cromwell: 'You have sat too long here for any good you have been doing. Depart, I say, and let us have done with you. In the name of God, go!'[49]

The following day the opposition, scenting blood, called for a vote of confidence to be held at the end of the day's proceedings. As devastating as Amery's speech, if not as well known, was that of Herbert Morrison, a senior Labour Party member in the role of chief prosecutor. He fired a volley of highly disquieting questions.

Was there a plan in operation for unity of command between the various forces in Norway? Is it the case that A.A guns were sent without predictors, and that they were sent a week late? Is it the case that other guns were sent without ammunition? Is it the case that machine guns were sent without spare barrels? Was there any proper liaison between the port occupied by us at Namsos and the port occupied by us at Aandalsnes; were there proper communications between those two points? Is it a fact that the military force was not supplied with snowshoes, the consequence being that troops were stuck on the roads, and were bombed there? Is it a fact that the Territorial Brigades were sent ... which were second Territorial Army units that had never had even brigade training?[50]

The effect was, as Colville had earlier suggested of similar allegations, an impression 'unpleasantly reminiscent of the Crimean War'.[51]

Other members plunged in the knife, including, damagingly, Lloyd George: 'I say solemnly that the Prime Minister should give an example of sacrifice, because there is nothing which can contribute more to victory in this war than that he should sacrifice the seals of office.'[52] Churchill, nominated by Chamberlain to sum up for the government, did so robustly and with considerable political skill, appearing to take his share of the blame, while limiting his liability. 'I take complete responsibility,' he said, 'for everything that has been done by the Admiralty, and I take my share of the burden.' He ended by attempting to deflect and delay censure by appealing for patriotic unity:

I say, let pre-war feuds die; let personal quarrels be forgotten, and let us keep our hatreds for the common enemy. Let party interest be ignored, let all our energies be harnessed, let the whole ability and forces of the nation be hurled into the struggle, and let all the strong horses be pulling on the collar. At no time in the last war were we in greater peril than we are now, and I urge the House strongly to deal with these matters not in a precipitate vote, ill debated and on a widely discursive field, but in grave time and due time in accordance with the dignity of Parliament.[53]

The House divided with 281 votes for the government and 200 against. But those against included thirty-three Conservatives, with sixty more abstaining. The results were greeted with unprecedented scenes in the Chamber: the singing of 'Rule Britannia', drowned out by the chant of 'Go! Go! Go!'[54] As Churchill was later to write, 'There was no doubt that in effect, if not in form, both the debate and the division were a violent manifestation of want of confidence in Mr Chamberlain and his Administration.'[55] Two days later, on 10 May, Chamberlain had resigned, and Churchill was on his way to Buckingham Palace where the King asked him to form a government.[56] On the same day, Germany invaded Holland and Belgium.

19   'A Good Dividend'?

Suddenly, from being the central focus of attention as the only land theatre in which active warfare was taking place between the Allies and Germany, the campaign in Norway became a sideshow. The main event, in which the Germans had been expected at some time to 'seek a decision', was now on the Western Front. The new circumstances posed several immediate challenges to the higher direction of the war, and to the campaign in Norway.

The first challenge was the coincidence of the attack with the change of Prime Minister, and with it changes to those responsible for strategy. One of Churchill's first moves as Prime Minister was to reorganise the War Cabinet, reducing its size to five members. Reflecting the coalition nature of his government, this comprised two Conservatives – Chamberlain (Lord President of the Council) and Halifax (Foreign Secretary) – and two from the Labour Party – Clement Attlee (Deputy Prime Minister) and Arthur Greenwood (Minister Without Portfolio). Churchill also created, and appointed himself to, a new post, Minister of Defence, abolishing the Military Coordination Committee and replacing it with a Defence Committee, which he himself chaired. This met either as the Defence Committee (Operations) or the Defence Committee (Supply). The former, which is of main concern to an account of the campaign in Norway, comprised the Deputy Prime Minister and the three service ministers: Anthony Eden (Secretary of State for War), A. V. Alexander (First Lord of the Admiralty), and Archie Sinclair (Secretary of State for Air); the Chiefs of Staff continued to be in attendance.[1] There were, thus, a number of ministers who were not intimately familiar with the higher direction of the war, or with the issues and complexities of the campaign in Norway and the strategy for it. There was also some scepticism about the quality of those chosen as service ministers. Sir John Reith noted the names and commented in his diary, 'This is obviously so that Churchill can ignore them more or less and deal direct with the chiefs of staff.'[2] Inevitably, there was a hiatus in the high-level direction of the war. Hankey found 'complete chaos this morning. No-one was gripping the war in its crisis ... [being too involved in] sordid wrangles over secondary [government] offices'.[3]

The second challenge was presented to the military machine in Whitehall. As has been seen, the service departments had been considerably overfaced by the challenge of the planning and management of even a single campaign. Now there were two campaigns to run, although for one of them a theatre-level commander and headquarters existed in the form of Lord Gort and HQ BEF. The Chiefs of Staff and their subordinates in the service department, however, were able to devote far less of their time and attention to what was clearly the secondary campaign – Norway – although the need for that time and attention was undiminished.

Thirdly, although it was uncertain as to what the impact of events on the Western Front might be on the campaign in Norway, it was clear that resources would need to be carefully husbanded. An immediate War Office assessment concluded that the air defence of Narvik should be drastically reduced. The Chiefs agreed, cutting the number of heavy guns from 144 to 48, including for the proposed defensive position at Bodø.[4] This was endorsed by ministers on 11 May, and Cork duly informed.[5] The same day, the Chiefs told Cork that the position at Bodø, and any forces further south, could not be maintained from Britain and that he would have to cover this with 'trawlers and other small local craft from Narvik'.[6] Cork's task was being seriously stretched. As if to emphasise this, the German advance reached Mosjøen that day, causing the precipitate withdrawal of the Norwegian troops and the evacuation of the two Independent Companies to Bodø.[7] The previous day, the Germans had carried out a bold outflanking movement by sea and air, landing a small force at Hemnesberget, fifteen miles south-west of Mo and thirty miles behind the Allied front line.[8]

Churchill's determination to achieve campaign success at Narvik was, however, undiminished, and he continued to press Cork to seize the town. On 13 May, French forces conducted a successful amphibious assault on the village of Bjerkvik, eight miles to the north, but Allied forces were making only slow progress in closing in on the town. A direct attack on Narvik was not in immediate prospect.

It is surprising that Britain's commitment to the Norwegian campaign continued for as long as it did. On 13 May German panzers crossed the Meuse, and Reynaud telephoned Churchill saying, 'We are defeated; we have lost the battle.'[9] On the same day, Dill received a letter from Lieutenant General Claude Auchinleck, who had taken over from Mackesy at Harstad, that questioned the whole strategy for Norway: 'I have yet to meet a sailor', he wrote, 'who thinks that a defended

242   'A Good Dividend'?

anchorage at Narvik is a necessity to the Navy, so it is *not* a question of
the Army protecting the anchorage for the use by the Navy on the high
seas, but of the Navy using the anchorage for the protection of the army
in the coastal waters of Norway'[emphasis in original]. He continued:

> If HMG think that the commitment involved in the preservation of Northern
> Norway is worth adding to their other commitments, I trust they will set aside
> *definitely* the forces required for the purpose. I feel very strongly that if they are
> not prepared to do this it would be better to come away now than to risk throwing
> good money after bad by failing to provide the necessary forces. ... If there is any
> chance of it being decided to evacuate Norway, the sooner the decision is taken
> the better, as every day must increase the difficulty of the operation of withdrawal
> [emphasis in original].[10]

Four days later – the day after Churchill, at a crisis meeting in Paris, was
shocked to be told by Gamelin that there was no strategic reserve[11] – the
Chiefs met to consider Auchinleck's 'bedrock minimum' force require-
ments. The long list included 200 air defence guns, a bomber squadron,
two Hurricane squadrons and an Army Cooperation Squadron.[12] It was
clearly unaffordable. The Chiefs replied that only about half the air
defence guns would be available and that air assets would be limited to
a single Hurricane squadron, one Gladiator squadron and 'possibly' an
Army Cooperation Flight. They also contemplated abandonment of
northern Norway, although 'not ... unless militarily inevitable under
the above limitations'.[13] At the War Office Dewing had been advising
that 'HMG must ... face the issue as to whether we should withdraw
from Norway.'[14]

   There was, however, a reluctance on the part of the Chiefs to confront
Churchill with this issue. It was not until 17 May that the matter was
raised and then, by Churchill, himself, telling the War Cabinet that
'consideration should be given to the bearing of the new situation in
France on our operations at Narvik' and that 'we should consider
whether Narvik was eating up what we needed for our own defence,
particularly in destroyers, anti-aircraft guns and fighters.'[15] Ironside
responded that the Chiefs of Staff had already looked at this and had
told Lord Cork that he must deal with the situation with the forces at his
disposal and that he could expect no more. Meanwhile, he said, the
situation in northern Norway appeared to be satisfactory. A number of
German prisoners had been taken, with comparatively few casualties
among the British forces, and it seemed likely that Narvik would be
captured 'at any moment'.[16]

   This was certainly what Churchill wanted to hear. As late as 19 May,
he was declaring his determination to hold to the policy in Norway,
telling Halifax, 'The main remaining value of our forces in Norway is

to entice and retain largely superior German forces in that area away from the main decision. Norway is paying a good dividend now and must be held down to the job.'[17] High among Churchill's reasons for seizing Narvik may have been his wish to put into effect Operation Paul, which he had personally nurtured. This was the scheme (following on the Air Ministry's wider plan, code-named Gardening, for air-delivered sea mines) to block the harbour and approaches to Luleå with mines and torpedoes. Churchill had first brought it to the attention of the War Cabinet on 18 March.[18] The plan was to launch planes from aircraft carriers off the northern Norwegian coast, using airfields on land near Narvik for refuelling. He had recently resurrected his scheme, telling Ismay on 14 May (and using the Gardening code), 'Bring to the notice of the Chiefs of Staff Committee the importance of planting vegetables in the approaches to Luleå. This is one of the most important objects for which we have gone to Narvik. ... Let a good plan be prepared to be used in about three weeks. When it is ready, I will bring it before the War Cabinet myself.'[19] This, however, still left Oxelösund, the other ore export port in the Baltic; the SIS plan to sabotage the port facilities was lying in tatters after the Swedes arrested its leader on 20 April.[20]

Churchill's commitment to the retention of Narvik – still strong on 19 May – underwent a swift change within twenty-four hours, which was influenced by the rapid deterioration in the situation in France. Leading German panzer troops had reached Amiens, just forty miles from the coast, and the War Cabinet acknowledged the distinct possibility of an evacuation if disaster was to be averted. At the same time came reports of intensive air attacks at Harstad. Halifax may also have played a part in persuading Churchill because at the War Cabinet on 20 May,

[t]he Secretary of State for Foreign Affairs and the Prime Minister suggested that the Chiefs of Staff should now consider carefully whether we were likely to get a dividend out of our occupation of Narvik, even after we had succeeded in capturing it. It was clear that the troops, ships and equipment occupied in the operation were urgently needed elsewhere.[21]

That evening, at the Defence Committee, Churchill seriously questioned the value of retaining Narvik after its capture: '[I]t would be impossible for us to make a land advance towards the ore fields. The expedition was consuming our resources and would not result in us getting any ore at any rate for a long time, [and] Narvik was not essential to us as a naval base.' A decision was left, pending the results of detailed planning and a report by the staffs.[22]

Within the next twenty-four hours, the case for withdrawal was greatly strengthened by two reports. The first report, from Auchinleck, was unequivocal. Having listed all the resources that were deemed to be necessary but which had not been provided, he concluded, 'I cannot with reduced forces suggested by you hold myself responsible for the safety of this force. ... If in spite of this, larger considerations lead HM Government to decide that Northern Norway must continue to be held with diminished resources laid down by them, I cannot answer for the consequences.'[23]

The second report, from the Joint Planners on the military implications of a complete withdrawal from Norway, was an admirable piece of clear thinking and rigorous strategic analysis. It showed starkly how the objective of remaining in Norway was simply unsupported by the ways and means available. While accepting that Narvik should be captured to destroy the port and railway, they were clear that the reduced resources available, especially in terms of air and air defence earmarked for Narvik, 'would be insufficient to make that place tenable in the face of the scale of air attack which the Germans could put out from bases in southern Norway'. 'Our present operations in Norway do not constitute a profitable military detachment,' they continued, 'there is no reason for [the Germans] to lock up large forces in Norway merely because we are at Narvik.' And they put the campaign in Norway in the context of the war as a whole, drawing attention to the failure to decide on clear priorities by concluding bluntly, '[I]t is therefore necessary to consider what is and what is not essential. The security of France and the United Kingdom is essential, the retention of Norway is not.' Their main recommendation was forthright: '[O]wing to our inability to provide adequate forces to hold Northern Norway our present forces must be withdrawn. It would be to our advantage to withdraw them as soon as possible.'[24]

The Chiefs accepted the report and recommended to the Cabinet on 22 May that Narvik should be evacuated after its capture. Churchill now said that he 'deprecated asking troops to incur heavy losses in assaulting a town which it was proposed to evacuate immediately afterwards,' although he may have recognised that it would have appeared callous if he had not made the point. Only Alexander, the First Lord, demurred, suggesting that the grave political implications of abandoning Norway needed further and full consideration. Churchill neatly sidestepped this opposition, saying that he did not seek an immediate decision but that '[p]lans for evacuating Norway should, however, be worked out at once, both by the Service Staffs in this country and by Lord Cork.' 'He had no doubt', he added, 'that this country would shortly be subjected to very heavy attack.'[25] It was clear that the Prime Minister no longer believed that Norway was paying a good dividend, but at the same time, he was reluctant to bite the bullet and order evacuation after Narvik's capture.

The decision was eventually made at the Defence Committee on 24 May, and, along with it, authorisation was given for Operation Paul, an operation which, whatever its military sense (the Joint Planners had recommended against it[26]), would to some degree offset the humiliation of withdrawal. Churchill 'urged that every effort should be made to carry [it] out. ... No political consideration should stand in the way of this operation ... [it] should be begun just before the end of the evacuation from Narvik.'[27]

A complicating factor was a tentative proposal, put forward by the Swedes to the former Norwegian Prime Minister, Johan Ludwig Mowinckel, that the north of Norway might become a neutral zone, occupied by the Swedes. The proposal, which became known as the Mowinckel Plan,[28] was quickly rejected by the Norwegian government and also, on 19 May, by Churchill and the British government, not least due to suspicion that the plan had originated in Berlin. It was not long, though, before London judged that there might be an advantage in keeping the plan in play. Only two days later, the War Cabinet was agreeing with Halifax who 'did not propose to close the door on the Mowinckel Plan until it was seen how the situation developed'.[29] Indeed, Halifax was clearly attracted by the idea, giving as a major reason for the capture of Narvik that '[o]nce we had captured Narvik, it would be a valuable lever in connection with the ... plan for the withdrawal of both Allied and enemy forces from Northern Norway.'[30] One altruistic motive was to give the Norwegians the opportunity to avoid complete capitulation. Less altruistic were its other perceived attractions: first, to buy time for the evacuation; second, to keep the Norwegians sweet (after all, they could still remove their merchant fleet from Britain); and third, to save face. At the War Cabinet on 31 May, Halifax said that 'the Mowinckel Plan, if it could be put through, would certainly be a way of getting us out of Norway without discredit. He was very unwilling to face the prospect of scuttling out of Norway and would like to try every possible means of saving our face in this matter.'[31] The Cabinet agreed that the Norwegians should be advised to enter into negotiations on the plan. The Norwegian government did so, but the process was to be overtaken by events.

That the decision, taken at the Defence Committee on 24 May, to evacuate was made with reluctance was illustrated by several second thoughts. Just three days later at a meeting of the War Cabinet, Alexander argued that 'the chances of invasion of this country would be increased if we left Narvik where we were containing much greater forces than our own.' Churchill said he was 'unmoved'.[32] On 30 May, the War Cabinet again reconsidered withdrawal on a number of grounds:

the adverse effect on British prestige, the containment of greater numbers of German forces, the possible loss of the Norwegian merchant fleet and the effect on neutrals.[33] As late as 2 June, Churchill himself admitted that, as a result of the success of the evacuation from Dunkirk, he had been having second thoughts about an immediate evacuation from Narvik, hoping to 'maintain a garrison there for some weeks on a self-contained basis', but that he had concluded it should go ahead.[34] Churchill still hoped to deliver his parting shot, Operation Paul, which he declared was 'indispensable',[35] but was told that the carriers would not be available for a fortnight due to the evacuation from Narvik.[36] Thereafter, the fall of France (and thus German access to the Lorraine iron ore fields), doubts about political repercussions and the need to conserve naval resources for the threat closer to home caused the scheme to be quietly dropped.

After 10 May, the German invasion of Belgium, the Netherlands and France had called for rapid strategic reassessment in Whitehall, not least the need to cut the losses of the Norwegian campaign. The need to do so quickly is, of course, easier to see in hindsight. It was far from obvious at the time that in mid-May the situation on the Western Front was as serious as it was. German troops did not cross the Meuse until 13 May, and even then, in Churchill's words, 'It was ridiculous to think that France would be conquered by 120 tanks.' [37] Nor was it clear, to Churchill at least, that Narvik was not on the point of capture – he was told that matters were progressing satisfactorily in northern Norway and that Narvik would be captured 'at any moment'. Nevertheless, there was sufficient evidence at the time for a serious reappraisal of the contribution of the campaign in Norway to success in the war as a whole.

Some in Whitehall had recognised sooner than others that the 'good dividend' was no dividend at all, but just an expensive drain on much needed resources. Some, no doubt, had arrived at the conclusion by instinct or through fear or other emotions. Some, however, most notably the Joint Planners, had done so by a hard-headed analysis of the ends, ways and means, applying sound judgment and concluding that, if the ways and means were not present and the risk of pursuing the stated ends was unacceptably high, then the ends must be altered. They then presented this in a way that persuaded even those who might be reluctant to accept their unpalatable conclusions.

That there were those who would find them unpalatable was inevitable: the Joint Planners' proposal was tantamount to admitting defeat. It was not just Churchill, who had invested so much personally in the campaign as a whole, and Narvik in particular, who was reluctant. Others, too, found it hard to accept that there was no way out: that if just a little more time was given, it would all come good; that just a little more risk could be taken; or that the ends were so important that they were worth just a little more sacrifice. Yet others, bearing in mind the amount of blood and treasure that had already been invested, were no doubt horrified at the prospect of it all going to waste. As the official historian shrewdly observed, 'The policy of continuing our efforts in North Norway is partly attributable to the momentum which a campaign gathers, making it hard for psychological as well as practical reasons to order its abandonment'.[38] In this aspect, the campaign in Norway was far from unique.

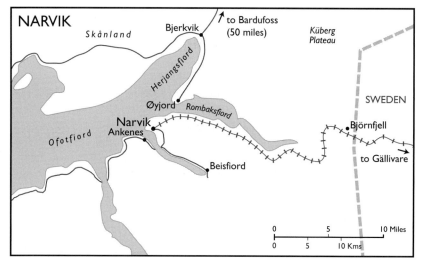

Map 20.1 Narvik

Strategic decision-making in London was based on perceptions of what was happening 'in theatre' and of the envisaged consequences of the strategic decisions. How close, though, were those perceptions to what was actually happening in northern Norway? To what extent were the strategic decision-makers in London in touch with the reality 'on the ground'? And what were the perceptions of commanders in theatre?

At Harstad, following the decision to evacuate from central Norway, and with domestic politics already dominating campaign strategy, the political necessity to capture Narvik, and the pressure to do so, had become intense. Back on 25 April, Cork had told Churchill that he was 'satisfied that under existing circumstances direct attack against Narvik is impracticable' and that he would advance on the town overland.[1]

Mackesy had produced his plan to do so: taking the two headlands which overlooked the town – Øyjord in the north and Ankenes in the south. But within forty-eight hours Cork had completely changed his mind. No doubt reflecting that Churchill would be far from satisfied with such a time-consuming approach, he reverted to his insistence on a direct attack.[2] Mackesy replied that his position was unchanged: a direct attack on Narvik had to be 'ruled out absolutely', as it would be 'a costly and bloody failure'.[3] On 28 April, Churchill, following the decision to evacuate central Norway, renewed the pressure on Cork: 'It is upon Narvik and the Gällivare ore-fields that all efforts must now be centred. . . . Here it is that we must fight and persevere on the largest scale possible', with a reminder that, '[t]roops already sent or coming to you amount to nearly thirteen thousand men'.[4]

The extent to which Churchill understood that numbers of men and force ratios were a very inadequate means of judging combat capability and fighting power is uncertain. A large number of the troops at Harstad were logisticians, essential to support the expedition to Gällivare. Few of them were of use for the capture of Narvik. Indeed, Harstad was suffering from a surfeit of unneeded support troops and equipment. Without a headquarters controlling movement 'into theatre', the pre-arranged plan was being followed mechanically, with vast numbers of men and stores bringing chaos to the little port. 'Everything was put ashore in complete confusion without regard to sorting or destination of the goods or to the capacity of the quays. . . . The docks soon became congested with a mixture of all kinds of baggage, supplies and stores.'[5] The equipment included 138 vehicles and 38 motor cycles, but only two mechanics to maintain them.[6] To add to the chaos, air attacks had, from the start, been a daily occurrence – there were to be a total of 140 such attacks – causing alarm and casualties.[7] Yet the capabilities badly needed, air defence and artillery, had been painfully slow in arriving, despite the urgent requests of Cork and Mackesy.[8] The first Bofors anti-aircraft guns did not arrive until 24 April, the first field guns until 29 April and the first heavy anti-aircraft guns until 6 May.[9] Administrative chaos continued: Bren gun carriers were diverted to Tromsø;[10] when vital snow shoes eventually arrived, 'even the smallest were far too big';[11] the rubber boots supplied were reported as 'leaking badly';[12] and among the less welcome deliveries was one of thirty tons of bulk stationery.[13] It appears that senior decision-makers in London were unaware of this chaotic state of affairs.

London did, however, understand that the potential scale of the operation at Narvik required a corps commander and headquarters. Lieutenant General Claude Auchinleck was selected, and it was recognised – the lesson having been learnt – that a proper headquarters was needed, not an ad hoc collection of spare individuals and that this might take some days to achieve. On this occasion, though, the most urgent need was getting a senior commander, with or without a staff, to Harstad to sort out the command relationship at the top of the force; indeed, such a move was long overdue. Ironside had come to understand the urgency, recording on 28 April, 'We have decided to send out Auchinleck with his staff at once and that command shall be passed when he gets there. ... We have no time to lose.'[14] The CIGS had again found himself frustrated by the War Office bureaucracy: 'I wish that I could have got Auchinleck there before,' he wrote on 5 May, 'but the Operations people prayed for more time.'[15] He was chiding himself four days later, with Auchinleck yet to arrive at Harstad: 'He ought to have been there before, and I should have insisted on his going.'[16] It was to be almost a fortnight from the decision to send him that Auchinleck arrived at Harstad.

In the meantime, relations between Cork and Mackesy had degenerated still further. One of the roots of this was a difference in their priorities. For Cork, the clear priority was the capture of Narvik. Mackesy, though, was 'preoccupied ... with the idea that the Narvik area would be untenable unless he could prevent the Germans continuing their northward progress'.[17] A specific incident led to a new low in their relationship. On 28 April, Brigadier General Béthouart arrived from Namsos to take command of French forces. At a meeting with Cork and Mackesy, according to the latter, Cork 'used all his persuasive powers to making a breach between General Béthouart and myself' and then 'took Béthouart off in his flagship for a reconnaissance of Narvik'.[18] According to Béthouart, Mackesy was invited, but declined.[19] Either way, the relationship was dysfunctional. Béthouart now had to tread with some delicacy. In his response to questioning from Cork about the feasibility of an assault, he said that although he considered that a direct attack might be unwise, there was certainly an opportunity to land troops elsewhere, for example, at Øyjord, and thereafter work towards Narvik.[20] With the thaw starting, the arrival of the French troops, Allied artillery now numbering twenty-four guns, the delivery of eight landing craft and the imminent arrival of a battery of anti-aircraft guns and a troop of tanks, this course was, indeed, a much more practical proposition than hitherto.[21] Béthouart may also have been influenced by the alternative: the long overland approach advocated by Mackesy. This would have been highly unattractive to him. All the French units were missing items of equipment 'badly loaded at Brest';[22] and by no means all of the Chasseurs Alpins were trained for winter warfare: only one section per company was equipped with skis, and the remainder were short of snow shoes.[23] Wet snow and slush were making things even more difficult. It seems that Mackesy was under some illusions about the capability of the French forces and Béthouart may have been reluctant to point out their inadequacies.

On 3 May Cork received a further spur from Churchill, 'Every day that Narvik remains untaken, even at severe cost, imperils the whole enterprise.'[24] Mackesy's plan for land forces converging on Narvik was making some progress: the South Wales Borderers, supported by Chasseurs Alpins ski troops, had been moved to the Ankenes peninsula on the south side of the Ofotfiord, and the Norwegian forces, with the remainder of the Chasseurs Alpins, were closing in, if slowly, from the north. It was clear to Cork, however, that this was not going to achieve the immediate result desired by Churchill. The CinC now gave orders for a direct assault to be carried out on 8 May, launched from the sea or across Rombaksfiord, 'as judged best'. He informed Churchill accordingly.[25] Mackesy, who had all along made it clear (to both Cork and the War Office) that if he received a direct order from Cork he would carry it out, agreed to do so and produced a plan.[26] Churchill ramped up the pressure: 'Urgency of Narvik is extreme. Trust you will use all available strength and press hard for decision.'[27]

A further, almost farcical, command crisis followed – an entirely unnecessary one, which, as a cameo, illustrates much that was at fault with British decision-making. Mackesy's plan was passed to 24 Brigade where Fraser, who had been wounded, had been temporarily replaced as brigade commander by Lieutenant Colonel Trappes-Lomax, commanding officer of the Scots Guards. On 5 May, following a reconnaissance by ship (which was attacked by aircraft and an accompanying Polish destroyer, *Grom*, was sunk), Trappes-Lomax wrote to Lord Cork requesting an interview in Mackesy's presence.[28] This was a most irregular request and, in the circumstances, both Cork and Mackesy should have smelt trouble. Cork should have told Mackesy to deal with the matter; Mackesy should have told Trappes-Lomax to come and discuss it with him in private. The first Mackesy knew of the reason for the request was when he and Trappes-Lomax were in the barge taking them out to Cork's ship, and Trappes-Lomax showed him a letter that he intended to present to Cork.[29] It was a strongly worded condemnation of the proposed operation, listing numerous reasons for its folly. Mackesy later claimed he was 'horrified' at this approach.[30]

At the interview Trappes-Lomax read out his letter, which, he said, had the support of all his subordinates, Captain Hamilton of the *Aurora*, and of Fraser, whom he had visited earlier in the day in hospital.[31] Indeed, Cork's own chief of staff, Captain Maund, concurred with the Army commanders in their desire to postpone the operation pending further study.[32] Trappes-Lomax 'demanded' that his views should be put before the government, and after the interview declared to Mackesy that he would refuse any order to carry out the operation.[33] Cork should have told Mackesy to go away and sort out the matter, and then either confirmed the order or bowed to the experts' advice and postponed it. Instead, and not for the first time, he decided to pass the buck and 'refer the matter to the judgment of His Majesty's Government'.[34] Once in London, the matter was escalated by the Chiefs of Staff to the War Cabinet. Unsurprisingly, the Cabinet wished to solicit Cork's own view on the subject, but, seeing where this might be leading, declared that 'It was most important not to send any message which would bring pressure to bear on Lord Cork and might cause him to take action against his better judgment,' adding that 'he would be fully supported', whatever his decision.[35] Cork, too, saw where this might be leading, and his reply was very carefully worded: 'I do not consider success certain, but believe that there is a good chance of success, whereas it is certain by not trying no success can be gained.' He raised an important strategic point: 'The real question is whether the capture of Narvik now is from [the] broader point of view worth risking a reverse,' adding that Narvik now had no practical utility and therefore only had value 'as a symbol of Victory'.[36] He also suggested that a final decision might await the arrival of General Auchinleck.[37]

The War Cabinet discussed this on the second day of the House of Commons debate, and its members may have had other things on their minds, but they told Cork that 'the capture of Narvik should be pressed with vigour' and that, since Auchinleck would not be arriving for several days, 'he should be left out of your calculations'.[38] By the time this reply reached Harstad, however, Cork had already postponed the attack until Auchinleck's arrival and in the meantime was going ahead with Mackesy's original plan to close in on the town overland.[39]

The whole Trappes-Lomax incident showed the weakness, indecisiveness and lack of clarity of British decision-making, exacerbated by operational pressure and command rivalry.

In the meantime, the Allied strength relative to the Germans had been steadily mounting. Two Norwegian battalions had been brought by sea from northern Norway, bringing their total force level in the Narvik area to five battalions.[40] The three battalions of Chasseurs Alpins had been joined by two battalions of the French Foreign Legion and, on 9 May, by a brigade of four Polish battalions, raised in France from immigrant workers, many with experience of fighting the Germans. By 13 May, together with the three British battalions, this totalled seventeen battalions which, with artillery and other combat support and logistics troops, added up to almost 30,000 men.[41] The German force comprised just three battalions of mountain troops, plus the naval detachments, which

Figure 20.1 Under increasing pressure: German Gebirgsjäger in the mountains above Narvik
(Bundesarchiv)

were now organised into some seven small battalions, together with several hundred reinforcements which had arrived over the past month by air and by rail through Sweden (under the guise of Red Cross workers and medical staff): a total of around 5,000 men.

Increasingly, this Allied combat power had been brought to bear. The Norwegians, commanded by Major General Fleischer, had intensified their offensive operations, attacking the Germans from the north and north-east. The Norwegians and Germans endured by far the harshest climatic conditions of the whole campaign while fighting each other in these mountains, well inside the Arctic Circle at altitudes up to 3,000 feet. And with their resupply interrupted, the Gebirgsjäger were, at times, literally starving.[42]

Although at first the Norwegians suffered a number of costly reverses, by the end of April, they started to be more successful, particularly in the mountains. According to Fleischer, 'Our units suffered much, but they became tough and ... learned how to take care of themselves. They became units that could be used in war.'[43] They were now joined by elements of the Chasseurs Alpins. Whereas Mackesy had little time for the Norwegian military – 'taken as a whole, I regarded them as utterly untrustworthy'[44] – and had not sought to establish the close personal relationship between commanders essential to success in coalition warfare,[45] Béthouart made it his business to get to know the Norwegians and to go at least some way towards fighting a joint campaign with them. He established a good relationship with Fleischer and attached a number of his troops to Norwegian units, and the two national contingents generally worked in close cooperation at the tactical level.[46] French troops, however, were taking more casualties from frostbite and snow blindness than from enemy action.[47] Nevertheless, this concentration of force resulted in the Germans being outnumbered on this front by six to one, with the Allies better supported by artillery and mortars. Moreover, even at the end of April, 3 Mountain Division was still reporting severe shortages of vital winter warfare equipment including skis.[48] Indeed, their position had become so dire that, on 6 May, Dietl reported to Falkenhorst that, without reinforcements and strong support from the Luftwaffe, he would not be able to hold the northern front.[49] At the same time, the Germans found the Allies' failure to attack on the southern flank 'incomprehensible'.[50] The Allies, however, were unaware of this situation.

Following the postponement of a direct attack on Narvik, placed in abeyance after the Trappes-Lomax protest, attention now focused on the possibility of an amphibious assault on the village of Bjerkvik, at the head of the Herjangsfiord. A few days earlier, separate proposals made by Béthouart and Fleischer for such an attack had been rejected by Mackesy, but the latter now accepted the plan, combined with a push from the north by Norwegian and French troops, and tasked Béthouart accordingly.[51] Béthouart's plan was for the assault to be led by two well-trained battalions of the Foreign Legion, recently arrived from Africa. At the planning meeting their initial reaction was that the plan was 'quite unworkable', but by the end they had become philosophical about the challenge. One of their officers remarked to Maund, 'Ah it's all very difficult. We are used to travelling on camels across the desert, and here you give us boats and we have to cross the water. It is very difficult, but it will be all right. I think so.'[52] It was Béthouart who commanded the operation which, after several postponements, took place on 13 May.

The assault, supported by gunfire from British warships and aircraft from *HMS Ark Royal*, was made from landing craft by the two battalions of Foreign Legionnaires, accompanied by five light tanks. They were fortunate that the defenders of Bjerkvik were German sailors and not Gebirgsjäger. The sailors were 'badly shaken by the bombardment, and gave ground quickly, abandoning most of their machine guns in the process'.[53] (Dietl was later to castigate the sailors as 'useless for combat and a danger to our troops'.)[54] The French then exploited their success, seizing the Øyjord peninsula – of considerable tactical importance, not least as an artillery observation position overlooking Narvik itself, and as a potential launching point for an amphibious assault on the town. The attack had been highly successful; Allied casualties totalled only thirty-six. It had also demonstrated the effectiveness of a coordinated Allied effort, with valuable lessons learnt for future amphibious assaults. It came close, too, to wider success. Unbeknown to the Allies, the German

Figure 20.2 Naval bombardment of Bjerkvik prior to the assault, 13 May
(Getty Images)

overall position in the Narvik area had become precarious. That evening, Falkenhorst reported to OKW that the situation in Narvik was critical. Dietl had told him that, without speedy reinforcement of his northern front, there was no alternative but to cross the border into Sweden.[55]

Apart from the capture of the town of Narvik, there were two other important strands to the plan to hold it. The first strand was the development of air operations. Initially, the Chiefs of Staff believed that the necessary air power could be provided by carrier-borne aircraft, but the experience further south had demonstrated the vulnerability of both the carriers and their outdated aircraft. It had rapidly become apparent that airbases in Norway were required, hence the attempt to establish one at Lesjaskog. Not until 1 May was an officer despatched to find suitable sites in the Narvik area. In large part, this delay resulted from the reluctance of the Air Ministry to become more involved in the campaign because of the prospect of the diversion of scarce assets needed closer to home. The reluctance was increased when it transpired that three squadrons of fighters would be required and that the aircraft needed would include highly valued Hurricanes.[56] Several sites were surveyed, and efforts made to establish three of them, although only one, Bardufoss, was to become fully operational.[57] With the bitter lessons of Lesjaskog in mind, considerable care was taken in the planning and preparation of flying operations at Bardufoss, especially its air defence, although this wise precaution delayed the airfield from becoming operational until 21 May.

The second strand of the plan was that of delaying the German advance northwards from Namsos. The Chiefs of Staff had finally decided on 5 May that Bodø should be considered as the forward defence of Narvik and that the Independent Companies should conduct a delaying action to its south. Following the evacuations from Namsos and Åndalsnes, the Chiefs of Staff had not anticipated the enemy pushing north of Trondheim in the immediate future: the German link-up with the garrison there had been achieved and it was judged that 'Germany is consolidating her position in southern Norway.'[58] Carton de Wiart's report that the roads were practically impassable had been accepted, but with the embellishment that, 'in a month's time movement ... will be possible.'[59] The danger of the Germans attempting some form of outflanking operation by sea, as they had done at the top of the Trondheim Fiord, or of their dropping parachute troops to seize a potential airfield, was acknowledged, and steps had been taken to reduce this risk: a company of Chasseurs Alpins had been shipped to Mosjøen, and a company of the Scots Guards had been similarly moved from Harstad to Bodø. The five Independent Companies were deployed, two each at Mosjøen and Bodø and one at Mo. A number of Norwegian detachments were positioned throughout the area. The Chiefs of Staff did not expect the speed of the German action. Having seen the swift and aggressive link-up operation from Oslo to Trondheim, they should not have been surprised.

By late April, Hitler again had become so concerned about the situation at Narvik that he had ordered 2nd Mountain Division to deploy to Norway to link-up from Trondheim with Dietl, a distance of about 350 miles in a straight line – far longer by road and track, many interrupted by fiords to be crossed by boat.[60] Like 3rd Mountain Division, the 2nd Division had combat experience from the campaign in Poland and contained some of the best troops in the German Army. Its commander, Lieutenant General Valentin Feurstein, was to show qualities of skill, determination and tenacity that were to match Dietl's. On 4 May Feurstein arrived at Trondheim where he was given his orders by Falkenhorst, now wisely co-located there with the Kriegsmarine and Luftwaffe commanders. Such was the urgency that, although the majority of his division had yet to arrive, Feurstein immediately set out for Mosjøen with what he had at hand: two Mountain Infantry battalions, a battery of artillery and an engineer platoon.[61] By 10 May, having advanced 100 miles across 'impassable' country, they were approaching the town, which was held by the remnants of a Norwegian Battalion and two British Independent Companies. On the same day, the Germans conducted their daring outflanking manoeuvre by ship and flying boats, landing 300 Gebirgsjäger with two artillery guns, two anti-aircraft guns and a mortar platoon at Hemnesberget. The plan was for a link-up by the main force, advancing north from Mosjøen. Thus, within a day of the German invasion of the Netherlands, France and Belgium, Cork's position had suddenly taken a turn for the worse. His allocation of air defence artillery had just been severely cut; he was now responsible for operations south of Narvik; the enemy were already at Mosjøen with an advance party just south of Mo; and preparations had yet to begin on his airbase and defensive position at Bodø or his airfield at Bardufoss.

On a brighter note for Cork, the much awaited new Army commander at Harstad, Lieutenant General Auchinleck, had finally arrived on 11 May. 'The Auk' had spent almost his entire career in the Indian Army, where he had made his reputation as a highly competent officer and an expert in mountain warfare. He had been recalled to Britain early in 1940 to set up a corps headquarters, ready to deploy to the BEF. Summoned to the War Office on 28 April, he was told of his appointment, but it was a week before he was given his orders, and a further two days before he set sail.

Figure 20.3 Lieutenant General Claude Auchinleck with his air component commander, Group Captain Maurice Moore
(Getty Images)

Auchinkleck's orders appointed him as Mackesy's designated successor, but he was given personal instructions by Dill that authorised him to take over from Mackesy, if he considered that 'local conditions necessitate'.[62] Although he knew Mackesy from the Quetta Staff College and 'had an excellent opinion of his abilities,'[63] it was clear to Auchinleck, soon after arrival, that local conditions did, indeed, necessitate a change – and that it was long overdue. The relationship between Cork and Mackesy was plainly toxic, and they were disagreeing on almost everything. The relationship had taken a considerable toll on Mackesy's physical and mental health. He was spending long periods confined to bed, for example, for the whole of 2 and 3 May, 'with a bad cough ... [from which] I never quite recovered until I left Harstad, and began suffering from insomnia, which became really serious later'.[64] Mackesy was also experiencing a crisis of self-confidence, exacerbated by the news of Auchinleck's impending arrival. He wrote to Cork on 8 May, 'I beg you to get me and my own staff ... removed as soon as possible.' Mackesy recalled later that on another occasion he 'really felt in despair'.[65] Command can be lonely, and it had become increasingly so for Mackesy. There was no one else of his rank at Harstad, and not only was he barely on speaking terms with his boss – their interaction was mostly confined to written memoranda – but also he and his senior staff officer, Colonel Dowler, did not get on with each other.[66] Furthermore, since coming under Cork's command on 21 April, Mackesy had been forbidden to contact the War Office except for administrative purposes.[67] He had received no personal communication, let alone any message of support, from the CIGS. Mackesy had disregarded the stricture about contacting the War Office on one occasion when he signalled Dill, an old friend, 'to make this personal appeal to you in order to ensure that someone in authority at home knows the facts'.[68] In such circumstances, visiting the troops under command can provide the necessary tonic, but geographical dispersion meant that this was not easy to achieve. Relations between Mackesy and Cork had reached a very low ebb. As Brigadier Fraser noted, the relationship had become 'quite impossible and a source of danger to the operation'.[69] It was clearly time for either Mackesy or Cork to be replaced. Had there been, from the start, an intermediate Army commander between the CIGS and Mackesy, or had a senior officer been despatched to ascertain the situation in early April, the situation might have been resolved. Whether it would have resulted in a different outcome at Narvik is a very different matter.

21   The Long Retreat

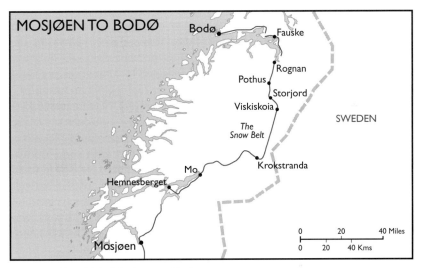

MOSJØEN TO BODØ

Bodø

Fauske

Rognan

Pothus

Storjord

Viskiskoia

The
Snow Belt

SWEDEN

Mo

Krokstranda

Hemnesberget

Mosjøen

0   20   40 Miles

0   20   40 Kms

Map 21.1 Mosjøen to Bodø

After relieving Mackesy on 13 May, Auchinleck moved swiftly. He established a cordial relationship with Cork[1] and persuaded him to set up a joint-services headquarters onshore, which the CinC had hitherto either not seen the use of or had been unable to bring himself to cohabit with Mackesy. Auchinleck also established contact with the Norwegian commanders, Ruge and Fleischer, and met with Béthouart whom he described as 'a most refreshing person to deal with'.[2]

Auchinleck focused his attention on the developing situation in the south. In the absence of a single commander for the Norwegian campaign as a whole, the campaign on land had been conducted as two separate operations: Cork had, initially, been concerned only with Narvik, and Massy only with operations to the south of Narvik. With the evacuations at the end of April, the situation to his south had suddenly become of great relevance to Cork. Although he was given detailed tactical-level instructions from London – of the 'deploy a company to Bodø', 'send a destroyer to Mo' type – he had been given no indication whatsoever of the overall plan or of the responsibility and authority for it.[3] So much so that, on 4 May, he was signalling to London, 'Request I may be informed of the general policy regarding Bodø, Mo and Mosjøen. . . . These areas do not, I presume, come under Narvik Command. Are there any other allied forces to the South of me?'[4] The signal had prompted the Chiefs to belated action, and three days later, Cork had been informed that, with immediate effect, he was indeed responsible for all the activities to the south, and in particular for the Independent Companies.[5]

The Independent Companies – forerunners of the Commandos – had had a suitably unconventional provenance. Immediately following the invasion of Norway, the War Office branch responsible for guerrilla activity – Military Intelligence (Research) – had started looking at the potential for such operations in Norway, with Lieutenant Colonel Colin Gubbins,[6] a specialist in irregular warfare, leading the project. Within a week, a proposal was made for the formation of ten large companies for the purpose. At that stage, with no stated operational requirement, let alone an approved plan for their employment, the idea met with some opposition. (Part of the proposal was for each company to have £4,000 in cash. The War Office's deputy permanent secretary, guardian of the budget, disapproved, commenting that it 'seems a very large sum for each of them to have'.)[7] The concept, however, was given the go-ahead, with authority on 20 April to immediately form and train up to ten of these 'Independent Companies',[8] with Gubbins appointed as the force commander.

The Independent Companies were the epitome of improvisation. It was originally intended to give the role to the Lovat Scouts – a Reservist unit largely made up of ghillies and deer stalkers from Scottish highland estates.[9] This approach was then changed to a call for volunteers from across the whole Territorial Army – a company from each division, a platoon from each brigade. Each company was established for about 300 men, with a high proportion of officers (even section commanders were officers). With plenty of volunteers, the quality of individuals selected was high, but in the time available, training for the role was minimal – in most cases, little more than one week. That was at least sufficient to test physical fitness; in one company alone, fifty-six aspirants considered to be physically unfit were 'returned to unit'.[10] Each company included signallers, demolition experts, a doctor, a Norwegian interpreter and a mountain warfare officer from the Indian Army. The companies were by far the best equipped forces deployed to Norway, with a high proportion of light machine guns, light mortars, radios to section level, Alpine rucksacks, snow shoes and special cold weather clothing.[11] The companies were designed for guerrilla warfare, yet the role in which they were about to find themselves was one of directly opposing a strong and well-equipped enemy in delaying operations, for which they were not designed, trained or equipped. The first five companies, code-named Scissorsforce, were deployed in the first week in May, two each to Mosjøen and Bodø, and one to Mo.[12]

On 8 May Cork received an alarming message from the War Office that 'our latest information is that road Grong-Mosjoen is not, repeat not, impassable',[13] and the following day he and Mackesy ordered Fraser and 24 Brigade (less one battalion) to establish a brigade defensive position at Mo.[14] The need looked all the more necessary when Mosjøen was lost on 11 May, and the two Independent Companies there, who had arrived only two days previously, were evacuated to Bodø. The first unit from 24 Brigade, the Scots Guards, arrived at Mo by ship on 12 May. The following day, however, Cork was having second thoughts, uncomfortable with the prospect of having to resupply Mo by sea in the face of air attack – it was at the head of a long, narrow fiord – and agreed with Auchinleck that the brigade position should instead be at Bodø.[15] Auchinleck now ordered Fraser with the remainder of 24 Brigade to move to Bodø and hold it 'permanently', but to hold Mo only 'as long as he could'[16]. However, fate took a hand. The Polish transport, *Chrobry*, carrying one of the battalions, the Irish Guards, was attacked by aircraft early on 15 May, causing a number of casualties, including the commanding officer and all three majors.[17] In scenes reminiscent of the legendary discipline shown on the sinking troopship *Birkenhead* off South Africa in 1852, the battalion paraded on deck and patiently awaited rescue. An escorting destroyer took them off and returned them to Harstad to refit.

The plan started to unravel further. The same day, Fraser, visiting Mo, reported to Auchinleck and Cork that to try and hold the place with only one battalion was militarily unsound.[18] The following day, the ship on which Fraser was travelling was badly damaged and had to make for Scapa for repairs.[19] Auchinleck reorganised his force, incorporating 24 Brigade into Scissorsforce and promoting Gubbins to brigadier as its commander. Contrary to Fraser's advice, he instructed Gubbins that the detachment at Mo was to 'hold on to its position and not withdraw ... [adding] I hope that when they [the Germans] come up against really determined opposition they will sit back and think of it'.[20] This hope represented, of course, a gross underestimation of the German capability, but Auchinleck had no experience of their performance in central Norway, nor had he seen the terrain for himself. Fate again took a hand. *HMS Effingham*, the ship carrying the South Wales Borderers to Bodø, ran aground. This battalion, too, had to be evacuated back to Harstad to refit, having lost most of its equipment – some of it, such as mortars, Bren gun carriers and a troop of tanks, irreplaceable.

A few misjudgements and misfortunes – as Clausewitz said, 'the kind you can never foresee' – had combined to produce a compounded error. The position in the Mo area, actually at the hamlet of Stien,[21] eight miles to the south of the town, required two battalions but was now held by just one: the Scots Guards (minus a company, still at Bodø, and another deployed to counter a threat nearer to Mo). It was supported by four 25-pounder guns, three Bofors anti-aircraft guns and a section of Royal Engineers.[22] A position ten miles further south, held by an Independent Company and a company of Norwegian troops, was attacked on 14 May by the troops who had landed at Hemnesberget, now joined by the overland advance of 2 Mountain Division. After a fierce engagement, the defenders withdrew the following day, joining the Scots Guards at Stien. The main German attack here came on the afternoon of 17 May. Although at first it was firmly held, communications to the guns were cut by German artillery and mortar fire, and the Gebirgsjäger, helped by the failure of the British to picket the heights and by the early withdrawal of Norwegian ski troops, steadily outflanked the position.[23] Reports were received (erroneous, as it transpired) of a parachute landing to the rear of the position.[24] In the early hours of 18 May, the commanding officer ordered the forward companies to withdraw to a depth position, but – as had happened so often in the Gudbrandsdal – the message did not get through to all the platoons. The retreat was, at times, chaotic. Without transport, any equipment that could not be carried was abandoned, and one company was completely cut off.[25] Later in the morning, Gubbins arrived at the depth position just south of Mo and reviewed the situation.[26] Apart from the missing company, casualties had amounted to only three killed, but a further seventy to eighty were wounded or missing;[27] the troops had nothing but their weapons and what they stood up in.[28] Gubbins decided that the position was untenable and ordered a withdrawal through Mo and a continuing delaying action to the north.[29] Supporting troops, including the exhausted Independent Company, were sent on ahead.[30] Finally, the bridges at Mo were blown, although this did not prevent Feurstein's troops from taking the town or hold up their further advance for long.

Sitting in Harstad, Auchinleck was bewildered by events, reporting to Dill, 'Why our soldiers cannot be as mobile as the Germans, I don't know, but they aren't apparently.'[31] He was naturally concerned at the failure to hold Mo: the position at Bodø was unprepared, and Bardufoss airfield was not due to become operational for several days. It was essential to buy time with a firm defence further south. Yet, as the Scots Guards withdrew on foot, harassed by air attacks, they were imposing little delay on the enemy. Auchinleck decided to hold the Germans some fifty miles (by road) to the north of Mo, just short of the high, treeless plateau known as the snow belt, where the road passed between walls of snow. Gubbins ordered Trappes-Lomax accordingly. When the latter was approaching Krokstranda, at the foot of the snow belt, he received a signal from Auchinleck, telling him, 'You have now reached good position for defence. Essential to stand and fight. ... I rely on Scots Guards to stop the enemy.'[32] Auchinleck, however, was uneasy about Trappes-Lomax's reliability, and when he spoke to Gubbins, 'again told him to remove any officer not fit to command and replace him at his discretion'.[33]

As a defensive position, the Krokstranda area showed more promise on Auchinleck's map than it did on the ground, not least because the only supply route – the narrow snow-belt road, twenty miles long – offered no protection from air attack and the fact that once the position was outflanked and the road was cut, the battalion would be trapped. In his assessment of the situation, Gubbins recognised that the position was 'precarious' and that the main defensive position should be at Storjord [just north of the snow belt][34] – a view shared by the commanding officer in his reply to Auchinleck.[35] After a conversation with Auchinleck's staff, Gubbins gave the commanding officer modified instructions for 'hitting hard', and only withdrawing if the safety of the force was 'seriously endangered'[36] but ordering him categorically to hold the enemy as far south as possible.[37]

En route to Krokstranda, the battalion was rejoined by the company from Bodø and by the company which had been cut off south of Mo. The latter had evaded the Germans by trekking through the mountains in deep snow for thirty-six hours, returning to the safety of the Mo-Bodø road from where it had been picked up by truck.[38] They were not the only ones to be suffering from exhaustion. After the battle at Mo, marching more than forty miles in two days, with intermittent air attacks, the whole battalion and the accompanying Norwegian detachment were exhausted, demoralised and jittery by the time they neared Krokstranda. An incident at a delaying position a few miles to the south was described by the Norwegian detachment commander:

Then something strange happened. From my command post, I saw one of the guards stand up on the other side of the road, throw away everything and vanish to the rear. One more did likewise, then others, and at the end, the whole field was strewn with rifles, pouches, and lambskin overcoats. I did not understand what had happened. ... It was never established what caused the panic.[39]

The equipment was later retrieved by the Norwegians and returned to the battalion.

The main attack at Krokstranda, on the ground and from the air, came on the evening of 21 May, the companies in the forward line of defence withdrawing to depth positions. The attack was resumed in the very early hours of 22 May,[40] outflanking an intermediate position and causing a further withdrawal to the depth position. Later in the day, Trappes-Lomax, despite orders from Gubbins, brought to him by a staff officer, not to retreat under any circumstances without his permission,[41] ordered a withdrawal to take place that evening in lorries prepositioned in the rear, over the snow belt to Viskiskoia, just short of Storjord.[42] This was flagrant disobedience, but the probability is that had he not done so, the whole battalion would have been outflanked and cut off.

At Viskiskoia, as the battalion's War Diary frankly records, '[T]he men were utterly exhausted and a certain demoralisation had set in, in consequence of fatigue, loss of kit, a succession of rear-guard actions and continuous menace from the air.'[43] The battalion's morale was not improved by news that their commanding officer, 'for whose personality and ability everyone had the highest respect, and in whom everyone had the greatest confidence', had been sacked.[44] Auchinleck had ordered his removal, both he and Gubbins having clearly lost confidence in him.[45] The force at Viskiskoia comprised only one, by now weakened, battalion, an Independent Company and about eighty Norwegians. Moreover, two of the light anti-aircraft guns were out of action, only one mortar remained, and the field guns were reduced to the direct-fire role for lack of any communication equipment. Gubbins ordered the position at Viskiskoia to be held until 27 May, but when he came forward on 23 May with a German air attack in progress, he quickly realised that it was untenable.[46] At 6 P.M. he ordered a withdrawal to an intermediate position, some five miles further north, from where the following evening a further twelve-mile withdrawal was ordered to a defensive position being prepared at Pothus by the Irish Guards.[47] When the Scots Guards eventually trudged wearily through the Irish Guards position that night, they did so in silence; there was none of the usual banter between the two battalions.[48]

With the Bodø position still in preparation – the South Wales Borderers, whose task it was, were still incomplete – a delaying action of several days was required. Pothus, sitting astride a river swollen by melting snow, was a natural defensive position and the troops were well dug in. Along with the Irish Guards (now commanded by a captain – their senior surviving officer) were four Independent Companies, a troop of artillery (still only in the direct fire role) and a Norwegian infantry company with a small mortar detachment. The force was commanded by Lieutenant Colonel Hugh Stockwell, former commander of No. 2 Independent Company. The German advance guard, as usual on bicycles, reached Pothus early on 25 May and were duly ambushed. The direct attack which followed was beaten off. But during the night, the Germans built a pontoon bridge upriver and, by the following morning, had manoeuvred infantry round to the flank of the position. By mid-morning it had become apparent that the position was being encircled, and Gubbins authorised Stockwell to withdraw. It was not until late afternoon that this could be coordinated and not until early evening that the withdrawal commenced. Yet again, not all companies received the executive order to withdraw, and again a company, this time of the Irish Guards, had to conduct an arduous march across the mountains to escape.[49] It is noteworthy, and a reflection on the difficulty of conducting a withdrawal in contact with the enemy but without radio or telephone communications, that in almost every battle fought by the British in the campaign, one company did not receive the order to withdraw and had to make its escape independently.[50]

The withdrawal – to Rognan, ten miles to the north, where fishing boats were waiting to take the force across the fiord – was aided by the appearance, for the first time, of two Gladiator aircraft from Bardufoss who brought down four enemy aircraft.[51] Pothus was to be the last battle fought by British troops in Norway. On 26 May Gubbins was informed by Auchinleck of the decision to evacuate, but he was forbidden to inform the Norwegians.[52] Gubbins now had to arrange the safe extraction of his force to Bodø from where they would be embarked. As the British headed for the key point of Fauske, and from there along the peninsula to Bodø, the Norwegians carried out a number of small rearguard actions, but the greatest threat was from the air. Following the Gladiators' appearance at Pothus, the Luftwaffe visited Bodø in strength the next day, first the airfield and then the town, with the latter reduced, in the words of one platoon commander, to 'a mass of chimney stacks – like a series of dead men's fingers sticking up'.[53] Fortunately for the British, the bombs missed the quays.[54] The German forces followed up, but not as aggressively as previously. The force divided at Fauske, with the main effort pressing north to relieve Dietl. Nevertheless, Gubbins was far from confident, telling Auchinleck, 'I would be very grateful indeed if the evacuation could be arranged for May 31 at the latest as I rather doubt that I can hold till June 1.'[55] After a brief rearguard action just east of Bodø to keep the Germans at bay and the destruction of a large amount of heavy weapons and equipment, the last British troops were embarked on 31 May.[56] The local Norwegian forces had only been informed of the evacuation three days before it began. Having established a strong position around Fauske, reinforced by a battalion from the Narvik area and being keen to fight on, they considered the British decision madness and protested strongly, but to no avail. Lacking the force to hold by themselves, they withdrew to a port twenty miles to the north, where a fleet of fishing boats took them off for the Lofoten Islands. Their bitterness at again being deserted by the British can be imagined.

For the British and Norwegians, the long retreat was over. For the Germans, the long advance was not. Having already travelled a remarkable 400 miles in twenty-eight days, 2 Mountain Division were determined to relieve their brothers-in-arms at Narvik. Ahead of them lay a further 100 miles of roadless, snow-covered tundra. Undeterred, Feurstein gathered a hand-picked force of his 2,500 toughest Gebirgsjäger and set them off on 2 June to reach Narvik on skis, resupplied only by air. A week later they were already halfway there when the Allied evacuation took place. A token force of a platoon carried on to demonstrate the capability, arriving five days later to a tumultuous welcome from their comrades.

The retreat north from Mosjøen to Bodø had lasted a fortnight and had been a series of defeats for the British. Auchinleck had only partially grasped the reasons when, with evident feeling, he confided his personal view in a letter to Dill.

It is lamentable that in this wild and underdeveloped country where we, with our wealth of experience, should be at our best, are outmanoeuvred and outfought every time. It makes me *sick* with shame. The French are all right, real soldiers. As I said, our new armies will have to be very different from our old if we are going to recover our lost ascendency in battle [emphasis in original].[57]

An analysis of the relative fighting power of the German and British forces is more revealing. The British operation had shown all the results of poor strategy, hasty planning, wishful thinking, erratic command and control, and an underestimation of the enemy and of the impact of air power. The resources supplied – for example, numbers of troops – were never enough for the task; the type of troops, both Regulars and the Independent Companies, were totally unsuited to the role they were given. Especially remarkable was the failure to learn the lessons of the operations around Trondheim. The British were again surprised at the physical and psychological impact of enemy air superiority, by the aggression, speed and momentum of the Germans, by their combination of fire and manoeuvre and by their ability to outflank defensive positions – all lessons of the operations in central Norway. Part of the reason for this

was that, at the time of those operations, the commanders in the north –
Cork and Mackesy – had had little interest in what was going on around
Trondheim; their responsibility was the capture of Narvik. Moreover,
Auchinleck brought with him no experience of fighting the Germans or
knowledge of Norway, hence his bewilderment ('Why our soldiers
cannot be as mobile as the Germans, I don't know, but they aren't
apparently.') Senior commanders had not found the opportunity to get
out of their headquarters, see the ground for themselves, visit the front-
line commanders and acquire a feel for the battlefield. As in the
operations in the south, those in the north showed up the impact of air
superiority, skilfully applied. Having had more time to consider the
lessons to be learnt, Auchinleck was to write in his report, 'The predominant factor in the recent operations has been the effect of air power . . .
the first general lesson to be drawn is that to commit troops to a
campaign in which they cannot be provided with adequate air support
is to court disaster.'[58]

In every component of fighting power the Germans had shown themselves superior to the British. Not least, they matched the right troops to
the terrain and climate, and provided them with the necessary support.
As Auchinleck also observed in his report, 'The enemy's thoroughness
and foresight in providing everything required for fighting were extraordinary.'[59] It was, of course, only extraordinary by British standards at the
time. Particularly notable was the poor standard of training of the British
compared to the Germans. The Independent Companies had only been
given about one week's training prior to deployment. The quantity and
quality of the training (in its widest sense) given to the Regular soldiers,
for example, the Scots Guards, was shown to have been totally
inadequate when matched against an enemy as competent as
Feurstein's Gebirgsjäger in the terrain and climate of northern Norway.
Neither the Scots nor Irish Guards had had more than rudimentary
collective training, and they had to fit that training in with their guard
duties in central London. In comparison to that of their German opponents, their training had been amateur. There were hard lessons to be
learnt, too, in leadership, discipline and morale.

While the long retreat north was taking place, plans for the assault on Narvik were moving ahead in parallel. Following the successful assault at Bjerkvik on 13 May, Cork was under immediate pressure from Churchill: 'I hope you will get Narvik cleaned up as soon as possible, and then work your way southwards with increasing force.'[1] Béthouart was tasked with the detailed planning, and the date was set for 21 May. But two days before, a postponement until 24 May was ordered: the assault craft were required for the construction of the airfield at Bardufoss, a prerequisite for the attack.[2] Now the Prime Minister expressed considerable irritation: 'I am increasingly disappointed by the stagnation which appears to rule the operations around Narvik, and the delay in occupying the town itself. . . . I should be much obliged if you would enable me to understand what is holding you back.'[3] Cork replied robustly, explaining the reasons, refuting the charge of 'stagnation' and saying the he did 'not require spurring'.[4] He also expressed some frustration at the apparent lack of strategic clarity in London: 'I have tried to make my views clear that what is going on here is not a struggle for the town of Narvik, but whether or not we can establish ourselves in this country.'[5] This point was reiterated in a signal he sent to the Chiefs of Staff, chiding them that 'it would be folly under existing conditions to switch off from essential preparations of aerodromes to that of attacking Narvik – a place which does not affect the main issue'.[6] But further delay was to come. On 23 May, with Hurricanes still awaited at Bardufoss, and the carriers *Furious* and *Glorious* back at Scapa refuelling, Auchinleck told Cork that it would be reckless to carry out the assault without air support.[7] The attack was postponed until 26 May. Then, on 24 May, Cork had to report to Churchill yet more delay 'due to the situation at Bodø'.[8] The attack was finally scheduled for the night of 27/28 May. These postponements were all necessary but appeared to Churchill to be just excuses for inaction.

Over this period, on 24 May, the evacuation order was received from London, and with it the instructions that 'the Norwegian Government have not repeat not yet been informed and greatest secrecy should be observed.'[9] Cork and Auchinleck decided that Béthouart must be informed and told him two days later.[10] The Norwegians were led to believe that Britain's military commitment to their country was undiminished. As late as 13 May, Anthony Eden had assured the Norwegian minister in London that 'the Allied action in Norway would be pursued with the utmost energy.'[11]

There were, thus, three military operations to be conducted: the first two, roughly simultaneously, the capture of Narvik and the withdrawal from Bodø, and the third, evacuation as soon as possible thereafter.

On the eve of the attack, the situation in and around Narvik had become highly favourable for the Allies. Despite the arrival of resupply and several hundred reinforcements, some by train via Sweden, some by seaplane, and about two companies by parachute,[12] Dietl's situation remained precarious.[13] His troops in the mountains to the north-east were exhausted and critically short of supplies, particularly ammunition and hot food.[14] Here, Norwegian attacks had successfully dislodged the Germans from part of the tactically important Kuberg plateau, threatening the German main base at Bjørnfjell, and the Chasseurs Alpins had gained ground along the shores of the Rombaksfiord. To the south, Brigadier General Bohusz-Szyszko's Polish Brigade, who had taken over on the Ankenes peninsula, had been involved in some bitter fighting and was now threatening further advances. Bardufoss had become operational on 21 May, initially with Gladiators and, from 24 May, with the Hurricane squadron (although this did not prevent the Luftwaffe from sinking the anti-aircraft cruiser *Curlew* near Skånland on 26 May). The snow had gone from the lower ground, and the Allies now had artillery, tanks, landing craft and air support. Moreover, many in the attacking force had the successful amphibious operation at Bjerkvik under their belts.

The plan for the capture of Narvik was for an amphibious assault from Øyjord across the Rombaksfiord – a distance of about a mile – by two battalions of the Foreign Legion and one of Norwegian troops, with ten light tanks supported by naval gunfire and three batteries of artillery at Øyjord. The assault was to be synchronised with attacks in the north by the Chasseurs Alpins and in the south against Ankenes and Beisfiord by the Polish Brigade. At the same time the Norwegians would increase pressure in the mountains to prevent reinforcement of the town. In a second phase, a company of Poles and the skiers from the Chasseurs Alpins would seize the railway line in the Germans' rear, cutting their line of retreat to the Swedish border. The attack would be timed for midnight in the knowledge that the German-held airfields at Stavanger and Trondheim were not equipped for night take-off. Although the Germans would be expecting an assault at some time, they would not know exactly when or where it would take place. The plan was a good one and benefited from the lessons learnt from the Bjerkvik operation a fortnight earlier. According to Maund, it was also, in outline, identical to the plan produced by Mackesy 'within a very few hours of his reaching Harstad'.[15]

The operation, mounted close to midnight on 27 May, did not go exactly to plan. As usual, the unexpected played a part. Fog descended over Bardufoss at a critical point in the early morning, closing the airfield, while clear weather remained over Narvik, allowing the Luftwaffe an unopposed run. Their main targets were the British ships. *HMS Cairo*, with Cork and Béthouart aboard, was hit twice, leaving thirty casualties. When the fog cleared later in the morning, the tables were turned, and the Hurricanes achieved complete local air superiority over the Narvik area, flying no less than ninety-five sorties in the course of the day. The amphibious landings were successful, and although German resistance was determined, and included several local counter-attacks, by the early evening the defenders had been forced to withdraw east towards their base at Bjørnfjell and the Swedish border. Delay, largely caused earlier by the Luftwaffe, prevented the second phase of the Allied operation from trapping the Germans before they escaped. An important, and often neglected, part of the operation was the continued offensive over the following days by French, Polish and, prominently, Norwegian troops, which kept the Germans, now critically short of ammunition and food, very much on the defensive.[16]

The attack had been a considerable success for the Allies – a joint-service and multinational amphibious operation which had required skill, determination and good cooperation in both planning and execution. Casualties, though, were not light. Sixty Norwegian soldiers and thirty-nine civilians were killed.[17] The French and Polish armies each had around 100 men killed.[18] The British lost forty men – all members of the Royal Navy.[19] Apart from some artillery and logistic support, the British army had been conspicuously absent from the operation. What the attack achieved in terms of its contribution to campaign objectives was, however, strictly limited. There was certainly an irony in the capture of a town only to evacuate it and hand it back, but the operation facilitated what was a difficult and risky evacuation, and this was its foremost military contribution. For the War Cabinet the main reason for the capture of the town was, of course, political. Narvik had become a famous name on a map and had thus acquired a totemic importance out of all proportion to its military value. It had become a touchstone of success or failure. Its capture offset, to some extent, the ignominy of evacuation and campaign failure. In the event, though, it was over-shadowed by the events on the Western Front where Belgium had capitulated on the same day (28 May) and a much larger and more dramatic evacuation was starting at Dunkirk. The capture of Narvik certainly had the air of, in one historian's words, 'a hollow victory'.[20]

Detailed planning for the evacuation from Narvik had begun in both London and Harstad from the moment the decision had been promulgated on 24 May. The initial assessment was that the evacuation of the 25,000 Allied troops and their equipment would take twenty-eight days, but this was clearly unacceptable. An accelerated programme concentrated the operation into a single week, albeit at the expense of leaving behind large quantities of equipment, including all the vehicles and, more importantly, all the heavy air defence guns. There was little room for error in this plan, and considerable risk. The greatest was the paucity of fighter aircraft. With increased Luftwaffe activity, there were insufficient fighters to assure air superiority over the Narvik area during almost twenty-four hours of daylight. As Auchinleck told Dill on 30 May, 'The fighters certainly help a lot, but they could not prevent a hundred big bombs on Skaanland yesterday.'[21] In fact, two days later the combined efforts of the Hurricane and Gladiator squadrons were to see off a major Luftwaffe attack,[22] and, over the final fortnight of the campaign, they claimed a remarkable thirty-seven confirmed and seventeen unconfirmed kills.[23] If they were not always able to achieve local air superiority, they were able, more often than not, to deny it to the enemy and, in doing so, to demonstrate what might have been achieved in central Norway.

One of the most contentious issues of the evacuation was the strict instruction, as part of the order from London on 24 May, that the Norwegians were not to be told of the intention to leave.[24] Not only did success depend entirely on secrecy, but there was also a fear that if the Norwegian government knew that the British were cutting and running, it might seek an immediate armistice. Elaborate deception measures were used to deceive the Norwegians that the withdrawals and evacuations already taking place were part of a move to transfer the main base to Tromsø, 'which will make possible reinforcement of North Eastern Norway if a German threat should develop'.[25] The deception extended to telling a departing British logistic unit that it was going to Tromsø, but taking it to Scapa, where it was held incommunicado to preserve security. All of this was most distasteful to the commanders in theatre. On 27 May Cork told London that 'General Béthouart represented to General Auchinleck, who completely agrees with him, that there may be extreme difficulty in withdrawing [British and] French troops now fighting side by side with Norwegians in contact with enemy without betraying them.'[26] The War Cabinet considered the subject on the same day but deferred a decision, doing so again two days later.[27] Meanwhile, Béthouart signalled his military superiors in Paris, 'I am operating with Norwegian troops whom, for reasons of national honour, I will not abandon in difficulties on the battlefield.'[28] On 30 May Auchinleck unburdened himself to Dill on the subject, 'The worst of all is the need for lying to all and sundry in order to preserve secrecy. The situation vis-a-vis the Norwegians is particularly difficult and one feels a despicable creature in pretending that we are going on fighting, when we are going to quit at once.'[29]

On the evening of 31 May the War Cabinet at last agreed that the Norwegian government could be informed, and the next day Dormer broke the news to them.[30] This was, unsurprisingly, greeted by 'a feeling of soreness and disillusionment'.[31] After much debate and heart-searching, King Haakon and the government decided to take exile in Britain and were taken off in a warship. General Ruge insisted on remaining with his army, knowing that this would mean imprisonment.

The evacuation of the 25,000-strong Allied force, which took place between 4 and 8 June, was a well-organised operation and no mean feat. It also had luck on its side. Over the five-day period of the evacuation, low cloud and rain prevented serious interference from the Luftwaffe. The ground troops managed to withdraw successfully, due in large part to the Norwegian troops who covered their retreat, and operational security was maintained throughout – possibly aided by the severance of the undersea cable linking telecommunications from Narvik to the south[32] One of the outstanding feats was the evacuation of the Hurricanes from Bardufoss. It had been expected that the planes would have to be abandoned, but the crews decided to attempt a landing on the carrier HMS *Glorious* – the first time Hurricanes had ever attempted a carrier landing – and they did so without mishap. The final convoy departed on 8 June. The Norwegian Army capitulated the following day, and within twenty-four hours, the Germans were back in what remained of Narvik.

There was one final tragedy to be played out in the British campaign in Norway. In mid-May Raeder and the Kriegsmarine staff proposed an offensive operation (Operation Juno) to interdict British sea communications with Norway, starting at the end of the month. As the situation in Narvik deteriorated, the plan expanded to include attacks on British shipping in the Narvik/Harstad area and to open and maintain a supply line for Feurstein's 2 Mountain Division, hurrying north. The task force for Operation Juno – the *Scharnhorst*, *Gneisenau*, *Hipper* and four destroyers – left Kiel on 4 June. Four days later, now with signals intelligence reporting a possible British evacuation, it sighted an aircraft carrier and two escorting destroyers en route from Narvik to Scapa. The carrier was *Glorious*, returning outside a convoy, accompanied by *Ardent* and *Acasta*. None of the carrier's reconnaissance aircraft was deployed. Within two hours, all three ships had been sunk and 1,500 lives lost. There were only forty-five survivors.[33]

The reason for allowing the three ships to travel outside a convoy was given in the official history as *Glorious*'s shortage of fuel.[34] The truth only emerged some fifty years later when a court ordered the publication of the findings of the board of enquiry. These show that the real reason was the captain's impatience to get home – bizarrely, to court martial his senior RAF subordinate and that, even more bizarrely, he was given permission to do. Deploying reconnaissance aircraft was standard practice, and the captain's failure to do so rightly attracts strong criticism, as does his failure to deploy a proper lookout.[35] It also emerged, separately, that the Admiralty failed to alert the Fleet to warnings from Bletchley Park of a possible German offensive action, or even officially to inform Coastal Command of the evacuation.[36] The fact that *Scharnhorst* was badly damaged in the encounter as a result of heroic action by *Acasta* and *Ardent*, and that *Gneisenau* was torpedoed by a submarine and badly damaged on the way home, was little compensation.

The sinking of *Glorious*, *Ardent* and *Acasta* was a tragedy which obscured the fact that the final operations of the campaign – the capture of Narvik and the evacuation – had otherwise been highly successful and the very antithesis of the chaotic fumbling of the deployments to Norway and of much of the subsequent campaign. Commanders in-theatre had successfully resisted pressure from London, and particularly from the Prime Minister, to rush the assault, and the results vindicated their judgment. Churchill, of course, did not share this perception. A week after the evacuation he wrote to the Secretary of State for War, 'I hope before any fresh appointment is given to General Auchinleck, the whole story of the slack and feeble manner in which the operations at Narvik were conducted, and the failure to make an earlier assault on Narvik town, will be considered. Let me know the dates when General Auchinleck was in effective command.'[37]

There had been one other notable casualty of the campaign, and of the ongoing campaign in France. On the eve of the attack on Narvik, and with the evacuation of Dunkirk just beginning, Churchill had replaced Ironside as CIGS with Dill. According to Churchill, there was a 'very strong feeling' in the War Cabinet and high military circles that Dill should succeed Ironside and that Ironside 'volunteered the proposal' that he should cease to be the CIGS and agreed instead to command Home Forces.[38] Much more likely is the account of Colonel Leslie Hollis, member of the Cabinet secretariat, who was present at the time. According to him, Churchill told Ironside that 'it had been decided' to appoint Dill in his place, and that he could become commander of Home Forces.[39] Either way, Ironside was out as CIGS.

23   Conclusions

In terms of its immediate outcome, the campaign in Norway was a decisive victory for the Germans. They had gained their strategic object-ive of the occupation of Norway, and done so in an astonishingly short time, inflicting a humiliating defeat on Britain and France in the process. They had achieved all of this at a remarkably low cost in terms of casualties: a total of around 4,000 Germans killed. Of these, the majority (2,375) had been lost at sea. The number of their soldiers killed in the land campaign amounted to only 1,317.[1] By comparison, the five-week campaign in Poland had cost the German Army some 16,000 killed.

Assessing the Allied casualty numbers is harder. In the land campaign, the official casualty figures include wounded and missing, totalling 1,869 British casualties and about 530 French and Polish combined.[2] British lives lost at sea totalled around 2,500. Norwegian lives lost amounted to around 860 military and 400 civilians.[3]

In summary, when compared to other campaigns in the Second World War, the overall number of casualties in the land campaign was very low.

In terms of materiel, the Allied armies' losses in weapons, vehicles and equipment were not heavy, but were nonetheless significant; the losses could be ill-afforded. In the air, the British lost 163 aircraft – many of them obsolete Gladiators.[4] The Luftwaffe lost more aircraft – a total of 242, one-third of them transports,[5] but this represented a much smaller proportion of its aircraft fleet. Overall, naval losses on each side were broadly comparable. The Royal Navy's losses included an aircraft car-rier, two cruisers (plus three badly damaged), seven destroyers (with eight badly damaged) and four submarines. In addition, the French and Polish also lost one destroyer each. German losses included three cruisers (plus two badly damaged), ten destroyers (plus six damaged) and six U-boats, with three battleships badly damaged. Given the respective sizes of the British and German navies, however, the German losses were hugely disproportionate and strategically significant, amounting to roughly half their surface fleet. Although German posses-sion of naval bases in Norway weakened British control of the northern approaches to the Atlantic and provided bases for damaging raids on the Murmansk convoys, the geostrategic advantage was partially offset by the British occupation of Iceland. The strategic threat posed to the Allies by the Kriegsmarine surface fleet was rendered decidedly limited. The extent to which these German losses were a factor in Hitler's decision not to attempt an invasion of Britain is debatable.

Other longer-term strategic outcomes were a mixed blessing for the victors. By denying Norway to the Allies, Germany secured its northern flank. But continued access to Swedish iron ore in winter turned out to be of limited value; firstly, the Germans' own highly effective sabotage of the port installations prior to the Allied attack rendered the port inoperative for twelve months; secondly, Germany now had access to the much larger French iron ore mines in Lorraine. Nor did the Norwegian economy provide much of strategic importance to Germany; the major asset – the mercantile fleet – was in British hands. The German victory did, of course, provide an immediate enhancement to German prestige and a commensurate lowering of that of the Allies, particularly in the eyes of neutral countries. The greatest impact was on Sweden and Finland, both of which were to come within the German orbit of influence. Further afield, however, the diplomatic implications of the German victory in Norway were completely eclipsed by that on the Western Front. Against these variable benefits, the requirement to garrison Norway in the face of a continuing perceived threat of British invasion and to police it in the presence of an increasingly active resistance movement became a considerable drain on German military resources. By 1945, the German garrison numbered almost 400,000 soldiers.[6]

A significant consequence of the campaign in Norway was the impact on Hitler's position in Germany. As the chief protagonist of Weserübung, and overall director of the campaign, its stunning success was a personal triumph for the Führer and portrayed as such to the German people. For Hitler, personally, the victory affirmed to himself his military genius, strengthened his faith in his intuition, vindicated his over-ruling of his military advisers, justified his micro-management of tactical detail, and encouraged his gambling instinct. These reactions were all to be confirmed by his victory on the Western Front, and all to stand him and Germany in extremely poor stead in the future. In the same vein, OKW – the German Armed Forces High Command – also saw its star in the ascendant as a result of Weserübung. Again, this was to serve Germany poorly in future campaigns.

For Britain, the major consequence was the demise of Chamberlain and his replacement by Churchill. Bearing in mind the part Churchill had played in the failure of the campaign, it was certainly ironic that he was the main political beneficiary and – bearing in mind the part that he was to play in Hitler's downfall – that the Führer had inadvertently brought him to power. A further beneficial effect for Britain was the way that Churchill, as Prime Minister, did business, not least his immediate reduction in the size of the War Cabinet, the formation of a Defence Committee with himself as chairman and his direct engagement with the Chiefs of Staff Committee and Joint Planners. The extent to which he, personally, learnt lessons from the campaign is more open to question.

For Norway, the outcome and consequences were grave. Apart from the military and civilian casualties, and the destruction of whole towns such as Namsos and Åndalsnes, the Norwegian people were subjected to five years of Nazi rule. There was, however, good reason for national pride in looking back on the spirit of resistance, both at the time of the invasion and during the occupation. A major long-term political consequence was the public mood of 'Never Again April 9th' and the government's decision to abandon neutrality and join the North Atlantic Alliance.

What, though, of the reasons for British campaign failure?

Two are obvious and have been analysed earlier: the catastrophic failure of intelligence which allowed Operation Weserübung to achieve complete strategic surprise and the domination of German air power which proved decisive. The combination of these two factors made it almost impossible for the Allies to retrieve the situation and turn it to their advantage. Many analyses of the campaign focus almost exclusively on these factors and, in doing so, obscure other flaws which together combined to prescribe disaster. As in most campaigns, it is necessary to go back to the very outset of campaign planning and examine the anatomy of the campaign to understand the factors which influenced its outcome.

A retrospective examination of the campaign in Norway can easily under-estimate the scale of the challenge presented by its context and circumstances. The international situation was not only particularly complex, ambiguous and uncertain, with many different and often conflicting factors to be taken into consideration, but also fast moving. What appeared to be a sensible course of action one day was highly questionable the next. Failure to take this into account exaggerates the perception of vacillation, indecision and inconsistency of purpose on the part of the policymakers and strategists. Moreover, the theatre of operations was, itself, full of highly testing geographic and climatic challenges – a country 1,000 miles from north to south, much of it mountainous and sparsely populated, with its northern area within the Arctic Circle. British ignorance about Norway and the Norwegians compounded these challenges. Faced with the complete strategic surprise with which operations commenced, and having been 'completely outwitted', the British had only limited options to retrieve the situation, particularly against an enemy as adept as were the Germans. Additionally, amphibious operations are amongst the most challenging and unforgiving in the military lexicon. Furthermore, this was, for the Allies, the first land campaign of the war, although not for the Germans; thus, the great advantage of experience lay with the latter. Finally, this was a campaign which pitted democracies against a dictatorship, with all the inherent practical advantages of the latter in facing fewer constraints, for example, in rapid decision-making or the need to act legally and ethically, and without the scrutiny of parliament and a relatively free media. In summary, the circumstances in both the planning and implementation phases of the campaign were highly challenging; the result was bound to reveal any weaknesses or lack of preparation, and of these there was no shortage.

Perhaps the greatest weaknesses of the British campaign can be found in an examination of the link between policy and plans. The British campaign in Norway had its roots in the War Cabinet's policy objective in September 1939 to prevent the movement of iron ore from Sweden to Germany (an economic policy objective). To this was added, from early December, the aim of providing support for the Finns against Russia. The policy objectives were clear; the strategy, however, was flawed. It became almost exclusively focused on how the desired objectives were to be delivered rather than giving due consideration throughout as to whether they could and should be achieved – and thus whether they were sensible and rational. Policy objectives came to be treated, not least by the government's senior military advisers, as imperatives. They gave insufficient attention to the question of whether these 'ends' of strategy were adequately supported by the ways and means available. Without this consideration, policy became divorced from reality. Inadequate attention was also paid to risk, particularly the compound risk, involved. For example, the plan for the original intervention in Norway in February and early March (Operations Avonmouth, Stratford and Plymouth) contained a high number of risks which, together, produced a compound risk that was nothing short of a long-odds gamble. Risks such as this were insufficiently emphasised to the War Cabinet, leaving its members with the impression that they could be tolerated.

Furthermore, without a continuous and relentless focus on strategy, ministers and their advisers lacked consistency of thinking and of contextual guidance for action. Instead, attention became fixated on what to do next and on eye-catching tactical schemes, whether or not they were coherent or led to the achievement of strategic objectives. This descended to a level close to Captain Maund's caricature of the apparent strategy as '"Let's attack here", "Let's go there", and if anyone else has an idea, "Let's go there, too."'[7]

Yet the answer was not to focus solely on the campaign and on achieving its policy objectives. To do so obscured the context of the campaign and its part in the overall policy for the war as a whole. This was the long-war policy – the approach that held that it was in the Allies' interests to postpone major offensive operations until military strength had been built up. Although, belief in this policy was not unanimous within the War Cabinet, or within the Alliance, there was no formal consideration as to whether the proposed campaign in Scandinavia, which grew to the size of a major military commitment, was consistent with the policy or whether it had superseded it or, indeed, whether the long-war policy was still appropriate. As so often happens, enthusiasm for the campaign developed a momentum of its own.

Many assessments of the reason for campaign failure in Norway focus on the very poor state of the British armed forces at the start of the war and the lack of investment that had brought this about. There is ample evidence of the weakness of all three armed services at this time and of the under-investment that was largely responsible for it. The outcome of the campaign might, indeed, have been very different had the services been stronger in terms of equipment and trained personnel. But this argument cannot be used as vindication for poor strategy. Strategists must cut their coat according to the cloth that is to hand. The art of good strategy is to improve one's position to the optimum with the ways and means that are available, not to attempt to achieve what would be appropriate were better ways and means to hand.

A major factor in the poor strategy and decision-making that characterised both the planning and implementation of the campaign can be found in the organisation for the higher management of the war. Although the comprehensive committee structure ensured the close examination of proposed courses of action and plans, it was over-bureaucratic and ponderous, occupying too much of the time of ministers and their principal advisers, often distracting them from more important activity and exhausting them in the process. In the month of April alone, the War Cabinet met thirty-one times, the Military Coordination Committee twenty-one times and the Chiefs of Staff Committee forty-two times: for the Chiefs, who attended all three groups (although, on occasions, represented by their deputies), a staggering total of ninety-four meetings. It was, of course, a structure and system totally unsuited to rapid decision-making. The existence of the Military Coordination

Committee, in particular, added a layer of management that accomplished little and, when operations began, was actively counterproductive to sound and timely decision-making. But seeing these organisations as organisms further helps explain the poor decisions. The relationships between the individuals on all these committees were often fractious – their personal chemistry did not result in the whole being greater than the sum of its parts; on the contrary, it bordered on the dysfunctional. As pressure increased, so fissures in group cohesion expanded and multiplied. The atmosphere in the Military Coordination Committee became acrimonious and actively detrimental to sound, rational decision-making, with, as the official historian recognised, 'much intervention ... in the detailed conduct of operations, intervention which was often disconcertingly sudden and sometimes seemingly impulsive'.[8] In addition, as is so often the case in failed campaigns, government departments (in this case, notably the War Office, Admiralty and Air Ministry) did not work in concert and harmony, nor achieve an integrated approach. In the case of the service ministries, their lack of unity of purpose, let alone unity of effort, is striking.

The Allied campaign failed most obviously at the tactical level, manifested particularly by the succession of ignominious defeats, withdrawals and evacuations, but the outcome was decided at the grand-strategic and theatre (or 'operational') levels. In fact, there were a number of local Allied successes at the tactical level – the naval battles at Narvik, 15 Brigade's action at Kvam and Otta, the capture of Narvik, the Hurricanes at Bardufoss – but these never added up to the achievement of any theatre, let alone grand-strategic, objectives. A distinction between grand strategy and theatre strategy was not commonly recognised. One of the consequences was that, as J. R. M. Butler observed, '[T]he distinction between the higher direction of the war and local strategy became blurred in practice.'[9] It was in the theatre-level strategy, planning and management of the campaign – the link and gearing between high-level strategy and tactics - that the Germans laid the foundations for campaign success. They thought about, and conducted, the campaign *as a campaign* – a set of military operations which lead to the achievement of strategic objectives – rather than just as a number of operations. Almost from the start of their planning, they had a commander and staff dedicated to campaign design, the same commander and staff who would be responsible for the conduct of the campaign (and thus for the consequences of their plans). When it came to the implementation of the campaign plan, and the rapidly evolving situation which developed ('no plan survives contact with the enemy'[10]), the theatre commander and staff were well placed to respond, and to develop, coordinate and sequence operations accordingly.[11] While, contrary to the original design, Falkenhorst was in direct command only of the Army element, he and his headquarters were the focal point at the theatre level for coordination and synchronisation of the plans and action of all three services. This did not prevent Hitler and the OKW from playing the dominant role in campaign direction, but fortuitously for the Germans, the Führer's micro-management did not have the damaging effect that it was to have in later campaigns. Finally, easily overlooked is the part that Headquarters XXI Group played in the highly challenging and completely successful logistical sustainment of the campaign. This delivered more than 29,000 troops and 2,000 tons of supplies by air and more than 100,000 troops, 100,000 tons of supplies, 20,000 vehicles and 16,000 horses by sea.[12] The logistics operation benefitted from a dedicated theatre headquarters, and a highly professional one. It is difficult to envisage their British opponents accomplishing this, even without an enemy.

From the outset, the Allies thought about their operations in Norway not as a campaign, but as a number of separate, discrete operations, for example, the land, sea and air operations or the operations in the north (around Narvik) and in central Norway (around Trondheim). Furthermore, combined strategy and planning with the French existed only in the most rudimentary, broad-brush way, with the Allied Military Committee effectively becoming sidelined. The British Army member, Lieutenant General Marshall-Cornwall, considered that their work was largely nugatory: 'I always felt that the results were hardly commensurate with our efforts, largely because the Chiefs of Staff were usually too busy to pay much attention to our reports or advice.'[13] In terms of British planning, no joint-service commander or staff was responsible for these operations, even when they grew into what should have been a coherent campaign. No single commander was responsible, even within the single services. In the Army, for example, planning responsibility was divided (in a most unclear way) between the CIGS, with his War Office staff, and the tactical commander, Major General Mackesy, with his divisional staff. The arrangement was wholly impractical.[14] Campaign planning required far more focus and detailed attention than could possibly be given by the hard-pressed War Office staff. Mackesy, with his very small staff in York, might have been expected to plan a small-scale, simple operation, but certainly not one as large and complex as was being envisaged in Scandinavia. The division of responsibility was never clarified. Who, for example, was responsible for the provision and coordination of detailed intelligence or logistics? After the invasion, an intermediate commander – Carton de Wiart – was appointed for land operations in central Norway, but without a headquarters; and a week later, Massy, in London, was appointed for the purpose – again without a headquarters. Anything approaching effective theatre-level command was absent throughout.

Theatre-level command was a major factor in German success. Firstly, it played an important role in preventing the Allies from regaining the initiative. At every stage after the invasion, and at every level, the Allies found themselves reacting to German moves – what Field Marshal Montgomery used to call 'dancing to the enemy's tune'.[15] The Chiefs of Staff and also, notably, Churchill understood the importance of seizing back the initiative, and the planned attacks at Narvik and Trondheim, though cack-handed, were at least attempts to do so. Theatre-level command and control, skilfully applied, allowed the Germans to coordinate and synchronise operations, and to marshal and apply their assets such as intelligence, logistics, communications, reserves and air power, quickly and efficiently – at least in comparison with the Allies. It also allowed them to cope far better with the uncertainties and friction of war than could the British, whose command and control remained at the military-strategic level. Combined with their military effectiveness and relentless aggression, this gave the Germans the ability to do things faster than could their opponents – what is referred to in military jargon as 'high tempo'. The Allies were constantly doing things too late – for example, the arrival of ground forces at Narvik; the provision of anti-aircraft guns just after the Germans had destroyed Namsos and Åndalsnes; the establishment of an air base at Lesjaskog just after the Luftwaffe had established the ability to destroy it; the reinforcement in central Norway just too late to make a difference. The Allies were, therefore, constantly 'beaten to the punch'. Furthermore, desperate Allied attempts to regain the initiative were a major factor in some of the truly dire administrative fiascos of the campaign, as semi-trained, inexperienced staffs tried to cut corners in responding to the demands to rush reinforcements and supplies to hastily planned operations. Lesjaskog stands out as an example.

The Allied campaign was also impaired by the friction and constraints inherent in coalition warfare. The British thought that the French were devious, unprincipled and 'cannot keep a secret'[16] – 'These French!!' chided Cadogan in his diary;[17] 'The PM told me', recorded Colville, '[that] he considered Laval the most unscrupulous and unreliable of all French politicians – which is saying a lot.'[18] In return, the French thought the British devious, but also negative, ponderous and overcautious. As one historian has observed, 'Underlying suspicion and resentment were never far below the surface.'[19] At the grand-strategic level, in the absence of rigorous strategy, the need to keep the Alliance together and functioning – arguably the highest policy priority – often adversely impacted on the adoption of sound plans. For example, the perceived fragility of the French government's position in the face of domestic public opinion was a major factor in the British decision to intervene on behalf of Finland and, at the end of March, to carry out the mining operation in Norwegian waters. French pressure also influenced the critical decision immediately after the invasion to give priority to Narvik over Trondheim. The main Alliance decision-making forum, the Supreme War Council, was often responsible for poor strategy, its meetings being judged by many participants to be successful if the atmosphere was cordial – 'Everything agreed and merry as a marriage bell'[20] – rather than whether sound policies and plans resulted.

The multinational dimension impacted adversely on operations in other ways, particularly in the British failure to seek to understand Norwegian culture, get to know Norwegian senior officers or adopt a joint approach with the Norwegian military. It was a whole month after the invasion before Norway was asked to be represented on the Supreme War Council or for Norwegian liaison officers to be invited into British service ministries.[21] From the outset of land operations, the British adopted a patronising and deceitful attitude towards the Norwegian forces, whom they considered to be primitive and untrustworthy. When General Ruge first made contact shortly after the invasion, the British should have sent a senior liaison officer to co-locate with him, seek his advice and coordinate a joint campaign. Instead, they used service attachés. And inexplicably when the military (army) attaché, hastily appointed after the invasion, was captured on 23 April, he was not replaced until mid-May, despite Ruge's urging.[22] Furthermore, with the exception of Paget and Auchinleck, British commanders mistrusted the local Norwegian commanders and conducted separate and uncoordinated operations. French commanders, notably Béthouart, were better at engaging with, and getting the best out of, their Norwegian counterparts.

A further factor in British campaign failure was an over-reliance on, and pride in, improvisation – what was, and some might say still is, a particularly British military characteristic. This was thought to be a key area of superiority over the German Army: 'They require all their rules to be there,' wrote Ironside, 'they shrink from improvisation.'[23] The underlying suggestion was that, other things being equal, the gifted amateur (particularly the gifted, gentleman amateur) would beat the dull professional (particularly the dull, foreign professional) any day. From the earliest stage of planning, the British tended to rely on ad hoc solutions, for example in the command, supply, transport, protection and preparation of its troops.[24] The practice continued as planning developed and the operation grew in size to one which might involve up to five divisions.

Too much reliance was placed on improvised groupings and commands: Mauriceforce, Sickleforce, Rupertforce, North West Expeditionary Force. A reverence for flexibility, adaptability and empiricism became undue faith in 'playing it off the cuff', which was actually no more than 'muddling through'; the ability to improvise became not a useful part of, but a substitute for, military doctrine and sound planning. Thus, commanders thought that there was no need to plan far ahead; forces would adapt to the situation and exploit opportunities as they developed. Troops which departed on one task to one location could be expected to be able to redeploy to another task somewhere else and cope with whatever they found when they got there (despite the fact that they were untrained to do so). Commanders could be deployed without staffs. Communications could be improvised. 'Experience would show' what could and could not be done. This was ill-judged. Paget was at pains in his report to underline 'the need to apply in the field what we have practised in peace, to foresee events by careful appreciation of possibilities and probabilities and thus go a long way towards the avoidance of "ad hoc" plans and improvisations.'[25] These were wise words.

The campaign also suffered from what has become a notable feature of more modern campaigns: oversensitivity to the perceived imperative that 'something must be done'. The media clamour for action – any action – built up to such an extent in March 1940 that it was hard to resist. The temptation for those responsible for policy to bow to the call proved to be too great and led to decisions which paid insufficient heed to the consequences. This was reckless. Hoare was later to reflect, with admirable humility, 'the fault … was the rashness of undertaking a military operation for which we were not prepared, and in failing to resist the outcry for action when waiting was the only wise course. The result was disastrous failure.'[26] If part of the reason for precipitate action can be found in J. R. M. Butler's comment that 'British Ministers [were] acutely sensitive to public opinion' and that 'Mr Chamberlain … often paid excessive attention to the probable effect of our measures on public opinion',[27] more recent campaigns would suggest that they have not been alone in this respect.

Finally, there was underestimation of the extent to which warfare is subject to Clausewitzian friction – 'the only concept that more or less corresponds to the factors that distinguish real war from war on paper'.[28] There was a naive faith that, whatever the plan, it would dominate events and that friction, if it existed, could somehow be controlled. This was hubris. Insufficient attention was paid by British decision-makers as to how the enemy might disrupt their plans, how operations dependent on perfect synchronisation might fall victim to the unexpected, how troops prepared for a single, limited task (garrisoning a town) might suddenly become involved in a completely different one (manoeuvre operations), how untested communications might fail and how language problems would result in misunderstandings. There was little attention, too, paid to the notion that '[w]ar is the realm of chance. No human activity gives it greater scope. No other has such incessant dealings with this intruder.'[29] Yet chance – luck – was, indeed, an incessant intruder throughout the campaign. For example, the weather at the time of the German invasion played a large part in its success, just as it did in covering the final British evacuation. Moreover, but for the technical failure of the German torpedoes, Narvik would be remembered not as a triumph for the Royal Navy, but as a disaster. However, such was the degree of wishful thinking and complacency among British decision-makers and their advisers that they appear to have assumed that if luck was involved, the coin would always come down heads-up. In this regard, we should remind ourselves of the particular susceptibility of warfare to Sod's Law – the apocryphal law that says that if something can go wrong, it will.[30] Sod would have derived considerable satisfaction from the British campaign in Norway.

Did the campaign at least have the redeeming feature of providing valuable lessons which led to success and saved lives later in the war? Various 'lessons learned' reports were produced by individuals and organisations – for example, a brief inquiry by Hankey into the intelligence failures surrounding the German invasion[31] and the War Office's report on the tactical and administrative lessons of the campaign[32] – but there was no official, overarching report such as that produced after the fall of France.[33] Churchill may have preferred it to remain that way. He had had, after all, to deal with the Dardanelles enquiry in 1916–1917. The lesson-learning process was not helped by the tendency for denial in the Army reports that were produced; for example, claiming that 'man for man the British soldier is far superior to his German counterpart'[34] or blaming defeat on a stab-in-the-back by ubiquitous, treacherous 'Quislings' and Fifth Columnists, with which Norway was allegedly 'riddled' and 'infested'.[35] Nevertheless, Sir Ian Jacob, a well-placed observer, later commented, 'I do not think it is too much to say that it was out of the confusion of the Norway campaign that the good organisation of later campaigns sprang.'[36]

As far as lessons from the air campaign are concerned, in the opinion of one air power expert, '[T]here is little evidence that experience was assimilated and applied to other campaigns.'[37] The most obvious lessons unique to the Norwegian campaign were those in the naval campaign, in tri-service operations and in amphibious warfare in particular. It was no coincidence that a Directorate of Combined Operations was immediately created, although ironic – and typical of the Norwegian campaign – that it was formed two days after the final evacuation was completed.[38] Nevertheless, it required several more operations, for example in Dakar, Crete and Dieppe, for the lessons identified from Norway to be learnt and applied. Further lessons about naval command and control, and inter-service cooperation, were learnt from an inquiry into the tragic loss of the *Glorious*.[39] Some lessons which should have been learnt from the campaign were not, including the vulnerability of surface ships to air attack, to which the sinking of the *Prince of Wales* and the *Repulse* in 1941 bore witness.[40] Less obviously, lessons were learnt and applied in the handling of intelligence, in particular enhancing the role of the JIC, improving signals intelligence and establishing the Inter-Service Topographical Department.[41] Finally, a study of this campaign suggests the value of a quick internal audit, while a campaign is ongoing, of the campaign conduct and the appropriateness of the machinery of government to manage it. Had such an audit been carried out in, say, January or March, it might have identified some of the critical deficiencies that were later to have such momentous consequences.

So where does the responsibility for campaign failure lie?

It was clear from an early stage that the War Cabinet was not well tuned to the demands of making strategy or for managing and directing a war, even a phoney war. Chamberlain's predilection for compromise and consensus and for avoiding unpleasantness and postponing difficult decisions, and his unfamiliarity with the military machine he was directing, were not conducive to hammering out coherent strategy, nor did his managerial leadership style provide the leadership, direction and drive necessary in war. Too often, he showed a reluctance to lay down the hard priorities which effective higher direction of a war demands and which inevitably results in some people being disappointed or offended. Too often he failed to keep the War Cabinet's focus on grand strategy, instead allowing his colleagues to indulge their enthusiasm for minor strategy and tactics. As Ian Jacob observed, he was 'always out of his depth in military matters,'[42] or, in Ironside's words, 'hopelessly unmilitary'.[43] His great disadvantage was not that he did not know the answers but that he did not know enough about the subject to know the right questions to ask. As Prime Minister he must bear the ultimate responsibility, including that for the unsuitable machinery of government – in particular, the unwieldy committee structure – which proved so cumbersome to planning, so debilitating to decision-makers and advisers and so counterproductive to rapid decision-making. Churchill rightly described the system as representing 'the maximum of study and the minimum of action. It was all very well to say that everything had been thought of. The crux of the matter was – had anything been done?'[44] Chamberlain was also responsible for appointing as the chairman of the Military Coordination Committee someone whose judgment and conduct, during his tenure of the appointment, not only led to a number of critically poor decisions but also exhausted and debilitated his colleagues – someone whom Chamberlain was unable to control: Churchill.

Within the War Cabinet, Churchill admirably embodied fighting spirit, but his immense frustration with the lack of it in his colleagues contributed to his increasingly erratic judgment. Indeed, a considerable responsibility for the failure of the campaign falls on Churchill – as he, himself, acknowledged. In his history of the Second World War he admitted, 'Considering the prominent part I played in these events, it is a marvel that I survived.'[45] In the draft for the book he had gone even further: '[I]t was a marvel – I really do not know how I survived',[46] and to Ismay he confided, 'I certainly bore an exceptional measure of responsibility for the brief and disastrous Norwegian Campaign.'[47] Yet, despite this self-deprecating aside, he uses the book to defend his reputation, assiduously offloading the blame for failures and his own errors of judgment onto the shoulders of others – political colleagues, advisers, senior commanders and Allies.

Churchill came to dominate both Chamberlain's War Cabinet and the Military Coordination Committee. But his exceptional powers of advocacy, and his remarkable ability to overcome opposition through a mixture of persuading, inspiring, cajoling and browbeating opponents, was not matched during this campaign by the wisdom of his judgment. In the Military Coordination Committee, decisions came to be made as a result of instinct, impulse and emotion rather than rationality. The intensity of Churchill's passion became his own worst enemy. His single-minded pursuit of what he called, 'my pet ... my first love'[48] – Narvik – amounted to a dangerous obsession that blinded him to logic, reason and the objective, dispassionate consideration of strategy. As a future CIGS was to remark of him, 'He is like a child that has set its mind on some forbidden toy. It is no good explaining to him that it will cut his fingers or burn him. The more you explain, the more fixed he becomes in his idea.'[49] Ironside, too, and independently, followed the same analogy: 'He is so like a child in many ways. He tires of a thing, and then wants to hear no more of it.'[50]

Churchill's domination of the Admiralty was at times pejorative. Chamberlain became aware: he 'does enjoy planning a campaign or an operation himself so much and he believes so earnestly in his own idea (for the moment) that he puts intenser pressure on his staff than he realises. The result is apt to be that they are bullied into a sulky silence – a most dangerous position in war.'[51] This was also true of Churchill's relationship with the Chiefs of Staff. As J. R. M. Butler so delicately put it, '[T]he guess may be hazarded that the Chiefs of Staff were sometimes induced by the forceful personality of the First Lord of the Admiralty to lend support to bold enterprises against their better judgement.'[52] Churchill may well have been ruefully recalling this set of Chiefs of Staff when he later asserted, 'Why, you may take the most gallant sailor, the most intrepid airman, or the most audacious soldier, put them at a table together – what do you get? *The sum of their fears.*' [Emphasis in original.][53]

Churchill's own description of his way of going about business has a certain black humour to it, but is nonetheless revealing. 'All I wanted', he wrote, 'was compliance with my wishes after reasonable discussion.'[54] Although he was careful never to give a direct order which overruled clearly stated military advice, his application of what he called 'mental reconnaissance in force'[55] too often came close to pressurising commanders – for example, Cork and Mackesy – into action that would have led to disaster. Within the Admiralty, he 'constantly interfered with operational matters'.[56] And his fascination with tactical-level detail and gadgetry – such as designs for fluvial mines, trench-cutting machines, concrete ships, dummy ships, fire ships, the allocation of Lewis guns to small craft, schemes for putting wax in soldiers ears to deaden the noise of battle[57] – not only distracted him from focusing on strategic issues but also, as Brian Bond has pointed out, meant that 'an enormous amount of time and energy was taken up in resisting an obsessive and obstinate First Lord'.[58] Ian Jacob, so often a perceptive observer, later remarked that the difference between Churchill as team member and team leader was 'the difference between a human dynamo when humming at the periphery and when driving at the centre'.[59]

Churchill showed, throughout the campaign from its earliest inception, an ignorance of, and disdain for, logistics worthy of the cavalry subaltern he once had been, and perhaps, at heart, still was. If, as is sometimes said, 'amateurs talk tactics; professionals talk logistics',[60] Churchill was a proudly consummate amateur. Finally, he was largely responsible for some of the worst strategic blunders of the campaign – for example, the critical decision to offload the troops and deploy the fleet on 7 April and the prioritisation of Narvik over Trondheim in the following days. It is hard not to conclude that, for Churchill, the amphibious operations at both places represented opportunities to exorcise the ghosts of Gallipoli and vindicate his judgment. It may seem obvious and commonplace to say so, but the Norwegian campaign was not his finest hour.

The other members of the War Cabinet, although they played a lesser role in campaign failure, cannot escape their individual and collective responsibility. They were too ready to accept the military advice they were given, apparently reluctant to cross-examine the Chiefs, even when the proposed military plans were manifestly flawed or obviously highly risky. At the same time, they were happy to dismiss the Chiefs' advice if it conflicted with their personal predilections or agendas, for example, telling the Chiefs that an assessment of the likelihood of a German invasion of Norway 'was a political matter which was for the War Cabinet to deal with, and which did not lie within the province of the Chiefs of Staff'.[61] Ministers also allowed themselves to be too easily distracted from discussion of grand strategy, their main business, by discussion of tactics – what Ironside characterised as 'playing with tin soldiers on a map'[62] – and with media presentation; in other words, a reluctance to be shifted from their comfort zone. They had not developed the habit of thinking strategically, so that when confronted with crisis, and the need to address it in strategic terms, they were unable to do so.

The War Cabinet had, however, developed a habit of mind which was not only dangerous but also infectious to those around them – that of wishful thinking. Liddell Hart commented on this at the time:

There has been too much wishful thinking in our foreign policy. And in our attitude to the military conditions underlying it. We need to approach these problems not with the desire to suit our conclusions to our interests, but in the spirit, and with the method of the scientist – whose predominant interest is to discover the truth.[63]

This wishful thinking had two particularly pernicious effects. One effect was the lazy assumption, conscious or subconscious, which gradually seems to have gained ground in the minds of many ministers (and their advisers), that the whole plan was an academic exercise – for various reasons, it would never really happen, and therefore did not really matter. The other effect was that, in the warm glow of optimism, there was a reluctance of those who were not swept along by it to confront it for fear of being branded as pessimists and doom-mongers. There was a dangerous absence of hard-headed realism. Reading the minutes of the War Cabinet and other top committees, one is struck by the prevalence of the phrase, 'It was hoped that ...' ('It was hoped that we should soon be able to block the railway between Narvik and the frontier';[64] 'It was hoped that Brigadier Morgan would reach Dombås by 21st April;[65] 'It was hoped that these bombers would be able to reach Trondheim aerodrome'[66]). Ministers seemed happy to accept such statements and to work on the basis of hope. In this vein, it is notable that, although the War Cabinet was full of individuals of very high intellect, they often failed to apply real intellectual rigour to the issues brought before them. Some ministers, notably Halifax, Stanley and Hankey, were, on occasions, prepared to question the viability of policy proposals, but even they deferred too easily to Churchill's apparent experience and powers of persuasion or to Chamberlain's desire for consensus and compromise. Halifax, for example, was thought by Rab Butler to have agreed to the final decision to mine Norwegian waters 'only . . . because of his loyalty to the PM'.[67] A perceptive, young civil servant at the Ministry for Economic Warfare (and future leader of the Labour Party), Hugh Gaitskell, provided a thought-provoking observation in his deprecation of Chamberlain and his ministers at the time: 'these old gentlemen, with their optimistic twaddle'.[68]

At times the War Cabinet appeared remarkably disengaged from strategic-level military planning and decision-making, exercising insufficient supervision. At other times, its members, notably Churchill, became over-involved in detailed orders at the operational and even tactical levels, also to the detriment of campaign success. That Cabinet members responsible for the direction and conduct of war have every right to involve themselves in decision-making, including military decision-making, at every level is not disputed. As historians such as Eliot Cohen and Hew Strachan have pointed out, there should be no such thing as a 'politics-free zone'.[69] But exercising this right to the optimum degree is an art, and one requiring fine judgment. As events in early 1940 showed, the penalties for getting this judgment wrong can be severe.

That Chamberlain's War Cabinet fell some way short of the ideal in its conduct of strategy and in the direction of the war was cruelly exposed by the Norwegian campaign, but it need not have been disastrous had the Cabinet been served by a strong team of military advisers – the Chiefs of Staff. Sadly, this was not the case. Indeed, as the planning developed, the Cabinet was increasingly ill-served in this respect, although the extent of this only became obvious when forces were deployed to Norway. The Cabinet – any Cabinet – could, with some justification, have every right to expect the Chiefs of Staff to be expert military advisers; to have a deep understanding of strategy; to give consistently sound and coherent defence-wide advice; to be up to date with developments in warfare; and to act with foresight, imagination and good judgment. On this occasion, however, all these expectations were misplaced.

The Chiefs were quick to criticise the War Cabinet's lack of strategic understanding – Ironside frequently confided in his diary his frustration with ministers' lack of strategic comprehension – but the Chiefs' own understanding was decidedly shallow. They appeared to hold three assumptions about the meaning of the word *strategy* (as a process) that was almost guaranteed to result in bad strategy – that is to say a course of action where the ends to be achieved are grossly out of balance with the available ways and means. The first of these assumptions was an overly hierarchical, simplistic perception of strategy as the servant of policy. Thus they saw their constitutional role as providing advice to ministers and then implementing their wishes. Such a process did not take into account the need for discourse and, if necessary, robust debate, albeit accepting that, following the principle of 'civilian primacy', when formal political direction is given, it should be followed. This, in turn, led to the assumption that strategy was a one-way street: the sole object of strategy was to produce a plan for the implementation of policy. This did not take into account the possibility that what might be desirable politically might also be unachievable. If this were the case, there was a requirement – indeed, a duty – to return to their political masters to adjust the ends to be achieved or to accept responsibility for the risks and consequences of not doing so. The third assumption followed: strategy was a one-off process and that once a decision had been reached, strategy ended and implementation took over. This disregarded the need for strategy to be continuous, dynamic and iterative if policy and plans are to remain relevant to evolving circumstances and events. Doctrine about the place and role of strategy had become blinkered dogma. It excluded common sense.

Thus, when the War Cabinet expressed a desire to proceed with proposals for the 'major project' (the expedition through Norway to Sweden), the Chiefs saw it as their business to provide a plan for doing so rather than also to warn that the necessary ways and means were grossly inadequate. When their advice was ignored and the risks increased still further, they did not return to ministers to re-present the risks and advise on the options for adjustment of the policy. At times, the Chiefs virtually dispensed with strategy altogether in arriving at their plan, justifying this by saying that 'the stakes are high, but the prize of success is great'.[70] Moreover, their consideration of risk was often cavalier in the extreme. They appeared loath to present the War Cabinet with a full picture of the risks involved, possibly because to do so would seem faint-hearted or defeatist, possibly because they did not want the War Cabinet to interfere with their plans, perhaps because they would have to admit the lack of preparedness of the forces involved. Whatever the motive, this was reckless behaviour. It was – and is – the role and duty of the Chiefs of Staff to confront wishful thinking with realism and 'to speak truth unto power'.

A further major flaw was the Chiefs' failure to recognise their own limitations. They seemed to believe that, by virtue of their exalted appointments, they knew best, failing to recognise or acknowledge the quality and wisdom of their own advisers, in particular the Joint Planners. The latter had a much better understanding of strategy than did the Chiefs, based not on any doctrine, but on common sense – the need to balance ends, ways and means, establish priorities and manage risk. The Joint Planners also brought incisive minds and intellectual rigour to the conduct of strategy and generally provided excellent advice based on sound judgment. Yet the Chiefs frequently ignored this advice, for example, favouring Narvik over Trondheim as the priority for action on the day of the invasion. The Joint Planners were also consistent in their warnings whenever they considered that the ways and means failed to support the ends – for example, over the vulnerability to air attack of proposed Allied land operations in central Norway. Again, the Chiefs frequently either dismissed these warnings – 'Experience would show whether or not substantial forces could be maintained in the face of air attack'[71] – or watered them down – 'We do not consider that undue weight should be given to the inherent difficulties of the enterprise'[72] – or, on at least one occasion, effectively suppressed the Joint Planners' report.[73]

On other occasions the Chiefs provided good advice but failed to press it with sufficient force. When their advice was ignored or rejected in meetings of the War Cabinet or Military Coordination Committee, they did not return to the charge, even when the result was clearly leading into danger. It was their duty to do so. They appear, however, to have believed that their duty had been done if their case had been presented or that, constitutionally, they were prohibited from vigorous debate with ministers. On occasions, this had far-reaching consequences. For example, when in late March the War Cabinet was showing signs of resurrecting the intervention in Norway, the Chiefs failed to emphasise, before it was too late, that the expedition had been stood-down, that some of the key units had actually been disbanded, that the necessary detailed planning had ceased and, thus, that it would take weeks to make ready a force. In a further example, on 9 April the Chiefs left a meeting with the Joint Planners, fully agreeing that Trondheim and Bergen should have priority over Narvik, only to go straight into a meeting of the War Cabinet which, with no apparent intervention by the Chiefs, agreed almost the opposite. They allowed ministers – and, perhaps, on occasions, themselves – to be seduced by large, impressive arrows on planning maps (today it would be PowerPoint) without taking due account of the fact that the arrows illustrated possible movement, not necessarily a feasible operation. Above all, the Chiefs came to be in thrall to the overbearing personality of Winston Churchill. They failed to stand up to him. It did not have to be like that. General Sir Alan Brooke, as CIGS, was later to show that it could be done.

The Chiefs also consistently failed to give Defence-wide advice. As the official historian observed, 'The Chiefs of Staff ... had not yet become fully accustomed to teamwork and still represented primarily the interests and viewpoints of their several Departments.'[74] Indeed, the campaign suffered from the fact that the individual Chiefs were often pulling in diametrically different directions, ignoring the needs of the other services (but not their shortcomings) and acting contrary to the interests of Defence as a whole. This amounted to single-service chauvinism.[75] J. R. M. Butler was unusually forthright in his verdict:

[T]heir views were as often as not conveyed to the War Cabinet by each Chief of Staff treating separately whatever appeared to belong mainly to the business of his own Department. Thus the directions issued from London for the conduct of the combined operations in Norway came from an Admiralty which had a greater immediate interest in blockade measures, a War Office all too conscious of its heavy commitments in France, and an Air Ministry whose first concern was the air defence of Great Britain.[76]

It is worth recalling Ismay's comments on this:

The Chief of the Naval Staff and the Chief of the Imperial General staff acted with sturdy independence. They appointed their respective commanders without consultation with each other; and, worse still, they gave orders to those commanders without harmonising them. Thereafter, they continued to issue separate orders to them. Thus confusion was worse confounded.[77]

In Moulton's view, 'The air staff ... seemed to take quiet satisfaction that an air force should beat a navy, even though it was a German air force and a British navy.'[78]

It might be pleaded in defence of the Chiefs that the need for a more joint approach had not been recognised at the time, that they were merely following past precedent and that their conduct in this matter was no worse than that of many of their predecessors (or, indeed, as it has turned out, many of their successors). All of this is true, but it does not reflect well upon their wisdom; de Lee refers to their failure to act together for the benefit of the whole as 'corporate autism'.[79] (As it happens, the German armed forces were not, themselves, free from inter-service jealousies and pettiness, nor was their inter-service cooperation as exemplary as is sometimes claimed.) It should also be noted that the Chiefs were under great pressure throughout the period, with their time taken up by endless meetings, and clearly considered that their time was best spent within the Whitehall bubble. As a result, none of them got out much to visit their services, and so they became increasingly out of touch with reality.[80]

Although it is over-easy in retrospect to criticise decision-takers for lack of foresight and imagination, it is equally difficult to defend the Chiefs' collective performance in these areas. First, as heads of their professions they might have been expected to recognise as their duty the need to take a close personal interest in how warfare was evolving, how Germany's military capability and concepts might be developing and what lessons this might hold for Britain. This does not seem to have been the case. As a result, such evolution, in particular in air power, hit them as something of a 'revolution in military affairs'. In their defence, they were not alone in this, and the charge is equally applicable to their predecessors. The same was true of the Chiefs' attitude towards German intentions. Although from time to time during the Phoney War they commissioned the JIC to produce papers on the subject, and Ironside may have been, as has been claimed, 'a careful consumer of military intelligence directorate reports',[81] they rarely appear to have discussed in Committee their collective thoughts about what the Germans might be planning. They do not seem to have constantly kept at the forefront of their minds the thought of warfare as a two-sided, adversarial activity in which the enemy always gets a vote. In chess terms, they seem to have assumed that they would probably, if not always, draw white, with the privilege of making the first move, and that there was no need to think more than one or two moves ahead. Nor did they seem to be able to envisage the tactical consequences of their strategic decisions, for example, the chaos at ports too small for their role as major bases, the capability of unprepared troops in Arctic conditions or the consequences at the tactical level of the kaleidoscopic, last-minute changes in strategic plans – in short, the impact of friction. As for the lack of a proper command structure for joint operations in Scandinavia, it is hard to defend the Chiefs' failure to address this in a timely fashion. Their complacent under-estimation of their German opponents is particularly striking, based less on rational analysis than on an apparently innate faith in British superiority. The Chiefs' plans could have worked well against the opponents that they were used to facing in imperial policing; their plans, however, could not and did not work well against as professional and formidable opponents as the Germans. There is more than a grain of truth in the reported observation of a French officer at Namsos that 'the British have planned this campaign on the lines of a punitive expedition against the Zulus, but unhappily we and the British are in the position of the Zulus.'[82]

Perhaps the issue over which the War Cabinet could feel most aggrieved with the Chiefs of Staff was the latter's assurance in early April that they had in place the intelligence assets and machinery to identify any German move against Norway in time to react. This was a catastrophic failure, although the exact details of the assets and machinery are unknown and thus also the degree to which the Chiefs were personally to blame or the extent to which they were let down by others.

Individually, too, the Chiefs' performance was not a strong one. As chairman of the Chiefs of Staff Committee, Newall lacked the strength of personality necessary to lead the group and provide it with cohesion. Beaverbrook's comment that Newall 'was an Observer in the last war and has remained an observer ever since' was unkind, but, as Alex Danchev has noted, it 'registered Newall's passiveness if not acquiescence'.[83] Newall was too easily dominated by Ironside, and by other senior officers in his own service, and he was insufficiently robust or forceful in representing the Chiefs' advice and warnings in meetings of the War Cabinet and Military Coordination Committee. His understanding of warfare as a whole was narrow, and he was so wedded to the Trenchard doctrine that it clouded the clarity of his vision of air power. As a result, he failed to see the impact that German air doctrine and capability might have on the campaign, and it was left to Slessor to represent the case to the Chiefs – a case that Newall allowed to be rejected. He recognised that Allied plans for intervention in Scandinavia were deeply flawed, describing them as 'hare-brained', yet he failed in his duty to provide forceful opposition to them, lacking the courage of his convictions. Throughout the planning and implementation of the campaign, he was more concerned about looking after the interests of his own service than he was about the successful outcome of the venture as a whole, although, to his credit, in doing so he preserved the RAF for the much more important battles to come. Had he forcefully argued this principle early on, a different policy might have resulted.

Pound, too, saw his primary duty in terms of loyalty to his service. And it is hard to find evidence of occasions when he made a contribution to strategy or provided advice that was not restricted to the Royal Navy and the maritime dimension. He was unsuited to his appointment as First Sea Lord and 'took the job because there was nobody else and he shouldered the burden as best he could'.[84] A large part of the burden was his political master, Churchill, whom he attempted to control – an exceptional challenge – but with very limited success. He could not curb Churchill's penchant for meddling in operational details (indeed, a penchant that he, himself, shared) or for making unsuitable appointments such as Lord Cork, nor did he protect members of his staff to whom Churchill took a dislike and sacked. In the words of Pound's biographer, 'To put it simply, Churchill was allowed to intervene in operations far more than Pound should have been prepared to accept.'[85] Pound must share with Churchill the responsibility for some of the most disastrous decisions of the campaign: the disembarkation of the troops and the deployment of the Fleet on 7 April, the removal of the flotilla from the Narvik approaches on 8 April and the cancellation of the attack on Bergen on 9 April. Pound was essentially a backward-looking sailor whose belief that Britannia ruled the waves was based more on pride in past glories and traditions than on the rational analysis that a broad and enquiring mind might have produced. He was 'wedded ... to the battle fleet concept, and ... little aware of the growing influence of air and under-water weapons'.[86] His beliefs impacted adversely on operations through-out the campaign. He was, in Correlli Barnett's words, 'an industrious journeyman, a narrow professional sailor, not very well informed about wider issues'.[87] In his defence, Pound was not a well man at the time, already suffering from painful osteoarthritis.

Ironside was totally miscast as CIGS. In A. J. P. Taylor's words, 'Few men have been less successful as CIGS, and none has been more con-scious of it.'[88] Ironside was not to blame for his ignorance of the White-hall machine, or his poor ability to argue his case when challenged, or his frustration with the military-political interactions which are such a con-stant refrain in his diary and which so exhausted him. It is, however, difficult to disagree with Slessor's verdict that Ironside had 'an apparent self-confidence as CIGS in war which unfortunately turned out to be unjustified'.[89] At the heart of this was Ironside's erratic judgment which, due to the strength of his personality, came to play a major role in the planning and conduct of the campaign. Few in the Army had greater command experience than had he, and he had held appointments such as commandant of the Staff College where he had had the opportunity to broaden and deepen his understanding of warfare; yet the advice he gave suggested that the learning process had somehow been stunted. Along with this, his natural imperturbability – a great virtue in a commander – had crossed the line into complacency. His was the dominant voice in the Chiefs of Staff committee, arguing for the intervention in Scandinavia despite the obvious lack of resources and seemingly heedless of the ever-mounting risk. He advocated enterprises with dubious chances of suc-cess, such as the expedition from Narvik to Gällivare, which depended on much wishful thinking in terms of providing the necessary trained troops, equipment and logistic support. This is all the more remarkable since he, himself, had commanded a force in the Arctic Circle for a year (at Murmansk, 1918–1919).

Once he had seized on an idea, Ironside's mind became closed to logical arguments against it, constantly rejecting the warnings of his staff and the Joint Planners. He had come to rely on his intuition rather than the advice of his subordinates and staff – a habit which may have served him well in the past on operations but was not to do so at the strategic level in Whitehall. For example, his low opinion of senior German officers, and by extension the German military, was outdated and stereotyped, but it was unshakeable until he was brought face-to-face with reality.[90] In the same way, he, like Churchill, became so carried away with the idea – which he saw as his own idea – of taking the war into Scandinavia and thereby inflicting a major defeat on Germany that it became an article of faith for him, and he lost the cold, dispassionate objectivity essential to the strategist. He seemed unaware of his own personal weaknesses, or, indeed, that he had any at all, perhaps lacking anyone in his life to point them out to him. For twenty years a general officer, he had been too senior for too long. Ironside's military assistant, Colonel Macleod, believed that 'Ironside was a military genius';[91] Ironside may have come to believe it as well. He was also subject to rapid mood swings and changes of mind, the latter almost to the extent of holding two apparently contradictory ideas in his head virtually simultaneously, close to the point of cognitive dissonance: one day vowing 'we shall have no side-shows – if I can prevent the starting of them',[92] but three days later recording, 'I told them, here was a legitimate side-show.'[93] Equally contradictory was his espousal of the priority of the Western Front ('Our front line is in France and we must fight in France. We cannot escape that.'[94]) but arguing that it was more important for our troops to be in Scandinavia ('[T]he reduction of the BEF by three divisions is unlikely to influence decisively the outcome of the battle.'[95]). Then again, at the same time that he was strongly advocating the operations in Scandinavia, he was writing in his diary, 'One is almost frightened at the boldness of the plan, knowing what slender means one has at the moment to carry it out.'[96] This appeared to be, for him, a characteristic approach to risk: an apparent thrill in taking a gamble, together with a frisson of amazement at having actually had the temerity to have done so. Ironside was also wont to confide in his diary what he should have been telling his political masters: 'The Cabinet will try to rush me and I shall have to resist';[97] '[W]e … have nothing left in England fit for fighting';[98] 'Nobody has dared to say that the Territorial Army is virtually untrained after seven months of training.'[99] Although he had little difficulty in persuading Newall and Pound, probably against their better judgment, that his schemes for land operations should be followed, he more than met his match with Churchill, and in this relationship he lacked the strength of character, intellect and sharpness of mind to prevail. Thus, for example, he was persuaded to accept the priority of Narvik over Trondheim and, later, accepted that part of the force en route to Narvik should be immediately diverted to Namsos.

As an experienced commander, Ironside's errors of operational judgment are the more surprising. The muddled orders that he personally gave to deployed commanders (Mackesy, Carton de Wiart and Morgan), the impractical command and control arrangements that were made for their forces, the expectation that the forces at Namsos and Åndalsnes could succeed without the necessary support – these were major errors, seemingly the result of a lack of foresight, clarity of mind and intellectual rigour. Ironside's handling of the command crisis at Narvik did not reflect well on his judgment. He gave Mackesy no encouragement or support, nor, when the crisis became evident, did he visit Harstad or send his deputy, or follow the well-proven formula of 'back or sack'. Instead, he allowed the situation to fester until Auchinleck's arrival on 11 May. Even more surprising is the lack of attention that he paid to the training of the forces for Norway. Ironside must have known how critical it would be for these units to be well trained and was well aware of their very low state of training, particularly that of the Territorial Army formations and units. It might be expected, therefore, that he would have shown great personal interest in their training, visited the formations concerned and demanded constant progress reports. There is, however, no evidence that he did any of these things. He was, of course, hugely overworked and subject to a punishing schedule of daily meetings in London, but the oversight is nevertheless striking. His failure to emphasise the Army's low state of training – 'When it is discovered, there might be a row. The blame may well fall on the soldiers'[100] – does not reflect well on his moral courage. By the time he was removed from office (27 May), Ironside was, by his own admission, exhausted. In a candid observation, he told a friend later in 1940, 'I never realised until I had thrown off the harness how tired I was and how much I wanted a let-up at the time.'[101] If, in comparison with the other Chiefs, he seems to have attracted a disproportionate amount of attention in this book, it was his misfortune to have inadvertently revealed so much in his diary.

In summary, the three key military-strategic advisers – the Chiefs of Staff – were not of the highest quality, and they made a poor team. Their inadequacy had a major impact on the planning and conduct of the campaign. What is surprising in retrospect is that they were appointed in the first place and that they were not replaced sooner. Sufficient signs of their lack of competence were there to be seen from early 1940, but Chamberlain either did not recognise the signs, or chose to ignore them. In a way, it may have been, politically, quite convenient having military advisers who lacked unanimity; who were less than forthright in their advice; who, if their advice was ignored, did not remonstrate; and who were inadvertently prepared to accept major risk on behalf of the policy makers and could therefore be blamed when things went wrong. Nevertheless, Churchill acted swiftly to replace Ironside and, later in the year, to remove Newall (aged only 54); Pound's ill health forced his resignation a month before his death in 1943. Their inadequacy resulted less from a failure to do what they saw to be their duty than from what they saw their duty to be. They were all products of the system and culture of their time. The system had failed to educate its most senior officers to act effectively at the military-strategic level and had failed to appoint the brightest and best to fill the top appointments. The military culture was one of lazy anti-intellectualism which favoured empiricism and the adoption of intellectual shortcuts over hard thinking and the deep understanding of concepts, such as strategy, that could only be acquired through rigorous study. It was also an over-hierarchical culture that discouraged challenge to orthodoxy and authority.[102] To succeed at the military-strategic level within such a system and culture required exceptionally high-calibre individuals, and it was fortunate for Britain that the Chiefs' successors were all of a higher calibre: Admiral Sir Andrew Cunningham; General Sir John Dill, followed by General Sir Alan Brooke; and Air Chief Marshal Sir Charles Portal. In this vein, it is probably no coincidence that all of these had attended the Imperial Defence College, whilst none of their predecessors had done so.[103]

In retrospect, from the very inception of planning to the conclusion of operations, the British campaign was mired in error and misjudgement. In John Terraine's words, 'From the beginning to end, the Allied operations in Norway ... display an amateurishness and feebleness that make the reader alternately blush and shiver.'[104] The two most obvious factors which decided the outcome – the failure of Allied intelligence and the domination of German air power – tend to mask the many other weaknesses which, by themselves, could have resulted in defeat, either in the aborted expedition prior to the collapse of Finland or in the campaign as it unfolded in April and May. The poor tactical performance in the land operations also masks the fact that, even if some of these individual operations had been more successful, the strategic outcome would probably have been the same. Good tactics can seldom redeem bad strategy. Finally, the campaign illustrates that good strategy is elusive. Many factors conspire to make it so, particularly at the grand strategic level, particularly in a democracy and particularly within a coalition. Indeed, in these circumstances, as more recent campaigns have shown, it is far easier for bad strategy to result.

In sum, as so often after a long period of peace, the British military capacity, in its widest sense, faced the audit of war and was found to be wanting. The result was a fiasco – a textbook example of how not to plan and conduct a military campaign.

Campaigns that end in ignominious failure and have few redeeming features tend to be forgotten quite quickly. There is, of course, a danger in this, not least of failing to learn from bitter experience. An examination of the anatomy of this campaign serves not only to provide a better understanding of the reasons for its failure, but, perhaps more importantly, to provide a better understanding of campaigns in general, and of some of the likely pitfalls that await the unwary. The 'ramshackle' British campaign in Norway in 1940 may have been a sorry tale, but it is also a cautionary one.

Appendix A Operational Code Names

Avonmouth	Plan for expedition to Narvik and the Swedish iron ore fields
Hammer	Plan for direct amphibious attack on Trondheim
Maurice	Operations against Trondheim from Namsos
Paul	Plan for the blockage of Luleå harbour with air-delivered mines
Plymouth	Plan for operation to counter German occupation of southern Sweden
R4	Plan to occupy Narvik, Trondheim, Bergen and Stavanger in conjunction with mining operations in Norwegian territorial waters
Royal Marine	Plan to place mines in River Rhine
Rupert	Operation to recapture Narvik
Scissors	Operations of the Independent Companies south of Narvik
Sickle	Operations against Trondheim from Åndalsnes
Stratford	Plan to occupy Trondheim, Bergen and Stavanger
Weserübung	German operation to occupy Norway and Denmark
Wilfred	Minelaying operation in Norwegian territorial waters

Appendix B Who's Who (September 1939–June 1940)

AUCHINLECK, Lieutenant General Claude, CinC North West Expeditionary Force, May 1940

AUDET, Major General Gérard, Commander French Forces at Namsos

BÉTHOUART, Brigadier General Antoine, Commander Chasseurs Alpins at Namsos, thereafter commander of French and Polish forces in Narvik area

BRAUCHITSCH, Colonel General Walther von, CinC German Army

BRIDGES, Sir Edward, Secretary to the Cabinet

BROOKE, Lieutenant General Sir Alan, Commander 2nd Corps, British Expeditionary Force

BUTLER, Richard A. 'Rab', Parliamentary Under Secretary of State for Foreign Affairs

CADOGAN, Sir Alexander, Permanent Under Secretary, Foreign Office

CARTON de WIART, Major General (promoted Lieutenant General) Adrian, Commander Mauriceforce

CHAMBERLAIN, Neville, Prime Minister (until May 1940) then Lord President of the Council

CHANNON, Henry 'Chips', Parliamentary Private Secretary to R. A. Butler

CHATFIELD, Admiral of the Fleet Lord, Minister for Coordination of Defence (until April 1940)

CHURCHILL, Winston, First Lord of the Admiralty (until May 1940) then Prime Minister

COLLIER, Laurence, Head of Northern Department, Foreign Office

COLVILLE, John, Assistant Private Secretary to the Prime Minister

CORK and ORRERY, Admiral of the Fleet, the Earl of, Commander Naval Forces Narvik Area, from 20 April Commander-in-Chief British Forces Narvik Area

DALADIER, Edouard, French Prime Minister (until March 1940) then Minister of Defence

DANCKWERTS, Captain Victor, Director of Plans, Admiralty and member of the Joint Planning Sub-Committee (the Joint Planners) (until March)

DANIEL, Captain Charles, Director of Plans, Admiralty and member of the Joint Planning Sub-Committee (the Joint Planners) (from March)

DEWING, Major General Richard, Director Military Operations and Plans, War Office

DIETL, Major General (promoted Lieutenant General) Eduard, Commander 3rd Mountain Division, German Army

DILL, Lieutenant General (promoted General) Sir John, Commander 1st Corps, British Expeditionary Force (until April 1940) then Vice Chief of the Imperial General Staff

DORMER, Sir Cecil, British Minister to Norway

EDEN, Anthony, Dominions Secretary (until May 1940) then Secretary for War

EVANS, Admiral Sir Edward, CinC (designate) Naval Forces Narvik Area (in March 1940)

FALKENHORST, General Nikolaus von, Commander Group XXI, German Army

FEURSTEIN, Lieutenant General Valentin, Commander 2nd Mountain Division, German Army

FLEISCHER, Major General Carl Gustav, Commander, 6th Division, Norwegian Army

FOLEY, Frank, Secret Intelligence Service Head of Station, Oslo

FORBES, Admiral Sir Charles, CinC Home Fleet

FRASER, Brigadier William, Commander 24th Guards Brigade

GAMELIN, General Maurice, Chief of Staff for National Defence, France

GORT, General Lord, CinC, British Expeditionary Force

GRIGG, Sir James 'PJ', Permanent Under Secretary, War Office

GUBBINS, Colonel (promoted Brigadier) Colin, Commander Scissorsforce

HALDER, General Franz, Chief of Staff of the Supreme High Command of the German Army

HALIFAX, Viscount, Foreign Secretary

HANKEY, Lord, Minister Without Portfolio (until May 1940) then Chancellor of the Duchy of Lancaster

HARVEY, Oliver, Principal Private Secretary to the Foreign Secretary (until December 1939) then Minister at the British Embassy, Paris

HOARE, Sir Samuel, Lord Privy Seal (until April 1940) then Secretary for Air (until May 1940)

HORE-BELISHA, Leslie, Secretary for War (until January 1940)

IRONSIDE, General Sir Edmund, CIGS

ISMAY, Major General Hastings, Deputy Secretary of the War Cabinet, Secretary of the Military Coordination Committee and Chiefs of Staff Committee and (from 2 May) member of the Chiefs of Staff Committee

JACOB, Lieutenant Colonel Ian, Assistant Military Secretary to the War Cabinet

JODL, Major General Alfred, Chief of Operations, Oberkommando der Wehrmacht

KEITEL, Colonel General Wilhelm, Chief of Oberkommando der Wehrmacht

KENNEDY, Brigadier John, Director of Plans, War Office and member of the Joint Planning Sub-Committee (the Joint Planners) (until January 1940)

LIDDELL HART, Basil, military historian, theorist and commentator

MACKESY, Major General Pierse, Commander 49th Division and land forces at Harstad

MASSY, Major General (promoted Lieutenant General) Hugh, Deputy Chief of the Imperial General Staff (until April 1940) then CinC North West Expeditionary Force (until May 1940)

MAUND, Captain Loben, Chief of Staff to Lord Cork

MORGAN, Brigadier Harold, Commander 148th Infantry Brigade

MORTON, Desmond, Head of Intelligence, Ministry of Economic Warfare

NEWALL, Air Chief Marshal Sir Cyril, Chief of the Air Staff and Chairman of the Chiefs of Staff Committee

PAGET, Major General Bernard, Commander Sickleforce

PEIRSE, Air Vice Marshal (promoted Air Marshal) Richard, Deputy Chief (then Vice Chief) of the Air Staff

PELLENGAHR, Major General Richard, Commander 196th Infantry Division, German Army

PHILLIPS, Brigadier Charles, Commander 146th Infantry Brigade

PHILLIPS, Rear Admiral (promoted Vice Admiral) Tom, Deputy Chief (then Vice Chief) of the Naval Staff

PLAYFAIR, Brigadier Ian, Director of Plans, War Office and member of the Joint Planning Sub-Committee (the Joint Planners) (from January 1940)

POUND, Admiral of the Fleet, Sir Dudley, First Sea Lord (Chief of the Naval Staff)

POWNALL, Lieutenant General Henry, Chief of Staff, British Expeditionary Force

RAEDER, Grand Admiral Erich, Commander-in-Chief of the German Navy

REYNAUD, Paul, French Minister of Finance (until March 1940) then Prime Minister

RUGE, Major General Otto, CinC Norwegian Army (from April 1940)

SIMON, Sir John, Chancellor of the Exchequer (until May 1940) then Lord Chancellor

SLESSOR, Air Commodore John, Director of Plans, Air Ministry and member of Joint Planning Sub-Committee (the Joint Planners)

STANLEY, Oliver, Secretary for War (January–May 1940)

TRENCHARD, Marshal of the Royal Air Force Lord, Former Chief of the Air Staff and 'Father of the RAF'

WHITWORTH, Vice Admiral William, Commander Battle Cruiser Squadron

WOOD, Sir Kingsley, Secretary for Air (until April 1940) then Lord Privy Seal (until May 1940)

WOYTASCH, Major General Kurt, Commander 181st Infantry Division, German Army

Abbreviations Used in the Endnotes

BL	British Library
CA	Churchill Archives
COHB	Cabinet Office Historical Branch
COS	Chiefs of Staff
HofC	House of Commons
IWM	Imperial War Museum
JPC	Joint Planning Sub Committee
LHC	Liddell Hart Centre for Military Archives
MCC	Military Coordination Committee
MO	Military Operations, War Office
NA	The National Archives
NAM	National Army Museum
SWC	Supreme War Council
TA	Territorial Army
WC	War Cabinet

Notes

Preface

1 Winston Churchill, *The Second World War, Volume I: The Gathering Storm* (London, Penguin, 1985), p. 547.

Chapter 1

1 John Harvey (ed), *The Diplomatic Diaries of Oliver Harvey 1937–1940* (London, Collins, 1970), pp. 34–35.
2 Viscount Templewood, *Nine Troubled Years* (London, Collins, 1954), p. 376.
3 Chamberlain to Ida Chamberlain, 10 September, Robert Self (ed), *The Neville Chamberlain Diary Letters, Volume 4: The Downing Street Years. 1934–1940*, (Aldershot, Ashgate, 2005), p. 443.
4 Chamberlain to Hilda Chamberlain, 15 October, Self, *Chamberlain Diary Letters*, p. 458.
5 Roderick Macleod and Denis Kelly (eds), *The Ironside Diaries 1937–1940*, (London, Constable, 1962), p. 106.
6 The exception was Andrew Bonar Law, Chancellor of the Exchequer.
7 Chamberlain to Ida Chamberlain, 8 October, Self, *Chamberlain Diary Letters*, p. 457.
8 Clement Attlee, *Clem Attlee: The Grenada Historical Records Interview* (London, Panther, 1967), p. 17.
9 Andrew Roberts, *The Holy Fox: A Life of Lord Halifax* (London, Weidenfeld, 1991), p. 303.
10 Peter Ludlow, 'The Unwinding Appeasement', in Lothar Kattenacker (ed), *Das 'Andere Deutschland' im Zweiten Weltkrieg* (Stuttgart, Ernst Kleh Verlag, 1977), p. 20.
11 D. J. Dutton, 'Sir John Simon', in *The Oxford Dictionary of National Biography* (Oxford University Press, 2004).
12 Robert Rhodes-James, *Chips: The Diaries of Sir Henry Channon* (London, Weidenfeld & Nicholson, 1967), entry for 3 September 1939, p. 213.
13 A. J. P. Taylor, *English History 1914–1945* (Oxford, Clarendon Press, 1965), p. 229.

14 J. J. Q. Adams, 'Samuel John Gurney Hoare, Viscount Templewood', in *The Oxford Dictionary of National Biography* (Oxford University Press, 2004).

15 John Colville, *The Fringes of Power: Downing Street Diaries 1939–1955*, (London, Hodder & Stoughton, 1985), p. 36.

16 Peter Hennesey, *Cabinet* (Oxford, Blackwell, 1986), p. 17.

17 Stephen Roskill, *Hankey: Man of Secrets, Volume 3* (London, Collins, 1970), pp. 421–423.

18 Technically, officers of this rank are never retired, merely 'taken off the active list'.

19 Chamberlain to Hilda Chamberlain, 17 September, Self, *Chamberlain Diary Letters*, p. 387.

20 According to Churchill, he 'had not raised the point' [of a place in the War Cabinet] with Chamberlain'. Churchill, *The Gathering Storm*, p. 365.

21 Attlee, *The Grenada Historical Records Interview*, p. 17.

22 Robert Self, *Neville Chamberlain: A Life* (Aldershot, Ashgate, 2006), p. 387.

23 Taylor, *English History*, p. 456.

24 Chamberlain to Ida Chamberlain, 8 October, Self, *Chamberlain Diary Letters*, p. 457.

25 Churchill, *The Gathering Storm*, p. 365.

26 Brian Bond, 'British War Planning for Operations in the Baltic', in Goran Rystad et al. (eds), *In Quest of Trade and Security: The Baltic in Power Politics 1500–1990, Volume II* (Lund, Probus, 1995), p. 127.

27 Churchill quoted by Arthur Marder, 'Winston Is Back: Churchill at the Admiralty 1939–1940', in *The English Historical Review*, Supplement 5 (London, Longmans, 1972), p. 31.

28 F. H. Hinsley, *British Intelligence in the Second World War: Its Influence on Strategy and Operations, Volume I* (London, HMSO, 1979), p. 117.

29 Admiral Sir Reginald Plunket-Ernle-Erle-Drax and Rear Admiral Sir Gerald Dickens. Minutes of meeting in First Lord's Room 18 September, National Archives (hereafter NA), ADM 205/2.

30 Patrick Salmon, *Deadlock and Diversion: Scandinavia in British Strategy During the Twilight War 1939–1940* (Bremen, Hauschild, 2012), abridged version of PhD thesis written in 1979, p. 59.

31 A. C. Bell, *Seapower and the Next War* (London, Longmans, 1938), pp. 15, 45, 146; Ivan Lajos, *Germany's War Chances* (London, Victor Gollancz, 1939), p. 116.

32 Churchill, *The Gathering Storm*, p. 73.

33 Patrick Salmon, 'British Plans for Economic Warfare against Germany 1937–39: The Problem of Swedish Iron Ore,' *Journal of Contemporary History*, 16 (1981), p. 59.

34 Martin Gilbert, *The Churchill War Papers, Volume I: At the Admiralty, September 1939–May 1940* (London, Norton, 1993), p. 116; Patrick Salmon, 'Churchill, the Admiralty and the Narvik Traffic, *Scandinavian Journal of History*, 4:4 (1986), p. 311.

35 War Cabinet (hereafter WC) Conclusions, 19 September, NA, CAB 65/1/20.

36 Gilbert, *At the Admiralty,* p. 121.

37 WC Conclusions, 29 September, NA, CAB 65/1/31.

38 WC Conclusions, 5 October, NA, CAB 65/1/38.
39 Or, to give it its full title, the Standing Ministerial Committee for the Coordination of Defence.
40 Hastings Ismay, *The Memoirs of General the Lord Ismay KG, PC, GCB, CH, DSO* (London, Heinemann, 1960), p. 109.
41 Taylor, *English History*, p. 390.
42 Ismay, *Memoirs*, pp. 74–75; Cato, *Guilty Men* (London, Victor Gollancz, 1940), p. 76.
43 Ibid., p. 75.
44 Ibid., p. 109.
45 Constitutionally, the appointment was the responsibility of the Prime Minister, but it had become the custom for the longest serving member to be appointed as chairman. This was to change when Churchill became Prime Minister.
46 Vincent Orange, *Slessor: Bomber Champion – The Life of Sir John Slessor* (London, Grub Street, 2006), p. 63.
47 John Slessor, *The Central Blue: Recollections and Reflections* (London, Cassell, 1956) pp. 240–241.
48 Orange, *Slessor: Bomber Champion*, p. 67.
49 W. G. F. Jackson and Edwin Brammall, *The Chiefs: The Story of the United Kingdom Chiefs of Staff* (London, Brassey's, 1992), p. 82.
50 Correlli Barnett, *Engage the Enemy More Closely: The Royal Navy in the Second World War* (London, Penguin, 2000), p. 59; Marder also uses the adjective 'plodding': Arthur Marder, *Winston Is Back*, p. 5.
51 Robin Brodhurst, *Churchill's Anchor: The Biography of Admiral of the Fleet Sir Dudley Pound OM GCB GCVO* (Barnsley, Leo Cooper, 2000).
52 Admiral of the Fleet Sir Andrew Cunningham to Stephen Roskill, 1 December 1949, NA, CAB 106/1170.
53 Marder, *Winston Is Back*, p. 29.
54 Brodhurst, *Churchill's Anchor*, p. 96.
55 Captain J. G. Stanning to D. McLachlan, 3 June 1968, CA, biographical material collected by Donald Mclachlan relating to Admiral of the Fleet Sir Dudley Pound, Churchill Archives (hereafter CA), DUPO 8/4.
56 Brian Farrell, 'Sir Alfred Dudley Pickman Rogers Pound', in *Oxford Dictionary of National Biography* (Oxford University Press, 2004).
57 Vice Admiral Sir John Godfrey, 'Admiral Dudley Pound, Admiral Andrew Cunningham and Mr Churchill' (unpublished), CA, DUPO 6/1, p. 303.
58 Edmund Ironside, *Tannenberg: The First Thirty Days in East Prussia* (London, Blackwood, 1925).
59 Wesley Wark, 'Sir Edmund Ironside: The Fate of Churchill's First General 1939–1940', in Brian Bond (ed), *Fallen Stars: Eleven Studies of Twentieth Century Military Disasters* (London, Brassey's, 1991), p. 144.
60 Macleod and Kelly, *The Ironside Diaries*, 10 September, p. 94.
61 'I made a night of it with Winston Churchill at Chartwell. I dined alone with him and then we sat talking till 5 a.m. this morning.' Macleod and Kelly, *The Ironside Diaries*, 25 July 39, p. 83; see also pp. 39, 115, 189; '[Ironside] stayed three days with me [at Chartwell]', 27–30 August, Churchill, *The Gathering Storm*, p. 357.

62 Wark, *Sir Edmund Ironside*, p. 144.

63 John Kennedy, *The Business of War* (London, Hutchinson, 1957), p. 18.

64 Basil Liddell Hart, Note 'Talk with Ironside', 24 March 1937, Liddell Hart Centre for Military Archives, King's College London (hereafter LHC), LH 11/1937/16.

65 P. J. Grigg, *Prejudice and Judgment* (London, Cape, 1948), p. 33.

66 Grigg to Lord Lothian, 23 September, NA, FO 800/397.

67 Kennedy, *The Business of War*, p. 25.

68 Chamberlain to Hore-Belisha, 14 December 1939; R. J. Minney, *The Private Papers of Hore-Belisha* (London, Collins, 1962), p. 266.

69 Ibid., p. 267.

70 Major General Henry Pownall.

71 Ironside letter to Roderick Macleod, 1 May 1954, National Art Museum (herafter NAM), Macleod, R.

72 Bernard Law Montgomery, *The Memoirs of Field Marshal the Viscount Montgomery of Alamein* (London, Collins, 1958), p. 51.

73 Kennedy, *The Business of War*, p. 52.

74 John Gooch, 'The British General Staff in the Era of the World Wars', in David French and Brian Holden Reid (eds), *The British General Staff: Reform and Innovation 1890–1938* (London, Cass, 2002).

75 Brian Bond, *British Military Policy between the World Wars* (Oxford, Clarendon, 1980) p. 379.

76 Macleod and Kelly, *The Ironside Diaries*, 4 September, p. 101.

77 Letter from Ironside to Colonel Macleod, 4 December 1942, NAM, Macleod, R.

78 Macleod and Kelly, *The Ironside Diaries*, 6 October, p. 120.

79 Howard Welch, 'The Origins and Development of the Chiefs of Staff Sub-Committee of the Committee of Imperial Defence 1923–1939' (Doctoral Thesis, King's College, University of London, 1973), p. 321.

80 Warrant for the Chiefs of Staff, 20 June 1939, NA, CAB 104/14; NA, CAB 21/710.

81 Paul Kennedy, *The Rise and Fall of British Naval Mastery* (London, Penguin, 2004), p. 273.

82 Air Staff Paper, 'The Situation of the Bomber Force in Relation to the Principle of Air Parity', 2 November 1938, NA, AIR 8/246, quoted by Talbot Imlay, *Facing the Second World War: Strategy, Politics and Economics In Britain and France 1938–40* (Oxford, UK, Oxford University Press, 2003), p. 89.

83 Brian Bond, *Chief of Staff: The Diaries of Lieutenant General Sir Henry Pownall, Volume 1* (London, Leo Cooper, 1972), 31 October and 14 November 1938, and 9 January 1940, pp. 168, 170, 181.

84 See, for example, Brian Bond and Williamson Murray, 'The British Armed Forces 1918–39', in Alan Millet and Williamson Murray (eds), *Military Effectiveness, Volume 2: The Interwar Period* (Cambridge, UK, Cambridge University Press, 2010), and David French, *Raising Churchill's Army: The British Army and the War against Germany 1919–1945* (Oxford University Press, 2000).

85 Barnett, *Engage the Enemy More Closely*, pp. 42–52; 'Report of 1st Meeting of the Committee on Defence Programmes and Acceleration', 3 November 1938, NA, CAB 27/648.
86 John Terraine, *The Right of the Line: The Royal Air Force in the European War 1939–1945* (London, Hodder & Stoughton, 1985), p. 70.
87 Ibid.
88 Bond, *Chief of Staff: The Diaries*, 21 September 1938.
89 Michael Howard, *The Continental Commitment: The Dilemma of British Defence Policy in the Era of the World Wars* (London, Maurice Temple Smith, 1972), p. 130.
90 Bond, 'The Calm Before the Storm', p. 62.
91 J. P. Harris, 'The British General Staff and the Coming of War, 1933–39', in Brian Bond and David French (eds), *The British General Staff: Reform and Innovation* (London, Frank Cass, 2002), p. 186.
92 'Report of 1st Meeting of the Committee on Defence Programmes and Acceleration', 3 November 1938, NA, CAB 27/648.
93 Macleod and Kelly, *The Ironside Diaries*, 16 August, p. 87.
94 Kennedy, *The Business of War*, p. 7.
95 Denis Richards, *The Royal Air Force 1939–1945, Volume 1: The Fight at Odds* (London, HMSO, 1953), p. 55.
96 Christina Goulter, *A Forgotten Offensive: Coastal Command's Anti-Shipping Campaign 1940–1945* (London, Frank Cass, 1995), pp. 100–111.
97 Ibid. According to one naval historian, 'The legacy of RAF control of ship- and shore-based naval aviation between 1919 and 1939 proved to be catastrophic.' Andrew Lambert, 'The Only British Advantage: Sea Power and Strategy, September 1939–June 1940', in Michael Clemmesen and Marcus Faulkner (eds), *Northern European Overture to War: From Memel to Barbarossa* (Leiden, Brill, 2013), p. 60.
98 Maurice Dean, *The Royal Air Force and Two World Wars* (London, Cassell, 1979), p. 73.
99 Bond, *British Military Policy between the World Wars*, p. 324; and Ironside. 'we must have it under command', Macleod and Kelly, *The Ironside Diaries*, 13 October 1939, p. 142.
100 Macleod and Kelly, *The Ironside Diaries*, 26 September 1939, p. 140.
101 Ibid., 13 October 1939, p. 142.
102 Hansard, House of Commons (hereafter HofC), 19 November 1932, Volume 270, Column 632.
103 Templewood, *Nine Troubled Years*, p. 429.
104 Quoted in Bond, *British Military Policy*, p. 322.
105 Harris, quoted in Montgomery Hyde, *British Air Policy between the Wars 1918–1939* (London, Constable, 1982), pp. 490–491.
106 Director of Plans (Slessor) Note by D Plans on General Staff Memoran- dum, 'Services Required from the RAF for the Field Force' (COS 924), June 1939.
107 Brodhurst, *Churchill's Anchor*, p. 186.
108 At this stage, technically, the Deputy Director of Air Plans, but effectively Director.

109 I. S. O. Playfair, *History of the Second World War: The Mediterranean and the Middle East, Volume 1: The Early Successes against Italy (to May 1941)* (London, HMSO, 1954).

Chapter 2

1 Chiefs of Staff (hereafter COS) (39)7, 4 September 39, NA, CAB 66/1/5.
2 Ibid.
3 J. R. M. Butler, *Grand Strategy, Volume 2, September 1939–June 1941* (HMSO, 1957), p. 93.
4 Chamberlain to Ida Chamberlain, 10 September, Self, *Chamberlain Diary Letters*, p. 443.
5 Howard, *The Continental Commitment*, pp. 73–74.
6 Usually referred to at the time as the 'long-war strategy'.
7 WC Conclusions, 11 September, NA, CAB 65/3/4.
8 Supreme War Council (hereafter SWC) Minutes, 12 September, NA, CAB 99/3.
9 Chamberlain to Ida Chamberlain, 8 October, Self, *Chamberlain Diary Letters*, p. 456; Halifax to Lothian, 27 September, quoted in Imlay, *Facing the Second World War*, p. 106.
10 Imlay, *Facing the Second World War*, quoting NA, CAB 24/287.
11 Butler, *Grand Strategy*, p. 5.
12 Marder, *Winston Is Back*, p. 32.
13 Churchill, *The Gathering Storm*, p. 413.
14 COS(39)34(JP), 16 September, NA, CAB 80/2.
15 COS(39)35, 16 September, NA, CAB 80/2.
16 Imlay, *Facing the Second World War*, pp. 50–52.
17 WC Conclusions, 19 September, NA, CAB 65/3/10.
18 Macleod and Kelly, *The Ironside Diaries*, 19 September 1939, p. 112.
19 CIGS 'Note for COS', 28 September 1939, NA, WO 106/1701.
20 CIGS Memo, 'British Strategy in the War', 7 September 1939, NA, WO 106/1701.
21 Chamberlain to Ida Chamberlain, 23 September, Self, *Chamberlain Diary Letters*, p. 451.
22 Brian Bond, Liddell Hart. *A Study of His Military Thought* (London, Cassell, 1977), pp. 65–69, 130.
23 Although it does not seem to have occurred to the British that the French might have reason to treat the word *project* with equal cynicism.
24 COS(39)105, 31 October, NA, CAB 80/4.
25 Ibid.
26 COS Minutes, 1 November, NA, CAB 79/2.
27 Desmond Morton, 'Supplies of Swedish Iron Ore', MEW Paper dated 27 November, NA, FO 371/23659.
28 WC Conclusions, 30 November, NA, CAB 65/2/33; the Admiralty preference was for a force to be landed or a ship to be stationed at Narvik. Salmon, 'Churchill, the Admiralty and the Narvik Traffic', p. 323.
29 WC Conclusions, 30 November, NA, CAB 65/2/33.
30 Title of opinion article, *The Times*, 8 December.

31 WC Conclusions, 11 December, NA, CAB 65/2/45.
32 Churchill, *The Gathering Storm*, p. 489.
33 WC Conclusions, 7 December, NA, CAB 65/2/41.
34 Macleod and Kelly, *The Ironside Diaries*, 13 December, p. 172.
35 Operation Lumps, NA, HS 2/263.
36 Gilbert, *At the Admiralty*, pp. 522–523.
37 Francis Bacon, 'Of the True Greatness of Kingdoms and Estates' (1597).
38 WC Conclusions, 18 December, NA, CAB 65/2/52.
39 Ibid.
40 COS(39)168, 20 December, NA, CAB 66/4/19.
41 Military Coordination Committee (hereafter MCC) Minutes, 20 December, NA, CAB 83/1.
42 Macleod and Kelly, *The Ironside Diaries*, 21 December, p. 186.
43 MCC Minutes, 20 December, NA, CAB 83/1.
44 COS Minutes, 16 November, NA, CAB 79/2.
45 Macleod and Kelly, *The Ironside Diaries*, 17 December, p. 172.
46 Ibid., 18 December, p. 186.
47 Ironside, 'The Situation in the Balkans', 23 September, NA, WO 106/1701.
48 SWC Minutes, 19 December, NA, CAB 99/3.
49 Macleod and Kelly, *The Ironside Diaries*, 20 December, p. 186.
50 Wark, 'Sir Edmund Ironside', p. 145.
51 Minister of Economic Warfare at the MCC meeting, 19 December, NA, CAB 83/1.
52 Quoted by Munch-Petersen, *The Strategy of Phoney War: Britain, Sweden, and the Iron Ore Question* (Stockholm, Militärshistorika Förlaget, 1981), p. 87.
53 WC Conclusions, 22 December, NA, CAB 65/4/29. The term *combined operations* meant operations conducted by two or more services – what today would be called *joint* or *joint service*. Nowadays, the term *combined* in NATO doctrine means 'multinational'.
54 Colville, *The Fringes of Power*, p. 66.

Chapter 3

 1 MCC Minutes, 19 December, NA, CAB 83/1.
 2 WC Conclusions, 27 December, NA, CAB 65/4/30.
 3 Macleod and Kelly, *'The Ironside Diaries'*, 5 November, p. 145.
 4 Ibid., 26 December, p. 189.
 5 Ibid., 28 December, p. 190.
 6 Ibid., 31 December, pp. 176–178.
 7 27 December; received in the Admiralty, 28 December, NA, ADM 116/4471.
 8 Macleod and Kelly, *The Ironside Diaries*, 30 December, pp. 174–176.
 9 COS Minutes, 28 December, NA, CAB 79/2.
10 COS(39)181, 31 December, NA, CAB 80/6.
11 COS(39)180(JP)(S), NA, CAB 80/106.
12 COS(39)181, 31 December, NA, CAB 80/6.
13 Ibid.
14 COS(39)182, 31 December, NA, CAB 80/6.

15 COS(39)181, 31 December, NA, CAB 80/6.
16 WC Conclusions, 2 January, NA, CAB 65/11/1.
17 Ibid.
18 Ibid.
19 Macleod and Kelly, *The Ironside Diaries*, 2 January, p. 192.
20 WC Conclusions, 3 January, NA, CAB 65/11/2.
21 COS(39)181, 31 December, NA, CAB 80/6.
22 COS(39)182, 31 December, NA, CAB 80/6
23 DCIGS to GOCs-in-C, NA, WO 106/2014.
24 Colville, *The Fringes of Power*, diary entries for 1 and 11 January, pp. 63, 69–70.
25 Bond, *Chief of Staff: The Diaries*, 11 January, pp. 280–282.
26 David Dilks (ed), *The Diaries of Sir Alexander Cadogan OM 1938–1945* (London, Cassell, 1971), 8 January, p. 243.
27 Munch-Petersen, *The Strategy of Phoney War*, pp. 101–102.
28 King Haakon to King George, 8 January, FO 419/34.
29 WC Conclusions, 10 January, NA, CAB 65/11/8.
30 Notes by Cabinet Secretary to WC Conclusions, NA, CAB 65/56/78.
31 WC Conclusions, 11 January, NA, CAB 65/11/9.
32 Dilks, *Cadogan Diaries*, 11 January, p. 245.
33 WC Conclusions, 12 January, NA CAB 65/11/10.
34 Martin Gilbert, *Finest Hour: Winston S. Churchill 1939–1941* (London, Heinemann, 1983), p. 131.
35 WC Conclusions, 12 January, NA, CAB 65/11/10.
36 Ibid.
37 DCIGS to GOCs-in-C Home Commands, NA, WO 106/2014B.

Chapter 4

1 Ismay, *Memoirs*, p. 105.
2 Self, *Neville Chamberlain*, p. 384.
3 Patrick Beesly, *Very Special Admiral: The Life of Admiral J H Godfrey CB* (London, Hamilton, 1980), p. 113.
4 Lieutenant Colonel R. Macleod, *Great Days or the War of Lost Opportunities* (NAM, Macleod, R.).
5 Franklyn Johnson, *Defence by Committee: The British Committee of Imperial Defence 1885–1959* (London, Oxford University Press, 1960), pp. 278–279.
6 Colville, *The Fringes of Power*, diary entry for 28 December, p. 60.
7 Taylor, *English History*, p. 466.
8 Ibid.
9 David Reynolds, *In Command of History: Churchill Fighting and Writing the Second World War* (London, Allen Lane, 2004), p. 320.
10 His official title was Personal Adviser to the First Lord in Scientific Matters.
11 Gilbert, *At the Admiralty*, p. 209.
12 Macleod and Kelly, *The Ironside Diaries*, 5 November, pp. 144–145.
13 Welch, *The Origins and Development of the COS Sub-Committee*, p. 11.
14 Churchill, *The Gathering Storm*, p. 374.
15 Kennedy, *The Business of War*, 9 November, p. 38.

16 Ismay, *Memoirs*, p. 109.
17 Lieutenant General Sir Ian Jacob in John Wheeler-Bennett (ed), *Action This Day: Working With Churchill* (London, Macmillan, 1968), p. 161.
18 Macleod and Kelly, *The Ironside Diaries*, 16 October, p. 125.
19 Ibid., 2 January, p. 191.
20 Major General Richard Dewing, 'Diary 1939–1941' (unpublished, LHC, GB 0099 Dewing) (Annotated: 'The majority of these notes were written up by me . . . in the summer of 1941, based on very rough notes made at the time events occurred and from my memory. They are only intended to remind me of my own doings and they are not necessarily fully accurate.'). 4 January.
21 Harvey, *Diplomatic Diaries*, 9 November, p. 328.
22 Macleod and Kelly, *The Ironside Diaries*, 21 November, p. 159.
23 Stephen Roskill, *Churchill and the Admirals*, (London, Collins, 1977), p. 94.
24 Admiral Sir William Whitworth to Admiral Sir Andrew Cunningham, 15 December 1942, Brodhurst, 'Churchill's Anchor', p. 265.
25 NA, ADM 199/1729.
26 Macleod and Kelly, *The Ironside Diaries*, 7 September, p. 105.
27 Ibid., 23 October, p. 134.
28 Kennedy, *The Business of War*, p. 43.
29 Macleod and Kelly, *The Ironside Diaries*, 20 November, p. 164.
30 See Brian Bond, 'Gort', in John Keegan (ed), *Churchill's Generals* (London, Warner Books, 1992), pp. 40–42.
31 Gilbert, *Finest Hour*, p. 120; Minney, *The Private Papers of Hore-Belisha*, pp. 269–272.
32 For a contrary view, see Marder, *Winston Is Back*.
33 Ibid., p. 29.
34 Ibid.
35 Ibid.
36 Ibid., p. 31.
37 Churchill, draft for *The Gathering Storm*, quoted in Reynolds, *In Command of History*, p. 117.
38 Arthur Marder, *From the Dreadnought to Scapa Flow, Volume 1* (Oxford University Press, 1961), p. 143.
39 Technically, officers of this rank are never retired, merely 'taken off the active list'.
40 Pound to Churchill, 31 December, NA, ADM 116/4471.
41 Salmon, *Deadlock and Diversion*, p. 59.
42 Martin Stephens, *The Fighting Admirals: British Admirals of the Second World War* (London, Leo Cooper, 1991), p. 35; for a rebuttal of this suggestion, see Brodhurst, *Churchill's Anchor*, pp.114–115.
43 Ibid., pp., 123, 254.
44 See, for example, Barry Gough, *Historical Dreadnoughts: Roskill and Marder. Writing and Fighting Naval History* (Barnsley, Seaforth Publishing, 2010), p. 219.
45 Terraine, *The Right of the Line*, p. 76.

Chapter 5

1 COS(39)181, 31 December, NA, CAB 80/6.
2 5th Battalion Scots Guards. Formed from volunteers from across the Army.

3 COS(39)181, 31 December, NA, CAB 80/6; COS(40)184, 2 January NA, CAB 80/7. The code names Avonmouth, Stratford and Plymouth were applied later.
4 COS(40)199, 16 January, NA, CAB 66/5/3 and WC Conclusions, NA, CAB 65/11/17.
5 WC Conclusions, 18 January, NA, CAB 65/11/17
6 COS(39)181, 31 December, NA, CAB 80/6.
7 WC Conclusions, 19 January, NA, CAB 65/11/17.
8 Dilks, *Cadogan Diaries*, 17 January, p. 247.
9 Macleod and Kelly, *The Ironside Diaries*, 17 January, p. 209.
10 Gilbert, *At the Admiralty*, pp. 667–675.
11 Ibid., pp. 692–698.
12 Joint Planners (hereafter JP) (40)12, 18 January, NA, CAB 84/10.
13 COS(40)214(JP)(S), 23 January, NA, CAB 80/104.
14 COS(40)218(S), 28 January, NA, CAB 80/104.
15 'A Brief Review of the General Strategical Situation', undated, but written at the end of December. See note from Grigg to Massy, 3 January: 'Thank you for your paper,' NA, WO 258/16.
16 Macleod and Kelly, *The Ironside Diaries*, 31 January, pp. 213–214.
17 COS(40)216(S), 24 January, NA, CAB 80/104.
18 Macleod and Kelly, *The Ironside Diaries*, 27 January, p. 213.
19 Slessor, *The Central Blue*, p. 247.
20 Macleod and Kelly, *The Ironside Diaries*, 25 January, p. 211.
21 Major General Carton de Wiart, 'British Military Mission to Poland, Despatch and Lessons of the Campaign', undated, NA, WO 106/1747; MI3 'Notes on the German Army, Number 6, October 1939, WO 287/226.
22 Macleod and Kelly, *The Ironside Diaries*, 27 September 1937, p.30
23 MI3, 'Expansion of the German Army', 22 January, NA, WO 190/891.
24 Allied Military Committee appreciation, 'Possible German Action in the Spring of 1940', Joint Intelligence Committee (hereafter JIC) (40) 4, 23 January, NA, CAB 81/96.
25 COS Minutes, 24 January, NA, CAB 79/3.
26 Ibid.
27 Macleod and Kelly, *The Ironside Diaries*, 25 January, p. 210.
28 Ibid., 27 January, p. 212.
29 COS(40)218, 28 January, NA, CAB 66/5/15.
30 Macleod and Kelly, *The Ironside Diaries*, 1 February, p. 214.
31 WC Conclusions, 2 February, NA, CAB 65/11/23.
32 SWC Minutes, 5 February, NA, CAB 99/3.
33 Macleod and Kelly, *The Ironside Diaries*, 5 February, p. 215.
34 Butler, *Grand Strategy*, p. 108.
35 SWC Minutes, 5 February, NA, CAB 93/3.
36 Dilks, *Cadogan Diaries*, 5 February, p. 253.
37 Macleod and Kelly, *The Ironside Diaries*, 5 February, p. 216.

Chapter 6

1 JP(40)29, 6 February, NA, CAB 84/10.
2 COS(40)233(JP)(S),9 February, NA, CAB 80/104.

3 Military Operations, War Office (hereafter MO) Comments on Statements Made at the SWC, unsigned, undated; NA, WO 193/772.
4 Ibid.
5 'We thought Tiny had told Gort verbally. He didn't. Hence soreness at GHQ', Dewing Diary, 7 February,
6 Alex Danchev and Daniel Todman (eds), *War Diaries 1939–1945: Field Marshal Lord Alanbrooke* (London, Weidenfeld and Nicholson, 2001), p. 38.
7 Bond, *Pownall Diaries*, 9 February, p. 281.
8 Ibid., 22 February, p. 285.
9 Wark, *Sir Edmund Ironside*, 8 February, p. 158.
10 DCOS(40)26(S), 12 February, NA, CAB 82/14, and Speaking Notes by MO3 for Deputy Chiefs of Staff Meeting, 14 February, NA, WO 193/772.
11 COS(40)243(JP)(S), 14 February, NA, CAB 80/104.
12 MO Briefing Note for COS Meeting, 15 February, NA, WO 193/772.
13 COS Minutes, 15 February, NA, CAB 79/85.
14 Only Hankey expressed any concern over the air situation that might materialise. WC Conclusions, 16 February, NA, CAB 65/11/30.
15 *News Chronicle*, 19 February.
16 *The Times*, 18 February.
17 *Daily Mail*, 18 February.
18 WC Conclusions, 18 February, NA, CAB 65/11/32.
19 Salmon, *Deadlock and Diversion*, 9 February, p. 139.
20 Macleod and Kelly, *The Ironside Diaries*, 16 February, p. 217.
21 DCOS Minutes, 16 February, NA, CAB 82/2.
22 WC Conclusions, 16 February, NA, CAB 65/11/31.
23 COS(40)247(S), 18 February, NA, CAB 80/104.
24 Note on the 1st Progress Report of the Inter-Service Planning Staff, 15 February, NA, WO 193/772.
25 NA, CAB(40)245(S), 19 February, NA, CAB 80/104.
26 Macleod and Kelly, *The Ironside Diaries*, 19 February, p. 219.
27 WC Conclusions, 17 February, NA, CAB 65/11/31.
28 WC Conclusions, 18 February, NA, CAB 65/11/32.
29 See Jukka Nevakivi, *The Appeal That Was Never Made: The Allies, Scandinavia and the Finnish Winter War 1939–1940* (London, Hurst, 1976), pp. 112–145; Salmon, *Deadlock and Diversion*, pp. 149–154.
30 WC Conclusions, 22 February, NA, CAB 65/11/36.
31 WC Conclusions, 23 February, NA, CAB 65/11/37.
32 Bridges to Bevir, 24 February, NA, PREM 1/419.
33 WC Paper, 'The Stoppage of Traffic in Norwegian Territorial Waters', 22 February, NA, CAB 66/5/40.
34 WC Conclusions, 22 February, NA, CAB 65/11/36.
35 Llewellyn Woodward, *British Foreign Policy in the Second World War, Volume 1* (London, HMSO, 1970), p. 87.
36 WC Conclusions, 23 February, NA, CAB 65/5/50.
37 WC Conclusion, 21 February, NA, CAB 65/11/35.
38 COS(40)254(JP)(S), NA, CAB 80/104.
39 Briefing Note (drafted by MO1; consulted MO2, DDMI, MI2, SD1, DDSD and MO3), 21 February, NA, WO 193/772.

40 Memorandum Director Military Operations and Plans to Director Staff Duties, 24 February, NA, WO 193/772.

41 Note on WC Paper, NA, CAB 66/5/40, 23 February, NA, WO 193/772.

42 Ironside to Gort, 10 February, NA, WO 106/1700.

43 DMO&P Memorandum, 27 February, NA, WO 193/772.

44 WC Conclusions, 29 February, NA, CAB 65/11/41.

45 Chamberlain to Ida Chamberlain, 2 March, Self, *Chamberlain Diary Letters*, p. 505.

46 WC Conclusions, 29 February, NA, CAB 65/5/55.

47 Chamberlain to Ida Chamberlain, 2 March, Self, *Chamberlain Diary Letters*, p. 505.

48 Notes to WC Conclusions, 29 February, NA, CAB 65/53/125.

49 WC Conclusions, 29 February, NA, CAB 65/5/52.

50 WC Conclusions, 1 March, NA, CAB 65/12/1.

51 Less accommodating partner: Eleanor Gates, *The End of the Affair: The Collapse of the Anglo-French Alliance 1939–40* (London, Allen & Unwin, 1981), p. 41; compromise peace: Imlay, *Facing the Second World War*, p. 67.

52 WC Conclusions, 1 March, NA, CAB 65/12/1

53 WC Conclusions, 1 March, NA, CAB 65/12/2.

54 *Daily Mirror*, 5 February.

55 *News Chronicle*, 7 February.

56 *Manchester Guardian*, 27 February.

57 *News Chronicle*, 4 March.

58 *The Times*, 5 March.

59 Reported in the *Manchester Guardian*, 2 March.

60 Roskill, *Hankey: Man of Secrets*, p. 455.

61 Ibid.

62 Ibid.

63 Colville, *The Fringes of Power*, diary entry for 2 February, p. 80.

64 Reported by Brigadier Ling, British Liaison Officer to the Finnish Forces, 7 February, COS(40)261(S), NA, CAB 80/104.

65 COS(40)261(S), 7 March, NA, CAB 80/104.

66 Ironside to Gort, 20 February, NA, WO 106/1700.

67 WC Conclusions, 8 March, NA, CAB 65/12/8.

68 Mackesy to Dewing, 8 March, NA, WO 106/1893.

69 WC Conclusions, 11 March, NA, CAB 65/12/10.

70 'Note for Admiral Pound', 6 March, Gilbert, *At the Admiralty*, p. 854.

71 WC Conclusions, 11 March, NA, CAB 65/12/10.

72 Macleod and Kelly, *The Ironside Diaries*, 11 March, p. 226.

73 Military Operations Branch, Notes on COS(40)258(JP)(S) for CIGS, 7 March, NA, WO 193/772.

74 Kennedy, *The Business of War*, pp. 48–49.

75 Macleod and Kelly, *The Ironside Diaries*, 12 March, p. 227.

76 WC Conclusions, 12 March, NA, CAB 65/12/11.

77 Kennedy, *The Business of War*, p. 48.

78 Ibid.

79 Ibid., pp. 49–50.

Chapter 7

1 Chamberlain to Ida Chamberlain, 16 March, Self, *Chamberlain Diary Letters*, p. 509.
2 Roberts, *The Holy Fox*, p. 191.
3 Gort to Harvey, *Harvey Diary*, 3 March, p. 339.
4 Gort to Stanley, 21 March, NA, WO 259/59.
5 Dilks, *Cadogan Diaries*, 14 March, p. 263; In Kennedy's view, '[T]here was only a remote chance of bringing it off. The great danger was that we should have had a fearful fiasco.' Kennedy, 'Diary 1940', LHC, Kennedy 4/2/2.
6 Notes to WC Conclusions, NA, CAB 65/56/136.
7 Churchill to Pound (and others), 11 December, Gilbert, *At the Admiralty*, p. 497.
8 Churchill, *The Gathering Storm*, p. 562.
9 Even one of Churchill's most ardent defenders considered that '[t]he Baltic, and increasingly the Norwegian facet, became almost an obsession with him.' Marder, *Winston Is Back*, p. 31.
10 For example, 28 and 29 January, 17 February, Macleod and Kelly, *The Ironside Diaries*, pp. 194, 218.
11 François Kersaudy, *Norway 1940* (London, Arrow, 1990), p. 26.
12 Taylor, *English History*, p. 469.
13 Salmon, *Deadlock and Diversion*, p. 93. See, for example, Chamberlain to Ida Chamberlain, 2 March, Self, *Chamberlain Diary Letters*, p. 505.
14 Wheeler-Bennett, *Action This Day*, pp. 159–161.
15 Ironside to Kennedy, 13 March, Kennedy, *The Business of War*, p. 50.
16 Memorandum by the Chiefs of Staff. Draft paper by CIGS for submission to the WC, 8 March, NA, WO 193/785.
17 Bond, *Pownall Diaries*, 7 March, p. 289.
18 Quoted in John Drewienkiewiecz, 'The Build-Up, Early Training and Employment of the TA in the Lead up to, and Early Days of, the Second World War' (Royal College of Defence Studies paper, 1992, unpublished), p. 8.
19 The Service Chiefs had been neither consulted nor informed prior to the announcement.
20 Butler, *Grand Strategy*, p. 28.
21 Peter Dennis, *The Territorial Army 1906–1940* (Woodbridge, Boydell, 1987), p. 251.
22 Drewienkiewiecz, 'The TA', p. 7.
23 Walter Hingston, 'A Territorial Battalion in Norway', *Army Quarterly*, LIX (1949), p. 87.
24 David Fraser, *And We Shall Shock Them: The British Army in the Second World War* (London, Bloomsbury, 1983), p. 31.
25 Dennis, *The Territorial Army 1907–1940*, p. 252.
26 Peter Caddick-Adams, 'Phoney War and Blitzkrieg: The Territorial Army in 1939–1940', *Royal United Services Institute Journal*, 143:2 (April 1998), p. 71.
27 Dewing, 'Diary', 4 March.
28 Army Council Meeting, 29 March, Drewienkiewiecz, 'The TA', p. 43.

29 Macleod and Kelly, *The Ironside Diaries*, 5 January, p. 194.

30 Ibid., 18 February, p. 218.

31 Ibid., 11 January, p. 196.

32 Ibid., 2 April, p. 243.

33 T. K. Derry, *The Campaign in Norway* (Uckfield, Naval and Military, 1952), p. 63.

34 Colonel Gubbins, Macleod to Howard-Vyse, 8 March, NA, WO 106/1701.

35 DCOS minutes, 29 February, NA, CAB 82/2.

36 COS(40)254, 8 March, NA, CAB 83/5, and MCC Minutes, 11 March, NA, CAB 83/3.

37 COS(40)218, 28 January, NA, CAB 66/5/15.

38 Macleod and Kelly, *The Ironside Diaries*, 5 February, p. 216.

39 Ibid., 19 February, p. 219.

40 Slessor, *The Central Blue*, p. 273.

41 Ibid., p. 261.

42 Salmon, *Deadlock and Diversion*, p. 74, Note 32; Roskill, *Churchill and the Admirals*, p. 93.

43 Donald Maclachlan, *Room 39: Naval Intelligence in Action 1939–1945*, (London, Weidenfeld & Nicholson, 1968), pp. 124–133.

44 Beesly, *Very Special Admiral*, p. 130.

45 'Plymouth Plan and 1st Maintenance Report', dated 11 March, NA, WO 193/773.

46 War Office, *Manual of Combined Operations, 1938* (London, HMSO, 1938), p. 20.

47 DMO Note to CIGS, 7 February, NA, WO 193/772.

48 Ismay, *Memoirs*, p. 104.

49 Derry, *The Campaign in Norway*, p. 59.

50 COS Minutes, 15 February, NA, CAB 79/85.

51 Amphibious Warfare HQ, *History of the Combined Operations Organisation 1940–1945* (London, 1956), NA, DEFE 2/699, p. 9.

52 Arguably, too much so. 'In the twenty years between the wars ... the Dardanelles was fought all over again ... at the Staff Colleges ... but on the whole people remembered the carnage on the beaches to the exclusion of all else.' Bernard Fergusson, *The Watery Maze: The Story of Combined Operations*, (London, Collins, 1961), p. 35. A leading study of the campaign was C. E. Callwell, *The Dardanelles* (London, Constable, 1919).

53 Richard Harding, 'Amphibious Warfare 1930–1939', in Richard Harding (ed) *The Royal Navy 1930–2000*, (London, Frank Cass, 2005), p. 43, quoting L. E. H. Maund, *Assault from the Sea* (London, Methuen, 1949), p. 4.

54 Harding, *Amphibious Warfare*, p. 63.

55 Amphibious Warfare HQ, *History*, p. 10.

56 'Albeit reinstated three months later'.

57 Ibid., p. 11.

58 DCOS Sub-Committee memorandum, 'Preparations for a Sea-Borne Expedition', 10 February, NA, CAB 82/2.

59 Macleod and Kelly, *The Ironside Diaries*, 20 February, p. 220.

60 Memo from Hankey to Chamberlain, 13 April, NA, PREM 1/404.

61 'Scandinavia: Plans and Preparations', JP(40)12, 18 January, NA, CAB 84/10.

62 Allied Military Committee paper, 'Possible German Intentions in the Spring of 1940', 23 January, NA, CAB 81/96.
63 COS(40)218(S), 28 January, NA, CAB 66/5/15.
64 JP(40)29, 6 February, NA, CAB 84/10.
65 Gilbert, *At the Admiralty*, 14 March, p. 884.
66 Kennedy, *The Business of War*, p. 46.
67 Ironside to Gort, 20 February, NA, WO 106/1700.
68 Macleod and Kelly, *The Ironside Diaries*, 25 January, p. 210.
69 WC Conclusions, 22 February, NA, CAB 65/11/36.
70 Ironside to Gort, 20 February, NA, WO 106/1700.
71 Kennedy, *The Business of War*, pp. 49–50.
72 Ibid., p. 48.
73 Macleod and Kelly, *The Ironside Diaries*, p. 229.
74 Ibid., 13 March, p. 228.
75 Brodhurst, *Churchill's Anchor*, p. 138.

Chapter 8

1 Hans-Martin Ottmer, *'Weserübung': Der Deutsche Angriff auf Danemark und Norwegen im April 1940* (München, Oldenburg Verlag, 1994), p. 7.
2 Michael Epkenhans, 'The Long and Winding Road to Weserübung', in Michael Clemmesen and Marcus Faulkner (eds), *Northern European Overture to War 1939–1941: From Memel to Barbarossa* (Leiden, Brill, 2013), p. 127.
3 Earl Ziemke, *The German Northern Theater of Operations 1940–1945* (Washington, US Government Printing Office, 1959), p. 9.
4 Ibid.
5 German Naval Staff, *War Diary of the German Naval Staff* (Operations Division), 13 January, Ike Skelton, Combined Arms Research Library, Fort Leavenworth, 5D807D1E13.
6 Ziemke, *The German Northern Theater*, 23 January, p. 14. Named after the North German river.
7 Walter Warlimont, *Inside Hitler's Headquarters 1939–45* (London, Weidenfeld & Nicholson, 1964), p. 71.
8 Ziemke, *The German Northern Theater*, p. 15.
9 Warlimont, *Inside Hitler's Headquarters*, p. 68.
10 Kersaudy, *Norway 1940*, p. 43.
11 Paul Leverkuehn, *German Military Intelligence* (London, Weidenfeld & Nicholson, 1954), p. 83.
12 Henrik Lunde, *Hitler's Pre-emptive War* (Newbury, Casemate, 2009) p. 63.
13 Ziemke, *The German Northern Theater*, p. 16.
14 Quoted in Kersaudy, *Norway 1940*, p. 46.
15 Ziemke, *The German Northern Theater*, p. 16
16 Klaus Maier, 'German Strategy', in Klaus Maier et al. (eds), *Germany and the Second World War, Volume 2: Germany's Initial Conquests in Europe* (Oxford, Clarendon, 2015), p. 191.
17 Ottmer, *'Weserübung'*, pp. 153–155.
18 Maier, 'German Strategy', p. 192.

19 Ziemke, *The German Northern Theater*, p. 18.
20 Charles Burdick and Hans-Adolf Jacobson (eds), *The Halder War Diary 1934–1942* (London, Greenhill, 1988), entry for 21 February.
21 Adam Claasen, *Hitler's Northern War: The Luftwaffe's Ill-Fated Campaign 1940–1945* (Kansas, University Press, 2001), p. 40.
22 Ziemke, *The German Northern Theater*, p. 19.
23 Warlimont, *Inside Hitler's Headquarters*, p. 60.
24 'Directive for Weserübung', 1 March, US Intelligence, 'The German Invasion of Norway and Denmark 1940', p. A-2.
25 Geirr Haarr, *The German Invasion of Norway* (Barnsley, Seaforth, 2009), p. 14.
26 German Naval Staff, *War Diary*, 4 March.
27 Ibid., p. 10.
28 Leverkuehn, *German Military Intelligence*, pp. 82, 85.
29 Adam Claasen, 'The German Invasion of Norway, 1940: The Operational Intelligence Dimension', *Journal of Strategic Studies*, 27:1 (March 2004), p. 114.
30 Ottmer, '*Weserübung*', pp. 47–53; Haarr, *The German Invasion of Norway*, p. 12.
31 Heinz Guderian, *Panzer Leader* (London, Michael Joseph, 1953), p. 105.
32 Ziemke, *The German Northern Theater*, p. 32.
33 Ibid., p. 20.
34 Warlimont, *Inside Hitler's Headquarters*, pp. 75–77; Geoffrey Megargee, 'Triumph of the Null: Structure and Conflict in the Command of German Land Forces, 1939–1945', *War in History*, 4 (1997), pp. 60–63.
35 Such as the Kriegsmarine's B-Dienst signals intelligence.
36 Ziemke, *The German Northern Theater*, p. 38.
37 Warlimont, *Inside Hitler's Headquarters*, p. 69.
38 Seventy-five ships: German Naval Staff, *War Diary*, 1 April.

Chapter 9

1 Butler, *Grand Strategy*, p. 114.
2 Dilks, *Cadogan Diaries*, 13 March, p. 262; Evelyn Wrench, *Geoffrey Dawson and Our Times* (London, Hutchinson, 1955), diary entry 13 March, p. 409.
3 Harvey, *Harvey Diary*, 14 March, p. 340.
4 *Sunday Pictorial*, 17 March.
5 *Algemeine Handelsblad*, quoted in the *Times*, 14 March.
6 Captain A. W. Clarke, Allied Military Committee, to Ismay, 'Allied Grand Strategy', 1 March, NA, CAB 21/1393.
7 Macleod and Kelly, *The Ironside Diaries*, 14 March, p. 229.
8 Templewood, *Nine Troubled Years*, p. 427.
9 WC Conclusions, 14 March, NA, CAB 65/12/12.
10 NA, CAB 65/56/138.
11 Macleod and Kelly, *The Ironside Diaries*, 14 March, p. 228.
12 Pound to Churchill, 31 December, NA, ADM 116/4471.
13 Gilbert, *Finest Hour*, p. 194.

14 WC Conclusions, 18 March, NA, CAB 65/12/13.
15 '"Royal Marine" which stands for Rhine Mines', Churchill to Gort, 26 December, Gilbert, *At the Admiralty*, p. 571.
16 Colville, *The Fringes of Power*, diary entry for 26 March, p. 90.
17 Macleod and Kelly, *The Ironside Diaries*, 14 March, p. 229.
18 Director of Military Operations and Plans memo to CIGS, 15 March, NA, WO 193/772.
19 'MO2 War Diary', NA, WO 165/48.
20 *Manchester Guardian*, 14 March.
21 Rhodes-James, *Channon Diaries*, 19 March, p. 237.
22 Hansard, HofC, 19 March, Volume 358, Column 1897.
23 Ibid., Col 1860.
24 Aaron Krishtalkia, 'Loyalty in Wartime: The Old Tories and British War Policy 1939–1940', in Brian Farrell (ed), *Leadership and Responsibility in the Second World War* (Quebec, McGill-Queen's University Press, 2004), p. 51.
25 Page Croft, 'Finland and After: Appreciation and Suggestion', 15 March, NA, ADM 199/1929.
26 *Daily Mirror*, 25 March.
27 *News Chronicle*, Opinion, 20 March.
28 *Daily Mail*, Opinion, 20 March.
29 Bond, *Pownall Diaries*, 17 March, p. 291.
30 Jacques Mordal, *La Campagne de Norvège* (Paris, Self, 1949), pp. 103–109.
31 WC Conclusions, 16 March, NA, CAB 65/6/15.
32 Ibid.
33 WC Conclusions, 19 March, NA, CAB 65/6/17.
34 WC Conclusions, 20 March, NA, CAB 65/6/18.
35 Salmon, *Deadlock and Diversion*, p. 177.
36 *Daily Express*, 20 March.
37 *Daily Mirror*, 21 March.
38 *News Chronicle*, 21 March.
39 Feiling, *Neville Chamberlain*, p. 430.
40 Joint Planning Sub Committee (hereafter JPSC) Minutes, 16 March, NA, CAB 84/2.
41 JP(40)61, 19 March, NA, CAB 84/11.
42 COS Minutes, 18 March, NA, CAB 79/3.
43 Gates, *The End of the Affair*, p. 43; Harvey, *Harvey Diaries*, 25 March, p. 342.
44 Kersaudy, *Norway 1940*, p. 53.
45 Ibid., p. 54.
46 Macleod and Kelly, *The Ironside Diaries*, 26 March, p. 234.
47 'Allied Grand Strategy', 23 March, NA, CAB 66/6/33; Bernard Kelly sees in the Chiefs' paper advocacy of abandoning the blockade and launching a pre-emptive assault on Germany. Bernard Kelly, *Drifting Towards War: The British Chiefs of Staff, the USSR and the Winter War, November 1939–March 1940* (London, Taylor & Francis 2009), p. 287.
48 WC Conclusions, 27 March, NA, CAB 65/6/21.
49 Macleod and Kelly, *The Ironside Diaries*, 27 March, p. 236.
50 Cabinet Note, 27 March, NA, CAB 65/56/145.

51 WC Conclusions, 27 March, NA, CAB 65/6/21.
52 J. M. Moulton, *The Norwegian Campaign of 1940: A Study of Warfare in Three Dimensions* (London, Eyre & Spottiswoode, 1966), p. 204.
53 Ibid., p. 58.
54 Telegramme, Halifax to Campbell, 27 March, NA, FO 800/312.
55 Paul Reyaud, *In the Thick of the Fight* (London, Cassell, 1955), p. 268.
56 Macleod and Kelly, *The Ironside Diaries*, 27 March, p. 237.
57 Reynaud, SWC Minutes, 28 March, NA, CAB 99/3.
58 Salmon, *Deadlock and Diversion*, p. 177, quoting Templewood Papers XI/2.
59 Macleod and Kelly, *The Ironside Diaries*, 27 March, p. 238.
60 SWC Minutes, 28 March, NA, CAB 99/3.
61 COS Minutes, 29 March, NA, CAB 79/85.
62 Ibid., 3 April.
63 COS(40)269(S), NA, CAB 80/104.
64 Deputy Chief of the Naval Staff to First Sea Lord, 28 March, NA, ADM 116/4471.
65 'MO2 War Diary', 29 March, NA, WO 165/48.
66 Memorandum from CIGS to Adjutant General, Quartermaster General and Permanent Under Secretary, dated March, NA, WO 193/773.
67 Signal from DMO to Director Staff Duties and Cs-in-C, 30 April, NA, WO 193/772.
68 Report by COS to WC, 1 April, NA, WO 193/773.
69 War Office to GOCinC Commands, 16 March, NA, WO 168/83.
70 Dewing, 'Diary', 2 April.
71 DMO to DCIGS, 2 April, NA, WO 106/1969.
72 DMO to DCIGS, 1 April, NA, WO 106/1650, and NA, WO 106/1969.
73 Bond, *Pownall Diaries*, 4 April, p. 296.
74 Memorandum by CIGS, COS(40)276(S), 3 April, NA, CAB 80/105.
75 COS Minutes, 4 April, NA, CAB 79/85.
76 *News Chronicle*, 29 January; also 'Coldest Weather since 1894', *Manchester Guardian*, 29 January.
77 Jacob to Ismay, 22 January 1959, LCH, Ismay papers 1/14.
78 'Evening Standard' report, 6 April.
79 Campbell letter to Halifax, 7 April, NA, FO 800/312; Harvey, *Harvey Diary*, 4 April, p. 346; and 2 April, Macleod and Kelly, *The Ironside Diaries*, 2 April, p. 237.
80 Note by Chamberlain, 31 March, NA, FO 800/312.
81 *Daily Mirror*, opinion, 28 March.
82 *News Chronicle*, opinion, 3 April.
83 WC Conclusions, 3 April, NA, CAB 65/12/15.
84 Frederick Leith-Ross, quoted in Salmon, *Deadlock and Diversion*, p. 178.
85 Salmon, *Deadlock and Diversion*, p. 177.
86 Templewood, *Nine Troubled Years*, pp. 430, 431.
87 Colville, *The Fringes of Power*, diary entry for 6 April, pp. 96–97.
88 Ibid.
89 WC Conclusions, 3 April, NA, CAB 65/12/15.
90 Halifax diary entry for 6 April, quoted in Salmon, *Deadlock and Diversion*, p. 176.

91 Colville, *The Fringes of Power*, diary entry for 6 April, p. 97.
92 Templewood, *Nine Troubled Years*, p. 427.
93 Churchill, *The Gathering Storm*, p. 526.
94 Ibid.
95 Mordal, *La Campagne de Norvège*, p. 133.
96 Gates, *End of the Affair*, p. 47.
97 Colville, *The Fringes of Power*, diary entry for 5 April, p. 95.
98 COS(40)278(S), NA, CAB 80/105.
99 Captains Torrance, Munthe and Croft and Major Palmer. Charles Cruick-shank, *SOE in Scandinavia* (Oxford University Press, 1986); Foreign Office to Dormer (British Minister, Oslo) 2 April, NA, FO 371/24819.
100 WC Conclusions, 5 April, NA, CAB 65/12/16.
101 COS Minutes, 4 April, NA, CAB 79/85.
102 Macleod and Kelly, *The Ironside Diaries*, 5 April, p. 246.

Chapter 10

1 Salmon, *Deadlock and Diversion*, 9 February, p. 139.
2 Lt Col Sutton-Pratt to Director Military Intelligence, 6 March, NA, WO 106/1899.
3 Hinsley, *British Intelligence*, p. 116.
4 Air Attaché, Stockholm to FO for DI Air Ministry, copy to Oslo, 26 March, NA, FO 371/24815.
5 Hitler's Pre-emptive War, NA, FO 116/4471.
6 Gilbert, *Finest Hour*, p. 298.
7 NA, FO 371/24815; Hinsley, *British Intelligence*, p.118.
8 Hinsley, *British Intelligence*, p. 119, quoting MI3b minute, 27 March, NA, WO 190/49.
9 Gilbert, *Finest Hour*, p. 199.
10 Hinsley, *British Intelligence*, p. 120.
11 COS Minutes, 3 April, NA, CAB 79/85.
12 WC Conclusions, 3 April, NA, CAB 65/12/15.
13 Michael Goodman, *The Official History of the Joint Intelligence Committee, Volume 1: From the Approach of the Second World War to the Suez Crisis* (London, Routledge, 2014), p. 70.
14 Dennis Richards, *RAF Bomber Command in the Second World War: The Hardest Victory* (London, Penguin, 2001), p. 33.
15 Gilbert, *Finest Hour*, p. 212, quoting NA, ADM 116/4471.
16 Hinsley, *British Intelligence*, p. 122.
17 Ibid.
18 Ibid.
19 Gilbert, *Finest Hour*, p. 213.
20 In fact, the force consisted of the battlecruisers *Scharnhorst* and *Gneisenau*, a cruiser (*Hipper*) and destroyer escort. Richards, *Royal Air Force 1939–1945*, p. 79.
21 Kenneth Macksey, *The Searchers: How Radio Interception Changed the Course of Both World Wars* (London, Cassell, 2003), p. 77.

22 Haarr, *The German Invasion of Norway*, p. 50.
23 Basil Collier, *Hidden Weapons: Allied Secret or Undercover Services in World War II* (Barnsley, Pen & Sword, 2006), pp. 65–71.
24 Hinsley, *British Intelligence*, p. 92.
25 Goodman, *Official History of the JIC*, pp. 63–65.
26 Hinsley, *British Intelligence*, pp. 42–43.
27 Ibid., p. 97.
28 Ibid., p. 93.
29 Goodman, *Official History of the JIC*, p. 64.
30 And even then, the Foreign Office representative was not allowed to see them. In the Admiralty and War Office, it had already become customary for the directors of intelligence to be given sight of JPC papers. JP(40)91, 19 March, NA, CAB 84/12.
31 Goodman, *Official History of the JIC*, p. 64; Hinsley, *British Intelligence*, pp. 92–93.
32 Hinsley, *British Intelligence*, pp. 94–97.
33 Goodman, *Official History of the JIC*, p. 63.
34 Marshal-Cornwall to Ismay, 27 December, NA, CAB 104/327.
35 Hinsley, *British Intelligence*, p. 5.
36 Ibid., p. 103.
37 Ibid., p. 119.
38 Victor Goddard, 'Epic Violet', drafts for 'Skies to Dunkirk: A Personal Memoir', p. 31, LHC, Goddard.
39 Hinsley, *British Intelligence*, p. 98.
40 Ibid., p. 92.
41 For example, the War Office. Wesley Wark, 'Beyond Intelligence: The Study of British Strategy and the Norway Campaign, 1940', in Michael Fry, *Power, Personalities and Policies: Essays in Honour of Donald Cameron Watt* (London, Cass, 1992), p. 245.
42 Kenneth Strong, *Intelligence at the Top: The Recollections of an Intelligence Officer* (London, Cassell, 1968), p. 18.
43 Patrick Howarth, *Intelligence Chief Extraordinary: The Life of the Ninth Duke of Portland* (London, Bodley Head, 1986), p. 116.
44 Ibid., p. 121.
45 Hinsley, *British Intelligence*, p. 100.
46 Ibid., p. 101.
47 Playfair to Derry, 10 January 1950, NA, CAB 106/1170.
48 Michael Smith, *Foley; The Spy Who Saved 10,000 Jews* (London, Hodder & Stoughton, 1999), pp. 173–184.
49 Arthur Walter, Andrew Croft, Malcolm Munthe. Arthur Walter, Imperial War Museum (hereafter IWM), Sound Archive 12555.
50 MO8, Notes on the Norwegian Army, January 1940, NA, WO 106/1842.
51 Report by Lieutenant Colonel CS Vale, 31 August 1937, NA, FO 371/21088.
52 Hinsley, *British Intelligence*, p. 140.
53 Ziemke, *The German Northern Theater*, pp. 10–12; Leverkuehn, *German Military Intelligence*, pp. 82, 85.
54 WO, *Manual of Combined Operations*, Part 2, Chapter 5, p. 26.

55 Macksey, *The Searchers*, p. 77.

56 His name was Harry Hinsley. Macksey, *The Searchers*, p. 77.

57 Ibid.

58 Hinsley, *British Intelligence*, pp. 104, 109; Claasen, *Hitler's Northern War*, pp. 85–86.

59 Anthony Clayton, *Forearmed: A History of the Intelligence Corps* (London, Brassey's, 1993), p. 76.

60 COS(40)218, 28 January, NA, CAB 80/7.

61 COS Minutes, 19 April, NA, CAB 79/3.

62 Goodman, *Official History of the JIC*, p. 72.

63 MI3b, Appreciation of the Situation in Norway by German Commander in Oslo at 0900 26 April, NA, WO 106/5731.

64 Strong, *Intelligence at the Top*, pp. 56–57.

65 MI3b assessment, 11 December, NA, WO 190/885.

66 COS(39)168, 20 December, NA, CAB 66/4/19.

67 Salmon, *Deadlock and Diversion*, p. 139.

68 Macleod and Kelly, *The Ironside Diaries*, 15 February, p. 217, and 20 February, p. 221.

69 Ibid., 20 February, p. 221.

70 ISSB Minutes, 27 February, NA, WO 283/1.

71 Notes to WC Conclusions, 1 April, NA, CAB 65/56/148, and 2 April, Macleod and Kelly, *The Ironside Diaries*, p. 243.

72 *News Chronicle*, 26 March.

73 *Daily Express*, 26 March.

74 Salmon, *Deadlock and Diversion*, p. 175.

75 *Evening Standard*, 30 March.

76 *Le Temps*, 27 March, quoted in Thomas Munch-Petersen, *The Strategy of Phoney War, Britain, Sweden, and the Iron Ore Question* (Stockholm, Militär-shistorika Förlaget, 1981), p. 195.

77 Allied Military Committee Paper, 'Possible German Action in the Spring of 1940', JIC(40), 23 January, NA, CAB 81/96.

78 War Office Weekly Intelligence Commentary No. 32, 28 March, NA, WO 208/2257.

79 Wark, *Beyond Intelligence*, pp. 246–248.

80 Bond, *Pownall Diaries*, 22 February, p. 285.

81 Hinsley, *British Intelligence*, p. 120.

82 Wark, *Beyond Intelligence*, p. 248.

83 Hinsley, *British Intelligence*, pp. 90–91.

84 Ibid., p. 125.

85 Quoted in Reynolds, *In Command of History*, p. 123.

Chapter 11

1 Kersaudy, *Norway 1940*, p. 49.

2 Falkenhorst, quoted by Kersaudy, *Norway 1940*, p. 49.

3 German Naval Staff, *War Diary*, 1 April; Part B, quoted by Kersaudy, *Norway 1940*, p.49.

4 David Kahn, *Hitler's Spies: German Military Intelligence in World War II* (London, Hodder & Stoughton, 1978), p. 96.

5 David Irving, *Hitler's War*, (London, Hodder & Stoughton, 1977), p.93

6 Ibid., quoting German Naval Staff, *War Diary*.

7 German Naval Staff, *War Diary*, 1 Apr, p. 1.

8 Ibid. 4 April, p. 25.

9 Admiral Carls, quoted by Walther Hubatsch, 'Problems of the Norwegian Campaign, 1940', *Royal United Services Institute Journal* 103:611 (1958), p. 340, DOI: 10.1080/03071845809429634.

10 Stephen Roskill, *The War at Sea 1939–1945, Volume 1: The Defensive* (London, HMSO, 1954), p. 164.

11 Rear Admiral R. B. Darke, quoted in W. S. Chalmers, *Max Horton and the Western Approaches: A Biography of Admiral Sir Max Kennedy Horton* (London, Hodder & Stoughton, 1954), p. 77.

12 Ibid., p. 76.

13 Ibid., p. 77.

14 Churchill, *The Gathering Storm*, p. 549.

15 '1st/5th Leicester's War Diary', NA, WO 166/4418.

16 '1st Battalion Scots Guards and 1st Battalion Irish Guards War Diaries', March 1940, NA, WO 166/4107, and NA, WO 166/4104.

17 'Hallamshire's War Diary', NA, WO 166/4323.

18 Ibid.

19 COS(40)269(S), CAB 80/104.

20 Roskill, *The War at Sea*, p. 159.

21 According to Roskill, due to non-receipt by any station of the squadron leader's transmission, Roskill, *The War at Sea*, p. 159; according to Barnett, due to a failure at the Admiralty to pass it on, Barnett, *Engage the Enemy More Closely*, p. 108.

22 Roskill, *The War at Sea*, pp. 159–160.

23 Barnett, *Engage the Enemy More Closely*, p. 109.

24 Ibid.

25 Captain Ralph Edwards, letter to Russell Grenfell, 17 April (no year given), CA, The Private Papers of Captain Russell Grenfell, GREN 1/2.

26 Ibid.

27 Ibid.

28 Ibid.; although Edwards believed that '[i]t was, in fact, the 1st Sea Lord's decision and not Winston's.' Ibid.; According to Roskill, '[T]here is no doubt that the decision was taken by Churchill, Roskill, *Churchill and the Admirals*, p. 98; According to Andrew Lambert, 'The decision was taken by Winston Churchill as First Lord of the Admiralty with his senior naval adviser, Admiral Sir Dudley Pound', Lambert, *The Only British Advantage*, p. 45.

29 Churchill, *The Gathering Storm*, p.533

30 See Roskill, *The War at Sea*, pp. 98, 161.

31 Massy to Derry, 'Notes on Official History Comments', NA, CAB 140/98.

32 Jacob, quoted in Roskill, *Churchill and the Admirals*, p. 98.

33 WC Conclusions, 8 April, NA, CAB 65/6/29.

34 Barnett, *Engage the Enemy More Closely*, p. 110.

35 Ibid.
36 Roskill, *The War at Sea*, p. 160.
37 Ibid.
38 'Naval Operations of the Campaign in Norway', Battle Summary Number 17, NA, ADM 186/798.
39 Whitworth, Battle Cruiser Squadron Results of Proceedings, 29 April, NA, ADM 199/379.
40 MCC Minutes, 8 April, NA, CAB 83/3.
41 Colville, quoted in Gilbert, *At the Admiralty*, p. 986.
42 Hoare, quoted in Gilbert, *At the Admiralty*, p. 986.
43 Ismay, *Memoirs*, pp. 118–119.
44 Dewing, 'Diary', 9 March.
45 COS Minutes, 9 April, NA, CAB 79/3.
46 Gilbert, *Finest Hour*, p. 217.
47 WC Conclusions, 9 April, NA, CAB 65/6/30.
48 A week before the invasion, four Military Intelligence officers had been deployed, one each to Trondheim, Stavanger, Bergen and Narvik, 'to prepare the way' for the British deployment. Charles Cruickshank, *SOE in Scandinavia* (Oxford University Press, 1986), p. 52; They appear to have been deployed without radio communications. Captain Torrance, the officer at Narvik, left the town on the arrival of the Germans and took refuge in a hut in the mountains above the town, where he remained for the next month, effectively cut-off from events below.
49 'Captain Torrance's Report on Occupation of Narvik 9 April–1 June', NA, WO 198/15.
50 WC Conclusions, 9 April, NA, CAB 65/6/30.
51 COS Minutes, 9 April, NA, CAB 79/3.
52 COS Minutes, 9 April, NA, CAB 79/3.
53 WC Conclusions, 9 April, NA, CAB 65/6/31.
54 Derry, *The Campaign in Norway*, p. 66.
55 Ibid.
56 COS(40)285(JP)(S), NA, CAB 80/105.
57 SWC Minutes, 9 April, NA, CAB 99/3.
58 Macleod and Kelly, *The Ironside Diaries*, 9 April, p. 250.
59 Ibid.
60 MCC Minutes, 9 April, NA, CAB 83/3.
61 Churchill, *The Gathering Storm*, pp. 536–537; Barnett, *Engage the Enemy More Closely*, p. 113.
62 Roskill, *The War at Sea*, p. 170.
63 Ibid., p. 171.
64 Captain Ralph Edwards, quoted by Barnett, *The War at Sea*, p. 114.
65 Macleod and Kelly, *The Ironside Diaries*, 9 April, p. 250.
66 Gilbert, *At the Admiralty*, p. 1001.
67 COS Minutes, 10 April, NA, CAB 79/3
68 Ibid.
69 Joint Planning Sub-Committee Minutes, 10 April, NA, CAB 84/2.
70 'New Appreciation of the Tactical Possibilities of Conducting an Opposed Landing at Narvik', prepared by MO8 for DMO, 10 April, NA, WO 106/1812

71 Dewing, 'Diary', 10 April.
72 Report from military attaché, Stockholm, 10 April, received 1600, NA, WO 106/1940.
73 MCC Minutes, 10 April, NA, CAB 83/3.
74 Roskill, *The War at Sea*, p. 170.
75 WC Conclusions, 10 and 11 April, NA, CAB 65/6/32 and CB 65/6/33.
76 Also sunk was *HMS Hunter*.
77 Barnett, *Engage the Enemy More Closely*, p. 116.
78 After Prince Rupert.
79 Dewing, 'Diary', 11 April,
80 Colville, *The Fringes of Power*, diary entry for 12 April, p. 102.
81 Edwards quoted in Roskill, *Churchill and the Admirals*, p. 102.
82 Macleod and Kelly, *The Ironside Diaries*, 1 A.M., 12 April, p. 253.
83 Roskill, *Churchill and the Admirals*, p. 102.
84 Dewing, 'Diary', 12 April.
85 WC Conclusions, 12 April, NA, CAB 65/12/21.
86 WC Conclusions, 12 April, NA, CAB 65/12/22.
87 The inshore waters along the Norwegian coast.
88 'Notes by the Chairman of the MCC for the Joint Planning Staff', 12 April, in Gilbert, *At the Admiralty*, p. 1043.
89 Dewing, 'Diary', 12 April.
90 Macleod and Kelly, *The Ironside Diaries*, 12 April, p. 255.
91 Since the British Mission in Norway was a legation, not an embassy, its head was a 'minister' not an 'ambassador'.
92 Mallet to Halifax, 12 April, NA, FO 371/24830.
93 Mallet to FO, 12 April, received 2130, NA, FO 371/24830.
94 Sargent's comment on memorandum from Collier to Halifax, 12 April, NA, FO 371/24834.
95 Macleod and Kelly assert that 'the CIGS was almost alone in refusing to regard the Narvik operation as a "walk-over"' (*The Ironside Diaries*, p. 259) However, Ironside wrote in his diary that night, '[T]here may still be 3,000 Germans there, but their centre has now gone and there should not be so much difficulty in mopping up the remains of the force.' Macleod and Kelly, *The Ironside Diaries*, 13 April, p. 256.
96 WC Conclusions, 13 April, NA, CAB 65/12/23.
97 Campbell to Halifax, 13 April, received 1615, NA, FO 371/23834.
98 MCC Minutes, 13 April 1700, NA, CAB 83/3.
99 MCC Minutes, 13 April 2230, NA, CAB 83/3.
100 Dewing, 'Diary', 13 April.
101 Ironside to Derry, 7 March 1950, NA, CAB 106/1170.
102 Macleod and Kelly, *The Ironside Diaries*, p. 257.
103 Ibid.
104 In which the previous visit on the night of 11 April was recorded.
105 'Military Operations Night Duty Officer's Log', NA, WO 106/1882; Ironside's statement in Macleod and Kelly, *The Ironside Diaries*, p. 257. His Military Assistant was Colonel Macleod, joint editor of *The Ironside Diaries*.
106 COS Minutes, 13 April, NA, CAB 79/85.

107 COS Minutes, 14 April, NA, CAB 79/85; MCC Minutes, 14 April, NA CAB 83/3.
108 Mordal, *La Campagne de Norvège*, p. 285.
109 Despatch by Rear Admiral Whitworth, Supplement to the London Gazette, 1 July 1947, Number 38005, p. 3054.
110 Cajus Bekker, *Hitler's Naval War*, (London, Purnell Books, 1974), p. 119.
111 Massy to Ironside, 13 April, NA, WO 216/780.
112 Dewing, 'Diary', 12 April.
113 Macleod and Kelly, *The Ironside Diaries*, 9 April, p. 249.
114 Churchill, *The Gathering Storm*, p. 523.
115 DD Plans to D Plans, 12 April, NA, AIR 8/292.
116 Clausewitz, *On War*, p. 101.
117 German Naval Staff, *War Diary*, 2 April.
118 Harald Høiback, *Command and Control in Military Crisis: Devious Decisions* (London, Cass, 2003), pp. 69–72.
119 Haarr, *The German Invasion of Norway*, pp.144–145. The total was probably well short of the figure of 1,000 given by some authors, eg, Kersaudy, *Norway, 1940*, p.71; Lunde, *Hitler's Pre-emptive War*, p. 220.
120 Hinsley, *British Intelligence*, p. 141.
121 Quoted in Roskill, *Churchill and the Admirals*, p. 119.
122 Kersaudy, *Norway 1940*, pp. 67–68.
123 Lunde, *Hitler's Pre-emptive War*, p. 222.
124 Laake had been 'handpicked for his job ... precisely because of his willingness to serve as a humble bureaucrat', Høiback, *Devious Decisions*, p. 88.
125 Margaret Reid, 'Norway Journal, in 'Private Papers of Miss MG Reid', IWM Document 15483; Smith, *Foley*, pp. 183–184.
126 Ibid.
127 Haarr, *The German Invasion of Norway*, p. 392.
128 On 13 April.
129 Führer Directive 'Weserübung', 11 April. US Office of Naval Intelligence, 'Fuehrer Directives and Other Top Level Directives of the German Armed Forces 1939–1941' US Army, Combined Arms Research Library, Fort Leavenworth.

Chapter 12

1 Pierse Mackesy, 'Brief Account of the Narvik Expedition 1940', NA, CAB 106/1168, p. 14.
2 Kennedy, *The Business of War*, pp. 49–50.
3 Dewing, *Diary*, 4 April.
4 Ibid., 31 January.
5 Mackesy, 'Brief Account', NA, CAB 106/1168, p. 3.
6 'Order of Battle of Rupertforce', NA, CAB 44/74.
7 William Fraser to Captain Macintyre, 10 February 1960, LHC, GB009, Fraser, William.
8 'Orders for Major General Mackesy', 5 April, NA, CAB 44/74; The orders specified, 'It is clearly illegal to bombard a populated area in the hope of

hitting a legitimate target which is known to be in the area but which cannot be precisely located and identified.' Derry, *The Campaign in Norway*, p. 145; Churchill, *The Gathering Storm*, p. 549.

9 Derry, *The Campaign in Norway*, p. 145.
10 Ibid., Appendix A, p. 248.
11 Derry, *The Campaign in Norway*, p. 247.
12 Mackesy, 'Brief Account', NA, CAB 106/1168, p. 15.
13 Derry, *The Campaign in Norway*, pp. 247–248.
14 Mackesy, 'Brief Account', NA, CAB 106/1168, p. 17.
15 Mackesy, Draft for 'Narvik 1940', IWM, Mackesy Papers.
16 Ibid., p. 19.
17 'My contacts with [him] had become intimate in the long months during which the active discussions of Baltic strategy had proceeded.' Churchill, *The Gathering Storm*, p. 550.
18 Derry, *The Campaign in Norway*, pp. 146–147.
19 Hansard, 'Norway Campaign: Cork Despatch', Section 1, 10 July 1947, Supplement to the *London Gazette*, 38011, p. 3167.
20 War Office, *Manual of Combined Operations, 1938*.
21 Churchill, *The Gathering Storm*, p. 551.
22 Butler, *Grand Strategy*, p. 141.
23 See, for example, Churchill, *The Gathering Storm*, pp. 536–537; Roskill, *Churchill and the Admirals*, p. 102.
24 Edwards, Diary 21 April, quoted in Brodhurst, *Churchill's Anchor*, p. 140.
25 Hansard, Whitworth, *Despatch*, p. 3055.
26 'Aurora to Southampton', 14 April 1327, NA, ADM 199/1929.
27 Derry, *The Campaign in Norway*, p. 147.
28 War Office to Avonforce: MO8, 13 April 1800; MI3, 13 April 1045; WO, 13 April 1800 NA: all WO 106/1835.
29 Derry, *The Campaign in Norway*, p. 147.
30 Hansard, 'Cork Despatch', Section 1.
31 D. Riley-Smith, 'Notes from My Diary 1–15 April 1940', in IWM, Mackesy papers, PJM Box 2.
32 Hansard, 'Cork Despatch', Section 1.
33 A signal requesting landing craft had been sent while at Scapa. Maund, *Assault from the Sea*, p. 32; Ellenberger to Latham (Cabinet Office), 19 January 1950, NA, CAB 106/1170, and Fraser to MacIntyre, January 1960 (sic), LHC Fraser GB 0099.
34 Mackesy, 'Report on Operations in Northern Norway, Appendix A to Hansard, 'Cork Despatch'; Derry, *The Campaign in Norway*, pp. 148–149; David Erskine, *The Scots Guards 1919–1955* (London, William Clowes, 1956), p. 9.
35 War Office to Avonforce, 14 April 1915, NA, WO 106/1835.
36 Cork to Admiralty, 16 April 1201, NA, ADM 199/485.
37 Admiralty to Cork and Mackesy, 17 April 1359, NA, ADM 199/1929.
38 Cork to Churchill, 18 April, 1317, NA, ADM 199/1929.
39 Minutes of conference held at 1800, 18 April. NA, ADM 199/485.
40 Ibid.
41 Macleod and Kelly, *The Ironside Diaries*, 15 April, p. 262.

42 Ibid., 18 April, p. 268.

43 Lieutenant General Auchinleck (appointed 28 April) arrives Harstad, with Deputy Director Military Operations, 11 May, DMO to DSD, 9 May, NA, WO 106/1811.

44 Avonmouth to War Office, 19 April 0943, received 1129, NA, ADM 199/1929.

45 Mackesy, 'Brief Account', NA, CAB 106/1168, p. 36.

46 Avonmouth to War Office, 16 April 1050, received 17 April 2330, NA, WO 106/1806.

47 Personal and Private from Churchill to Cork, 19 April 1926, NA, ADM 199/485.

48 Avonmouth to War Office, 20 April 1451, NA, ADM 199/1929.

49 Churchill, *The Gathering Storm*, p. 571; Admiralty to Cork and Mackesy, 20 April 2027, NA, WO 106/1806.

50 Mackesy to Cork, 21 April, NA, WO 168/83.

51 According to Mackesy, 'Brigadier Fraser supported their views.' Mackesy, 'Brief Account, p. 34, NA, CAB 106/1168.

52 Mackesy to Cork, 21 April, in Mackesy, 'Brief Account', NA, CAB 106/1168, p. 35.

53 Cork to Admiralty, 21 April 2229, received 2359, received in the Private Office 0040, NA, ADM 199/1929; Gilbert, *At the Admiralty*, p.1116.

54 Gilbert, *Finest Hour*, p. 261.

55 Churchill to Cork, 22 April 1429, NA, ADM 199/1929.

56 Ibid.

57 Kersaudy, *Norway 1940*, p. 127.

58 They did not attempt to do so! Lieutenant Philip Francklin, RN (pilot of the Fleet Air Arm Walrus plane), 'The Norwegian Campaign', unpublished.

59 Maund, *Assault from the Sea*, p. 35.

60 Notes of Conference 22 April, IWM, PJM Box 1.

61 Derry, *The Campaign in Norway*, p. 154.

62 Gebirgsdivision 3, 'Kriegstagebuch 1940', IWM, AL 1368.

63 Ibid.

64 Cork to Admiralty, 25 April 2209, NA, CAB 106/1168; Hansard, 'Cork Despatch', Section 2.

65 Ibid., p. 571.

66 Bernard Ash, *Norway 1940* (London, Cassell, 1964), p. 113; see also Nvakivi, *The Appeal That Was Never Made*, pp. 155–156.

67 Moulton, *The Norwegian Campaign*, p. 225.

68 Ziemke, *The German Northern Theatre of Operations*, p. 90; Harvey suggests that a 'window of opportunity' existed up to 16 April, but not beyond. Maurice Harvey, *Scandinavian Misadventure: The Campaign in Norway 1940* (Tunbridge Wells, Spellmount, 1990), p. 207; In Haarr's view, 'A subsequent swift attack [on 15 April, following a bombardment] such as Lord Cork wanted, would very likely have won the town … [but would have been followed by] a series of bloody counter-attacks.' Geirr Haarr, *The Battle for Norway* (Barnsley, Seaforth, 2010), p. 201.

69 Hamilton to Admiral Forbes, 29 May, NA, CAB 106/1170; Hamilton and Cork were related. William Boyle (Lord Cork and Orrery), *My Naval Life* (London, Hutchinson, 1942), p. 192.

70 For example, Lunde, *Hitler's Pre-emptive War*, p. 278, and Roskill, *Churchill and the Admirals*, p. 107.
71 Major Linback-Larsen quoted in Lunde, *Hitler's Pre-emptive War*, p. 405.
72 Letter Hubbacks to Derry, 24 May 1950, NA, CAB 106/1170.
73 Letter Maund to Derry, 15 May 1950, NA, CAB 106/1170. Cork and his chief of staff had fallen out with each other. In the opening paragraphs of his Despatch, Cork pointedly makes it clear that Maund was not his choice for the job. *Cork, 'Despatch', Section 1.*
74 Piers Mackesy, 'Churchill on Narvik', *Journal of the Royal United Services Institute*, 115 (1970), pp. 28–33.
75 Derry, *The Campaign in Norway*, p. 153.
76 Halder, *War Diary*, 13 April.
77 German Naval Staff, *War Diary*, 13 April, p. 116.
78 Halder, *War Diary*, 13 April.
79 Jodl, quoted by Kersaudy, *Norway 1940*, p. 144.
80 Warlimont, *Inside Hitler's Headquarters*, pp. 79–80.
81 Ottmer, *Weserübung*, pp. 141–144; Ziemke, *The German Northern Theater*, p. 64.
82 Warlimont, *Inside Hitler's Headquarters*, p. 78.
83 Gebirgsdivision 3, 'Kriegstagebuch'.
84 For Dietl's orders from Falkenhorst, see Ottmer, *Weserübung*, pp. 161–165. Dietl was promoted lieutenant general by Hitler on 16 April.
85 Alex Buchner, *Narvik; Die Kämpfe der Gruppe Dietl im Früjahr 1940* (Neckargemünd, Vowinckel, 1958), p. 12.
86 Høiback, *Devious Decisions*, p. 84.
87 German Naval Staff, *War Diary*, 20 April.
88 Lunde, *Hitler's Pre-emptive War*, p. 290.
89 Gebirgsdivision 3, 'Kriegtagebuch 1940'. The Junkers 55 aircraft, which landed the troops on a frozen lake, were stranded and eventually destroyed.
90 Buchner, *Narvik*, p.40; Lunde, *Hitler's Pre-emptive War*, pp. 290–291.
91 Claasen, *Hitler's Northern War*, p. 100.
92 Haarr, *The German Invasion of Norway*, p. 370, quoting a Norwegian source.
93 Theodor Boch, *The Mountains Wait* (London, Michael Joseph, 1943), pp. 95–98.
94 Torrance, Report, NA, WO 198/15.
95 Gebirgsdivision 3, 'Kriegstagebuch 1940'
96 Buchner, *Narvik*, p. 32; Lunde, *Hitler's Pre-emptive War*, p. 279.
97 Buchner, *Narvik*; Lunde, *Hitler's Pre-emptive War*, p. 279.
98 Buchner, *Narvik*, p. 32.
99 Gebirgsdivision 3, 'Kriegstagebuch 1940'
100 Buchner, *Narvik*, p. 40.
101 Ibid., pp. 32, 51.
102 Cork, 17 April, NA, ADM 199/485.
103 Cork Report, Appendix C, NA, ADM 199/485.
104 Ismay, *Memoirs*, p. 111.
105 Avonforce to War Office, 17 April 2105, received 18 April 0030, NA, CAB 44/74.
106 Mackesy, 'Brief Account', NA, CAB 106/1168, p. 20.
107 The view was widely shared not just in Mackesy's force but also throughout the British forces in Norway.

Chapter 13

1 Signal Foley to FO, 13 April, NA, WO106/1802.
2 PM to Ruge via Foley, 13 April, NA, FO 371/24834.
3 MCC Minutes, 14 April, NA, CAB 83/3.
4 Note by the Chairman of the MCC, 13 April, Gilbert, *At the Admiralty*, p. 1043
5 MCC Minutes, 14 April, NA, CAB 83/3.
6 15 April, quoted in Gilbert, *At the Admiralty*, p. 1070.
7 Churchill, *The Gathering Storm*, p. 562.
8 Ibid., p. 599.
9 MCC Minutes, 13 April, NA, CAB 83/3.
10 Forbes to Admiralty, 14 April 1157, NA, WO 106/1859.
11 MCC Minutes, 15 April, NA, CAB 83/3.
12 Macleod and Kelly, *The Ironside Diaries*, 17 April, p. 265.
13 Commander 18th Cruiser Squadron's War Diary, 1–15 April, ADM 199/385.
14 Further south, submarines accounted for the light cruiser *Karlsruhe* (sunk on 9 April) and the pocket battleship *Lützow* (badly damaged on 10 April). Fleet Air Arm aircraft sunk the light cruiser *Königsberg* in Bergen harbour on 10 April.
15 Derry, *The Campaign in Norway*, p. 34.
16 Admiralty to Forbes, 15 April 0121, NA, WO 106/1859.
17 Forbes to Admiralty, 17 April 0250, NA, WO 106/1859; Donald Macintyre, *Narvik* (London, Pan Books, 1962), p. 38.
18 'Examination of the Possibility of a Direct Attack on Trondheim', JP(40)105, NA, CAB 84/12.
19 COS Minutes, 15 April, NA, CAB 79/85.
20 Ibid.
21 Macleod and Kelly, *The Ironside Diaries* 15 April, pp. 262–263.
22 COS Minutes, 15 April, NA, CAB 79/85.
23 Ismay, *Memoirs*, p. 111; Churchill, *The Gathering Storm*, p. 539.
24 Macleod and Kelly, *The Ironside Diaries*, 14 April, p. 260.
25 Minute by Bridges, 25 April, NA, PREM 1/404.
26 Minute by Sir Horace Wilson (Head of the Civil Service), 25 April, NA, PREM 1/404; the operation was at first named Boots.
27 MCC Minutes, 16 April, NA, CAB 83/3.
28 'General Dewing came to CMHQ and put before General Crerar an outline of the proposed operations ... and the request that the Canadians "in view of the lack of other trained troops" might participate.' 'Preliminary Narrative. "The History of the Canadian Military Forces Overseas 1939–1940"', Chapter 4, NA, WO 106/1971.
29 Orange, *Slessor: Bomber Champion*, p. 69.
30 According to Macintyre, 'Fighter escort by RAF aircraft was had been arranged, but no fighters materialised.' Macintyre, *Narvik*, p. 127.
31 Report of Captain *HMS Suffolk*, 26 April, NA, ADM 199/475.
32 Macintyre, *Narvik*, p. 128.

33 Ibid., pp. 132–133.
34 Edwards, 'Diary', 18 April, CA, GREN 1/2; see also 19 April, Macleod and Kelly, *The Ironside Diaries*, p. 269.
35 Edwards, 'Diary', 18 April, CA, GREN 1/2.
36 Kersaudy, *Norway 1940*, p. 136, quoting from an interview in 1979 with Admiral of the Fleet Lord Mountbatten.
37 Macleod and Kelly, *The Ironside Diaries*, 18 April, p. 268.
38 Convened at 1300 for a meeting at 1400, 19 April. Macleod and Kelly, *The Ironside Diaries*, p. 269.
39 COS Minutes, 19 April, NA, CAB 79/85
40 Churchill, *The Gathering Storm*, p. 564.
41 Chamberlain to Hilda Chamberlain, 4 May, Self, *Chamberlain Diary Letters*, p. 527.
42 COS Minutes, 19 April, NA, CAB 79/85.
43 WC Conclusions, 20 April, NA, CAB 65/12/29.
44 Capt D(6) to Admiralty, 15 April 0915, NA, FO 371/24831.
45 Dewing, *Diary*, 19 April.
46 'Notes for an Appreciation of the Situation in Central Scandinavia', DMO&P, annotated, 'It has been accepted in principle by the Military Coordinating [sic] Committee on 19 April 1940', NA, CAB 106/1173.
47 MCC Minutes, 19 April, NA, CAB 83/3.
48 Slessor to Derry, 11 April 1950, NA, CAB 106/1170.
49 Official History Comments to TK Derry, NA, CAB 140/98.
50 WC Conclusions, 20 April, NA, CAB 65/12/29.
51 Churchill, *The Gathering Storm*, p. 570.
52 OKW Situation Map, 11 |April, quoted in Cabinet Office Historical Branch (hereafter COHB), 'Notes on the Norwegian Campaign', NA, CAB 146/3; Buchner, *Narvik*, p. 51.
53 Ziemke, *The German Northern Theater*, p. 77.
54 Derry, *The Campaign in Norway*, p. 87; see also Haarr, *The Battle for Norway*, p. 104.
55 German Naval Staff, *War Diary*, 10 April, p. 80.
56 Ibid., 12 April, p. 104.
57 Haarr, *The Battle for Norway*, p. 14.
58 Lunde, *Hitler's Pre-emptive War*, p. 399; According to Høiback, about 2,000 Norwegian civilians were involved in this work at Vaernes and nearby Lade airfields. Without their help, the airfields would have been unusable; the strategic consequences could have been immense. *Devious Decisions*, p. 130, Note 131.
59 Group XXI War Diary quoted in COHB, 'Notes on the Norwegian Campaign', NA, CAB 146/3; Lunde, *Hitler's Pre-emptive War*, p. 291.
60 Ibid.
61 War Office Weekly Intsum, NA, WO 208/2257.
62 Derry, *The Campaign in Norway*, p. 67.
63 MO Intsum, 16 April, NA, WO 106/1857.
64 War Office to Mauriceforce, 21 April, NA, WO 168/93.
65 Intsum, 22 April, NA, WO 106/1916.
66 Keitel to Falkenhorst, 23 April, NA, CAB 106/1173.

67 German Naval Staff, *War Diary*, 22 April.
68 Lord Strabolgi, *Narvik and After: A Study of the Scandinavian Campaign* (London, Hutchinson, 1940), p. 129.
69 Ibid., p. 77.
70 Churchill, *The Gathering Storm*, p. 558.
71 Derry, *The Campaign in Norway*, p. 77.
72 Ibid., p. 80.
73 'The Conjunct Expedition to Norway, April–June 1940', NA, WO 106/1859.
74 Quoted in Roskill, *The War at Sea*, p. 187.
75 Derry, *The Campaign in Norway*, p. 77.
76 Ismay, *Memoirs*, p. 122.

Chapter 14

1 WC Conclusions, 19 April, NA, CAB 65/12/28.
2 WC Conclusions, 20 April, NA, CAB 65/12/29.
3 MCC Minutes, 19 April, NA, CAB 83/3.
4 COS Minutes, 19 April, NA, CAB 79/85.
5 Macleod and Kelly, *The Ironside Diaries*, 18 April, p. 267.
6 Claasen, *Hitler's Northern War*, p. 101.
7 The landing operation was code-named Henry.
8 Derry, *The Campaign in Norway*, p. 85.
9 Walter Hingston, *Never Give Up: The History of the Kings Own Yorkshire Light Infantry* (London, Lund Humphries & Co, 1950), p. 61.
10 Ibid.
11 MO2 Situation Report, 19 April, NA, WO 106/1836.
12 WO 106/1830.
13 Gary Sheffield, 'Carton de Wiart and Spears', in John Keegan (ed), *Churchill's Generals* (London, Warner Books, 1992), p. 324. While at Namsos, Carton de Wiart was promoted to lieutenant general.
14 E. T. Williams, 'Adrian Carton de Wiart', *Oxford Dictionary of National Biography* (Oxford University Press, 2004).
15 Ibid.
16 Duff Hart-Davis, *Peter Fleming: A Biography* (Oxford, University Press, 1974), pp. 222–224. Peter Fleming's brother, Ian, was also an author.
17 Adrian Carton de Wiart, *Happy Odyssey: The Memoirs of Lieutenant General Adrian Carton de Wiart* (London, Cape, 1950), p. 166.
18 R. F. H. Nalder, *The Royal Corps of Signals: A History of Its Antecedents and Development (Circa 1800–1955)* (London, Royal Corps of Signals Institution, 1958), pp. 19–20.
19 Hart-Davis, *Peter Fleming*, pp. 225–226; Sheffield, *Carton de Wiart and Spears*, p. 330.
20 'Instructions to Major General Carton de Wiart' by CIGS, dated 14 April. Derry, *The Campaign in Norway*, pp. 249–250.
21 Derry, *The Campaign in Norway*, p. 85; '4 feet of snow makes deployment off-roads impossible', reported by Fleming to MI2 on 14 April, NA, WO 106/1836.

22 Derry, *The Campaign in Norway*, p. 86.
23 Carton de Wiart, *Happy Odyssey*, p. 168.
24 Ibid., p. 169.
25 War Office to Carton de Wiart, 16 April 0020, NA, WO 106/1859.
26 Carton de Wiart, *Happy Odyssey*, p. 167.
27 Leland Stowe of the *Chicago Daily Press,* whose articles were reproduced in the *Daily Telegraph*.
28 Derry, *The Campaign in Norway*, p. 87.
29 Carton de Wiart to CIGS, 25 April, NA, WO 106/1856.
30 Ibid, p. 115.
31 Lieutenant Sneddon, 'Report on Norwegian Forces in Namsos Area', 28 April, NA, WO 168/8.
32 Lincoln's War Diary, 18 April, NA, WO 168/59.
33 '[U]ne pigaille', Mordal, *La Campagne de Norvège*, p. 284.
34 Carton de Wiart, *Happy Odyssey*, p. 169.
35 *Nubian* to Admiralty, 21 April 0530, received 0628, NA, WO 106/1938; received by Ironside 'about 0800', 21 April, Macleod and Kelly, *The Ironside Diaries*, p. 276.
36 Marie-Emile Béthouart, *Cinque Années d'Espérance: Mémoires de Guerre* (Paris, Plon, 1968), p. 25.
37 Carton de Wiart to War Office (through *HMS Nubian* and Admiralty), 21 April 0530, received 0628, NA, WO 106/1938.
38 Carton de Wiart, *Happy Odyssey*, p. 169.
39 Churchill, *The Gathering Storm*, p. 579.
40 Group XXI War Diary, quoted in COHB, 'Notes on the Norwegian Campaign', NA, CAB 146/3.
41 Ibid., Moulton, *The Norwegian Campaign*, p. 170.
42 Ziemke, *The German Northern Theater*, p. 80.
43 Derry, *The Campaign in Norway*, p. 93; Hansard, Supplement to the London Gazette, Number 37584, 28 May 1946. 'Despatch of Lieutenant General HRS', Part 2.
44 '1/4 KOYLI War Diary', 21 April, NA, WO 168/61; Hingston, *Never Give Up*, pp. 68–74.
45 Brigadier Phillips' Report No. 2 to Under Secretary of State, War Office, 25 April, NA, CAB 44/73.
46 Lieutenant Colonel Newton, CO Lincolns, 'Report on Operations 19–23 April, 26 April, NA, WO 168/59.
47 'Lincoln's War Diary', 22 April, NA, WO 168/59.
48 Derry, *The Campaign in Norway*, p. 93, quoting Lieutenant Colonel Newton, 'Report on Operations 19–23 April', NA, WO 168/59.
49 Hingston, *Never Give Up*, p. 75.
50 'Lincoln's War Diary', 23 April, NA, WO 168/59; '1/4 KOYLI War Diary', 24 April, NA, WO 168/61.
51 146 Brigade to War Office, 27 April, NA, WO 106/1785.
52 Carton de Wiart to CIGS, 25 April, NA, WO 106/1856.
53 *Nubian* to Admiralty, From Carton de Wiart for War Office, 21 April 2135, NA, WO 106/1912.

54 Maurice to War Office, 23 April 1338; 'NWEF War Diary', NA, WO 168/2.
55 *Nubian* to Admiralty, From Maurice for War Office, 23 April 1740, received by Admiralty 1851, NA, WO 106/1938; Macleod and Kelly, *The Ironside Diaries*, 17 April, p. 265.
56 'Report of Commanding Officer *HMS Maori*', 26 April, NA, ADM 199/476.
57 'COS Weekly Resume', 25 April–2 May, COS(40)324, NA, CAB 80/10
58 Hansard, 'Massy Despatch', Part 2.
59 Some brigade transport (without drivers) had arrived on the night of 22/23 April in the *Blackheath*, WO 106/1830.
60 Ibid.; 'Conversation of Captain Lindsay and Lieutenant Scott-Haston with Deputy Director Military Intelligence', 10 May 1940, NA, WO 106/1938; 'untrained gunners', Christopher Buckley, *Norway, The Commandos, Dieppe* (London, HMSO, 1952) p. 115.
61 Hansard, 'Massy Despatch', Part 2.
62 Ibid., Parts 1 and 2; Derry, *The Campaign in Norway*, p. 178.
63 *Massy*, 'Despatch', *Part 1*
64 Derry, *The Campaign in Norway*, p. 96.
65 Ibid., p. 141; The evacuation of French forces commenced on the night of 29/30 April. Hansard, 'Massy Despatch', Part 1.
66 'MO8 Situation Report', 24 April 0600, NA, WO 106/1913.
67 'War Office Summary of Casualties', NA, CAB 106/1157; and Derry, *The Campaign in Norway*, p. 143.
68 Buckley, *Norway, The Commandos, Dieppe*, p. 113.
69 E. R. Hooton, *Phoenix Triumphant: The Rise and Rise of the Luftwaffe* (London, Arms & Armour, 1994), p. 229.
70 Carl von Clausewitz, *On War*, edited and translated by Michael Howard and Peter Paret (Princeton University Press, 1976), p. 119.
71 'For the want of a nail the shoe was lost/For the want of a shoe the horse was lost/For the want of a horse the rider was lost/For the want of a rider the battle was lost/For the want of a battle the kingdom was lost/And all for the want of a horseshoe nail', attributed to Benjamin Franklin.

Chapter 15

1 B. H. Dowson, 'An Account of the Activities of the 8th Foresters', 6 April–7 May 1940, NA, WO 168/62.
2 Dudley Clarke, *Seven Assignments* (London, Cape, 1948), p. 92.
3 Derry, *The Campaign in Norway*, p. 99; Clarke, *Seven Assignments*, p. 93.
4 Derry, *The Campaign in Norway*, p. 251.
5 Ibid., p. 99.
6 Clarke, *Seven Assignments*, p. 84.
7 'Plans and First Maintenance Report, issued to Brigadier Morgan', NA, WO 106/1950.
8 Moulton, *The Norwegian Campaign*, p. 172. The operation was code-named Primrose.
9 For the defence of Åndalsnes.

10 According to Lieutenant Colonel Clarke, mapping was restricted to 'a dozen motor maps on a scale of 16 miles to the inch'. Clarke, *Seven Assignments*, p. 95.
11 Morgan to War Office, 19 April 0045, NA, WO 106/1928.
12 Hansard, 'Massy Despatch', Part 3.
13 King-Salter papers, NA, CAB 106/1161.
14 *Black Swan* to Admiralty for War Office, 19 April 1320, NA, WO 106/1870.
15 British and French MAs to CIGS, 18 April 1730, NA, CAB 106/1161.
16 Foley to FO, 13 April, FO 371/24834.
17 '148 Brigade War Diary', NA, WO 168/26.
18 Derry, *The Campaign in Norway*, p. 104.
19 Major Brown, Number 13 Military Mission to Norway, IWM, Private Papers of Brigadier AW Brown, Document 13781; 'Record of Conference at Norwegian GHQ at 1200 20 April' by Lieutenant Colonel Clarke, NA WO 106/1815.
20 'The MA told me that he had decided, on his own responsibility, not to show this to the CinC'. Brown, Private Papers.
21 For protestations, see Clarke, *Seven Assignments*, pp. 119–120.
22 'Sickleforce War Diary', NA, WO 168/93.
23 E. G. C. Beckwith, 'The 8th Battalion Sherwood Foresters TA. Campaign in Norway 1940' (1958), unpublished, IWM, 42488.
24 Beckwith, 'The 8th Sherwood Foresters', 20 April.
25 Ex-Platoon Sergeant Major Leslie John Sheppard, Leicesters, IWN Sound Archive 8773.
26 'Group XXI War Diary', quoted in COHB, 'Notes on the Norwegian Campaign', NA, CAB 146/3.
27 Ziemke, *The German Northern Theater*, p. 73.
28 '148 Brigade War Diary', NA, WO 168/26.
29 Matthew Richardson, *Fighting Tigers: Epic Actions of the Royal Leicestershire Regiment* (Barnsley, Leo Cooper, 2002), p. 105.
30 C. Housley, *First Contact: A History of the 8th Battalion, The Sherwood Foresters 1939–45* (Nottingham, Milquest, 1997), p. 37.
31 W. E. Underhill, *The Royal Leicestershire Regiment 17th Foot: A History of the Years 1928–1956* (Royal Leicestershire Regiment, 1957), p. 22; Richardson, *Fighting Tigers*, p. 107.
32 'Leicesters War Diary', 21 April, NA, WO 168/63.
33 Hansard, 'Massy Despatch', Part 3.
34 Ibid., p. 23.
35 Joseph Kynoch, *Norway 1940: The Forgotten Fiasco* (Shrewsbury, Airlife, 2002) p. 42.
36 Clarke, *Seven Assignments*, p. 131.
37 '[T]otally intermingled': 'Major Dowson's Account', NA, WO 168/62; Total numbers: Moulton, *The Norwegian Campaign*, p. 179.
38 E. G. C. Beckwith, *The 8th Sherwood Foresters TA: Campaign in Norway 1940* (1958), IWM, 42488, 22 April.
39 King-Salter, 'Report 11–27 April 1940' (undated), NA, CAB 106/1161.
40 '148 Brigade War Diary', 22 April, NA WO 168/26.

41 Clarke, *Seven Assignments*, p. 127.

42 Ibid., p. 128.

43 'Acting on orders, they withdrew', C. N. Barclay, *The History of the Sherwood Foresters. Nottinghamshire and Derbshire Regiment 1919–1957* (London, William Clowes, 1959), p. 52.

44 Sergeant Major Leslie John Sheppard, Leicesters, IWM, Sound Archive 8773.

45 Derry, *The Campaign in Norway*, p. 109.

46 Moulton, *The Norwegian Campaign*, p. 181, quoting a German source.

47 '"Get out of it – every man for himself", or words to that effect, were our orders.' Ex-Sergeant Frank Cox, Foresters, 'An Epic Escape: The Diary of Frank Cox', *Firm and Forester*, 8:4 (October 1985), IWM, 9085; and 'We were given the order "Every man for himself" … we came across a German machine gun post … we didn't have any rifles by then, everybody had been told to ditch them … we were at panic stations'. Private William Moss, Foresters, IWM, Sound Archive 9270.

48 'Major Dowson's Account', 22 April, NA, WO 168/62.

49 '148 Brigade War Diary', NA, WO 168/26; Richardson, *Fighting Tigers*, p. 108; Beckwith, *The 8th Sherwood Foresters*, p. 23, April; 'Major Dowson's Account', NA, WO 168/62; 'The Operations in Norway – Åndalsnes (First Narrative)', p. 22, NA, CAB 44/72.

50 H. Dolphin, Foresters, 1WM, Sound Archive 8912.

51 Hansard, 'Massy Despatch', Part 3.

52 'Report on Signal Communications', Paget Force, NA, WO 198/11; '149 Brigade War Diary', NA, WO 168/26; 'The Operations in Norway 1940 – Åndalsnes (First Narrative)', p. 27, NA, CAB 44/72.

53 'Diary of Major Jefferis' Duty in Norway', 22 April, NA, WO 106/1875.

54 Beckwith, *The 8th Sherwood Foresters*, 23 April.

55 There were, however, incidences of effective fire with Boyes anti-tank rifles against these light tanks. For example, Leslie John Sheppard, IWM, Sound Archive 8773.

56 'Group XXI War Diary', quoted in COHB, 'Notes on the Norwegian Campaign', NA, CAB 146/3; Private S. Barthorpe, 8th Foresters, IWM, Sound Archive 9081.

57 'Group XXI War Diary'; 'cut off', Massy, 'Despatch', Part 3

58 'The Operations in Norway 1940 – Åndalsnes (First Narrative)', NA, CAB 44/72.

59 'Major Dowson's Account', WO 168/82.

60 Quoted by Derry in notes for the official history, NA, CAB 106/1175.

61 Lunde, *Hitler's Pre-emptive War*, p. 328, quoting Tage Ellinger, *Den Forunderlige Krig* (Oslo, Gyldendal Norsk Forlag, 1960), pp. 27–28

62 Derry, *The Campaign in Norway*, p. 112.

63 O. Sheffield, *The York and Lancaster Regiment, Volume 3: 1919–1953* (Aldershot, Gale & Polden, 1956), pp. 32–33.

64 '1st Battalion, KOYLI, War Diary,' NA, WO 168/53.

65 Derry, *The Campaign in Norway*, p. 264.

66 Julian Paget, *The Crusading General: The Life of General Sir Bernard Paget GCB DSO MC* (Barnsley, Pen & Sword, 2008), pp. 8–12.

67 General Sir Cameron Nicholson, Private Papers, IWM, 9768.

68 Lieutenant Colonel R. O. Wilberforce, Private Papers, IWM, 12931.

69 Nicholson, Private Papers, IWM, 9768; Paget, *The Crusading General*, p. 29.

70 'The Operations in Norway 1940 – Åndalsnes (First Narrative)', 23 April, NA, CAB 44/72.

71 Derry, *The Campaign in Norway*, p. 114.

72 Ibid., p. 131.

73 Paget, 'Sickle Report', NA, WO 106/1904.

74 Ruge, quoted by Haarr, *The Battle for Norway*, p. 82.

75 Air Ministry 'Review of the Campaign in Norway' (unsigned, undated), NA, AIR 41/20.

76 Hansard, 'Massy Despatch', Part 3.

77 NA, CAB 44/72, p. 50.

78 '1 KOYLI War Diary', NA, WO 168/53.

79 HQ 196 Division, 25 April, quoted in O. Munthe-Kaas, 'Operations in Romerike, Hedemark, Gudbrandsdal & Romsdal', NA, CAB 106/1175.

80 Paget, *The Crusading General*, p. 34.

81 NA, CAB 44/72, p. 68.

82 '1 KOYLI War Diary', NA, WO 168/54.

83 Sheffield, *The York and Lancaster Regiment*, p. 37.

84 Ibid.

85 Hansard, 'Massy Despatch', Part 3.

86 William Synge, *The Story of the Green Howards 1939–1945* (Richmond, Yorkshire, The Green Howards, 1952), pp. 15–19.

87 Hansard, 'Massy Despatch', Part 3; 'sea mines and depth charges': Mike Calvert, 'BEF, Back Every Fortnight, Norway 1940', *Royal Engineers Journal*, 88 (1974), pp. 37–40.

88 Hogg to WO for Massy, 26 April 2245, NA, WO 106/1928.

89 Brigadier Hogg, Report, 4 May, NA, WO 106/1905.

90 Deployment of Anti-Aircraft Units, NA, WO 106/1807.

91 Hogg to WO for Massy, 27 April 1100, received 2300, NA, WO 106/1916.

92 Paget to WO, 28 April 0745, received 1131, NA, WO 106/1916.

93 Hansard, 'Massy Despatch', Part 3.

94 Paget, *The Crusading General*, p. 37.

95 Ibid.; Høiback, *Devious Decisions*, p. 12; Ruge had then written in his diary, 'The crisis is over.'

96 Paget, *The Crusading General*, p. 37.

97 Clarke, *Seven Assignments*, p. 152.

98 '1 KOYLI War Diary', 30 April, NA, WO 168/53; Hingston, *Never Give Up*, pp. 102–103; Derry, *The Campaign in Norway*, pp. 134–136.

99 Cameron Nicholson, Nicholson Papers, IWM, 9768 p. 36.

100 '[North of Dombås] we passed small groups of unarmed British soldiers, heading North'. Lieutenant Michelet, one of Ruge's staff, quoted by Haarr, *The Battle for Norway*, p. 158.

101 Reid, Journal, IWM, 15483.

102 Mike Calvert, IWM, Sound Archive 9942

103 Royal Navy source quoted by Derry, *The Campaign in Norway*, p. 138.

104 Buckley, *Norway, The Commandos, Dieppe*, p. 91.
105 Judging by the number of graves in Commonwealth War Graves Cemeteries in Norway, the number of those killed in the two regiments was remarkably small: 12 Leicesters and 25 Sherwood Foresters. Housley agrees with the figure for the Foresters and gives a figure of 185 taken prisoner with a further 69 interned in Sweden. Housley, *First Contact*, p. 78. The equivalent figures for the Leicesters are not known.
106 Ziemke, *The German Northern Theater*, p. 77.
107 In this fighting, the Norwegians lost 46, 240 were wounded and 800 went missing; the Germans lost 175 and 360 were wounded. Lunde, *Hitler's Pre-emptive War*, p. 336.
108 Moulton, *The Norwegian Campaign*, p. 191.
109 The effective use of artillery in 196 division also reflected the influence of its commander, Major General Pellengahr – a gunner by trade.
110 Ian Playfair, *The Mediterranean and Middle East, Volume 2*, p. 27. Although written of a later campaign, the remark is applicable to the campaign in Norway.
111 Albeit that at this stage of the war such inter-Arms and inter-Service cooperation was still relatively rudimentary to that which was achieved later.
112 British doctrine laid down the need for soldiers to act on their own initiative (see, for example, War Office, 'Training Regulations', 1934), but in practice, for various reasons, control by detailed orders was used, especially in Territorial Army battalions. See French, *Raising Churchill's Army*, pp. 128–129.
113 In contemporary military jargon: high tempo.
114 Bernhard Kroener, 'The Manpower Resources of the Third Reich in the Area of Conflict Between Wehrmacht, Bureaucracy and War Economy 1939–1941', in Bernhard Kroener, Rolf-Dieter Mueller, and Hans Umbricht (eds), *Germany and the Second World War*, Volume 5b (Oxford, Clarendon, 2015), p. 944.
115 Ibid.
116 Major H. N. Burr, 'Norwegian Expedition. 1 KOYLI. Captain McGrath's Notes', IWM, Papers of Brigadier E. Cass, 87/28/1.
117 Derry, *The Campaign in Norway*, p. 93.
118 MI3, 'Notes on the German Army', Number 5, 11 October 1939, and Number 10, 23 December 1939, NA, WO 287/226.
119 Drewienkiewicz, *The TA*, p. 48.
120 'Leicesters War Diary', WO 166/4374.
121 'Lincolns War Diary', WO 168/4426.
122 Housley, *First Contact*, pp. 12–13.
123 Ex-Platoon Sergeant Major Leslie John Sheppard, Leicesters, quoted in Richardson, *Fighting Tigers*, p. 109.
124 NA, CAB 44/72.
125 Col Hibbert, 1/4 KOYLI, NA, WO 106/1938.
126 Hingston, *Never Give Up*, p. 56.
127 '49 Division Training Instruction', 21 March, NA, WO 168/83.
128 Drewienkiewicz, *The TA*, p. 29, quoting 'Report from General Officer Commanding 3 Corps to Under Secretary of State', 21 January 1940.

129 '49 Division Training Instruction', 21 March, NA, WO 168/83.
130 Drewienkiewiecz, *The TA*, p. 44.
131 'Leicesters War Diary', NA, WO 166/4418. The Hallams received a draft of 120 men as late as 7 March. 'Hallamshires War Diary', WO 168/60.
132 French, *Raising Churchill's Army*, p. 63.
133 Ibid.
134 Ex-Second Lieutenant John Shields, Leicesters, IWM, Sound Archive 8333; Even in 15 Brigade this was an issue: One company commander later recalled his feeling of impotence in the face of a far better armed and equipped enemy: 'I began to feel bitter about the whole bloody thing. We weren't equipped and we were just good strong Yorkshiremen who were being sacrificed, as far as I could see. I wasn't defeatist but there was nothing you could bloody well do.' Major A. W. Vickers, 1 KOYLI, IWM Sound Archive 9271.
135 Major Dowson, Foresters, IWM, Sound Archive 08911.
136 War Office publication, 'Infantry Training', 1937, p. 55.
137 Hingston, *Never Give Up*, p. 78.
138 Fraser, *And We Shall Shock Them*, p. 54.
139 And thus without air defence, air support, artillery, mortars, anti-tank guns, communications, logistic support and no more than a handful of attached ski troops.
140 'General Paget stated it as his opinion that his troops could not endure for more than four days unless adequate air support was forthcoming'. Hansard, 'Massy Despatch', Part 1.
141 'Fighting power defines our ability to fight, and comprises: a conceptual component (the thought process), a moral component (the ability to get people to fight), and a physical component (the means to fight)'. UK Defence Doctrine, (Version 5, December 2014, www.gov.uk/government/uploads/system/uploads/attachment_data/file/389755/20141208-JDP_0_01_Ed_5_UK_Defence_Doctrine.pdf
142 Moulton, *The Norwegian Campaign*, p. 190.
143 The rearguard action at Dombås on 30 April gave a taste of what could be achieved by British-Norwegian mutual support.

Chapter 16

1 CS 18 to Admiralty, 20 April 2139, NA, WO 168/93.
2 WC Conclusions, 21 April, NA, CAB 65/12/30.
3 Ibid.
4 WC Conclusions, 20 April, NA, CAB 65/12/29.
5 WC Conclusions, 21 April, NA, CAB 65/12/30.
6 War Office Appreciation, 'Operations in Scandinavia', 21 April, NA, CAB 83/3.
7 Churchill to Chamberlain, 21 April 2359, Gilbert, *At the Admiralty*, p. 1117.
8 Clarke, *Seven Assignments*, pp. 76–77.
9 Hansard, 'Massy Despatch', Part 1.
10 Danchev and Todman, *Alanbrooke Diaries*, 18 April, p. 53.

11 Assistant Director Ordinance Services, 'HQ 5 Corps War Diary', NA, WO 168/17.
12 MO2 Situation Report, 22 April 0630, NA, WO 106/1836.
13 COS Minutes, 22 April, NA, CAB 79/3.
14 Ibid.
15 Macleod and Kelly, *The Ironside Diaries*, 22 April, p. 278.
16 Harvey, *Diaries*, 22 April, p. 350.
17 SWC Minutes, 22 April, NA, CAB 99/3.
18 Macleod and Kelly, *The Ironside Diaries*, 22 & 23 April, p. 279.
19 Admiral Auphan, quoted by Kersaudy, *Norway 1940*, p. 154.
20 Colville, *The Fringes of Power*, diary entry for 23 April, p. 106.
21 Macleod and Kelly, *The Ironside Diaries*, 23 April, p. 279.
22 WC Conclusions, 23 April, NA, CAB 65/12/32; COS Minutes, 23 April NA, CAB 79/85.
23 WC Conclusions, 23 April, NA, CAB 65/12/32.
24 Macleod and Kelly, *The Ironside Diaries*, 23 April, p. 279.
25 'MO 8 War Diary', 22 April 2055, NA, WO 165/55.
26 Macleod and Kelly, *The Ironside Diaries*, 23 April, pp. 279–280.
27 Carton de Wiart to WO, 23 April 1338, 'NWEF War Diary', NA, WO 168/2.
28 Carton de Wiart to WO, 23 April, 1740, received in the Admiralty 1851, NA, WO 106/1938.
29 MCC Minutes, 23 April, NA, CAB 83/3
30 Ibid.
31 COS Minutes, 23 April, CAB 79/85.
32 Colville, *The Fringes of Power*, diary entry for 23 April, p. 107.
33 MCC Minutes, 23 April, NA, CAB 83/3.
34 Macleod and Kelly, *The Ironside Diaries*, 23 April, p. 279.
35 Dilks, *Cadogan Diaries*, 24 April, p. 273.
36 Morgan to War Office, 24 April 1015, 'Sickleforce War Diary', NA, WO 168/93.
37 MCC Minutes, 24 April, NA, CAB 83/3.
38 Ibid.
39 WC Conclusions, 24 April, NA, CAB 65/12/33
40 COS(40)301(JP)(S), NA, CAB 80/105.
41 Colville, *The Fringes of Power*, diary entry for 24 April, p. 107.
42 Dewing, 'Diary', 25 April.
43 Cadogan, 'Diary', 25 April.
44 Ziemke, *The German Northern Theater*, p. 78.
45 COS(40)303(S), 25 April, NA, CAB 80/105.
46 Macleod and Kelly, *The Ironside Diaries*, 26 April, p. 284.
47 COS Minutes, 25 April, NA, CAB 79/85.
48 Macleod and Kelly, *The Ironside Diaries*, 26 April, p. 283.
49 COS(40)303(JP)(S), 26 April, NA, CAB 80/105.
50 COS Minutes, 26 April, NA, CAB 79/85.
51 COS(40)303(JP)(S), 26 April, NA, CAB 80/105.
52 COS Minutes, 26 April, NA, CAB 79/85.
53 Squadron Leader Whitney-Straight to Air Ministry, 25 April 1755, received 26 April 0652, NA, WO 106/1916.

54 'Report on Sickleforce by Lieutenant Colonel Festing', 26 April 0012, NA, WO 106/1916.

55 Paget to Massy, 26 April 0345, received 0710, NA, WO 106/1916.

56 Churchill, *The Gathering Storm*, p. 581.

57 MCC Minutes, 26 April, NA, CAB 83/3.

58 Macleod and Kelly, *The Ironside Diaries*, 26 April, p. 279.

59 WC Conclusions, 26 April, NA, CAB 65/12/35.

60 Ibid.

61 Macleod and Kelly, *The Ironside Diaries*, 26 April, p. 286.

62 SWC Minutes, 26 April, NA, CAB 99/3.

63 SWC Minutes, 27 April, NA, CAB 99/3.

64 MCC Minutes, 27 April, NA, CAB 83/3.

65 WC Conclusions, 27 April, NA, CAB 65/12/36.

66 MCC Minutes, 27 April, NA, CAB 83/3.

67 Ibid.

68 Chamberlain to Hilda Chamberlain, 20 April, Self, *Chamberlain Diary Letters*, p. 521.

69 Ibid.

70 Ismay, *Memoirs*, p. 111.

71 Colville, *The Fringes of Power*, diary entry for 25 April, p. 108.

72 Chamberlain to Ida Chamberlain, 27 April, Self, *Chamberlain Diary Letters*, p. 522.

73 Slessor, Official History Comments, NA, CAB 140/98.

74 Jacob in Wheeler-Bennett, 'Action This Day', pp. 160–161.

75 Macleod and Kelly, *The Ironside Diaries*, 26 April, p. 283.

76 Jacob in Wheeler-Bennett, 'Action This Day', pp. 200–201.

77 Eric Seal letter to Arthur Mader, quoted in Gough, *Historical Dreadnoughts*, pp. 234–235. Seal added, 'To infer … that he assumed control is, in the circumstances almost malicious. It is certainly unwarranted and false.'

78 Ibid.; Churchill certainly had easy access to the war room: both his office and his flat were in the Admiralty building.

79 For example, in the period 5 February–12 March.

80 Dewing, 'Diary', 3 May.

81 Slessor, *The Central Blue*, p. 279.

82 Nigel de Lee, 'Command in Central Norway, 1940: A Cautionary Tale', in Gary Sheffield and Geoffrey Till (eds), *Challenges of High Command in the Twentieth Century* (Strategic and Combat Studies Institute, *The Occasional*, 38 (December 1999), p. 57.

83 Clausewitz, *On War*, p. 119.

Chapter 17

1 Clausewitz, 'On War', pp. 595–596.

2 James Corum, *The Roots of Blitzkrieg: Hans von Seekt and German Military Reform* (Kansas University Press, 1992), pp. 148–149.

3 The fact that Germany was predominantly a land power, as opposed to a sea power, may have influenced this approach. Germany would come to regret its lack of strategic bombers.

4 Peter Oppenheimer, 'From the Spanish Civil War to the Fall of France: Luftwaffe Lessons Learned and Applied', *Journal of the Institute for Historical Review*, 7:2 (1986), p. 133.

5 Ibid.; General Wilhelm Speidel quoted in James Corum, 'The Luftwaffe's Army Support Doctrine', *Journal of Military History*, 59 (January 1995), p. 53.

6 Hugh Thomas, *The Spanish Civil War* (London, Penguin, 1990), p. 370; see also James Corum, Uncharted Waters: Information in the First Modern Joint Campaign – Norway 1940', *Journal of Strategic Studies*, 27:2 (2004), p. 350.

7 Brian Armstrong, 'Through a Glass Darkly: The Royal Air Force and the Lessons of the Spanish Civil War 1936–1939', *RAF Air Power Review*, 12:1 (2009), pp. 32–55. Armstrong's study is recommended for further reading on this subject.

8 Ibid.

9 JIC Sub-Committee Air Warfare in Spain, Report Number 4, 21 September 1937, NA, CAB 56/5.

10 Air Staff Position Paper, 18 November 1939, NA, CAB 21/903.

11 Group Captain (later Air Vice Marshal Sir) Victor Goddard, quoted in Hinsley, *British Intelligence*, pp. 78–79. Nor was Goddard alone in this. The army intelligence officer lecturing at the Imperial Defence College (Commandant: Air Marshal Sir Arthur Longmore) on the subject of the German armed forces 'was forbidden to include . . . any comments on the employment of the German Air Force in war.' Strong, *Intelligence at the Top*, p. 18.

12 Tony Mason, 'British Air Power', in John Olsen, *Global Air Power* (Washington DC, Potomac Books, 2011), pp. 7–63.

13 And at the Imperial Defence College, 'The RAF officers were urged on by the Air Staff to fight lustily for the new principle. . . . That some of the RAF officers did not entirely agree with this attitude was fairly obvious, but they had to subscribe to the new doctrine.' Gerald Dickens, *Bombing and Strategy: The Fallacy of Total War* (London, Sampson Low, Marston & Co, 1946). This state of affairs, in all three Services, is not totally unheard of in more recent times.

14 Malcolm Smith, *British Air Strategy between the Wars* (Oxford, Clarendon, 1984), p. 175.

15 Jackson and Brammall, *The Chiefs*, p. 165.

16 Claasen, *Hitler's Northern War*, p. 84.

17 D Air Plans, 'Note on the action to be taken in reply to a German air attack against the UK', 11 October 1939, NA, AIR 8/292.

18 Goulter, *A Forgotten Offensive*, p. 111.

19 Dean, *The RAF and Two World Wars*, p. 80.

20 Slessor, *The Central Blue*, p. 277.

21 COS(39)181, 31 December, NA, CAB 80/6.

22 Terraine, *The Right of the Line*, p. 91.

23 Richards, *Hardest Victory*, p. 38.

24 Richards, *The Fight at Odds*, p. 89.

25 WC Conclusions, 18 February, NA, CAB 65/5/45, and 23 February, NA, CAB 65/1/37.
26 Air Ministry, 'Review of the Campaign in Norway', NA, AIR 41/20.
27 Martin Middlebrook and Chris Everitt, *The Bomber Command War Diaries* (Leicester, Midland Publishing, 1996), p. 36; James Corum, 'The German Campaign in Norway 1940 as a Joint Operation', *Journal of Strategic Studies*, 21:4 (December 1988), p. 74. In conceptual terms, closing down Alborg would have been a decisive point on the path to unlocking the German centre of gravity.
28 Following the Franco-British bombing policy. See Derry, *The Campaign in Norway*, p. 53.
29 Assistant Chief of the Air Staff to CinC Bomber Command, 27 April, NA, CAB 106/1173.
30 Denis Richards, *Portal of Hungerford: The Life of Marshal of the Royal Air Force Viscount Portal of Hungerford, KG GCB OM DSO MC* (London, Heinemann, 1977), p. 143.
31 Air Ministry, 'Review of the Campaign in Norway', NA, AIR 41/20.
32 Middlebrook and Everitt, *The Bomber Command War Diaries*, p. 33.
33 'Disposition of German Aircraft on Norwegian Airfields', Air Historical Branch, NA, CAB 106/1171.
34 Claasen, *Hitler's Northern War*, p. 102.
35 Hooton, *Phoenix Triumphant*, p. 229.
36 'The Campaign in Norway', Draft and Documents, Introduction to Part 1, NA, CAB 106/1173.
37 Air Ministry, 'Review of the Campaign in Norway', NA, AIR 41/20, pp. 54–55.
38 AVM Sholto Douglas (ACAS(T)) to H W Fraser (DMC), 24 April, NA, CAB 106/1173.
39 Richards, *The Royal Air Force 1939–1945*, p. 94.
40 Middlebrook and Everitt, *The Bomber Command War Diaries*, p. 38.
41 Claasen, *Hitler's Northern War*, p. 87.
42 Middlebrook and Everitt, *The Bomber Command War Diaries*, p. 38.
43 Harvey, *Scandinavian Misadventure*, p. 179.
44 Goulter, *A Forgotten Offensive*, pp. 100, 102.
45 Claasen, *Hitler's Northern War*, p. 75.
46 Hansard, 'Massy Despatch', Part 1.
47 Quoted in Richards, *The Royal Air Force 1939–1945*, p. 105.
48 WC Conclusions, 2 May, NA, CAB 65/7/2.
49 Ruge to Ironside, 15 April, NA, WO 198/14.
50 Ziemke, *The German Northern Theater*, p. 56.
51 Derry, *The Campaign in Norway*, p. 234.
52 Air Ministry (ACAS (I)), *The Rise and Fall of the German Air Force 1939–1945* (London, Air Ministry, 1948), pp. 40–41.
53 Corum, 'Norway 1940 as a Joint Operation', p. 64.
54 For example, Leicesters, NA, WO 168/63, and Sherwood Foresters NA, WO 168/62.
55 The Luftwaffe flew a total of 330 sorties against Namsos; 720 against Åndalsnes. Hooton, *Phoenix Triumphant*, p. 229.
56 Ironside to Colonel Macleod, 18 June 1957, NAM, Macleod, R.

57 'Report of the Bartholomew Committee', LHC, GB0099, Bartholomew.
58 Claasen, *Hitler's Northern War*, p. 118.
59 War Office, *Field Standard Regulations, Volume 2*, 1935.
60 WC Conclusions, 2 May, NA, CAB 65/7/2.
61 Corum, 'Norway 1940 as a Joint Operation', p. 50.
62 Chamberlain to Ida Chamberlin, 27 April, Self, *Chamberlain Diary Letters*, pp. 573–574; for further analysis of the air campaign, see Harvey, *Scandinavian Misadventure*, pp. 170–201, and Alastair Byford, 'False Start: The Enduring Air Power Lessons of the Royal Air Force's Campaign in Norway April–June 1940', *RAF Air Power Review*, 13:3 (Autumn/Winter 2010), pp. 119–138.

Chapter 18

1 Churchill Personal Minute 1310, 26 April, NA, ADM 199/487; WC Conclusions, 28 April, NA, CAB 65/6/51.
2 SWC Minutes, 27 April, NA, CAB 99/3.
3 Anglo-French Meeting, 26 April, NA, ADM 205/4.
4 Quoted in Gilbert, *Finest Hour*, p. 277.
5 WC Conclusions, 2 May, NA, CAB 65/7/2.
6 Macleod and Kelly, *The Ironside Diaries*, 30 April, p. 289.
7 WC Conclusions, 28 April, NA, CAB 65/6/51; committee chaired by Sir Austin Hudson MP, Civil Lord of the Admiralty.
8 'Edward's Diary', 30 April, CA, GREN 1/2.
9 COS Minutes, 4 May, NA, CAB 79/4.
10 WC Conclusions, 6 May, NA, CAB 65/13/3.
11 COS(40)309(S), 28 April, NA, CAB 80/105; COS(40)314(S), 30 April, NA, CAB80/105.
12 Massy to Carton de Wiart, 29 April 0410, NA, WO 106/1911; Carton de Wiart to Massy, 30 April 1100, NA, WO 106/1911; Massy, 'Despatch', Parts 1 and 2.
13 DMO Brief for CIGS, 29 April, NA, WO 106/1957.
14 MCC Minutes, 29 April, NA, CAB 83/3.
15 COS(40)309(JP)(S), 30 April, NA, CAB 80/105.
16 COS(40)313, 2 May, NA, CAB 80/105.
17 COS(40)314(S), 30 April, NA, CAB 80/105.
18 COS(40)312(S), 30 April, NA, CAB 80/105.
19 COS Minutes, 2 May, NA, CAB 79/85.
20 COS(40)313(S), 2 May, NA, CAB 80/105.
21 DMO brief, 3 May, NA, WO 106/1980.
22 MCC, Note by the Chairman, MC(40)94, 4 May, NA, CAB 83/5.
23 COS(40)318, NA, CAB 80/10.
24 DMO to CIGS, 5 May, NA, WO 106/1980.
25 COS Minutes, 5 May, NA, CAB 79/4.
26 Gilbert, *Finest Hour*, pp. 278–279.
27 Ibid., p. 279.
28 Rhodes-James, *Chips*, 1 May, p. 244.

29 Harold Macmillan, *The Blast of War 1939–1945* (London, Macmillan, 1967), p. 65.
30 Harold Nicholson, *Diaries and Letters* (London, Collins, 1966), 30 April, p. 74.
31 Ibid., 1 May, p. 74. Mr Taper and Mr Tadpole were 'party fixers' in Disraeli's 1844 novel *Coningsby*.
32 Colville, *The Fringes of Power*, diary entries for 26 and 27 April, pp. 111–112.
33 Ibid., 1 May, p. 115.
34 *Daily Express*, 12 April.
35 *Daily Telegraph*, 16 April.
36 *Daily Mirror*, 22 April.
37 *Daily Express*, 1 May.
38 Hansard, HofC, 2 May, Volume 260, Columns 906–913.
39 Rhodes-James, *Chips*, 2 May, p. 244.
40 Macleod and Kelly, *The Ironside Diaries*, 3 May, p. 293.
41 *Manchester Guardian*, 6 May.
42 Keyes to Churchill, 30 April, NA, PREM 1/418.
43 Macmillan, *The Blast of War*, p. 66.
44 Nicholson, *Diaries and Letters*, 7 May, p. 77.
45 Hansard, HofC, 7 May, Volume 360, Columns 1125–1130.
46 Ibid.
47 Nicholson, *Diaries and Letters*, 7 May, p. 77.
48 L. S. Amery, *My Political Life, Volume 3: The Unforgiving Years 1929–1940* (London. Hutchinson, 1955), p. 365.
49 Hansard, HofC, 7 May, Volume 360, Columns 1140–1150.
50 Hansard, HofC, 8 May, Volume 360, Column 1261.
51 Colville, *The Fringes of War*, 24 April, p. 107.
52 Hansard, HofC, 8 May, Volume 360, Column 1283.
53 Ibid., Columns 1347–1365.
54 Nicholson, *Diaries*, 8 May, p. 79.
55 Churchill, *The Gathering Storm*, p. 595.
56 Ibid., pp. 599–600.

Chapter 19

1 Churchill was the only formal member; other ministers were invited to attend.
2 Quoted in Martin Gilbert, *The Churchill War Papers, Volume 2: Never Surrender* (London, Heinemann, 1994), p. 13.
3 Hankey to Hoare, 12 May, quoted in Gilbert, *Never Surrender*, pp. 14–15.
4 COS(40)340, 10 May, NA, CAB 80/10.
5 Minutes of Meeting of Ministers, 11 May, NA, CAB 65/7/13.
6 COS Minutes, 11 May, NA, CAB 79/4.
7 War Office to Auchinleck, 10 May 1545, NA, WO 107/1827.
8 The British had received advanced warning of this but had delayed the despatch of warships to intervene. By the time the warships arrived, the Germans had landed. A platoon of No. 1 Independent Company, which

happened to be in the area, fought a fierce but unsuccessful defensive action. Derry, *The Campaign in Norway*, p. 181.

9 Winston Churchill, *The Second World War, Volume 2: Their Finest Hour* (London, Penguin, 1985), p. 38.

10 John Connell, *Auchinleck: The Biography of Field Marshal Sir Claude Auchinleck* (London, Cassell, 1959), p. 114.

11 Churchill, *Their Finest Hour*, p. 43.

12 COS (40)356 of 15 May, NA, CAB 80/11.

13 WC Conclusions, 17 May, CAB 79/4.

14 DMO to MO8, 15 May, NA, WO 106/1911.

15 WC Conclusions, 17 May, NA, CAB 65/7/21.

16 Ibid.

17 Woodward, *British Foreign Policy*, p. 130.

18 WC Conclusions, 18 March, NA, CAB 65/12/13.

19 Gilbert, *Never Surrender*, pp. 32–33.

20 NA, HS 2/264; two previous attempts to carry out the plan had been aborted. Munch-Petersen, *The Strategy of Phoney War*, p. 111.

21 WC Conclusions, 20 May, NA, CAB 65/7/26.

22 Defence Committee Minutes, 20 May, NA, CAB 69/1.

23 From NWEF to War Office, 21 May, COS(40)374, NA, CAB 80/11.

24 COS(40)372(JP), NA, CAB 80/11.

25 WC Conclusions, 23 May, NA, CAB 65/13/16.

26 COS(40)376(JP), 23 May, NA, CAB 80/11.

27 Defence Committee Minutes, 24 May, NA, CAB 69/1.

28 Also referred to as the Dahlerus Plan.

29 WC Conclusions, 21 May, NA, CAB 65/7/27.

30 WC Conclusions, 23 May, NA, CAB 65/13/16.

31 WC Conclusions, 31 May, NA, CAB 65/13/28.

32 WC Conclusions, 27 May, NA, CAB 65/13/22.

33 WC Conclusions, 30 May, NA, CAB 65/13/26.

34 WC Conclusions, 2 June, NA, CAB 65/13/30.

35 Churchill to Ismay, 3 June, NA, CAB 21/1471.

36 WC Conclusions, 3 June, NA, CAB 65/13/31.

37 Dilks, *Cadogan Diaries*, 16 May, p. 284.

38 Derry, *The Campaign in Norway*, p. 172.

Chapter 20

1 Cork to Admiralty, 25 April 1201, NA, WO 168/83.

2 Cork to Mackesy, 27 April, NA, WO 168/83.

3 Mackesy to Cork, 27 April, NA, CAB 106/1170.

4 Admiralty to Cork, 28 April 0148, NA, ADM 199/1929.

5 'Administrative History of the Operations in Scandinavia', NA, WO 198/17.

6 Rupert to War Office, 23 April, NA, WO 106/1793.

7 Hansard, 'Cork Despatch', Section 2.

8 Cork Report, Annex B, NA, ADM 199/485.

9 NA, WO 106/1798; 'Cork Report', Section 2, NA, ADM 199/485; PREM 3/ 328/3.
10 Erskine, *The Scots Guards*, p. 30.
11 Rupert to War Office, 13 May, NA, WO 106/1791.
12 MO8 Report, 14 May, NA, WO 106/1783.
13 Ibid.
14 Macleod and Kelly, *The Ironside Diaries*, 28 April, p. 288.
15 Ibid., 5 May, p. 295.
16 Ibid., 9 May, p. 297.
17 Brigadier Fraser Letter to Captain Macintyre, 10 February 1960, LCH, GB 0099, Fraser, William.
18 Mackesy, 'Brief Account', NA, CAB 106/1168.
19 Béthouart, *Cinque Années d'Espérance*, p. 39.
20 Ibid.
21 Derry, *The Campaign in Norway*, p. 193; Landing craft: Maund, *Assault from the Sea*, p. 37.
22 Béthouart, *Cinque Années d'Espérance*, p. 45.
23 Lunde, *Hitler's Pre-emptive War*, p. 352; Mackesy, 'Brief Account', p. 54, NA, CAB 106/1168.
24 Churchill to Cork, 3 May 0031, received 0233, NA, WO 168/83.
25 Cork to Mackesy, 3 May, WO168/83; Cork to Churchill, 3 May 1147, received 1749, NA, ADM 199/1929.
26 Mackesy to Cork, 3 May, and Mackesy to Dill, 29 April, both NA, WO 168/83.
27 Admiralty to Cork, 4 May, 0038, NA, ADM 199/1929.
28 Or, according to Mackesy, 'demanding an interview with me in the presence of Lord Cork'. Mackesy, 'Brief Account', NA, CAB 106/1168.
29 Ibid.
30 Ibid.
31 Cork Report, Appendix C, NA, ADM 199/485.
32 Derry, '*The Campaign in Norway*', p.196.
33 Mackesy told Trappes-Lomax to go and talk to Fraser again. Having done so, Trappes-Lomax returned to tell Mackesy that 'he now realised that his duty lay in doing as ordered'. Mackesy, 'Brief Account', NA, CAB 106/1168. Prior to the meeting with Cork, Fraser had told Trappes-Lomax that 'it was nonsense to talk of resigning.' Fraser, 'Diary' 5 May. LHC, GB0099, Fraser, William.
34 WC Conclusions, 6 May, NA, CAB 65/13/3
35 Ibid.
36 Cork to Admiralty, 7 May 0631, received (in full) 1941, NA, ADM 199/1929.
37 Ibid.
38 WC Conclusions, 8 May, NA, CAB 65/13/5.
39 Derry, *The Campaign in Norway*, p. 196.
40 Refsdal, *The Campaign in North-Norway*, pp. 30–32.
41 NA, Cabinet Historical Section, 'The Conjunct Expedition to Norway April– May 1940', Section B, Army Historical Branch, MOD.
42 'Survey of Supply Situation of Narvik Group in Group XXI War Diary', 20 May 1940, quoted in COHB, 'Notes on the Norwegian Campaign', NA, CAB 146/3; Buchner, *Narvik*, p. 51.

43 Quoted in Haarr, *The Battle for Norway*, p. 241.
44 Mackesy, 'Brief Account', NA, CAB 106/1168.
45 ... although according to Mackesy, and contrary to Fleischer's assertion, Mackesy and Fleischer had met at least once – at Lavangen on 30 April. Ibid, p. 49.
46 Haarr, *The Battle for Norway*, p. 242; although, see Lunde, *Hitler's Pre-emptive War*, p. 481.
47 Derry, *The Campaign in Norway*, p. 157.
48 Gebirgsdivision 3, 'Kriegstagebuch', 29 April.
49 Ibid, p. 85; and Ziemke, *The German Northern Theater*, p. 92.
50 Buchner, *Narvik*, p. 59.
51 'Meeting between General Mackesy and General Béthouart', 7 May, IWM, Mackesy Papers, PJM Box 1.
52 Maund, *Assault from the Sea*, pp. 39–40.
53 Ziemke, *The German Northern Theater*, p. 93.
54 Ibid., p. 94.
55 Ibid., pp. 92–93.
56 COS(40)313(S), 2 May, NA, CAB 80/105; COS Minutes, 3 May, NA, CAB 79/4
57 Derry, *The Campaign in Norway*, p. 205.
58 COS(40) 313(S), 2 May, NA, CAB 80/105.
59 Massy, 'Outline Appreciation on Operations in Norway', 1 May, COS(40) 316(S), NA, CAB 80/105.
60 At the time, no roads linked Fauske and Narvik.
61 'Group XXI War Diary', quoted in COHB, 'Notes on the Norwegian Campaign', NA, CAB 146/3.
62 Ibid., p. 104.
63 Roger Parkinson, *The Auk. Auchinleck: Victor of Alamein* (London, Grenada, 1977), p. 47.
64 Mackesy, 'Brief Account', NA, CAB 106/1168.
65 Ibid. 27 April.
66 Dowler to Derry, 11 March 1950, NA, CAB 106/1170.
67 Mackesy to Derry, 26 March 1950, NA, CAB 106/1170.
68 Mackesy to War Office, Personal for General Dill, 27 April, 1050, Mackesy, NA, CAB 106/1168.
69 William Fraser, 'Diary', LHC, GB0099, Fraser, William

Chapter 21

1 Parkinson, *The Auk*, p. 48.
2 Connell, *Auchinleck*, pp. 116–118.
3 Hansard, 'Cork Despatch', Section 5.
4 Cork to Admiralty, 4 May 1645, NA, PREM 328/2.
5 Admiralty to Cork, 7 May 1645, NA, WO 106/1945; WO to Rupertforce, 7 May, NA, WO 106/1944.
6 Peter Wilkinson and Joan Bright-Astley, *Gubbins and SOE* (London, Leo Cooper, 1992), p. 50.

7 Deputy Under Secretary to DCIGS, 16 April, NA, WO 106/1782.

8 Derry, *The Campaign in Norway*, pp. 62, 168–169.

9 Michael Leslie-Melville, *The Story of the Lovat Scouts 1900–1980* (Edinburgh, Saint Andrews Press, 1987), pp. 123–125.

10 'Number 2 Independent Company War Diary', NA, WO 168/106.

11 Derry, *The Campaign in Norway*, p. 168.

12 The other five companies were formed and 'stood-to' for operations in Norway, but never deployed.

13 War Office to FO Narvik, Rupertforce and Colonel Gubbins, 8 May 1725, NA, WO 106/1827.

14 Derry, *The Campaign in Norway*, p. 182.

15 NA, CAB 120/654; Connell, *Auchinleck*, p. 115; William Fraser, 'Scandinavian Adventure', LHC, GB009, Fraser, William, 2/3

16 Auchinleck to Fraser, 13 May, NWEF Operational Instruction No. 1, IWM, Mackesy Papers, PJM Box 3.

17 Derry, *The Campaign in Norway*, p. 184.

18 Fraser to Auchinleck (D6 to RA Narvik), 15 May 0744, NA, AIR 20/2295.

19 Fraser returned to Harstad on another ship on 22 May, but the following day, as a result of the wound received a fortnight earlier and after 'a most cursory glance' by the senior medial officer, he was considered unfit to continue and ordered back to Britain. Fraser 'Norwegian Adventure', 2/3.

20 Auchinleck to Gubbins, 16 May, IWM, Gubbins 2/3.

21 Referred to, in many British accounts, as Dalkslubben – a hill feature near the village.

22 Erskine, The Scots Guards, p. 35.

23 Lunde, *Hitler's Pre-emptive War*, p. 439; Derry, *The Campaign in Norway*, pp. 185–186.

24 '1st Battalion Scots Guards War Diary', NA, WO 168/56.

25 Derry, *The Campaign in Norway*, p. 186; Erskine, *The Scots Guards*, pp. 38–39; The acting commanding officer at this stage was Major Graham, the Battalion Second in Command; Lieutenant Colonel Trappes-Lomax was commanding the whole of Bodo-force and was based in Mo.

26 'Scissorsforce War Diary', NA, WO 168/103.

27 Erskine, *The Scots Guards*, pp. 39–40.

28 H. L. Graham, 'The First Battalion in Norway, 1940', *Scots Guards Magazine* (1959), p. 55.

29 'Scissorsforce War Diary', NA, WO 168/103.

30 The company from Bodø rejoined the battalion later in the day.

31 Connell, *Auchinleck*, p. 122.

32 Auchinleck to Trappes-Lomax, 19 May 2011, received about 0400, IWM, Gubbins, 2/3.

33 Connell, *Auchinleck*, p. 125.

34 Gubbins, 'Brief Appreciation of the Situation', 21 May, NA, WO 198/8.

35 Derry, *The Campaign in Norway*, p. 188.

36 'Scissors War Diary', 20 April, NA, WO 168/103.

37 Gubbins to Trappes-Lomax, 21 May 1200, NA, WO 198/8; Gubbins Papers, LHC, 12618.

38 Erskine, *The Scots Guards*, pp. 41–42.
39 Captain Ellinger, quoted in Lunde, *Hitler's Pre-emptive War*, p. 445.
40 '1st Battalion Scots Guards War Diary', NA, WO 168/56.
41 Gubbins to GOC Home Forces, 13 September 1940, IWM Gubbins 2/3.
42 '1st Battalion Scots Guards War Diary', NA, WO 168/56; Erskine, *The Scots Guards*, p. 43.
43 Erskine, *The Scots Guards*, p. 43.
44 Ibid., p. 45
45 Auchinleck to Gubbins, 23 (amended to 22) May 2350, IWM, Gubbins papers, 2/3
46 '1st Battalion Scots Guards War Diary', NA, WO 168/56; Derry *The Campaign in Norway*, p. 189.
47 '1st Battalion Scots Guards War Diary', NA, WO 168/56; Erskine, *The Scots Guards*, p. 45.
48 Erskine, *The Scots Guards*, p. 46; Desmond Fitzgerald, *History of the Irish Guards in the Second World War* (Aldershot, Gale & Polden, 1949), p. 25.
49 Derry, *The Campaign in Norway*, pp. 191–192.
50 Leicesters at Lake Mjøsa, 21 April; Lincolns at Vist, 22 April; 1 KOYLI at Kvam, 26 April; York & Lancasters at Kjørem, 27 April; Green Howards at Otta, 28 April; Scots Guards at Mo, 17 May; Irish Guards at Pothus, 26 May.
51 Cork Report, Section 5, NA, ADM 199/485.
52 Derry, *The Campaign in Norway*, p. 213.
53 Second Lieutenant Tomas Harvey, Scots Guards, IWM, Sound Archive 8844.
54 '30 to 40 aircraft', Maxton to Harstad, 28 May 0640, NA, AIR 36/13.
55 Connell, *Auchinleck*, p. 139.
56 Derry, *The Campaign in Norway*, pp. 213–215.
57 Auchinleck to Dill, quoted in Connell, *Auchinleck*, pp. 130–131, 141.
58 Auchinleck Report, in Hansard, 'Cork Despatch', Appendix B.
59 Ibid.

Chapter 22

1 PM to Cork, 14 May 1730, NA, PREM 3/328/4.
2 Cork to Admiralty 19 May 1517, received 1759, NA, ADM 199/1929.
3 PM to Cork, 20 May sent 1848, NA, ADM 199/1929.
4 Cork to PM, 21 May 1506, received 1731, NA, PREM 3/328/4.
5 Ibid.
6 Cork to Chiefs of Staff, 21 May 1602, NA, ADM 199/486.
7 Cork Report, Appendix B, NA, ADM 199/485.
8 Cork to Churchill, 24 May 2214, received 25 May 0717, NA, ADM 199/1929.
9 Connell, *Auchinleck*, p. 133.
10 Cork Report, Section 7, NA, ADM 199/485; Although Churchill had informed Reynaud 'privately' on 24 or 25 May of the decision to evacuate, the War Cabinet did not authorise the French government to be officially informed until 31 May – after the capture of Narvik, and on the eve of

evacuation. COS Minutes, 25 May, NA, CAB 79/4, and WC Conclusions, 30
May, NA CAB 65/13/26.

11 Kersaudy, *Norway 1940*, p. 205.
12 For example, on 24 May sixty five Gebirgsjäger from 137 Mountain Regiment arrived by parachute. Gebirgsdivision 3, 'Kriegstagebuch'.
13 Lunde gives the number of reinforcements as 133 in the first half of May, an
   additional 239 between 15 and 22 May and a further 671 in the last week in
   May. Lunde, *Hitler's Pre-emptive War*, p. 467.
14 Buchner, *Narvik*, pp. 108–109.
15 Maund to Hankey, 11 October 1940, IWM, Mackesy Papers, PJM Box 3.
16 Ziemke, *The German Northern Theater*, p. 101.
17 Haarr, *The Battle for Norway*, p. 271.
18 FO Narvik to Admiralty, 29 May, NA, WO 106/1921; Lunde, *Hitler's Pre-
   emptive War*, p. 504, quoting Witold Bieganski, *Poles in the Battle of Narvik*
   (Warsaw, Interpress Publishers, 1969). The figures quoted possibly include
   casualties before 27 May.
19 FO Narvik to Admiralty, 29 May, NA, WO 106/1921.
20 Nigel de Lee, 'Spring Fever: British Planning and Preparation for Operations
   in Norway in 1940' (paper presented at the Second International Strategy
   Conference, Carlisle Barracks, Pennsylvania, February 1991; unpublished),
   p. 93.
21 Connell, *Auchinleck*, p. 140.
22 Richards, *The Royal Air Force 1939–1945*, p. 103.
23 Air Ministry Weekly Intsum, 6 June, NA, WO 106/1802.
24 Admiralty to Cork, 24 May, NA, PREM 3/328/4.
25 HQ North West Expeditionary Force Instruction, 31 May, NA, WO 168/83
26 Cork to Admiralty, 27 May, NA, WO 106/1813.
27 WC Conclusions, 27 May, NA, CAB 65/13/22 and 29 May, 65/13/25.
28 Béthouart to Audet, NA, WO 106/1813; Béthouart, *Cinque Années d'Espérance*, p. 62.
29 Connell, *Auchinleck*, p. 140.
30 Hansard, 'Cork Despatch', Section 7.
31 Ibid.
32 R. F. H. Nalder, *The Royal Signals: A History of Its Antecedents and Development
   (circa 1800–1955)* (London, Royal Corps of Signals Institution, 1958), p. 18.
33 Derry, *The Campaign in Norway*, p. 225.
34 Ibid., p. 244; Roskill, *The War at Sea*, p. 195.
35 James Levy, 'The Inglorious End of the Glorious. The Release of the Findings of the Board of Enquiry into the Loss of HMS Glorious', *Mariners
   Mirror*, 86:3 (August 2000), pp. 303–309; and Barnett, *Engage the Enemy
   More Closely*, p. 136.
36 Hinsley, *British Intelligence*, p. 141; Roskill, *The War at Sea*, p. 198; Barnett,
   Engage the Enemy More Closely, pp. 135–136.
37 Churchill to Eden, 15 June, CA, Churchill Papers, CHAR 20/13.
38 Churchill, *Their Finest Hour*, pp. 64–65.
39 James Leasor and Leslie Hollis, *War at the Top. Based on the Experiences of
   General Sir Leslie Hollis.* (London, Michael Joseph, 1959), p.83.

Chapter 23

1 Maier, 'German Strategy', p. 218; Ottmer, *Weserübung*, p. 145.
2 Derry, *The Campaign in Norway*, p. 230.
3 Lunde, *Hitler's Pre-emptive War*, p. 542.
4 Hooton, *Phoenix Triumphant*, p. 229.
5 German Quartermaster-General's Return, quoted by Air Historical Branch to Derry, 4 October 1950, NA, CAB 106/1171.
6 Kersaudy suggests 500,000. *Norway, 1940*, p. 226.
7 Maund letter to Derry, 15 May 1950, NA, CAB 106/1170.
8 Derry, *The Campaign in Norway*, p. 237.
9 Butler, *Grand Strategy*, p. 129.
10 Helmut von Moltke (the elder), 'No plan of operations extends with any certainty beyond the first contact with the main hostile force.' Quoted by Daniel Hughes and Harry Bell, *Moltke on the Art of War: Selected Writings* (Novato, Presdio, 1993), p. 92.
11 Thus, in modern military jargon, exercising 'operational art'.
12 Lunde, *Hitler's Pre-emptive War*, p. 311.
13 James Marshall-Cornwall, *Wars and Rumours of Wars: A Memoir*, (London, Leo Cooper, 1984), p. 130.
14 For an alternative view, see Fraser, *And We Shall Shock Them*, pp. 49–50.
15 Stephen Brooks (ed), *Montgomery and the Eighth Army* (London, Bodley Head, 1991), p. 33.
16 Colville, *The Fringes of Power*, diary entry for 15 February, p. 83.
17 Cadogan, in Dilks, *Cadogan Diaries*, 27 March, p. 265
18 Colville, *The Fringes of Power*, 24 January, p. 74
19 Nick Smart, *British Strategy and Politics During the Phoney War: Before the Balloon Went Up* (Westport, Praeger, 2003), p. 128.
20 Cadogan, in Dilks, 'Cadogan Diaries', 5 February, p. 253.
21 COS Minutes, 9 May, NA, CAB 79/4.
22 Haarr, *The Battle for Norway*, p.265; In mid-May, Colonel Pollock was appointed as head of a British military mission to the Norwegian Government.
23 Macleod and Kelly, *The Ironside Diaries*, 29 September 1937, p. 31.
24 For example, 'Reliance must be placed on improvised transport in the first instance, MT being shipped later.' NA, WO 260/28.
25 Paget, 'Sickle Report', NA, WO 106/1904.
26 Templewood, *Nine Troubled Years*, pp. 430–431.
27 Butler, *Grand Strategy*, pp. 117, 150.
28 Clausewitz, *On War*, p. 119.
29 Ibid., p. 101.
30 Although warfare is particularly susceptible to Sod's Law, it is by no means governed by it: Sod's Law is no exception to Sod's Law.
31 Hankey's inquiry, April 1940, NA, PREM 1/435.
32 Director of Military Training, 'Notes on the Tactical and Administrative Lessons of the Campaign in Norway', 7 June 1940, NA, WO 231/1.
33 'Lessons Learned from Flanders 1940', Committee chaired by General Sir William Bartholomew, LHC, GB 0099, Bartholomew.

34 Hansard, 'Massy Despatch', Part 4.

35 For example, 'The place is riddled, I am convinced, with spies', Auchinleck
    to Dill, Lunde, *Hitler's Pre-Emptive War*, p. 480);
    'There was strong feeling amongst most of us that the country was riddled
    with Boche agents. No proof – merely a feeling.' Brigadier Hogg, 'Operations
    at Aandlasnes 25 April–2 May 1940. Lessons and Deductions.' NA, WO 168/
    10; 'Country is riddled with agents and Army has disloyal elements.' MA
    Stockholm to War Office, 15 April, NA, WO 106/1940; 'Norway must have
    been stinking with Nazis.' Ironside, quoted by Wark, *Sir Edmund Ironside*,
    p. 239; 'spies or German sympathisers … infested the country.' Hansard,
    'Massy Despatch Draft, (subsequently amended), NA FO 371/47545.

36 Jacob to Derry, 5 March 1951, NA, CAB 106/1170.

37 Byford, 'False Start', p. 137.

38 'History of the Combined Arms Organisation', NA, DEFE 2/699; Fergusson,
    The Watery Maze, pp. 47, 52.

39 Hinsley, *British Intelligence*, p. 268; Stephen Roskill, 'Marder, Churchill and
    the Admiralty 1939–1942', *Royal United Services Institute Journal*, 4:117
    (December 1972), p. 51.

40 Ironically, *HMS Prince of Wales* was commanded by Vice Admiral Tom Phil-
    lips, Vice Chief of the Naval Staff at the time of the Norwegian Campaign.

41 Hinsley, *British Intelligence*, pp. 136–140, 161, 267–276.

42 Jacob, *Action This Day*, p. 163.

43 Macleod and Kelly, *The Ironside Diaries*, 7 April, p. 247.

44 Quoted in Leslie Hollis, *One Marine's Tale* (London, Andrew Deutsch,
    1956), p. 66.

45 Churchill, *The Gathering Storm*, p. 650.

46 Reynolds, *In Command of History*, p. 126.

47 Churchill to Ismay, 26 May 1946, NA, CAB 127/50.

48 Churchill, *The Gathering Storm*, p. 562.

49 General Sir Alan Brooke, quoted in Kennedy, *The Business of War*, p. 275.

50 Macleod and Kelly, *The Ironside Diaries*, 22 April, p. 278.

51 Chamberlain to Hilda Chamberlain, 20 April, Self, *Chamberlain Diary Letters*,
    p. 520.

52 Butler, *Grand Strategy*, p. 150.

53 Quoted in Macmillan, *The Blast of War*, p. 562.

54 Roskill, *Churchill and the Admirals*, p. 287.

55 Churchill, *The Gathering Storm*, p. 550.

56 Brodhurst, *Churchill's Anchor*, p. 141.

57 Gilbert, *At the Admiralty*, pp. 387, 478–480 ; Colville, *The Fringes of Power*,
    diary entry for 29 May, p. 144; Marder, 'Winston Is Back', p. 8; Roskill,
    Churchill and the Admirals, p. 120; Gough, *Historical Dreadnoughts*, p. 249.

58 Bond, *British War Planning for Operations in the Baltic*, p. 133; for examples,
    see Maclachlan, *Room 39*, pp. 74, 124–133.

59 David Reynolds, 'Churchill in 1940: The Worst and Finest Hour' in Robert
    Blake and William Roger Louis (eds), *Churchill* (Oxford University Press,
    1996), p. 253.

60 Attributed to General Omar Bradley.

61 WC Conclusions, 2 January, NA, CAB 65/11/1.
62 Macleod and Kelly, *The Ironside Diaries*, 30 April, p. 289.
63 Liddell Hart, 'Notes', 11 April 1940, LHC, LH/11/1940/23.
64 WC Conclusions, 2 May, NA, CAB 65/7/2.
65 MCC Minutes, 19 April, NA, CAB 83/3.
66 WC Conclusions, 15 April, NA, CAB 65/12/25.
67 Colville, *The Fringes of Power*, diary entry for 6 April, p. 96.
68 Gaitskell to Dalton, 17 March, Ben Pimlot, *The Political Diary of Hugh Dalton. 1918–1940, 1940–1960* (London, Cape, 1986), p. 325; in similar vein, see also Cato, *Guilty Men*.
69 Eliot Cohen, *Supreme Command: Soldiers, Statesmen and Leadership in Wartime* (London, Simon & Schuster, 2003); Hew Strachan, *The Direction of War: Contemporary Strategy in Historical Perspective* (Cambridge University Press, 2013), pp. 210–234.
70 COS(40)218, 28 January, NA, CAB 66/5/15.
71 COS Minutes, 15 April, NA, CAB 79/85.
72 COS(40)218, 28 January, NA, CAB 66/5/15.
73 COS(40)243(JP)(S) of 14 February, NA, CAB 80/104.
74 Derry, *The Campaign in Norway*, p. 60.
75 Malcolm Smith talks of 'a political civil war among the services' in the inter-war years. *British Air Strategy between the Wars* (Oxford, Clarendon, 1984), p. 304.
76 Butler, *Grand Strategy*, p. 60.
77 Ismay, *Memoirs*, p. 111.
78 Moulton, *The Norwegian Campaign*, p. 208.
79 Nigel de Lee, 'Scandinavian Disaster: Allied Failure in Norway in 1940' in Gary Sheffield and Geoffrey Till (eds), *The Challenges of High Command: The British Experience* (Basingstoke, Palgrave Macmillan, 2003), p. 59.
80 See, for example, Orange, *Slessor: Bomber Champion*, p. 65.
81 Wark, 'Beyond Intelligence', pp. 244–248.
82 Colville, *The Fringes of Power*, diary entry for 3 May, p. 116.
83 Alex Danchev, 'The Central Direction of the War, 1940–41' in John Swetman (ed), *Sword and Mace: Twentieth Century Civil-Military Relations in Britain* (London, Brassey's, 1986), p. 70.
84 Brodhurst, *Churchill's Anchor*, p. 286.
85 Ibid., p. 139.
86 Roskill, *Churchill and the Admirals*, p. 93.
87 Barnett, *Engage the Enemy More Closely*, p. 733.
88 A. J. P. Taylor, review article, *The Observer*, 11 November 1962.
89 Slessor, *The Central Blue*, p. 242.
90 See Macleod and Kelly, *The Ironside Diaries*, 26 April, pp. 284–285, and 7 May, p. 296.
91 Macleod, 'Calais 1940' (undated, unpublished), NAM, Macleod, R.
92 Macleod and Kelly, *The Ironside Diaries*, 17 December, p. 172.
93 Ibid., 21 December, p. 186.
94 Ibid., 13 December, p. 172.
95 'Memorandum by the Chiefs of Staff. Draft paper by CIGS for submission to the WC', 8 March, NA, WO 193/785.

 96 Macleod and Kelly, *The Ironside Diaries*, 5 February, p. 216.
 97 Ibid., 8 February, p. 216.
 98 Ibid., 18 February, p. 218.
 99 Ibid., 2 April, p. 243.
100 Ibid., 11 January, p. 196.
101 Ironside to Lindsay [only name given], 31 December 1940, IWM, Ironside letters 2096.
102 For example, '[O]fficers have found for too long that it does not pay to express ideas contrary to orthodoxy and the letter of the manuals. The habit of watching their step has become too deeply ingrained.' Lieutenant Colonel Eric Dorman-Smith to Liddell Hart, 'Notes on Talk with Gort and Others at Staff College', 5 October 1936, LHC, LHH 11/1936/81.
103 I am grateful to Professor David French for pointing this out.
104 Terraine, *The Right of the Line*, p. 115.

Bibliography

Acworth, Bernard, *The Navy and the Next War. A Vindication of Sea Power* (London, Eyre and Spottiswoode, 1934).

Adams, Jack, *The Doomed Expedition* (London, Leo Cooper, 1989).

Adams, J. J. Q.,'Samuel John Gurney Hoare, Viscount Templewood', in *Oxford Dictionary of National Biography* (Oxford University Press, 2004).

Addison, Paul, *The Road to 1945. British Politics and the Second World War* (London, Pimlico, 1994).

Air Ministry (ACAS [I]), *The Rise and Fall of the German Air Force 1939–1945* (London, Air Ministry, 1948).

Amery, Leo, *My Political Life. Volume 3. The Unforgiving Years 1929–1940* (London, Hutchinson, 1955).

Armstrong, Brian, 'Through a Glass Darkly. The Royal Air Force and the Lessons of the Spanish Civil War 1936–1939', *RAF Air Power Review*, 12:1 (2009) 32–55.

Ash, Bernard, *Norway 1940* (London, Cassell, 1964).

Assmann, K, *The German Campaign in Norway* (London, HMSO, 1948).

Attlee, Clement, *Clem Attlee. The Grenada Historical Records Interview* (London, Panther Books, 1967).

Barclay, C. N., *The History of the Sherwood Foresters. Nottinghamshire and Derbyshire Regiment. 1919–1957* (London, William Clowes, 1959).

Barnett, Correlli, *Engage the Enemy More Closely. The Royal Navy in the Second World War* (London, Penguin, 2000).

Beesly, Patrick, *Very Special Admiral. The Life of Admiral JH Godfrey CB* (London, Hamilton, 1980).

Bekker, Cajus, *Hitler's Naval War* (London, Purnell Books, 1974).

The Luftwaffe War Diaries (London, Corgi Books, 1969).

Bell, AC, *Seapower and the Next War* (London, Longmans, 1938).

Béthouart, Marie-Emile, *Cinque Années d'Espérance. Mémoires de Guerre* (Paris, Plon, 1968).

Boch, Theodor, *The Mountains Wait* (London, Michael Joseph, 1943).

Bond, Brian, *British Military Policy Between the World Wars* (Oxford, Clarendon, 1980).

'British War Planning for Operations in the Baltic', in Rystad, Goran et al. (eds), *In Quest of Trade and Security. The Baltic in Power Politics 1500–1990, Volume II* (Lund, Probus, 1995), pp. 108–138.

Chief of Staff: The Diaries of Lieutenant General Sir Henry Pownall. Volume 1 (London, Leo Cooper, 1972).

'Gort', in Keegan, John (ed), *Churchill's Generals* (London, Warner Books, 1992). pp.34–50.

Liddell Hart. A Study of His Military Thought (London, Cassell, 1977).

Boyle, William (Lord Cork and Orrery), *My Naval Life* (London, Hutchinson, 1942).

Brodhurst, Robin, *Churchill's Anchor. The Biography of Admiral of the Fleet Sir Dudley Pound OM GCB GCVO* (Barnsley, Leo Cooper, 2000).

Buchner, Alex, *Narvik. Die Kämpfe der Gruppe Dietl im Früjahr 1940* (Neckargemünd, Vowinckel, 1958).

Buckley, Christopher, *Norway, The Commandos, Dieppe* (London, HMSO, 1952).

Burdick, Charles, and Jacobson, Hans-Adolf (eds), *The Halder War Diary 1934–1942* (London, Greenhill, 1988).

Butler, J. R. M., *Grand Strategy. Volume 2. September 1939–June 1941* (London, HMSO, 1957).

Byford, Alastair, 'False Start: The Enduring Air Power Lessons of the Royal Air Force's Campaign in Norway April-June 1940', *RAF Air Power Review*, 13: 3 (2010), 119–138.

Caddick-Adams, Peter, 'Phoney War and Blitzkrieg: The Territorial Army in 1939–1940', *Royal United Services Institute Journal*, 143:2 (1998), 67–74.

Callwell, C. E., *The Dardanelles* (London, Constable, 1919).

Calvert, Michael, 'BEF, Back Every Fortnight, Norway 1940', *Royal Engineers Journal*, 88, (March 1974), 32–40

Carton de Wiart, Adrian, *Happy Odyssey. The Memoirs of Lieutenant General Adrian Carton de Wiart* (London, Cape, 1950).

Cato, *Guilty Men* (London, Victor Gollancz, 1940).

Chalmers, W. S., *Max Horton and the Western Approaches. A Biography of Admiral Sir Max Horton* (London, Hodder & Stoughton, 1954).

Churchill, Winston, *The Second World War. Volume I: The Gathering Storm* (London, Penguin, 1985).

The Second World War. Volume 2: Their Finest Hour (London, Penguin, 1985).

Claasen, Adam, 'The German Invasion of Norway, 1940. The Operational Intelligence Dimension', *Journal of Strategic Studies*, 27:1 (2004), 114–114.

Hitler's Northern War. The Luftwaffe's Ill-Fated Campaign 1940–1945 (Lawrence, KS, University Press of Kansas, 2001).

Clarke, Dudley, *Seven Assignments* (London, Cape, 1948).

Clausewitz, Carl von, *On War*, Howard, Michael, and Paret, Peter (eds, trans) (Princeton, NJ, Princeton University Press, 1976).

Clayton, Anthony, *Forearmed. A History of the Intelligence Corps* (London, Brassey's, 1993).

Cohen, Eliot, *Supreme Command. Soldiers, Statesmen and Leadership in Wartime* (London, Simon & Schuster, 2003).

Collier, Basil, *Hidden Weapons. Allied Secret or Undercover Services in World War II* (Barnsley, UK, Pen & Sword, 2006).

Colville, John, *The Fringes of Power. Downing Street Diaries 1939–1955* (London, Hodder & Stoughton, 1985).

Connell, John, *Auchinleck. The Biography of Field Marshal Sir Claude Auchinleck* (London, Cassell, 1959).

Corum, James, 'The German Campaign in Norway 1940 as a Joint Operation', *Journal of Strategic Studies*, 21:4 (1988), 50–50.

'The Luftwaffe's Army Support Doctrine', *Journal of Military History*, 59 (1995), 53–53.

The Roots of Blitzkrieg. Hans von Seekt and German Military Reform (Lawrence, KS, University Press of Kansas, 1992).

'Uncharted Waters: Information in the First Modern Joint Campaign – Norway 1940', *Journal of Strategic Studies*, 27:2 (2004), 345–345.

Croft, Andrew, *A Talent for Adventure* (London, SPA Limited, 1991).

Crow, Duncan (ed), *Clem Attlee. The Granada Historical Records Interview* (London, Panther Record, 1967).

Cruickshank, Charles, *SOE in Scandinavia* (Oxford University Press, 1986).

Danchev, Alex, and Todman, Daniel (eds), *War Diaries 1939–1945. Field Marshal Lord Alanbrooke* (London, Weidenfeld and Nicholson, 2001).

Danchev, Alex, 'The Central Direction of the War', 1940–41', in Swetman, John (ed), *Sword and Mace. Twentieth Century Civil-Military Relations in Britain* (London, Brassey's, 1986), pp. 57–57.

Dean, Maurice, *The Royal Air Force and Two World Wars* (London, Cassell, 1979).

de Lee, Nigel, 'Command in Central Norway, 1940: A Cautionary Tale', in Sheffield, Gary, and Till, Geoffrey (eds), *Challenges of High Command in the Twentieth Century* (Strategic and Combat Studies Institute, *The Occasional*, 38, (1999), 52–60.

'Scandinavian Disaster: Allied Failure in Norway in 1940', in Sheffield, Gary and Till, Geoffrey (eds), *The Challenges of High Command. The British Experience* (Basingstoke, Palgrave Macmillan, 2003).

Dennis, Peter, *The Territorial Army 1906–1940* (Woodbridge, Boydell, 1987).

Derry, T. K., *The Campaign in Norway* (Uckfield, Naval and Military, 1952).

Dickens, Gerald, *Bombing and Strategy. The Fallacy of Total War* (London, Sampson, Low, Marston & Co, 1946).

Dilks, David (ed), *The Diaries of Sir Alexander Cadogan OM 1938–1945* (London, Cassell, 1971).

Dix, Anthony, *The Norway Campaign and the Rise of Churchill, 1940* (Barnsley, Pen and Sword, 2014).

Douglas, Roy, *The Advent of War 1939–1940* (London, Macmillan, 1978).

Dutton, D. J., 'Sir John Simon', in *Oxford Dictionary of National Biography* (Oxford University Press, 2004).

Ehrman, John, *Cabinet Government and War 1890–1940* (Cambridge University Press, 1958).

Ellinger, Tage, *Den Forunderlige Krig* (Oslo, Gyldendal Norsk Forlag, 1960).

Epkenhans, Michael, 'The Long and Winding Road to Weserübung', in Clemmesen, Michael, and Faulkner, Marcus, *Northern European Overture to War 1939–1941. From Memel to Barbarossa* (Leiden, Brill, 2013, pp.115–158.

Erskine, David, *The Scots Guards 1919–1955*, (London, William Clowes, 1956)

Farrell, Brian, *The Basis and Making of British Grand Strategy. Was There a Plan?* (Lampeter, Edwin Mellon, 1998)

'Sir Alfred Dudley Pickman Rogers Pound', in *Oxford Dictionary of National Biography* (Oxford University Press, 2004).

Fergusson, Bernard, *The Watery Maze. The Story of Combined Operations* (London, Collins, 1961).

Fitzgerald, Desmond, *History of the Irish Guards in the Second World War* (Aldershot, Gale & Polden, 1949).

Fraser, David, *And We Shall Shock Them. The British Army in the Second World War* (London, Bloomsbury, 1983).

Freedman, Lawrence, *Strategy. A History* (Oxford University Press, 2013).

French, David, *Raising Churchill's Army. The British Army and the War Against Germany 1919–1945* (Oxford University Press, 2000).

Gates, Eleanor, *The End of the Affair. The Collapse of the Anglo-French Alliance 1939–40* (London, Allen & Unwin, 1981).

Gates, L. H., *The History of the Tenth Foot 1819–1950 [The Lincolnshire Regiment]* (Aldershot, Gale & Polden, 1952).

Gilbert, Martin, *The Churchill War Papers. Volume I. At the Admiralty. September 1939 – May 1940* (London, Norton, 1993).

The Churchill War Papers. Volume 2. Never Surrender (London, Heinemann, 1994).

Finest Hour. Winston S Churchill 1939–1941 (London, Heinemann, 1983).

Gooch, John, 'The British General Staff in the era of The World Wars', in French, David, and Holden Reid, Brian (eds), *The British General Staff: Reform and Innovation 1890–1938* (London, Cass, 2002). pp.192–203.

Goodman, Michael, *The Official History of the Joint Intelligence Committee. Volume 1. From the Approach of the Second World War to the Suez Crisis* (London, Routledge, 2014).

Gough, Barry, *Historical Dreadnoughts: Roskill and Marder. Writing and Fighting Naval History* (Barnsley, Seaforth, 2010).

Goulter, Christina, *A Forgotten Offensive. Coastal Command's Anti-Shipping Campaign 1940–1945* (London, Frank Cass, 1995).

Graham, H. L., 'The First Battalion in Norway, 1940', *Scots Guards Magazine* (1959), 48–60.

Grigg, P. J., *Prejudice and Judgment* (London, Cape, 1948).

Guderian, Heinz, *Panzer Leader* (London, Michael Joseph, 1953).

Haarr, Geirr, *The German Invasion of Norway* (Barnsley, Seaforth, 2009).

The Battle for Norway (Barnsley, Seaforth, 2010).

Hansard, 'Despatch of Admiral of the Fleet, the Earl of Cork and Orrery', *Supplement to the London Gazette*, Number 38011, 10 July 1947.

'Despatch of Lieutenant General HRS Massey', *Supplement to the London Gazette*, Number 37584, 28 May 1946.

'Despatch of Rear Admiral WJ Whitworth', *Supplement to the London Gazette*, Number 38005, 1 July 1947.

Harding, Richard 'Amphibious Warfare 1930–1939' , in Richard Harding, (ed) *The Royal Navy 1930–2000*, (London, Frank Cass, 2005), pp. 42–68.

Harris, J. P., 'The British General Staff and the Coming of War, 1933–39', in Bond, Brian, and French, David, *The British General Staff. Reform and Innovation* (London, Frank Cass, 2002). pp. 175–191.

Hart-Davis, Duff, *Peter Fleming. A Biography* (Oxford University Press, 1974).

Harvey, John (ed), *The Diplomatic Diaries of Oliver Harvey 1937–1940* (London, Collins, 1970).

Harvey, Maurice, *Scandinavian Misadventure. The Campaign in Norway 1940* (Tunbridge Wells, Spellmount, 1990).

Hennesey, Peter, *Cabinet* (Oxford, Blackwell, 1986).

Higham, Robin, *The Military Intellectuals in Britain 1918–1939* (New Brunswick, Rutgers University Press, 1966).

Hingston, Walter, *Never Give Up. The History of the Kings Own Yorkshire Light Infantry* (London, Lund Humphries & Co, 1950).

'A Territorial Battalion in Norway', *Army Quarterly*, LIX (1949), 87–96

Hinsley, F. H., *British Intelligence in the Second World War. Its Influence on Strategy and Operations, Volume I* (London, HMSO, 1979).

Hitler's Strategy (Cambridge University Press, 1951).

Høiback, Harald, *Command and Control in Military Crisis. Devious Decisions* (London, Cass, 2003).

Hollis, Leslie, *One Marine's Tale* (London, Andrew Deutsch, 1956).

Hooton, E. R., *Phoenix Triumphant. The Rise and Rise of the Luftwaffe* (London, Arms & Armour, 1994).

House, Jonathan, *Combined Arms Warfare in the Twentieth Century* (Kansas University Press, 2001).

Housley, *First Contact. A History of the 8thBn, The Sherwood Foresters 1939–45* (Nottingham, Milquest, 1997).

Howard, Michael, *The Continental Commitment. The Dilemma of British Defence Policy in the Era of the World Wars* (London, Maurice Temple Smith, 1972).

Howarth, Patrick, *Intelligence Chief Extraordinary. The Life of the Ninth Duke of Portland* (London, Bodley Head, 1986).

Hubatsch, Walther, 'Problems of the Norwegian Campaign, 1940', *Royal United Services Institute Journal*, 103:611 (August 1958), 336–336.

Hughes, Daniel, and Bell, Harry, *Moltke on the Art of War: Selected Writings* (Novato, Presdio, 1993).

Imlay, Talbot, *Facing the Second World War: Strategy, Politics and Economics in Britain and France 1938–40* (Oxford University Press, 2003).

Ironside, Edmund, *The High Road to Command: The Diaries of Major-General Sir Edmund Ironside, 1920–1922* (London, Leo Cooper, 1972).

Tannenberg. The First Thirty Days in East Prussia (London, Blackwood, 1925).

Irving, David, *Hitler's War*, (London, Hodder & Stoughton, 1977).

Ismay, Hastings, *The Memoirs of General the Lord Ismay KG, PC, GCB, CH, DSO* (London, Heinemann, 1960).

Jackson, W. G. F., and Brammall, Edwin, *The Chiefs: The Story of the United Kingdom Chiefs of Staff* (London, Brassey's, 1992).

Jacob, Ian, in Wheeler-Bennett, John (ed), *Action This Day. Working with Churchill* (London, Macmillan, 1968), pp.158–217.

Johnson, Franklyn, *Defence by Committee. The British Committee of Imperial Defence 1885–1959* (Oxford University Press, 1960).

Kahn, David, *Hitler's Spies. German Military Intelligence in World War II* (London, Hodder & Stoughton, 1978).

Kelly, Bernard, *Drifting Towards War: The British Chiefs of Staff, the USSR and the Winter War, November 1939-March 1940* (London, Taylor & Francis 2009).

Kennedy, John, *The Business of War* (London, Hutchinson, 1957).

Kennedy, Paul, *The Rise and Fall of British Naval Mastery* (London, Penguin, 2004).

Kersaudy, François, *Norway 1940* (London, Arrow, 1990).

Knight, Nigel, *Churchill. The Greatest Briton Unmasked* (Newton Abbott, David and Charles, 2008).

Krishtalkia, Aaron, 'Loyalty in Wartime: The Old Tories and British War Policy 1939–1940', in Farrell, Brian (ed), *Leadership and Responsibility in the Second World War* (Quebec, McGill-Queen's University Press, 2004). pp.39–67.

Kroener, Bernhard, 'The Manpower Resources of the Third Reich in the Area of Conflict Between Wehrmacht, Bureaucracy and War Economy 1939–1942', in Militärgeschichtliches Forschungsampt (ed), *'Germany and the Second World War. Volume 5/1. 'Organization and Mobilization of the German Sphere of Power'* (Oxford, Clarendon, 2015). pp.787–1127.

Kynoch, Joseph, *Norway 1940. The Forgotten Fiasco* (Shrewsbury, Airlife, 2002).

Lajos, Ivan, *Germany's War Chances* (London, Victor Gollancz, 1939).

Lambert, Andrew, 'The Only British Advantage: Sea Power and Strategy, September 1939 – June 1940', in Clemmesen, Michael, and Faulkner, Marcus, *Northern European Overture to War 1939–1941. From Memel to Barbarossa* (Leiden, Brill, 2013). pp.45–74.

Leasor, James, and Hollis, Leslie, *War at the Top. Based on the Experiences of General Sir Leslie Hollis* (London, Michael Joseph, 1959).

Leslie-Melville, Michael, *The Story of the Lovat Scouts 1900–1980* (Edinburgh, Saint Andrews Press, 1987).

Leverkuehn, Paul, *German Military Intelligence* (London, Weidenfeld & Nicholson, 1954).

Levy, James, 'The Inglorious End of the Glorious. The Release of the Findings of the Board of Enquiry into the Loss of HMS Glorious', *Mariners Mirror*, 86:3 (August 2000), 303–303.

Ludlow, Peter, 'The Unwinding Appeasement', in Kettenacker, Lothar (ed), *Das 'Andere Deutschland' im Zweiten Weltkrieg* (Stuttgart, Ernst Kleh Verlag, 1977). pp.9-48.

Lunde, Henrik, *Hitler's Pre-emptive War* (Newbury, Casemate, 2009).

Macintyre, Donald, *Narvik* (London, Pan Books, 1962).

Mackesy, Pierse, 'Churchill on Narvik', *Royal United Services Institute Journal*, 115 (December 1970), 28–28.

Macksey, Kenneth, *The Searchers. How Radio Interception Changed the Course of Both World Wars* (London, Cassell, 2003).

Maclachlan, Donald, *Room 39: Naval Intelligence in Action 1939–1945* (London Weidenfeld & Nicholson, 1968).

Macleod, Roderick, and Kelly, Denis (eds), *The Ironside Diaries 1937–1940* (London, Constable, 1962).

Macmillan, Harold, *The Blast of War 1939–1945* (London, Macmillan, 1967).

Maier, Klaus, 'German Strategy', in Maier, Klaus et al. (eds), *Germany and the Second World War, Volume 2, Germany's Initial Conquests in Europe*, (Oxford, Clarendon, 2015). pp.181–196.

Marder, Arthur, *From the Dreadnought to Scapa Flow. Vol 1* (Oxford University Press, 1961).

'Winston Is Back: Churchill at the Admiralty 1939–1940', in *The English Historical Review*, Supplement 5 (London, Longmans, 1972).

Marshall-Cornwall, James, *Wars and Rumours of Wars. A Memoir* (London, Leo Cooper, 1984).

Mason, Tony, 'British Air Power', in Olsen, John, *Global Air Power* (Washington DC, Potomac Books, 2011). pp.7-63.

Maund, L. E. H., *Assault from the Sea* (London, Methuen, 1949).

Megargee, Geoffrey, *Inside Hitler's High Command* (Kansas University Press, 2000).

'Triumph of the Null: Structure and Conflict in the Command of German Land Forces, 1939–1945', *War in History*, 4 (1997), 60–60.

Middlebrook, Martin, and Everitt, Chris, *The Bomber Command War Diaries* (Leicester, Midland Publishing, 1996).

Millet, Alan, and Murray, Williamson (eds), *Military Effectiveness. Volume 2. The Interwar Period* (Cambridge University Press, 2010).

Minney, R. J., *The Private Papers of Hore-Belisha* (London, Collins, 1962).

Montgomery, Bernard, *The Memoirs of Field Marshal the Viscount Montgomery of Alamein*, (London, Collins, 1958).

Montgomery Hyde, H., *British Air Policy Between the Wars 1918–1939* (London, Constable, 1982).

Mordal, Jacques, *La Campagne de Norvège* (Paris, Self, 1949).

Moulton, J. M., *The Norwegian Campaign of 1940. A Study of Warfare in Three Dimensions* (London, Eyre & Spottiswoode, 1966).

Munch-Petersen, Thomas, *The Strategy of Phoney War. Britain, Sweden, and the Iron Ore Question* (Stockholm, Militärshistorika Förlaget, 1981).

Munthe, Malcolm, *Sweet is War* (London, Gerald Duckworth, 1954).

Murray, Williamson, and Millet, Alan (eds), *Military Innovation in the Interwar Period* (Cambridge University Press, 1996).

Nalder, R. F. H., *The Royal Signals. A History of Its Antecedents and Development (circa 1800–1955)* (London, Royal Corps of Signals Institution, 1958).

Nevakivi, Jukka, *The Appeal That Was Never Made: The Allies, Scandinavia and the Finnish Winter War 1939–1940* (London, Hurst, 1976).

Nicholson, Harold, *Diaries and Letters 1939–1945* (London, Collins, 1966).

Oppenheimer, Peter, 'From the Spanish Civil War to the Fall of France: Luftwaffe Lessons Learned and Applied', *Journal of the Institute for Historical Review*, 7:2 (Summer 1986), 133–133.

Orange, Vincent, *Churchill and His Airmen* (London, Grub Street, 2012).

Slessor: Bomber Champion - The Life of Sir John Slessor (London, Grub Street, 2006).

Ottmer, Hans-Martin, *'Weserübung'. Der Deutsche Angriff auf Danemark und Norwegen im April 1940* (München, Oldenburg Verlag, 1994).

Paget, Julian, *The Crusading General. The Life of General Sir Bernard Paget GCB DSO MC* (Barnsley, Pen & Sword, 2008).

Parkinson, Roger, *The Auk. Auchinleck. Victor of Alamein* (London, Greda, 1977).

Pimlot, Ben, *The Political Diary of Hugh Dalton. 1918–1940, 1940–1960* (London, Cape, 1986).

Playfair, I. S. O., *History of the Second World War. The Mediterranean and the Middle East. Volume 1. The Early Successes Against Italy (to May 1941)* (London, HMSO, 1954).

Probert, Henry, *High Commanders of the Royal Air Force* (London, HMSO, 1991).

Refsdal, Per, *The Campaign in North-Norway 1940* (Harstad, Trykksentraien, 1990).

Reynaud, Paul, *In the Thick of the Fight* (London, Cassell, 1955).

Reynolds, David, 'Churchill in 1940: The Worst and Finest Hour', in Blake, Robert, and Louis, William, Roger (eds), *Churchill* (Oxford University Press, 1996). pp.240–256.

  In Command of History. Churchill Fighting and Writing the Second World War (London, Allen Lane, 2004).

Rhodes-James, Robert, *Chips. The Diaries of Sir Henry Channon* (London, Weidenfeld & Nicholson, 1967).

Rhys-Jones, Graham, *Churchill and the Norwegian Campaign* (Barnsley, Pen and Sword, 2008).

Richards, Denis, *Portal of Hungerford. The Life of Marshal of the Royal Air Force Viscount Portal of Hungerford KG GCB OM DSO MC* (London, Heinemann, 1977).

  RAF Bomber Command in the Second World War. The Hardest Victory (London, Penguin, 2001).

  The Royal Air Force 1939–1945. Volume 1. The Fight at Odds (London, HMSO, 1953).

Richardson, Matthew, *Fighting Tigers. Epic Actions of the Royal Leicestershire Regiment* (Barnsley, Leo Cooper, 2002).

Roberts, Andrew, *The Holy Fox. A Life of Lord Halifax* (London, Weidenfeld, 1991).

Roskill, Stephen, *Churchill and the Admirals* (London, Collins, 1977).

  Hankey. Man of Secrets. Volume 3 (London, Collins, 1970).

  'Marder, Churchill and the Admiralty 1939–1942', *Royal70l United Services Institute Journal*, 117:4 (December 1972), 40–40.

  The War at Sea 1939–1945, Volume 1, The Defensive (London, HMSO, 1954).

Salmon, Patrick (ed), *Britain and Norway in the Second World War* (London, HMSO, 1995).

  'British Plans for Economic Warfare Against Germany 1937–39: The Problem of Swedish Iron Ore', *Journal of Contemporary History*, 16 (1981), 53–72

  'Churchill, the Admiralty and the Narvik Traffic', *Scandinavian Journal of History*, 4:4 (1979), 305–305.

  Deadlock and Diversion. Scandinavia in British Strategy during the Twilight War (Bremen, Hauschild, 2012).

Self, Robert, *Neville Chamberlain. A Life* (Aldershot, Ashgate, 2006).

  (ed) *The Neville Chamberlain Diary Letters. Volume 4. The Downing Street Years. 1934–1940* (Aldershot, Ashgate, 2005).

Sheffield, Gary, 'Carton de Wiart and Spears', in Keegan, John (ed), *Churchill's Generals* (London, Warner Books, 1992). pp.323–350.

Sheffield, O., *The York and Lancaster Regiment Volume 3. 1919–1953* (Aldershot, Gale & Polden, 1956).

Slessor, John, *Air Power and Armies* (Oxford University Press, 1936).
   The Central Blue. Recollections and Reflections (London, Cassell, 1956).
Smart, Nick, *British Strategy and Politics During the Phoney War. Before the Balloon Went Up* (Westport, Praeger, 2003).
Smith, Malcolm, *British Air Strategy Between the Wars* (Oxford, Clarendon, 1984).
Smith, Michael, *Foley. The Spy Who Saved 10,000 Jews* (London, Hodder & Stoughton, 1999).
Stephens, Martin, *The Fighting Admirals. British Admirals of the Second World War* (London, Leo Cooper, 1991).
Strabolgi, Lord, *Narvik and After. A Study of the Scandinavian Campaign* (London, Hutchinson, 1940).
Strachan, Hew, *The Direction of War. Contemporary Strategy in Historical Perspective* (Cambridge University Press, 2013).
Strong, Kenneth, *Intelligence at the Top. The Recollections of an Intelligence Officer* (London, Cassell, 1968).
Synge, William, *The Story of the Green Howards 1939–1945* (Richmond, Yorkshire, The Green Howards, 1952).
Taylor, A. J. P., *English History 1914–1945* (Oxford, Clarendon Press, 1965).
Tedder, Arthur, *Air Power and War* (London, Hodder and Stoughton, 1954).
Templewood, Viscount, [Samuel Hoare], *Nine Troubled Years* (London, Collins, 1954).
Terraine, John, *The Right of the Line. The Royal Air Force in the European War 1939–1945* (London, Hodder & Stoughton, 1985).
Thomas, Hugh, *The Spanish Civil War* (London, Penguin, 1990).
Thompson, David, 'Norwegian Military Policy, 1905–1940: A Critical Appraisal and Review of Literature', *Journal of Military History*, 61 (July 1997), 503–503.
Underhill, W. E., *The Royal Leicestershire Regiment 17^{t}h Foot: A History of the Years 1928–1956* (Royal Leicestershire Regiment, 1957).
Waage, *The Narvik Campaign* (London, Harrap, 1964).
Wark, Wesley, 'Beyond Intelligence. The Study of British Strategy and the Norway Campaign, 1940', in Fry, Michael, *Power, Personalities and Policies. Essays in Honour of Donald Cameron Watt* (London, Cass, 1992). pp.233–257.
   'Sir Edmund Ironside: The Fate of Churchill's First General 193–1940', in Bond, Brian, *Fallen Stars. Eleven Studies of Twentieth Century Military Disasters* (London, Brasseys, 1991). pp.141–163.
Warlimont, Walter, *Inside Hitler's Headquarters 1939–45* (London, Weidenfeld & Nicholson, 1964).
Wilkinson, Peter, and Bright-Astley, Joan, *Gubbins and SOE* (London, Leo Cooper, 1992), p. 50.
Williams, E.T., "Carton de Wiart, Sir Adrian (1880–1963)," rev. Gary Sheffield, in *Oxford Dictionary of National Biography*, ed. H. C. G. Matthew and Brian Harrison (Oxford: OUP, 2004); online ed., ed. David Cannadine, September 2010, http://ezproxy-prd.bodleian.ox.ac.uk:2167/view/article/32316 (accessed November 29, 2016).

Wilt, Alan, *War from the Top. German and British Military Decision Making During World War II* (London, Taurus, 1990).

Woodward, Llewellyn, *British Foreign Policy in the Second World War, Volume 1* (London, HMSO, 1970).

Wrench, Evelyn, *Geoffrey Dawson and Our Times* (London, Hutchinson, 1955).

Ziemke, Earl, *The German Northern Theater of Operations 1940–1945* (Washington DC, US Government Printing Office, 1959).

OFFICIAL PUBLICATIONS

Amphibious Warfare HQ, *History of the Combined Operations Organisation 1940–1945* (London, 1956), NA, DEFE 2/699.

War Office, *Manual of Combined Operations*, (London, 1938).
Field Standard Regulations, Volume 2, (London, 1935).
The Employment of Air Forces with the Army in the Field, (London, 1938).
Infantry Training, (London, 1937).

UNPUBLISHED WORKS

Beckwith, EGC, *The 8th Battalion Sherwood Foresters TA. Campaign in Norway 1940* (1958) (Imperial War Museum).

de Lee, Nigel, *Spring Fever. British Planning and Preparation for Operations in Norway in 1940* (Paper delivered at International Strategy Conference, Carlyle Barracks, Pennsylvania, February 1991).

Dewing, Major General Richard, 'Diary 1939–41' (Liddell Hart Centre, King's College London).

Drewienkiewiecz, John, *The Build-Up, Early Training and Employment of the TA in the Leadup to, and Early Days of, the Second World War* (Royal College of Defence Studies paper, 1992).

Francklin, Philip, *Notes on the Norwegian Campaign*.

Fraser, William, *Scandinavian Adventure*, (Liddell Hart Centre, King's College London).
Diary, (Liddell Hart Centre, King's College London).

Gebirgsdivision 3, *Kriegstagebuch 1940* [War Diary of 3rd Mountain Division], (Imperial War Museum).

German Naval Staff (Operations Division), *War Diary*, (Combined Arms Research Library, Fort Leavenworth).

Mackesy, Pierse, *A Brief Account of the Narvik Expedition, 1940*, (Imperial War Musum).

Macleod, Roderick, *Calais 1940*, (National Army Museum).
Great Days or the War of Lost Opportunities, (National Army Museum).

US Office of Naval Intelligence, *Fuehrer Directives and Other Top Level Directives of the German Armed Forces 1939–1941*, (Combined Arms Research Library, Fort Leavenworth, Kansas).

Welch, Howard, *The Origins and Development of the Chiefs of Staff Sub-Committee of the Committee of Imperial Defence 1923–1939* (Doctoral thesis, King's College London, 1973).

Index

Abwehr, 80–1, 83, 85, 111
Ålborg, 84, 221–2, 226
Ålesund, 156, 162
Alexander, AV, 240, 244–5
Allied Military Committee, 8, 76, 87, 103, 108, 280
Amery, Leo, 238
Åndalsnes, 119, 126, 162–4, 166, 168, 172, 174, 178, 182–3, 189, 191, 196–7, 205, 209–11, 213–14, 217, 224–5, 228, 236, 256, 276, 281, 297
Ankenes, 249, 251, 269
Attlee, Clement, 2, 4, 240
Auchinleck, Lieutenant General Claude, xi, 241–3, 249, 252, 257–9, 261–8, 271, 273, 297
Audet, Major General Gerard, 174, 178, 207, 233

Bardufoss, 234, 256–7, 262, 265, 268–70, 272, 279
B-Dienst, 131, 150, 169
Beatty, Admiral of the Fleet Sir David, 14, 167
BEF. *See* British Expeditionary Force
Bergen, 35, 47, 61, 65, 73, 83, 94, 100, 112, 114, 117–22, 124, 133, 137, 169, 217, 221–3, 291, 295
Berney-Ficklin, Brigadier HPM, 161
Béthouart, Brigadier General Antoine, 174, 250, 253–4, 259, 268–71, 282
Bjerkvik, xi, 142, 241, 254, 258, 268–70
Bjørnfjell, 146, 150, 269–70
Bletchley Park. *See* Government Code and Cypher School
Boden, 23, 32–3, 53, 61
Bodø, 233–5, 241, 256–7, 260–6, 268
Bohusz-Szyszko, Brigadier General Zygmunt, 269
Bomber Command, 9, 16, 46, 220, 222–4
Brauchitsch, Colonel General Walther von, 112, 147

Braüer, Curt, 132
Bridges, Sir Edward, 66–7, 92, 209
British divisions and brigades
    15th Infantry Brigade, 160, 190, 193, 197–8, 203, 209–10, 279
    24th Guards Brigade, 114, 136, 138, 169, 181, 251, 261
    49th Infantry Division, 114, 135–7, 171, 200–1
    146th Infantry Brigade, 114, 126, 137–8, 155–6, 169, 171–2, 174, 178–9, 181, 201–2, 209, 217
    147th Infantry Brigade, 172
    148th Infantry Brigade, 114, 172, 181, 183–5, 189, 197–8, 200–1, 203, 209–10, 217
British Expeditionary Force, 12, 16, 30, 35–6, 44, 53, 55–6, 59–61, 69–71, 88–9, 91, 96, 136, 160–1, 167, 190, 209, 212, 233–4, 241, 257, 296
Brooke, Lieutenant General Sir Alan, 55, 207, 292, 298
Butler, 'Rab', 98, 235–6

Cadogan, Sir Alexander, 36–7, 54, 67, 87, 281
Calvert, Captain Mike, 197
Canadian forces, 25, 31, 161
Carls, Admiral Rolf, 79, 112
Carton de Wiart, Lieutenant General Adrian, xi, 170–5, 177–9, 182, 191, 205, 207, 209, 225, 233, 256, 280, 297
Cavendish-Bentinck, Victor, 104
Centre of Gravity, 218
Chamberlain, Neville, vii, xi, 1–4, 14, 20–2, 27, 29, 34–6, 39–42, 44, 48, 53, 60–9, 76–7, 88–93, 96–9, 101, 119, 123, 125, 128, 156, 160, 162, 164, 185, 205, 208, 210, 212–15, 229–31, 235–40, 275, 283, 285–6, 289, 297
Channon, Henry 'Chips', 88, 235, 237

Chatfield, Admiral of the Fleet Lord, xi, 3–4, 9, 27, 42, 64, 96, 104
Churchill, Winston, vii–viii, xi, 3–5, 7–8, 12–13, 21–30, 33–5, 37, 39–45, 47–9, 57, 60, 62, 64–5, 68–9, 73, 76, 88–9, 94, 96, 98, 100, 104, 107–8, 112–13, 115–20, 122–8, 138–9, 142–6, 153, 156–7, 159–60, 162, 164, 166, 168, 176, 205–6, 208–15, 230–1, 234–5, 237–46, 249, 251, 261, 268, 273, 275–6, 281, 284, 286–7, 289, 292, 294, 296, 298
Clarke, Lieutenant Colonel Dudley, 182, 187, 197
Clausewitz, Carl von, 129, 180, 217–18, 262, 283
Coastal Command, 16–17, 44, 101, 120, 220, 225, 273
Collier, Laurence, 97, 100
Colville, John, 36, 40, 63, 88, 98, 208–9, 211, 215, 236, 238, 281
Condor Legion, 218
Cork and Orrery, Admiral of the Fleet, the Earl of, xi, 45, 88, 138–9, 141–7, 152–3, 241–2, 244, 248–52, 257–61, 267–8, 270–1, 287, 294
Cunningham, Admiral Sir Andrew, 298

Dahl, Colonel Thor, 185–6, 188
Daladier, Edouard, 26, 52–3, 62, 89, 91, 97–8, 119
Danckwerts, Captain Victor, 19, 45, 73
Dardanelles. *See* Gallipoli
Defence Committee, 240, 243, 245, 276
Dewing, Major General Richard, 43, 56, 61, 64, 74, 95, 117, 121–4, 126, 136, 163, 216, 235, 242
Dietl, Lieutenant General Eduard, xi, 146–52, 165, 254, 256, 265, 269
Dill, General Sir John, 13, 207–8, 236, 241, 258, 262, 266, 271–3, 298
Dombås, 182–3, 185, 191–4, 197, 236, 288
Dormer, Sir Cecil, 124, 132, 272
Dowding, Air Chief Marshal Sir Hugh, 9, 46
Dowler, Colonel Arthur, 258
Dunkirk, 237, 246, 271, 273

Eden, 1, 230, 240, 269
Edwards, Captain Ralph, 115, 122–3, 231
Egersund, 83, 112, 133
Ends, Ways and Means, 33, 42, 54, 63, 84, 128, 159, 246, 291
Eriksen, Colonel Birger, 131

Evans, Admiral Sir Edward, 65–6, 73, 138, 203

Fåberg, 187
Falkenhorst, General Nikolaus von, xi, 81–5, 105, 110, 112, 133, 166, 191, 194, 220, 229, 254–6, 280
Feurstein, Lieutenant General Valentin, 256, 262, 266–7, 272
Fighter Command, 9, 16, 46
Fighting Power, 110, 199–200, 203–4, 249, 266–7
Fischer, Colonel Hermann, 186
Fisher, Admiral of the Fleet Sir John, 5, 11, 14
Fleet Air Arm, 16–18, 121, 161, 177, 220, 222, 225
Fleischer, Major General Carl Gustav, 141, 154, 253–4, 259
Fleming, Captain Peter, 170, 178
Foley, Frank, 133, 155
Forbes, Admiral Sir Charles, 73, 114, 116, 120, 131, 139, 157–8, 162, 167, 273
Fornebu, xi, 222–4
Fraser, Brigadier William, 137–8, 143, 251, 261
French formations and units
  Chasseurs Alpins, 71, 81, 94–5, 114, 119, 121, 136–7, 142, 168, 172, 174, 178, 208–9, 233, 250–3, 256, 269
  Foreign Legion, 160, 252, 254, 269

Gablenz, Colonel Freiherr Carl-August von, 222
Gaitskell, Hugh, 289
Gallipoli, 5, 35–6, 67, 75, 146, 153, 163, 166, 284, 288
Gällivare, 26, 29, 31–2, 47–8, 51, 53, 58, 63, 94, 106, 114, 123–4, 136–7, 206, 230, 249, 295
Gamelin, General Maurice, 22, 37, 44, 92, 107, 207, 213, 230, 234, 242
German formations and units
  1st Mountain Division, 166
  2nd Mountain Division, 166, 256–7, 262, 266–7, 272
  3rd Mountain Division, xi, 141, 148, 151, 165, 253–4, 256
  138th Mountain Regiment, 151, 165, 179
  139th Mountain Regiment, 148
  181st Infantry Division, 165
  196th Infantry Division, 186

German formations and units (cont.)
  Group XXI, 81–3, 105, 186, 280
Getz, Colonel Ole Berg, 173, 176, 178
Godfrey, Rear Admiral John, 104
Gordon-Finlayson, General Sir Robert, 56
Göring, Hermann, 83, 225, 229
Gort, General Lord, 12, 17, 44, 61, 63, 67, 77, 241
Government Code and Cypher School, 101–2, 106, 273
Green Howards, 190, 194, 197
Greenwood, Arthur, 240
Grigg, Sir James 'PJ', 13, 69, 122, 236
Gubbins, Brigadier Colin, 260–5
Gudbrandsdal, 155, 183, 193, 198–9, 228, 262

Haakon, King, 37, 131, 133, 197, 272
Halder, General Franz, 80, 82, 147
Halifax, Viscount, xi, 2, 4, 8, 20–1, 23, 25, 27, 29, 34, 36–7, 39, 44, 48, 60, 63, 66–7, 76, 90, 92, 98, 100, 123, 125, 236, 240, 243, 245, 289
Hallams. See York and Lancaster Regiment
Hamburg, 81, 83, 133
Hamilton, Captain Louis, 147, 251
Hankey, Lord, xi, 3–4, 27, 63, 76, 91, 109, 240, 284, 289
Harstad, 137–9, 143, 146, 157, 225, 241, 243, 249–50, 252, 256–8, 261–2, 265, 270–2, 297
Harvey, Oliver, 44, 87, 207
Hitler, Adolf, viii, 2, 20, 22, 46, 50, 79–83, 85, 88–9, 98, 101, 110, 129, 133, 146–8, 154, 166, 180, 218, 220, 256, 275–6, 280
Hoare, Sir Samuel, xi, 2–4, 18, 24, 27, 87, 93, 96–8, 107, 116
Hogg, Brigadier D, 191, 196
Hore-Belisha, Leslie, 4, 13–14, 30, 35, 42, 44, 88
Horton, Vice Admiral Sir Max, 113
Hotblack, Major General Frederick, 160
Hubbacks, Commander Gordon, 145, 147
Hvinden-Haug, Major General Jacob, 185

Independent Companies, 233, 235, 241, 256–7, 260–2, 264, 266–7
Industrial Intelligence Centre, 7
Inskip, Sir Thomas, 9
Inter-Service Planning Staff, 74, 121, 136, 214
Inter-Service Training and Development Centre, 75, 121, 138, 147

Irish Guards, 136, 261, 264, 267
Ironside, General Sir Edmund, xi, 12–14, 17–18, 22–4, 26–7, 30, 33–4, 36–7, 39, 42–4, 48–53, 55, 58, 60–1, 63, 65–6, 68–72, 74, 76–7, 87–8, 91–3, 96, 99–100, 104, 107–8, 117, 119–26, 128, 137, 143, 153, 157, 159–60, 162–4, 169, 172, 185, 206–8, 210–11, 213, 215–16, 228, 231, 233, 235–7, 242, 250, 273, 295–7
Ismay, Major General Hastings, 39, 43, 63, 65, 74, 103, 117, 153, 159, 167, 211, 215, 235

Jacob, Lieutenant Colonel Ian, 68, 96, 115, 215, 284–5, 287
Jodl, Major General Alfred, 79, 81–3, 148
Joint Intelligence Committee, 58, 100–2, 104, 107, 285, 293
Joint Planners, 19, 21, 25, 32, 43, 49, 52, 55–6, 61, 72, 74, 76, 90, 94, 102, 104, 118–20, 125, 127, 158–9, 167, 210–11, 216, 221, 227, 233, 235, 244–6, 276, 291, 296, 302–4
Joubert de la Ferté, Air Marshal Philip, 123, 161

Keitel, Colonel General Wilhelm, 79–81, 166
Kennedy, Brigadier John, 14, 19, 42, 65–6, 78
Keyes, Admiral of the Fleet Sir Roger, 166, 237
Kings Own Yorkshire Light Infantry, 169, 176, 190, 193–4, 197, 201
King-Salter, Lieutenant Colonel Edward, 183, 185, 187
Kirknesvag, 176
Kjørem, 194
Koht, Halvdan, 132
KOYLI. See Kings Own Yorkshire Light Infantry
Krancke, Captain Theodor, 80, 82
Kristiansand, 83, 112–13, 133
Krokstranda, 263–4
Kvam, 193–4, 279

Laake, General Kristian, 133
Lake Mjøsa, 185–8
Laurantzon, Major General Jacob, 165, 173
Leicestershire Regiment, 181, 183, 185, 187–8, 200–1
Lesjaskog, xi, 192–3, 212, 226, 255, 281
Liddell Hart, Basil, 22, 288

Lillehammer, 155, 182, 184–8, 205, 209, 217
Lincolnshire Regiment, 169, 176–7
Lindemann, Professor Frederick, 40
Lindsay, Captain Martin, 170
Lloyd George, David, 2, 238
Lovat Scouts, 260
Ludlow-Hewitt, Air Chief Marshal Sir Edgar, 9, 46
Luftwaffe, 16, 18, 80, 82–4, 134, 146, 151, 156–7, 161, 169, 174, 178, 180, 191–2, 199, 204, 212, 218–20, 222–3, 225, 227–8, 254, 256, 265, 269–72, 274, 281
Luleå, 7, 24, 26, 47, 88, 94, 97, 230, 232, 243
Lund, Brigadier Otto, 137

Mackesy, Major General Pierse, xi, 64, 66, 73–4, 135–9, 141–7, 152–5, 173, 182, 241, 249–54, 258–9, 261, 267, 270, 280, 287, 297
Macmillan, Harold, 88, 236
Marshall-Cornwall, Lieutenant General James, 103, 280
Massy, Lieutenant General Hugh, 49, 100, 128, 164, 178, 192, 207, 209–11, 213–14, 233, 235
Maund, Captain Loben, 121, 138, 145, 147, 251, 254, 270, 278
MI(R), 170, 260
MI3, 100, 103, 107
MI5, 102
MI6. See Secret Intelligence Service
Military Coordination Committee, 8–9, 19, 25, 29, 42–3, 72–3, 76, 96, 116, 119, 121–2, 124–6, 128, 139, 156–7, 159–60, 163, 168, 206, 209–10, 212–15, 233–5, 240, 278–9, 286, 291, 294
Ministry of Economic Warfare, 22–3, 25, 27, 102, 104
Mo-i-Rana, 233–4, 241, 256–7, 260–3
Molde, 124, 183, 191, 197
Molotov-Ribbentrop Pact, 21
Moore, Group Captain Maurice, xi, 257
Morgan, Brigadier Harold, 181–3, 185–8, 191, 193, 205
Morrison, Herbert, 238
Morton, Desmond, 7, 104
Mosjøen, 178, 233–4, 241, 256, 258, 260–1, 266
Mowinckel, Johan Ludwig, 245

Namsos, xi, 119, 123–6, 138, 155–7, 160, 162–3, 166, 168–70, 172, 174–5, 177–9, 182–3, 198, 205, 207–11, 213–14, 217, 224–5, 228–9, 233, 236, 238, 250, 256, 276, 281–2, 293, 297
Narvik, xi, 7–8, 23–4, 26–7, 29, 31–4, 36–7, 47–8, 52–3, 57, 60, 62, 64–5, 68, 73, 77, 80, 83, 87, 89, 92, 94, 97, 101, 112–27, 129, 131, 133, 136–9, 141–51, 154–6, 159–60, 162, 164, 166, 169–70, 172, 174, 179, 205–8, 212–13, 217, 221, 225, 229–31, 233–6, 241–6, 248–9, 251–4, 256–9, 261, 266–70, 272–3, 279–82, 284, 286–8, 291, 295, 297
Newall, Air Chief Marshal Sir Cyril, xi, 9–10, 12, 14–15, 18, 34, 37, 46, 51, 57–60, 65–6, 69, 77, 91, 117–18, 120, 122–3, 128, 207, 211, 216, 294, 296, 298
Nicholson, General Sir William, 14
Nicholson, Harold, 236
Nicholson, Lieutenant Colonel Cameron, 191
North West Expeditionary Force, 207, 283
Norwegian formations
  2nd Division, 185, 198
  4th Brigade, 198
  5th Brigade, 198
  6th Division, 141, 147, 252–3, 270, 274

Oberkommando der Wehrmacht. See OKW
OKW, 79–80, 82, 84–5, 133, 255, 275, 280
Operations
  Avonmouth, 47–8, 73–4, 94–5, 97, 113–14, 121, 135, 138, 169, 221, 277
  Catherine, 5, 45, 88, 138
  Hammer, 160, 162–4, 167, 174, 177, 190, 205, 208–10, 215–16, 227
  Juno, 272
  Maurice, 122, 124, 158, 168, 170, 174–5, 177, 179, 198, 204–5, 208–9
  Paul, 243, 245–6
  Plymouth, 47, 49, 55, 73–4, 96, 114, 206, 277, 300
  R4, 97, 113, 115, 127
  Royal Marine, 88, 90, 92–3, 97–9, 116
  Rupert, 122, 126, 138, 231, 283
  Scissors, 261
  Sickle, 174–5, 185, 190, 193, 196, 198, 204–5, 212

Operations (cont.)
  Stratford, 47, 55, 61, 73, 94–5, 97,
    113–14, 169, 172, 179, 181, 221,
    277
  Wilfred, 57, 87, 92–3, 97
Oslo, xi, 25, 76, 80, 83, 99–100, 105,
    112, 117–18, 120, 123–4, 131–3,
    155, 163, 173, 182, 186, 198, 205,
    222–4, 226, 236, 256, 274
Østerdal, 186, 193, 197–8
Otta, 189, 194–5, 210, 279
Oxelösund, 24, 243
Øyer, 184, 188
Øyjord, 249–50, 254, 269

Paget, Major General Bernard, xi, 161,
    190–1, 193–4, 196–7, 212
Peirse, Air Marshal Richard, 51
Pellengahr, Major General Richard, 186,
    194, 197, 200
Petsamo, 52–3
Phillips, Brigadier Charles, 169–70, 173,
    176–7, 179, 209
Phillips, Vice Admiral Tom, 94, 100–1,
    115, 123, 126, 157, 207, 221
Playfair, Brigadier Ian, 19
Polish formations and units
  Brigade, 136, 252, 269–70, 274
Portal, Air Chief Marshal Sir Charles, 223,
    298
Pothus, 264–5
Pound, Admiral of the Fleet Sir Dudley, xi,
    11–12, 15, 35, 45, 49, 64–5, 78,
    88–9, 115–18, 120, 123, 127, 143,
    153, 157, 160, 162, 207, 210, 216,
    294–6, 298
Pownall, Lieutenant General Henry, 36, 55,
    69, 89, 108

Quisling, Vidkund, 79, 82, 133, 149, 154,
    173, 284

Raeder, Grand Admiral Erich, 79, 82,
    84–5
Reid, Margaret, 133, 155, 360
Reynaud, Paul, 91–3, 97, 99, 112, 119,
    208
Rombaksfiord, 251, 269
Roope, Lieutenant Commander Gerard,
    116
Roosevelt, Franklin, 40, 112
Rosyth, 114–15, 137–8, 169, 181, 183,
    201
Royal Marines, 3, 34, 75, 156, 169, 178,
    183

Ruge, Major General Otto, 125, 133, 156,
    184–7, 192–3, 196–7, 203, 225, 259,
    272, 282

Sargent, Sir Orme, 125
Scapa Flow, 1, 114, 118, 131, 137, 161,
    175, 225, 230–1, 261, 268, 271–2
Schwerpunkt/Point of Main Effort, 30, 134,
    166, 186, 207, 214, 220–1, 265
Scots Guards, 65, 136, 251, 256, 261–4,
    267
Secret Intelligence Service, 24, 102–3, 105,
    133, 155, 243
Seeckt, General Hans von, 218
Sherwood Foresters, 181–2, 185, 187–8
Ships
  British
    Acasta, 272–3
    Afridi, 178
    Arab, 179
    Ardent, 272–3
    Ark Royal, 92, 254
    Aurora, 138–9, 144, 147, 251
    Bittern, 179
    Cairo, 270
    Cedarbank, 186, 205, 207
    Cossack, 57, 238
    Curlew, 269
    Effingham, 262
    Empress of Australia, 170
    Furious, 114, 127
    Glorious, 92, 268, 272–3, 285
    Glowworm, 115–16, 131, 152
    Gurkha, 157
    Hardy, 122, 152
    Nubian, 174
    Renown, 117, 121, 131
    Rodney, 122, 157
    Royal Oak, 1
    Southampton, 138–9, 151
    Suffolk, 161
    Warspite, 122, 127, 139, 142, 147, 150,
      156
  French
    Bison, 178
    Ville d'Alger, 175
  German
    Altmark, 57, 69
    Blücher, xi, 131, 274
    Gneisenau, 101, 106, 117, 131, 272–3
    Graf Spee, 45, 57, 69
    Hipper, 116, 131, 272
    Karlsruhe, 122
    Königsberg, 122, 222
    Lützow, 122, 131

Rio de Janeiro, 113, 132
Scharnhorst, 101, 117, 131, 272–3
Norwegian
  Eidsvold, 149
  Norge, 149
Polish
  Chrobry, 261
  Grom, 251
  Orzel, 112
Simon, Sir John, xi, 2, 4, 21, 62, 213
Sinclair, Sir Archibald, 89
SIS. *See* Secret Intelligence Service
Slessor, Air Commodore John, 10, 14,
    19, 72, 106, 128, 158–9, 161, 164,
    216
Smyth, Brigadier HEF, 190, 194
South Wales Borderers, 136, 251, 262, 264
Spanish Civil War, 18, 218
Stanley, Oliver, 8, 60, 63, 67, 97–8, 100,
    116, 119, 123, 162, 164, 205, 208–9,
    229, 289
Stannard, Lieutenant Commander
    Richard, 179
Stavanger, 25, 47, 59–61, 65, 73, 84, 94–5,
    100, 114, 117, 120, 133, 137, 156,
    158–9, 161, 181, 217, 221, 223,
    225–6, 269
Steinkjer, 174, 176–7, 180, 205, 208, 236
Stien, 262
Stockwell, Lieutenant Colonel Hugh,
    265
Storjord, 263–4
Supreme War Council, 8, 19, 26, 48, 52–3,
    55, 60, 90–1, 93–4, 98, 107, 112,
    119, 207–8, 213, 230, 282
Sylt, 90

Talbot, Captain AG, 73
Territorial Army, 17, 51, 69–71, 96, 114,
    137, 163, 201, 238, 260, 296–7
Thyssen, Fritz, 26–8, 90
Torrance, Captain JW, 150
Trappes-Lomax, Lieutenant Colonel
    Thomas, 251–2, 254, 263–4

Trenchard, Marshal of the Royal Air Force,
    Lord, 14, 18, 44, 219, 294
Tretten, 188–9, 194, 209–10
Tromsø, 80, 146, 197, 249, 271
Trondheim, 25, 31–2, 47, 56, 59, 61, 65,
    73, 83, 94, 107, 112, 114–20,
    122–7, 131, 133, 137, 146, 149, 151,
    156–69, 172–3, 175, 177, 179–80,
    182, 185–6, 198, 205–12, 217, 221,
    223, 225, 234, 236–7, 256, 266, 269,
    280–2, 287–8, 291, 297

Valdres, 198
Venning, General Sir Walter, 56
Verdalsøra, 175
Viskiskoia, 264
Vist, 176, 178

Wallenberg, Marcus, 37
War Cabinet, viii, xi, 2–4, 7–9, 19–21, 23,
    25–7, 29, 31, 33, 35, 37, 39–43,
    46–9, 52, 57, 59–63, 65, 67–9, 71–2,
    75–7, 87–9, 91, 97–8, 100, 103–4,
    108, 113, 115, 117–18, 120, 123,
    125, 142, 144, 155, 160, 163–4, 168,
    174, 182, 205, 208–10, 213–14,
    221–2, 225, 230–1, 235, 240, 242–3,
    245, 252, 270–1, 273, 276–8, 285–6,
    288–92, 294
Warburton-Lee, Captain Bernard, 122,
    127, 238
Wegener, Admiral Wolfgang, 6, 79
Weserübung, 80, 82–5, 105, 110, 112, 133,
    147, 220, 222, 275–6
Whitworth, Vice Admiral William, 113,
    115–16, 122, 127
Wilberforce, Captain Richard, 191
Wood, Sir Kingsley, xi, 4, 27, 40, 48, 59,
    96
Woytasch, Major General Kurt, 165,
    175–6, 180

York and Lancaster Regiment, 137, 169,
    177, 190, 193–4